Interwoven Lives

Interwoven Lives

Indigenous Mothers of Salish Coast Communities

CANDACE WELLMAN

WSU PRESS

Washington State University Press
Pullman, Washington

WSU PRESS
WASHINGTON STATE UNIVERSITY

Washington State University Press
PO Box 645910
Pullman, Washington 99164-5910
Phone: 800-354-7360
Email: wsupress@wsu.edu
Website: wsupress.wsu.edu

First printing 2019

Library of Congress Cataloging-in-Publication Data

Names: Wellman, Candace, author.
Title: Interwoven lives : indigenous mothers of Salish coast communities / Candace Wellman.
Description: Pullman, Washington : Washington State University Press, [2019] | Includes bibliographical references and index.
Identifiers: LCCN 2018044846 | ISBN 9780874223644 (alk. paper)
Subjects: LCSH: Salish Indians--Marriage customs and rites--Washington (State)--Whatcom County. | Interracial marriage--Washington (State)--Whatcom County--History--19th century. | Whatcom County (Wash.)--Race relations--History--19th century.
Classification: LCC E99.S2 W387 2019 | DDC 305.8009797/7309034--dc23
LC record available at https://lccn.loc.gov/2018044846

Maps by Chelsea Feeney, cmcfeeney.com

On the cover: "Mt. Rainier." Oil painting by James Tilton Pickett of Portland, Oregon. Courtesy of the Whatcom Museum, Bellingham, Washington, #1975.60.1.

Dedication

To Mike, Christine, Ame, Jim, Amy, Ron, Jake, and
Addy who have supported and endured

To the Gonzaga Girlz Rita, Suzann, Judy, and Sue
who have always believed in me

To my own grandmothers, great-grandmothers,
and those who came before them

And to my Coast Salish mentors
who have guided my journey

Contents

Illustrations and Maps

Acknowledgments

THIS BOOK COMPLETES the publication of eight Whatcom County biographies and the context of cross-cultural marriages between Euro-Americans and indigenous women in American and Washington Territory history. Over the past twenty years, more than two hundred people have assisted this effort to bring a group of important indigenous women out of the historical shadows to have their contributions to the birth of new communities recognized. Many contributors were thanked in the previous volume and I now thank those who aided in the research and writing of the second four biographies. During the two decades of my research and writing, a few of these have "walked on" and I remain always thankful for their gift of wisdom and knowledge during their lifetimes. Many photographs are being published for the first time and I am grateful for those who preserved them to be seen today.

Chief Tsi'lixw (William) James, Frances Lane James, George Adams, Juanita Jefferson, Adelina Singson, Tammy Cooper-Woodrich, Catalina Renteria, Dr. Wayne Suttles, Mike Vouri, Tim Wahl, Roger Newman, Mary Helen Cagey, Ernestine Gensaw, Lorraine McConaghy, Janet Oakley, Jennifer Mueller, Carole Teshima, Marilee Hagee, Sam Pambrun, Dr. Jean Barman, and Dr. Alexandra Harmon all provided many years of support, personal research, and knowledge of this subject and the people. Thanks to David Busch, and to Mrs. Mary Kazda who taught me to write.

Thanks also to the following individuals and sources.

Wynn chapter: Lisa Mowat, Janet Beard, Becky Wynn-Thill, Echo Oxford Dorr, Maxine Stremler, Lori Apana, and Mary Wood.

Patterson chapter: Peggy and James McDonald, Mary Michaelson, Carol Rasmussen, Troy Lugenbill, Earngy Sandstrom, Phillip Wahl, Denise McClanahan, Margaret Hellyer, Carolyn Ruggrath, Karen Parsons, Allan Richardson, Boyd Pratt, Joan Fitch, Patricia Johnson, and Kris Kirby of the Snoqualmie Museum.

Allen chapter: Frank Allen, Mandie Jimmie, Jim and Linda Allen, Kathy Pool, Patricia Roppel, Don Hauka Jr., James LeMaster, Centralia (IL) Regional Library, C.E. Brehm Memorial Library (Mt. Vernon, IL), and Red Bud (IL) Public Library.

Pickett chapter: Martha Boltz, Pat Wood, JoEllen McConnell, George and Ridgely Copland, Dr. Elizabeth Upton, Dr. Melissa Upton Cyders, Llyn De Danaan, Gene MacKenzie, and Robert Krick. Edradine Hovde of the Pickett House was indispensable.

The depth of my research would not have been possible without the collections and staff of the Washington State Archives, Northwest Region, and the WWU Center for Pacific Northwest Studies, both in Bellingham, Washington. The Whatcom County Historical Society and Whatcom Writers and Publishers cheered me on through all the years. Other institutions whose staffs assisted me with this volume were Lummi Nation Archives, Seattle Archdiocese Archives, State Library of Virginia, Virginia Historical Society, Oregon Historical Society, University of Washington Libraries Special Collections, and the U.S. Military Academy Archives.

Many bookstores and book clubs were greatly instrumental in the success of *Peace Weavers*, the first volume of biographies, and I am so grateful for their confidence.

My thanks again go to Beth DeWeese, Robert Clark, Ed Sala, Caryn Lawton, and Kerry Darnall of WSU Press whose support through publication of *Peace Weavers* and *Interwoven Lives* is unwaveringly enthusiastic and always available to me.

My apologies to anyone I have omitted. Feel free to let me know and I will instantly tender my gratitude.

Thanks and apologies also go to the descendants of Thomas and Fanny Barrett whose story could not be included but who have given me great insight into their own cross-cultural family's past and present.

Preface

"Half-histories are half-truths. And half-truths are lies."
—George Adams, Nooksack elder

THERE IS A SAYING that historians are always surprised that their subject waited for them. For me, it really was a surprise to find that writing biographies of "ordinary" native women of the nineteenth century was an unusual task. The biographical research project that became *Peace Weavers: Uniting the Salish Coast through Cross-Cultural Marriages* (2017) and now *Interwoven Lives* began in 1998 while I was a volunteer research assistant at the Washington State Archives, Northwest Region, in Bellingham, Washington. I helped many people plan and carry out projects and became deeply familiar with the content of public and private collections there and at the Center for Pacific Northwest Studies in the same building.

Those collections, questions from genealogy society members, family historians, and a project of an East Coast journalist about the native wife of General George E. Pickett coalesced into the impetus for a three-year project to write a local history book or article. Those experiences brought attention to the symbiotic relationships I saw between the incoming half dozen settler women to Whatcom County in the early 1850s and the young indigenous women who married other settlers and army officers. Evidence showed an atmosphere of mutual learning and friendship among women at the mill and mine communities, where little conflict occurred between the Coast Salish residents at Lummi Peninsula and settlers. This continued even during the territory's 1855–56 Treaty War though armed conflict occurred elsewhere.

As I researched my project, gradually the "first white women" of Bellingham Bay became less interesting. Local historians had written about them in other books to some degree, though still less than their husbands, who were assumed to have achieved everything important in the early decades of white settlement in the Coast Salish neighborhood. As I encountered more and more cross-cultural marriages of influential men, those native wives became more interesting. Few were mentioned by name, but they were the overwhelming majority of the new community's wives. And yet, local history books contained little or nothing about them and what they might have contributed or endured as women caught between cultures and forced to adapt. It was always about "the first white women" and "the first white children," as it was in other frontier locales. Read fifty to seventy years after the books were published, the histories showed obvious cultural bias in content, interpretation, and wording which, with new readers' frequent assumption that everything already written was accurate, has led to egregiously erroneous misconceptions. Clearly, the preponderance of Native wives during the birth of Bellingham and their importance was an inconvenient history that historians had not wanted to explain. I left the very nice white ladies behind.

I started with a group of twenty-two women to profile in short accounts for the book, despite assumptions by local and regional historians that information about their lives would be impossible to find. Most assumed that the women were nameless girls "bought" from acquiescent parents. That they were not "really" married if there was no official paper. That they were simply housekeepers and bed partners for lonely men. That they made no meaningful contributions to the new community. That all were young women from the nearby Lummi village. That they never spoke English. That their children were misfits. That their husbands abandoned them for white wives at the first opportunity. That the husbands' families elsewhere had no interest in them or their children. I tested those widespread assumptions.

I made an early decision to also thoroughly research the men's backgrounds, sometimes for three generations or more. All marriages are influenced by each spouse's personal and family history, as well as culture and regional subculture. That history for these men affected how they viewed marriage in general, their own role as husband, their wife's role, their children's roles, and how they treated their family members. That decision and its research resulted in many surprises that enriched the picture of the marriages. Husbands would not be "dropped from the sky" into the local milieu, nor would they cease to exist if they left. Everyone's lives would be followed.

The basis for choosing a woman to profile was she and her husband had to live at Bellingham Bay in the 1850s to 1860s period, even if there were subsequent marriages or moves that took her elsewhere. The cache of information continued to grow as I broke through the assumption there was no information available. Families, both Native and white-identified, began to contribute oral history, documents, photographs, and their own genealogical research after they understood I planned something different from the biased accounts and stereotypes of the past. I was mentored by knowledgeable people from several tribes, as well as by the late respected anthropologist Dr. Wayne Suttles.

As years passed beyond the planned three, I reduced the initial list to sixteen, then to twelve, ten, and finally eight complete biographies written in what became a twenty-year project. The lengthy process of research and writing was not because there was so little to find, but because there was so much. At the same time, the list of frontier communities founded by intermarried couples grew for the region and nation and is probably grossly incomplete. I also heard from more and more descendants seeking help to bring their great-great-great grandmothers out of the family's dark shadows where they had been relegated around the turn of the twentieth century. The new dominant white majority changed the perception of important pioneering couples into people on the fringe whose early accomplishments they minimized. Therefore, the eight women and their husbands whose lives are brought to light in *Peace Weavers* and *Interwoven Lives* do not complete the broader picture that full biographies of many others would provide.

I chose not to speculate very often into what emotions or motivations the women might have because I am not of their time nor their culture. I was also leery of attributing the same to the husbands who were products of their time and culture unless I had credible evidence to do so.

Research into other communities will yield newly discovered community mothers. The telling of those other lives must be left to those great-great-great granddaughters (and sons) who live in both cultures and whose books may be fuller and different from what I have written.

As in the first four biographies published in *Peace Weavers*, the *Interwoven Lives* biographies follow the same guidelines.

- Four categories of sources for biographical content and cross-checking events were used: primary documents and other materials from public and private collections; professional historians' work; research by local historians and independent scholars; and personal research by family historians and genealogists.

- Endnotes were included to enable a descendant or researcher to find the sources. No dialogue was created. I assume that corrections will be made to my own work as new information is uncovered, particularly when a single source appeared to be the only one existing.
- Requests by contributors for anonymity were honored.
- Requests about the publishing of indigenous personal names were respected. Names are personal possessions, passed down and owned. If the current name owner could not be found to seek permission, the name was only used if it had been repeatedly published in other recent works. Baptismal names were the norm for interaction with settlers. I deeply apologize if my use of a personal name has offended the current name owner.
- Most geographical places have names in more than one language. I used the one that seemed most logical for the context.
- Terms differ today in Canada and Washington. "First Nations" and "bands" are preferred in Canada, while "tribes" is used in the United States. As well, "country marriage" among Hudson's Bay Company employees means the same as "tribal custom marriage" in the American Northwest.
- Lastly, I pledged to families that the women would be treated as individuals and never as "case studies." I hope I have achieved that.

Introduction

In late summer 2017, controversy over a small concrete bridge erupted in Bellingham, Washington, Whatcom County's "City of Subdued Excitement." For weeks, locals argued in person and in print about the bridge's name, although it had not been questioned for ninety-seven years. Articles and photographs headlined the Bellingham Herald's front page. The controversy took residents back to the era of Captain George E. Pickett (later a Confederate general) and his cross-cultural marriage.

Events on the other side of the country in Charlottesville, Virginia, triggered the local brouhaha. A white supremacy march and counter-protest surrounding the removal of the city's heroic statue of Confederate General Robert E. Lee ended in the death of a young woman. Conversations started across the United States about the appropriateness of keeping statues of Confederate heroes in public parks.

In 1920 the Daughters of the American Revolution (DAR) set Bellingham's informal name of "Pickett Bridge" into a bronze plaque affixed to the short span over Whatcom Creek. In 1858 Captain Pickett, commander of Fort Bellingham, contracted out to local settlers the construction of the original log bridge. It linked the two small settlements on Bellingham Bay for movement of ordnance in case of attack. Called the "military bridge" when built, it was designed as part of a crude road that would connect Fort Bellingham to Fort Steilacoom near today's Tacoma, but which was never completed. Settlers, grateful for the bridge which made a walk between settlements safer, called it the "Pickett Bridge." They fondly remembered the captain for his local accomplishments and friendship despite his later service for the Confederacy.

At the start of the 2017 controversy, Bellingham's mayor ordered the plaque and signs pointing the way to the Pickett House Museum removed to prevent feared vandalism during the national debate about Confederate monuments. The signs to the house where the captain and his Alaskan Haida wife lived were soon replaced, but the argument continued about whether the plaque should be restored or whether it improperly glorified a Confederate "traitor." Some wanted the bridge renamed while others wanted it left as it was in tribute to Pickett's command of Fort Bellingham.

The *Herald* printed a resident's proposal to rename it the "Morning Mist Bridge" in tribute to Pickett's indigenous wife. In truth, "Morning Mist" was not her name, but rather a fictitious one invented by a novelist in 1937. The personal name of the young Alaskan native woman who married Pickett, gave birth to their son, and died within a year is unknown. Residents called her "Mrs. Pickett," the form accorded any fort commander's wife.[1]

The incident illustrates how misinformation passed along and repeated in print, because of inadequate critique of sources full of myth and stereotype, created legend. It also demonstrates the lack of accurate knowledge about indigenous women who crossed the cultural frontier to marry men from an alien society. Local historians who knew the true history of the Pickett family groaned in frustration that no suggestion was made to reexamine the Pickett "legend" to obtain a more accurate interpretation before action was taken. Their discussions centered on the possibility that historical misinformation could literally be set in concrete.[2]

Hidden from public knowledge for 150 years has been the number of indigenous women who married early Euro-American residents of Whatcom County. For the first twenty years of the county's legal existence, such intermarriages represented 80 to 90 percent of the couples building the new community. Historians buried the women's names and contributions in favor of praise for the half-dozen early white wives and the first white children. The cluster of intermarriages around Bellingham Bay was, in fact, simply the Salish Sea continuation of a custom reaching back to the Spanish Caribbean settlements of the 1500s. With the exception of some recognition given to Hudson's Bay Company wives in Oregon, indigenous women at other clusters in the American Northwest and across the country have largely been ignored. They were key to the establishment of many new communities on successive American frontiers. Cities as distant and disparate as Detroit, Michigan; Santa Fe, New Mexico; and Wenatchee, Washington, began with intermarried couples.

By 1514, 40 percent of Spanish Caribbean settlers are believed to have married Taino women, birthing the "mestizo" identity in the New World. Further north in the 1600s, the French colonized Acadia

(Nova Scotia), where many men intermarried and joined existing First Nations kin networks. This continued as Canada's fur trappers moved across the continent. The Catholic Church's missionaries routinely tolerated tribal custom marriages of isolated colonists and fur trappers until they chose to receive a formal blessing when clergy was available.[3]

Not so the British colonists who peopled the thirteen American colonies. Though many traders and others on the leading edge of colonial settlement married indigenous women, the couples were rarely accorded respectability because intermarriage didn't fit the cultural or religious norms imported from England. Colonists had no problem adopting practical indigenous technology or foods in the "wilderness," but they were uninterested in the indigenous world view, lifestyle, or spirituality. Or, above all, racial equality. So, when Patrick Henry and Thomas Jefferson proposed forming an American ethnicity by intermarriage, their idea fell flat.

Occasionally, white women married and children were adopted into a tribe after capture. Some offered "rescue" chose to stay with their indigenous families, which colonists could not understand. Published in 1953, *The Light in the Forest* by Conrad Richter was a children's novel about a captured and adopted boy who was unhappily returned home as a teenager. The book and subsequent movie brought an alternate view of loving tribal family life to American children steeped in Hollywood western movies in which Indians were always the uncivilized enemy.[4]

British colonists of every social class did not kindly tolerate their fellows who looked half-Indian, even if they adhered to European ways. This resulted in some mixed-blood men identifying with their mothers' cultures, and becoming leaders in the early republic's rebellions—for example, Cornplanter of the Seneca and Osceola of the Seminole. Alex McGillivray of the Creek rebellion was also French and Scottish. He was educated in Charleston, appointed a U.S. Army brigadier general, negotiated treaties, and owned a plantation. In the end, he led attacks against white encroachers on Creek lands. John Ross of the Cherokee who led the resistance to leaving their homeland was only one-eighth Cherokee.[5]

In the 1700s to mid-1800s, the North American frontier was in fact (if not in the American psyche), a multicultural, multinational domain with multiple colonizers and concurrent group histories and cultural conflicts. These interactions centered around ravenous Euro-American appropriation of indigenous territory and the indigenous struggle to adapt and survive. At the leading edge of all geographical movements by the invasive colonizing powers were cross-cultural marriages: American, Mexican, British, French, and Russian in Alaska.[6]

The Doctrine of Discovery by which European nations claimed the superior right of ownership and occupation of lands they encountered for the first time morphed into the popular Manifest Destiny idea whereby Americans would take legitimate possession of the land "from sea to shining sea." British colonizers saw native people as mere "occupants" of wasted land, a concept dating back to sixteenth century British and French writings that depicted the newly "discovered" continent as empty. Colonists would take over the "new" lands and re-make them. At the heart of the American government's agricultural colonization lay a belief that all land was by definition too good for Indians, including those who farmed. Migrating settlers told themselves they were moving into a wilderness, not a large, established neighborhood. Immersed in this pervasive national belief, Whatcom County's *Blaine Journal* in 1888 supported proposals to break up the Lummi Reservation and sell any land not a "requirement" for the tribe to "actual settlers." Concluded the editor: "It is a shame to have all that fine country lying idle."[7]

Cross-cultural communities rose at the edge of settlement as European and then American powers pushed the frontier ever further west, south, and north from Mexico. Besides Detroit and Santa Fe, they also included Chicago, St. Louis, San Antonio, and Green Bay, Wisconsin.

American mythic figures who lived on or ahead of the settlement edge often married history's unrecognized and unnamed indigenous women. Native wives supported their husbands' work and should share credit for their ability to move among the tribes unmolested. Yet history often mentions only that the "hero" was married to an Indian. Husband Jim Bridger of the Rocky Mountain Fur Company discovered a pass through the Rockies that is today the primary east-west highway I-80. William Bent, son of a Missouri Supreme Court justice, established a fort that supplied travelers of many nations. Kit Carson was a legendary guide, scout, and Santa Fe Trail trader. Sam Houston, governor of both Tennessee and Texas, lived with and was adopted by the Cherokee, and married into the tribe. He adopted many of their ways and wore parts of their dress until his death. Oregon settler and trapper Joe Meek was instrumental in the establishment of Oregon Territory. All of these well-known men married indigenous women.

As intermarried British Hudson's Bay Company (HBC) employees retired in the Pacific Northwest, they established communities in Oregon's Willamette Valley as well as many early Washington communities: the San Juan Islands, Vancouver, Spokane, Walla Walla's predecessor Frenchtown, Okanogan, Colville, and Chewelah. When American settlers moved north of the Columbia River, a new society, though far-flung, awaited them. More cross-cultural marriage clusters and first settlers led to new towns: Wenatchee, Shelton, Bellingham, Ferndale, Lynden, Dungeness (Port Angeles), Puyallup, and others. Former HBC employee families farmed in scattered locations in Pierce and Lewis Counties. One of Seattle's most touted city fathers, Henry Yesler (with a wife in the East), married the daughter of Duwamish leader Suquardle ("Curley"). Among those who married early Seattle-ites were a granddaughter and a niece of Sealth "Chief Seattle."[8]

Like all marriages, many did not last a lifetime. Native wives died from childbirth, home accidents, abuse, and illnesses for which they had no immunities. Sometimes they left their husbands and went home.

American military officers married native women as forts opened in the Pacific Northwest, as they had at scattered posts across the West. There were always a few who retired and stayed in budding communities. Others left their native wives and children behind because it was easy to do so. Lieutenant (later General) Philip Sheridan abandoned his Yakama wife Wal-lup-quat and their daughter Emma at The Dalles (Oregon) and another wife at his next post. Lt. James W. Forsyth of Fort Bellingham (later commander of the Wounded Knee Massacre) left his Swinomish wife Mary and daughter Teresa behind when he departed for the Civil War. He never contacted them again or sent support, despite commanding Fort Walla Walla a few years after the war. (Mary later married Lummi Chief Henry Kwina.)

Feelings could be harsh. Said Emma Sheridan's son Ben Olney: "I never heard my mother mention Phil Sheridan's name without crying and declaring that she would kill him if she ever saw him, because of his treatment of her mother, going away and leaving her as he did."[9]

When Americans wrote their local histories, the early indigenous wives of settlers across the Pacific Northwest and the rest of the country were, with rare exceptions, generally marginalized or erased in favor of the "first white woman in town." Indigenous community mothers, often from elite families, were an inconvenient piece of history. They did not fit the myth of courageous white women helping the "menfolk" conquer and remake the empty wilderness into an Eden. Community history needed to fit the Manifest Destiny mythology with white Americans as the superior civilized people. The founding mothers had to fit that, too.

In the northwest corner of Washington, local histories followed this pattern for many years, though American intermarriage clusters still existed in Whatcom County, on March Point in Skagit County, on the Olympic Peninsula, and in the San Juan Islands. In her two volumes of Whatcom County history and biographies published in 1926, Lottie Roeder Roth called Thomas Wynn's elite Lummi wife Jenny only an anonymous "native of this county" (see chapter 1). That nebulous description has often been interpreted as a white settler birth. Percival Jeffcott's 1949 book, *Nooksack Tales and Trails*, included this condescending passage about intermarriages: "Many times in these stories we have found it necessary to tell of the conjugal alliances made by prominent white men on the Bay, with the intriguing dark-eyed native maidens of this region. Knowing that man's natural instincts are ever stronger than his mental reservations, we are prompted in these cases to neither condone nor condemn, though often the innocent were caused to suffer as a result."[10]

On March 25, 1965, the *Bellingham Herald*'s anniversary edition profiled Whatcom County's communities without ever mentioning the presence of Lummi or Nooksack people, or the indigenous wives of several towns' first families. The county's general histories, and those of other locales, consistently lacked recognition of intermarried women's contributions to peace between the two nations who had to adapt to each other's presence in the birth of a new community. Recognizing those women's sometimes critical influence did not fit with a focus on male accomplishments, by both male and female local historians, or with the mythic, idealized white female settlers. Even worse were the erroneous stereotypes like Jeffcott's that attached to intermarried couples' children. Writers influenced by popular literature, such as Walt Whitman's 1849 work "The Half-Breed," consistently presented the offspring as lonely misfits who could function in neither culture. In fact, as adults the progeny seem to have led lives as personally successful or unsuccessful as nonnative children. (See *Peace Weavers* and this volume for numerous examples.)

The end result has been the assumption by current historians or genealogists that "nothing is known" and "there is nothing to find" about nineteenth century indigenous wives. Those assumptions hide the true picture in what are probably hundreds of towns and cities across the Northwest and the nation.

The northwest corner of Washington State is a gloomy, rainy place, and it is a gloriously sunny, warm place. Sometimes it has three or four different kinds of weather in the same day. Residents may begin casual conversation on the street with the colloquialism, "The mountain's out today." Whatcom County is vertically shallow, starting at the Canadian border twenty-five miles north of Bellingham and ending twenty miles south of the city at the edge of the Skagit Valley. But it is very wide and the eastern half features only trails and logging roads and is part of North Cascades National Park. On the west, it is bounded by almost circular Bellingham Bay in the Salish Sea, whose deep-green microorganism soup supports everything from miniature crabs to orcas and seals. On days of filtered sunshine, the bay is fringed by islands of every shade of green that front the remaining San Juan archipelago behind them. The Japanese Current flows to the bay from across the North Pacific, through the Strait of Juan de Fuca, and past the islands to keep the water a steady fifty degrees year around. Too cold for swimming, but too warm to freeze. It also moderates the land temperatures to allay weather extremes year around, except for the high winds of November that sweep in from all directions. In the winter, Arctic winds from the Yukon can howl down British Columbia's Fraser River Canyon and pour out across the agricultural fields of the northern county as blizzards or ice storms. To the east about thirty miles from the bay stands massive Mount Baker, shielding sixty more miles of backcountry to Okanogan County. The still-steaming volcano's snowy presence, nearly 11,000 feet high, dominates the region's skyline south to Seattle and north to Lower Mainland British Columbia, and it too affects the weather. Residents pile outerwear of every type and weight into the back seats of their cars, just in case the weather changes.

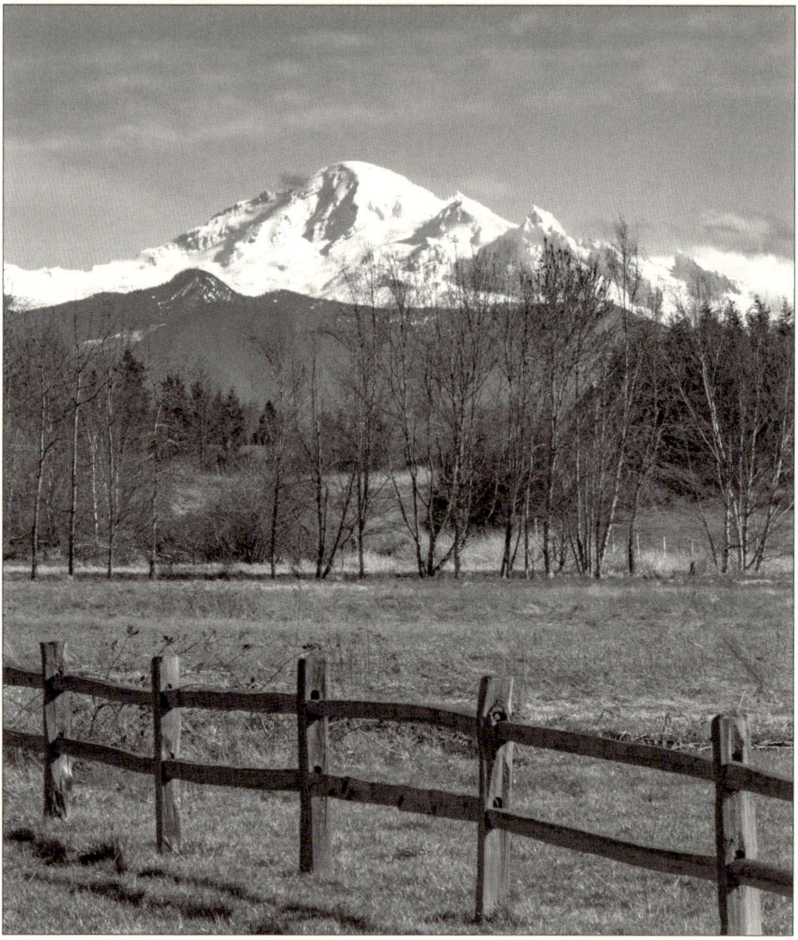

Mount Baker volcano (10,781 feet) from north of Bellingham. It occasionally steams in the twenty-first century, but in summer 1868 it erupted. Streaming lava was visible west to Victoria, BC, and it added heavy smoke to that of British Columbia wildfires during Whatcom County's summer. *Kathleen Kitto, photographer. #2017.15.118. Courtesy of Whatcom Museum, Bellingham, WA.*

Together this geography leads to unpredictable weather patterns, but also harbors an environment rich in resources of every kind. The Cascade Mountains and foothills birth millions of evergreen trees sought by loggers, and the salmon streams' progeny still sustain the Coast Salish. Mount Baker dominates the thoughts of skiers and snowboarders in the winter, and hikers in the summer. The salt water calls to boaters, fishermen, and windsurfers as it always has to the Lummi and Nooksack. In other words, the geography of Whatcom County has played a large part in six millenia of Coast Salish cedar- and salmon-based life, in the nineteenth century arrival of permanent Euro-American settlement, and in present-day culture.

Into this place in December 1852 came two erstwhile fortune-seekers from gold rush California, in search of a waterfall usable for a saw mill. From the stump- and mud-choked new territorial capital Olympia, Coast Salish men had transported them down Puget Sound to Port Townsend in a high-prowed cedar canoe. Several Lummi men told them about a waterfall on Bellingham Bay and canoed them to *Tam'whiq'sen,* the major village.

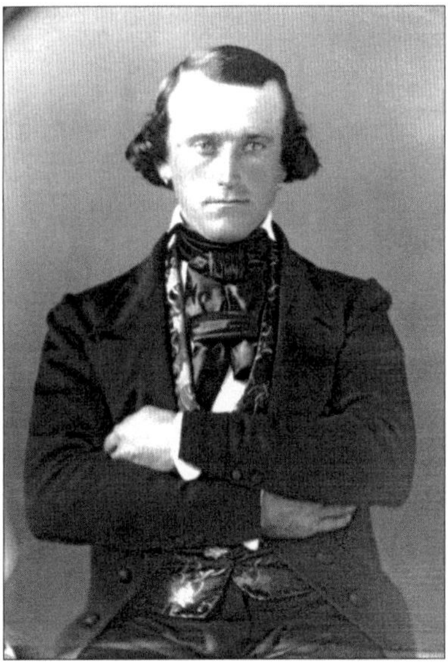

Henry Roeder. *Unknown photographer. #3882. Courtesy of Whatcom Museum, Bellingham, WA.*

Henry Roeder and Russell Peabody obtained permission to occupy the salmon-bearing waterfall around the curve of the bay, which indicates they had some comprehension that the place was not "empty" or "wasted." Despite that, they would not have seen it as "owned" by the Coast Salish families whose territory it had been for some six thousand years. The elder who gave permission, Chow'it'sut, may not have understood that the smelly and arrogant men intended to permanently take and occupy the site. The Lummi were used to seeing the HBC men from Fort

Victoria west on Vancouver Island roaming the Salish Sea. Roeder and Peabody probably didn't realize that other Lummi elders might not have been so generous. However, they were "Boston men" (Americans) and the Lummi are said to have thought the men's presence might offer some advantages to offset those the HBC ("King George men") provided to the villages further north in British territory.

Roeder (then twenty-eight years old) and Peabody (thirty-two) knew little about lumber mills. Previous efforts to reap their fortunes in California had not made them rich or even prosperous. They had tried mining, freighting, and a salmon business before they gave up. Perhaps this place would offer more. Immense trees presented an endless supply of wood for the Roeder Mill, though they would soon discover the falls did not supply a steady, year-round supply of water. With frequent fires leveling swaths of wooden shacks and stores in San Francisco, Roeder and Peabody anticipated an endless demand for their lumber.

The Roeder Mill was a beachhead for the invasion of Lummi and Nooksack territories by Americans and immigrants. Thousands of men arrived in four waves; nearly all were bachelors, or claimed to be. The lopsided in-migration gave birth to a community nearly devoid of women from their own society, unlike the ballyhooed towns started by wagon train families. Mill workers came from California first to work alongside Lummi men in Roeder's enterprise. After two workers stumbled across a coal seam a mile away around the bay, a San Francisco syndicate opened the Sehome Mine in 1854. Management from California worked with arriving experienced miners. Two years later, a U.S. Army company arrived to build Fort Bellingham for protection of the settlement and Coast Salish villages against seasonal raiders (see chapter 1). Two years after that, in 1858, thousands of pack-laden gold miners hurrying to the Fraser River Canyon's gold discoveries stumbled off ships onto Sehome Mine's wharf. They occupied every spare bed and empty floor in the nearby cabins, or camped on the beach awaiting completion of the Whatcom Trail to the Fraser. When the British started to require a license issued only in Victoria, they quickly departed and boomtown merchants took all the new frame buildings with them, leaving only a three-story brick building to anchor the "town."

Men from all four of these in-migrations to Bellingham Bay chose to stay in the resource-rich environment to build new lives and families. Those initial waves of bachelors, along with a handful of married white couples, established the embryonic community that is today the city of Bellingham with a population over eighty thousand. Six small towns plus Lummi and Nooksack homelands dot the western half of the county. Those towns and farmland replaced cedars and firs that reached twelve feet in diameter. Salmon still return to Whatcom Falls, but now to a hatchery at the base.

Familiar with cross-cultural marriages in settlements and forts in the new Washington Territory and at Victoria, Roeder and Peabody themselves presented examples to the incoming bachelors of the acceptability of intermarriage. Later, Roeder abandoned his Lummi wife and children when his fiancée arrived from Ohio. Peabody's wife went home to her village *Sumath* near the Canadian border up the Whatcom Trail when he left for California. Neither of Whatcom's city fathers' marriages to native women lasted, but they set an early pattern for other bachelors.

When Whatcom and Sehome bachelors found that the settlements lacked marriage-age women of their own culture, nearly all who stayed took neighborhood brides. This included all three army officers. Some wives, like two in this book, came from farther away when they met their husbands before they came to the bay. For the first twenty years of settlement the vast majority of married couples were cross-cultural. Many wives were the daughters of prominent families, whose marriages had the negative effect of taking them out of the gene pool when they were needed to help recover epidemic-decimated populations. On the other hand, in their culture, a woman almost always married outside her own village and moved to her husband's family longhouse. Parents might see their married daughter only once or twice a year, but the daughters who married settlers lived relatively close to home.

Unlike some other locations in the West, friendships and symbiotic relationships between settlers and Coast Salish villagers developed because of these intermarriages when nearly everyone had become in-laws. Men and women from both cultures traded knowledge and expertise. Coast Salish men worked at the mill and mine. The army at Fort Bellingham depended on Lummi scouts and runners for the defense of settlers and villagers alike.

The women in this book came from four places distant from one another, unlike those in *Peace Weavers*. These four wives who found themselves in Whatcom and Sehome after marriage were Coast Salish

(Lummi and Snoqualmie), Interior Salish (Nlaka'pamux), and Alaskan Haida. If not their languages, their ways of life shared some elements. Their peoples shared a tradition of marrying their upper-class daughters to suitable, elite husbands. The girls were dissuaded from premarital sex and pregnancy, usually by chaperonage after their puberty seclusion period. The men of Bellingham Bay in this book who married elite daughters were considered acceptable serious suitors.

After a young woman's elders judged a prospective son-in-law to be of equal social status, good character, and able to contribute advantages to the alliance, the couple married. A ritual involving mutual exchange of goods and services obligated the husband to his wife's parents and extended family and vice-versa. For example, the annual salmon harvest was critical to winter survival. Lummi sons-in-law, the geographically closest, would have been expected to participate in the fishery, though with the new white husbands the expectation and participation may not have been consistent, and there were men who ignored all their obligations. The intermarriages that went well benefited both the husband, who wanted companionship and housekeeping, and his wife's parents who had their own agendas, such as access to cash jobs for brothers and cousins, mediation with authorities, and mutual assistance. The family expected their daughter to be treated well. "Indian divorce" was an option if she was not. Families knew that marriages did not always work out.

Intermarried husbands became sheriffs, school superintendents, legislators, county commissioners, and judges, and held other civic positions in the years immediately following Whatcom County's formation in 1854. Most of those men became less publicly visible in the 1870s, giving way to men of more education and interest in government. Their retreat coincided with the arrival of a new wave of homesteading settlers. In 1873 the coal mine flooded and the struggling Roeder Mill burned, so city fathers had to work hard to attract newcomers to replenish the decimated population left without the army and the mine and mill workers. Newly arrived white couples and Protestant ministers were less tolerant of tribal custom marriages than Catholic missionaries had been. A generation of incoming and local white daughters was by then of courting age and the desirability of Coast Salish brides to new white bachelors declined. The opposite effect helped the tribes as more young women married into their own culture again.

Changing the balance of local social relations, this large influx of "properly married" people pressured the "Old Settlers" to regularize their tribal custom marriages with legally recorded civil or church ceremonies. Suddenly, instead of being proud partners of community builders, indigenous wives were branded "mistresses."

By the 1870s territorial laws allowed for marriage to Indians, an issue that had been argued and legislated in contradictory amendments to the original marriage law since the 1850s. Official marriages backed by certificates and entries in the county auditor's book would be the only ones recognized if the new majority had their way in Whatcom and other counties with a large number of tribal custom marriages. An 1878 Third District Court divorce case involving a white couple supported this position when the judge ruled that their common law marriage had no legality (see Appendix A). After that precedent, county grand juries started to indict "Old Settlers" on charges of fornication to make them comply. Though many intermarried couples succumbed to the pressure and had second ceremonies in the 1870s, a number of them refused. Some cannily bypassed the system by obtaining just marriage licenses so they had "paper." Those who refused new civil or church ceremonies believed that to do so would disrespect their wives, their children, and the obvious commitment the spouses had made years before. In Whatcom County, a grand jury containing some of their friends indicted nine prominent men on a charge that in effect declared their wives "concubines" and "mistresses." The defendants included Henry Barkhousen, a respected former county auditor, election judge, and homesteader married to Julia Seya'hom, whose father was a treaty signer and for whom the Sehome settlement was named. Barkhousen adamantly opposed disrespecting Julia by complying. If a jury convicted him of the felony, their children born over twenty-plus years of marriage would be officially illegitimate.

In the face of resistance, looming trials, and requests for clarification, Territorial Supreme Court Chief Justice Roger Greene issued an opinion between court sessions that legalized all tribal custom marriages. He declared that a wedding was for the benefit of church or government, but was not itself the marriage contract (see Appendix B for more detail).

Peace Weavers: Uniting the Salish Coast through Cross-cultural Marriages presented the lives of four intermarried Coast Salish women who wed more than one husband during their long lifetimes: Caroline Davis Kavanaugh, Mary Fitzhugh Lear Phillips, Clara Tennant Selhameten, and Nellie Carr Lane. Three, and perhaps all, were at least distantly related because—as a result of the custom of marrying outside one's home village—Coast Salish peoples can be described as a giant extended family reaching from about Whistler, British Columbia, to the Columbia River. The four women lived complex lives and three left descendants who in their turn contributed to their own communities.

Interwoven Lives presents four women with single marriages but more diverse outcomes. They also came from more diverse backgrounds and family cultures: Lummi, Haida, Nlaka'pamux, and Snoqualmie. Each of the four husbands came from families who had already participated in one of the major American migrations before they continued the westward movement. They also had diverse family histories: Philadelphia Quakers, Tennessee/Missouri cattlemen, Illinois prairie farmers, and Virginia blue bloods.

Chapter one traces the life of Jenny Wynn, daughter of an elite Lummi and his Songhees wife. Thomas Wynn's ancestor was a leader of the Quaker migration to Pennsylvania in the 1600s.

Chapter two profiles Snoqualmie Elizabeth Patterson, daughter of the most powerful native leader in western Washington. James Patterson was part of the American cattlemen's migration to the head of the Oregon Trail in Missouri and beyond.

Chapter three relates the life of Mary Allen, daughter of an Nlaka'pamux leader on the Fraser River in British Columbia. Solomon Allen was born to agrarian migrants from the upper South to the Old Northwest of Illinois in the early 1800s.

Chapter Four concludes the biographies with a more accurate history of Mrs. George Pickett, her marriage, and son after a twenty-year re-examination of the evidence. Captain (later General) Pickett's family was among the first Huguenot colonists to leave Europe for Virginia.

Map 1: Mid-Nineteenth Century Washington and British Columbia

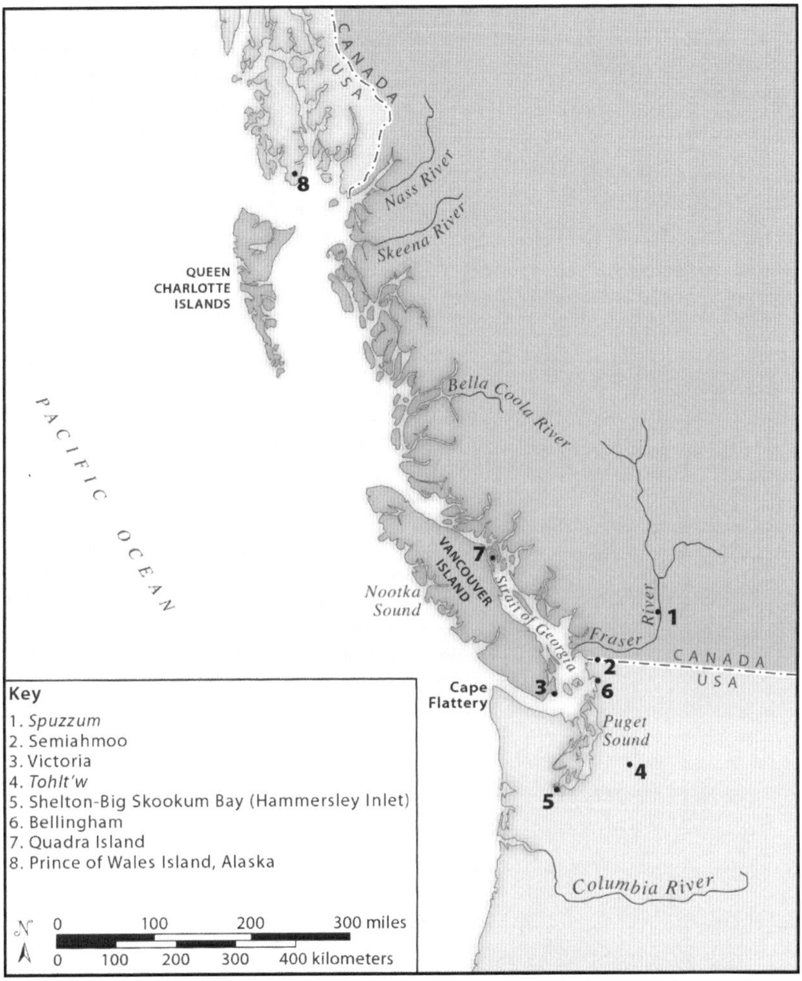

In the 1840s–1850s, *Laich'wil'tach* raiders from Quadra Island (#7) and further north attacked lower Fraser River villages of the Lummi, Samish, Swinomish, and Semiahmah, as well as the new settlements at Whatcom and Sehome. *Map by Chelsea Feeney*

Map 2:
The "Fourth Corner" of Washington

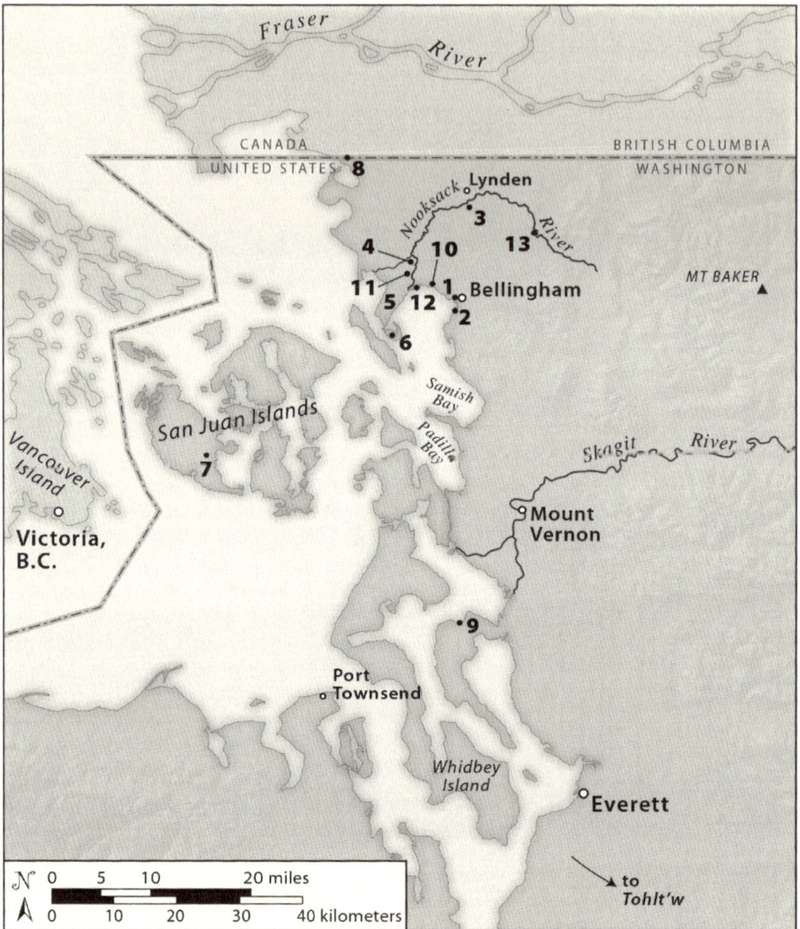

Key

o present day
• historic location

1. Whatcom
2. Sehome
3. *Sqweha:lich*
4. *Chah'choo'sen*
5. Lummi Peninsula
6. Portage Island
7. Camp Pickett
8. Semiahmoo
9. Utsalady, Camano Island
10. Fort Bellingham
11. Ferndale
12. Marietta
13. The Crossing/Everson

The northwest corner of Washington and adjacent regions of Canada were the setting for most events in the married lives of the indigenous women of *Interwoven Lives* and its predecessor, *Peace Weavers. Map by Chelsea Feeney*

CHAPTER 1

Jenny, Defender of the People

FROM MILES AWAY, Jenny and Tom Wynn heard the booms when two-hundred-foot Douglas firs and cedars exploded in flames and crashed to the ground, spewing incandescent embers into the swirling winds. Bits of the six-hundred-year-old patriarchs flew miles ahead of the fire and smoke born in Canada that consumed Whatcom County mile after mile during the summer of 1868.

Over three terrible days, the fire swept through the small prairies, trees, and brushy bottom along the Nooksack River, embers igniting eight-foot-thick stumps, sawdust, and everything in their path. Wild animals, livestock, and people found safety together on the beach ahead of the towering flames.

Armed only with shovels and pails, the Wynns refused to allow the wild inferno to take their farm. They battled the fire day and night, choking and nearly blinded by the thick smoke, slapping at sparks on their hair and clothes.

Perhaps the oldest children were safe at Lummi Reservation with their grandmother or with neighbors who fled into town when their farms burned, but Jenny's toddler Harry was with her. Years later when people asked him to describe his Lummi mother, he told their story.

When things were at their worst, Jenny saw that she must think of Harry's survival even if she could not save herself. She dug a small pit in the clearing between house and barn, and trusted in her people's traditional final defense. Jenny wrapped her frightened, choking little son in wet blankets and placed him down in the pit. If the unthinkable happened, Harry might survive.

The Wynns emerged unhurt, with only the market garden and some fences lost. The epic fire moved on to other farms and the settlements around the bay. It continued south for hundreds of miles until the vast Columbia River and autumn rains halted its advance.[1]

JENNY

Jenny's people, a group of extended Coast Salish families who called themselves the *Lhaq'temish* (Lummi), had occupied Lummi Island and other territory surrounding the lower Nooksack River since the late 1700s. Their extensive resource territories overlapped those of related families around the Salish Sea. The shared resource locations and customary cross-village marriages softened boundaries and tied distant families together in a vast network.

During the century before Jenny's birth, epidemics and unpredictable raids by distant, unrelated northern tribes drastically reduced the Coast Salish population. A number of families gradually made the permanent move from their winter longhouses in the San Juan Islands to the mainland. They never forgot their island origin thousands of years earlier, and the agony of abandoning their homeland, their *illahee*. Their history told them that they had been given Lummi (Nooksack) River salmon rights, so they consolidated midway down the fishing territory where sheltered places offered better defense. They would be safer from attack, and epidemic survivors could begin again among their mainland relatives and friends. They became the *Lhaq'temish* or *Xwe'lumi*. The "island" *Chah'choo'sen* between the lower river channels included *Ske'laxen* (Ske-laken) and *Si'lat'sis* prairies where an existing village (possibly including some of Jenny's paternal ancestors) was absorbed by the Lummi or its residents moved upriver to Nooksack territory. The main village grew at *Tam'whiq'sen* (later called Gooseberry Point) at the south end of Lummi Peninsula. By Jenny's time, her uncle Chow'it'sut's four-hundred-foot-long potlatch house dominated the north end of Portage Island, facing *Tam'whiq'sen* across a three-quarter-mile-wide channel and connected by a salal-covered sandy *swulesen*, dry at low tide and submerged at high (see Map 2).[2]

Spanish and British expeditions visited the Lummi in 1791–92 and were greeted by men in high-prowed cedar canoes who evaluated the peculiar strangers' intentions before any trade took place. After they left, new epidemics killed many. Population and cultural changes increased as contact with Europeans continued.

Jenny's father Sea'nult is called by most sources one of the seven sons of Lummi noble Saw'rem'ken. His mother, one of three co-wives, was said to be the daughter of a Nooksack leader upriver. Sea'nult had a reef net operation with his half-brother Tsi'lixw off Village Point on Lummi Island where he captained a crew that harvested several thousand salmon a day when the runs entered the Salish Sea. Jenny's father also had a fish weir above the mouth of the *Noos'kwiem*, the creek and wetlands that drained the *Chah'choo'sen* prairies. The Hudson's Bay Company (HBC) bought the men's excess catch for salting. Sea'nult built a cedar longhouse for his family and visitors on a bluff not far from his fish weir and sited it near one of the defensive hideouts on the *E'lik* ridge (later location of Marietta, chapter 3) If a runner brought an attack alarm from the Semiahmah village twenty miles north ("Semiahmoo"), a crane whistle summoned the family to run to the camouflaged shelter. The complex web of love, responsibilities, and privileges among the group of Lummi half-brothers and cousins, their wives, and in-laws, tightly wove Jenny's family into her community.[3]

Jenny's mother may have been baptized "Mary Ann" and was by all accounts the daughter of an important couple from one of the seven elite Songhees families who lived at the southeast Vancouver Island village, *Kosampson*. Jenny said that her mother's father was Chee-ah-thluch ("King Freezy"), the British Columbia treaty signer and HBC messenger. *Kosampson* and neighboring villages surrounded the site of today's Victoria, British Columbia. Songhees resource territory overlapped that of the Lummi in the Salish Sea, and a few villages in the area belonged to S'Klallam families from across the wide strait. Many marriages tied the Northern Straits Salish-speaking villages together.[4]

Sheltered in *Kosampson*'s bay for at least four thousand years, Jenny's Songhees people looked south across the Strait of Juan de Fuca toward the jagged peaks of the Olympic Mountains rising behind the smoke from S'Klallam villages. People on spirit quests went to the nearby swift water gorge that whites came to call Esquimalt. When Jenny's family visited, they may have joined others gathered at a nearby hilly meadow to play games, picnic, and sunbathe among the oak trees and grass. Those who canoed past Laurel Point saw the grave boxes fronted by life-sized carved memorial figures, a custom different from the tree burials of Jenny's Lummi family.

Epidemics decimated the Songhees from the thousands who once lived there. When Jenny's parents married in the 1820s, only forty families remained at *Kosampson*, even more vulnerable when Northern raiders came south along Vancouver Island's shore. By the time Jenny was grown, British colonists had appropriated all the places she had visited in her mother's homeland, and pushed her relatives onto a harborside reserve near the HBC's Fort Victoria, where trade and employment with the British had become important to the Songhees economy.[5]

Jenny was her mother's fifth child, born about 1840–45 at Sea'nult's longhouse on the lower Nooksack River. The Catholic missionary priest Father Casimir Chirouse baptized T'charlia/Whe'cha'leah "Jeanne" because her parents, like most Lummi, had converted. He probably chose the popular St. Jeanne d'Arc (Joan of Arc) for her baptismal name, a heroic one. As a married woman, she used Jenny (and rarely, Jane) in white society.[6]

Sea'nult, an early convert to Catholicism, fathered nine children and had them all baptized. Jenny's oldest sister was said to have died young and brother William died at age twenty during the tumultuous first year of white settlement in Whatcom County. Her brother Frank (who became the Wynn children's favorite uncle) was about ten years older than Jenny. Her sister Julia married Nooksack John Martin, and became mother to a future Lummi chief, August Martin. Another sister may have been the abandoned first wife of Henry Roeder (see endnote). Jenny's closest relationship was with her sister Mary, about six years older. After Jenny's birth came four half-sisters.[7]

Jenny frequently told her children stories about her eloquent uncle Chow'it'sut who greeted Henry Roeder and Russell Peabody when they arrived looking to use Whatcom Falls. Chow'it'sut was wealthy in both material goods and friends, many of whom had helped build his potlatch house just across the sand and salal bridge (*swulesen*) from the Lummi village to Portage Island. Jenny described her uncle's lavish, exciting potlatches to which invited guests traveled for days. There were "huge" quantities of food and presents, as well as opportunities for her to visit and play with cousins from distant villages. She loved the "stern" man she knew as good and honest, and firmly believed she was the favorite niece of the larger-than-life uncle who had no children of his own. A century later, an elder saw the imposing figure as an orator and "promotions man" who, though usually shrewd, had dealt naively with the white interlopers.[8]

A childhood event spawned one of Jenny's most-told and proud memories, passed down by her daughter Julia Wynn Smith and other listeners. She never forgot the day two large canoes of raiders came to kidnap and steal at her father's Village Point reef net site on Lummi Island. Sea'nult and an older man (probably Tsi'lixw) owned new

HBC muzzle-loading guns, the only ones at the fishery. The raiders did not bring guns, she said, but the fighting was fierce. After an arrow wounded the elder, he continued to load the guns for Sea'nult. Jenny, her older sister, and a servant girl had run into the woods where, huddled in a hollow stump, they heard the shouts and cries of the fight. The frightened young girls hid for more than a day, hearing shouts from time to time. Hungry, the sisters sent the other girl out to look and she found that the shouts were their father's, searching for them with other men. The raiders had left, but taken some women and children with them, and several Lummi men had died.[9]

The raiders came from somewhere up Vancouver Island, perhaps from Quadra Island midway up the larger island's coast. Jenny said that because her grandfather was a Songhees leader, her mother bore greater status in island villages than an unrelated person might. Time was critical, because the stolen people might never be seen again if they were moved. The Lummi men conferred and sent Jenny's "tiny" mother to negotiate a ransom. With her went furs and other valuables to the Songhees village where she enlisted family members to go with her on the dangerous rescue mission. With her negotiating skill and the generous ransom, Jenny's mother and her escort returned the captives to their families. The lesson of the mother's courageous example was not lost on her daughter.[10]

Jenny's Lummi village, like other Coast Salish ones, followed the seasonal work cycle. The Sea'nult family women grew crops on *Si'lat'sis* and *Ske'laxen* prairies where they had traditional rights, probably native carrots and onions, plus potatoes adopted from the HBC. Keeping track of the different short harvest seasons, they gathered bog cranberries and other wild berries and plants at near and distant locations for food, medicine, and raw materials. The Sea'nult family's women and girls probably spent large amounts of time making valuable goods for trade, gifts, and family use: white *ske'xe* (wool dog) blankets, finely woven baskets, hats, and clothing. While summer potlatches included weddings and namings, winter months at Lummi Peninsula were the time for important spiritual ceremonies and for Jenny and other children to learn their family's history and private knowledge around the longhouse fires.

Family grandmothers and "aunties" taught Jenny and her sisters the behaviors expected from respectable girls. When she was with her Nooksack and Songhees elders she would have learned from them also.

The values were much the same as those elite white Americans taught their own daughters: generosity, honesty, humility, reserve, industry, and good manners. When learned and lived out, the values turned girls from wealthy and influential families at Lummi into women their extended families and villages could take pride in, because everyone had a stake in their futures. Through proper behavior and a good marriage, girls like Jenny would add to their extended family's material and non-material wealth. As Jenny reached adult status, chaperones probably accompanied her until she married Tom Wynn. It was the practice of "the best" families, just as it was for wealthy Euro-American families.[11]

Although Jenny left no personal account, her coming-of-age would have called for a seclusion period of weeks to months. This common practice among Native Americans honored the girl and her new status as a woman, as well as the strength of her new female power and influence. The concentrated learning time prepared adolescent Coast Salish girls for adulthood and included child care, cooking, and herbal remedies, as well as the refinement of individual abilities. Incoming whites often thought that the seclusion must be a time of deprivation and isolation. On the contrary, female elders pampered the girls and brought them everything they needed. Girlfriends and female relatives visited every day. The custom was something American authorities would neither understand nor be willing to accommodate in the future.[12]

Important family values that Jenny learned from babyhood would mirror those her future husband learned during his Quaker youth: family interdependence and closeness, priority on generosity, subordinating the nuclear family's role to the community, and recognition of the individual's place within past and future. Jenny and Tom Wynn may never have been able to clearly discuss all of their common beliefs. However, their temperaments and actions demonstrated shared family values that strengthened a forty-one-year marriage and left generations of descendants committed to their communities.[13]

Thomas (Tom) Wynn

Oral family history informed and shaped Tom Wynn as it did Jenny. Three major stories of courage spanned Wynn(e) history before Tom was born which, added to their Quaker culture, formed the core of his family's identity.[14]

The first was the history of Welshman Dr. Thomas Wynne, born in 1627, who first worked as a cooper (barrel-maker), then apprenticed with a physician and earned a surgeon-barber license at age thirty-two (then considered middle-aged). After joining the controversial new Quaker religion, he proselytized and converted people to beliefs the king and Anglican Church considered heretical and treasonous. Without influential friends, Dr. Wynne served six years in filthy, cold, and unventilated Ruthin Prison with wealthy convert William Penn.[15]

After both were freed, the Quakers began to leave for America when Penn inherited a large land grant and vowed to build a colony for the "Friends." Dr. Wynne bought five thousand of Penn's acres across the Schuylkill River from the Philadelphia townsite and along with most of his family left Wales on Penn's ship the *Welcome* in 1682. Smallpox broke out during the hellish eight-week crossing. By the time the survivors docked, Dr. Wynne was William Penn's personal doctor and best friend.[16]

Wynne helped Penn negotiate with the *Lenni Lenape* (Delawares) for land they had owned for some six thousand years. The Quakers reputedly treated the Delaware with the same respect their religion accorded others, even allowing women to speak in meetings, a precedent for colonists to come. They still coveted the land, but used negotiation to foster cooperation and friendship instead of the conflict inevitably caused by compulsion. All the same, the "generous" payment extinguished Delaware possession of their land when they had no concept of exclusive ownership. For decades Delaware villages were left untouched, contributing to the Quakers' wide reputation for fair dealings. However, like most Europeans, the Quakers believed that indigenous people should make way for colonists whose culture must ultimately dominate.[17]

Peace between Quakers and the Delaware lasted many years, even though the church did not see them as potential members and colonists. Quaker "meetings" never dropped their commitment to the Indians and took their side in many disputes. Church beliefs in fair treatment also led the Wynnes and others to free their slaves in the 1700s after years of debate to become an early voice of abolitionism. Quakers also adopted pacifism and forbade members to enter military service.

Dr. Wynne spent the rest of his life as a founding father of Philadelphia and its medical community, and served in civic offices. He built a summer house on his land beside an old Indian trail that had been widened and named the Conestoga Road, connecting Philadelphia to the Merion Meeting House and the interior. Wynne mortared a keystone dated 1690 into a stone wall and named the house and estate "Wynnestay." It played a future role in Washington Territory's Tom Wynn's history as large as any individual did. After Dr. Wynne's only son Jonathan enlarged the house, it passed down to each generation's "Thomas Wynne." As the sixth "Thomas Wynn(e)" in the direct line, Tom grew up on the estate. He told his children of the events that took place within the stone house's walls in much the same way Jenny's family told their history around the longhouse fire in a place they had also occupied for many generations.[18]

The second example of Wynne family courage was set by the fourth owners of Wynnestay during the Revolution. Tom Wynn's great-grandfather (Thomas Wynne #3) and his wife Margaret gave generations of Wynnes the following story also enshrined in history books.[19]

Despite church rules that threatened disenrollment for military service, this Thomas Wynne immediately joined the fledgling Continental Army when independence was declared. Four months later, the British captured Lt. Wynne on Manhattan Island and sent him to a prison ship with much of General George Washington's army. For the next four years, he battled to stay alive in one of the wretched "sinkholes of filth, vermin, infectious disease and despair," so similar to the Ruthin Prison of Dr. Thomas Wynne's experience.[20]

Margaret and the children spent the war alone at Wynnestay. They watched the Continental Congress with its wagons full of records flee the capital city, leaving the Wynnes and their neighbors at the mercy of the British forces. Every British Army unit heading inland passed directly in front of the house.[21]

Redcoat foragers moved freely up and down the road and harassed residents. On December 11, 1777, two Pennsylvania militia regiments trying to protect the Wynnes and other farmers came under attack near Wynnestay. Margaret had never offered resistance while the British soldiers cut up her carpets and mattresses searching for valuables before they grabbed food and liquor. However, that day Lt. Wynne had already spent a year on the prison ship and apparently Margaret was fed up with pacifism. The peaceable Quaker housewife brought the livestock inside the house, barricaded the windows and doors, and took up arms. When she refused to open the door, the British foragers fired into Wynnestay's fieldstone walls.[22]

There are two versions of what happened next. In one, the Continentals heard gunfire and came running, then shot three of His Majesty's finest. In the version believed by most descendants and many others, Margaret shot the invaders. To these must be added a more intriguing scenario. It is possible that Tom Wynn's grandfather, Thomas #4, then fourteen years old, killed them but the militia took credit to protect him from British revenge. Using a heavy flintlock gun, it was hardly possible for Margaret alone to have killed three men of the world's best fighting force. Everyone agrees that they buried three soldiers in the corner of her yard in fear that the British officers would find the bodies. If young Thomas was also a shooter, retribution might have been swift and lethal. The British graves, surrounded by stones, reminded Wynne children of their family's courage as they do today.[23]

Lt. Wynne's military service seems to mark a turning point in the Wynnes' active Quaker church participation. After Thomas #5 (father of Whatcom County's Tom) married non-Quaker Hannah Sharp, the family remained Quaker, but grew progressively less religious as the years passed. Though Wynnestay was a large house, it was traditional Quaker in style with two rooms below and two rooms above. With Tom's newly widowed grandmother Elizabeth living with eight children in the four rooms, there was no space for Thomas (#5) and Hannah to build their own family. They moved into a new house on the farm, of which only 119 acres remained of the original five thousand. The new home bore the name "Wynnstay" on the gate (dropping the "e") and Tom's parents started using just "Wynn" for their surname.[24]

Tom's grandmother Elizabeth kept the big house for herself, apparently for a more unusual reason, resulting in the third family story passed down by Tom and other Wynn(e)s. Wynnestay lay just outside Chester County, a major Quaker center of the Underground Railroad. The 1600s house still had no staircase, just a panel in the keeping room's ceiling that slid back for a ladder to the upper rooms and then into the attic. Later generations believed that Tom's grandmother Elizabeth and his uncle Samuel hid runaway slaves in the attic behind its panel. Twentieth-century examination found a rubble-filled room under the porch and a seventy-five-foot tunnel to the springhouse and creek flowing to the Schuylkill River, typical of Underground Railroad sanctuaries. The tantalizing question remains: Did Tom Wynn's grandmother live out her Quaker principles by helping runaway slaves at her own peril and that of her son's family in the other house?[25]

Three daughters and a son came before Hannah gave birth on June 3, 1819, to Tom Wynn. He was the sixth Thomas Wynn(e) in his line after Dr. Wynne's only son Jonathan. Of the ten children born, five girls and two sons (Tom and Delaney) survived to adulthood. Tom's father inherited the farmland (without the original Wynnestay house) and the family prospered.[26]

Tom spent his childhood on the working farm, surrounded by siblings and nearby cousins within the geographical and cultural world of the Friends, and just down the road from the influential Merion Meeting House. Child-centered Quakers wanted their offspring to see home as a refuge, so they disciplined with reason and rewards, rather than punishment. They taught children to believe that people would reciprocate if treated fairly and kindly. In the pursuit of equality, Quakers encouraged their daughters and wives to speak out in meetings and family. As adults, the Friends were expected to practice the highest business and work ethics within the idea of the "good neighborhood" where people joined forces to erect buildings and do community service. There was little tolerance for idleness. Tom absorbed it all.[27]

The repressive "Quietism" church movement of Tom's childhood resulted in some cultural traits that stood out among both easterners and his future communities in the West. Quaker language became more economical and simple: blunt without superfluous words, yet colorful with invented expressions such as "flabbergasted," "cattywampus," and "bamboozle." In the pursuit of simplicity, observant Quakers abandoned the enjoyment of music and singing, which they came to regard as sins equal to theft and lying. This, along with the silence that reigned at services until someone felt compelled to speak, led outsiders to increasingly refer to the Quakers as the "quiet people."

During Tom's school years, his church developed conflicted attitudes toward education. Members wanted literacy, but not enough to work against equality. Tom did not attend respected Lower Merion Academy near home. In addition to a "common school" down the road, there was a hexagonal Quaker school building at Wynnestay where the numerous cousins may have gathered. Quakers, including Tom's family that descended from a respected physician, turned their children from the professions toward agriculture and the practical trades.[28]

Tom needed a trade because his older brother Delaney would inherit the farmland. He (or his father) chose blacksmithing, which may have been a family trade already. The advantage was its crucial importance to city and rural people alike, and it was portable. Tom probably worked at the smithy next to his parents' home, ready for customers traveling the major route now called Lancaster Road.[29]

Tom's parents continued to loosen their spiritual ties to Quakerism, probably because the Lower Merion Meeting labeled their mixed marriage "mongrel." Their meeting house had become a divisive place of argument and harshness. Marriage rules had become so strict that young people like Tom and his siblings, who now lived in an increasingly diverse place, found it all but impossible to fulfill church requirements with the spouse they wanted. Some of his siblings apparently rebelled and joined the Episcopal Church and the family moved burials to a new city cemetery. Family accounts say the Wynns remained "very straight-laced." They were always concerned with appearances, and willing to purchase goods of the finest craftsmanship whatever the cost. Still culturally Quaker, Tom's parents expected their children to live with them unless they married. Tom and his unmarried siblings stayed home.[30]

Within this atmosphere that might make young and single Quaker men like Tom think about moving on, gold fever struck.

The California Gold Rush hit Philadelphia newspapers in late November 1848. They published the adventures of early rushers, including the skilled craftsmen "hurrying on, expecting to realize fortunes." At age twenty-nine, bachelor Tom Wynn decided to join the other "go-ahead boys."[31]

A Quaker blacksmith had more travel funds available than many. He could go most cheaply overland, but faced the possibility of injury or cholera. Wealthier passengers chose Panama steamers, but the possibility of a boiler explosion or permanent malaria offset the advantages of speed and comfort. Tom's choice was typical of eastern seaport residents: a sailing ship on the safer Cape Horn route. He sailed on one of thirty-one ships departing from Philadelphia in 1849 loaded with miners, craftsmen, and merchandise. They were sent off with the tears of relatives and friends who didn't know if they'd ever see the young men again.[32]

Tom left the city where any longtime resident knew his history as soon as he said his name. He left the fieldstone houses and farm that sheltered his family for eight generations. He leapt into the unknown just as Dr. Thomas Wynne had done in 1682. He packed his Quaker values in his trunk.

Most of the Cape Horn ships were rickety tubs rolling in the swells, fitted with tiers of sleeping hammocks for a voyage lasting three and a half months minimum and six months for the unlucky. The year Tom sailed, no ships sank and few people died, although thousands of young men felt like they would during their first bout of seasickness. Hundreds died crossing Panama, and thousands died of cholera on the Great Plains. Tom's choice was the smart one, even if he rode the seas for 13,000 miles. Underway, he faced the reality that even the cleanest ships declined into filthy, miserable places below decks where constant human contact led to quarrels, often liquor-fueled. The staggering racial, ethnic, social class, and personality differences added to stress from the unfamiliar strict shipboard discipline. Ship cuisine for Tom and the others was much different from Mother's, sometimes inedible and inevitably boring. To break the tedium of thousands of empty hours, the men gambled, wrote, played practical jokes, sang, danced, and held prayer meetings. Anything to fill the hours.[33]

At Cape Horn, Tom's ship faced unforgiving currents colliding where the oceans met, along with floating ice and ceaseless winds in the worst stretch of water on the planet. Passengers could be caught for months in a nightmare of seasickness, constant damp, and then fog and lack of wind on the final leg. All were good conditioning for the tumultuous life Tom was about to encounter in San Francisco.

The final weeks out, forty-niners turned the ships into floating factories for mining equipment. One fellow said: "the puffs of the bellows, with the dingy smoke rising and curling above, the heavy blows of the blacksmith...were seen and heard." Nothing documented that Tom worked beside the carpenters and tinsmiths, but few mining "companies" would waste the talents of an experienced blacksmith, and the work would allow him to start his new life with a fatter wallet.[34]

When Tom first saw San Francisco, it looked far different from the orderly Quaker brick and stone of home. The miners' tent city ("Happy Valley") stretched inland two miles behind the dunes, plagued by non-existent sanitation, fleas, and rats. Not far away was "Pleasant Valley," which housed foundries, light manufacturing, and shipbuilding, plus worker tents and cabins. It is likely that Tom gravitated toward the second to live and work. Most Americans had never confronted a virtual Babel of languages and ethnicities living and working together in chaos and self-interest. For Tom Wynn, raised within his disciplined and caring Quaker "good neighborhood," it was probably a cultural shock.

The year he arrived, the city held nearly 35,000 men in a masculine culture of late nights and heavy drinking. Lanterns and tossed cigarettes took their toll on wooden buildings and only dynamite stopped four major fires in the first two years of the gold rush. Rebuilding, plus normal city and port needs, put heavy demands on Tom and the city's other blacksmiths. The fires demonstrated to men like Henry Roeder a permanent need for high-quality Pacific Northwest lumber.[35]

Tom Wynn, broad-shouldered and muscled at nearly thirty-four, encountered the short, dandified, and brusquely authoritative Roeder in May 1853. In town to buy machinery and hire men to operate his new saw mill at Whatcom Falls, Roeder hoped his new venture would finally make him a rich man. Impressed by the powerful, yet quietly dignified blacksmith, Roeder explained his needs and what he was offering. He convinced Wynn to take a chance and come north with a few others. Tom left for Washington Territory shortly thereafter, probably in Roeder's tow.[36]

The clear-eyed Pennsylvanian redhead with the bushy mustache and luxuriant mutton chops was a quiet sort. Roeder, the earringed, profane, and often unpleasant younger man was a contrast. Despite Tom Wynn's sojourn among salty tongues, his version of profanity ran to "drat" and "by gum." Freedom was the essence of the California atmosphere—freedom from Eastern rules, prejudices, and customs, but it came with a cost. In the future, others referred to Tom Wynn time and again as "the Quaker blacksmith," an indication of how deep his identity ran.[37]

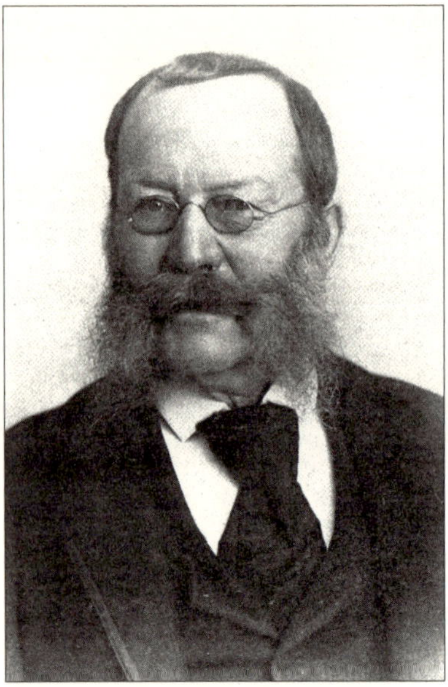
Thomas Wynn. *Unknown photographer.* From *Lottie Roeder Roth,* History of Whatcom County, Vol. 2. *Courtesy of Whatcom Museum, Bellingham, WA.*

Upon arrival at Whatcom Falls, Tom saw the crude mill going up beside the graduated cascade that ended in a large tidal pool. Immense evergreens dwarfed scattered tents and a few crude cabins that clung to the waterway's banks. Lummi people dominated the scene as Jenny's relatives and others took advantage of the new economic opportunity by supplying mill construction labor and canoe transportation while living in Tsi'lixw's secondary longhouse nearby. The women sold food, cedar mats, and baskets to the newcomers, a godsend since the closest merchant that year was a two-day canoe trip to Port Townsend.[38]

Tom's son said his father decided to take a land claim on Whidbey Island in addition to working at the mill, probably at Penn's Cove prairies where a group of farmers had settled the past three years. He never registered the claim so lost it. To the casual visitor, it showed more immediate promise than Whatcom, but a large coal seam was accidentally discovered a mile around the bay from the Roeder Mill. The San Francisco syndicate owners would need a blacksmith and it was clear that there were multiple demands for blacksmith services on Bellingham Bay.[39]

A more substantial settlement than the one at the falls rose at the Sehome Mine as fast as workmen could build it in early 1854. A major boost to the settlements was the mine store and a saloon. Tom probably handled work from the mine and Roeder's mill for some time. He entered the public record in the fall of 1854 when he served as a grand juror from newly-formed Whatcom County. The county commissioners had to pay the cash-poor jurors to attend the district court in Port Townsend, where the men enjoyed the regional gathering's camaraderie, shops, restaurants, and saloons.[40]

Jenny and Tom

Listed as "She-ah-delt-hu, Subchief," Jenny's father was among thirteen Lummi headmen who signed the Point Elliott Treaty in the dark, cold, and wet days of January 1855. It was a business contract between sovereign nations, not a treaty of surrender, although attendees could clearly see guns (and their implication) in the hands of military around the treaty grounds. The Lummi reserved their precious island as well as *Chah'choo'sen*, the "island" between the branches of the Nooksack/Lummi River at its delta, much of which is today's town of Ferndale. Within the reservation borders yet to be ratified and surveyed lay the *Nooskwiem*, the mystical place of bluff, prairie, salt marsh, wild hay, lake and creek—the place of Sea'nult's fish weir and longhouse.[41]

Not long after the treaty meetings, Tom Wynn sought out Jenny's parents to request marriage with their daughter. It was Tom's responsibility to canoe out and approach Jenny's family to talk of marriage, and the Wynn children said their father followed all the protocols. He was familiar with local marriages to high-born indigenous women, including those of Roeder, Peabody, and Virginia blue-blood coal mine manager/lawyer E. C. Fitzhugh. Years later, Jenny's daughter Julia asked her father what brought the unlikely pair together. He replied in his word-thrifty Quaker way: "I saw her and I liked her." No one recorded what Jenny thought of her parents' decision to send her off with the red-headed near-stranger.[42]

Romantic love as a reason to marry was not a priority for elite Lummi families, and neither was it among the Quakers. Better reasons for both groups were to gain an affectionate partner for life and interfamily ties that would benefit both family and the community. Readiness to work hard was important. Romantic love was a bonus.

Tom's Quaker-infused demeanor probably played a part in gaining the approval of Jenny's family elders since he was not one of the settlement's "headmen," although as a skilled craftsman he might have been perceived as equally important in a different way. If Tom had married at home, his family and Quaker meeting members would have had to formally approve the match just as Jenny's did. His youth had been spent in a culture that supported strong female leadership, and women's freedom to voice their ideas and be consulted in difficult community decisions. Perhaps apparent in Tom's behavior, this attitude made him a good match for Jenny, whose status carried with it an expectation of leadership.[43]

An exchange of gifts and service obligations similar to Quaker marriage arrangements marked Jenny and Tom's tribal custom wedding. Sea'nult became his *me'n,* an interchangeable term for father and father-in-law, very similar to the Quaker terms for the same relationships. Evidence indicates that the wedding most likely took place in February to March 1855. As many other important families did that January, her entire family may have accompanied Sea'nult to the treaty negotiations far up Puget Sound at Mukilteo. The chaperonage custom would make the chance of Jenny becoming pregnant before marriage nonexistent. She gave birth to Marshall on January 3, 1856 at Sehome. Tom had now linked his future to the Northwest. His Pennsylvania family began to call Tom and his family "The Wynns of the West."[44]

Jenny and Tom settled into married life at the Sehome Mine, probably in one of the two-room whitewashed cabins for the skilled workers. Several of the other native wives spoke her language and some were probably at least distantly related to her. In the diverse neighborhood along the bluff above the wharf and beach, the women's dialects mixed with English and Chinook Jargon, spiced by Irish and British accents, Southern drawls, and Tom's Quakerisms. The small community, tucked between the noise of mill and mine, was enlivened only sporadically by the unexpected arrival of a steamer with mail and visitors, or *Laich'wil'tach* raiding parties in the vicinity.[45]

Bachelors highly valued the few resident wives, nearly all of whom took in boarders since the men were willing to pay whatever it took to live in a home and eat home cooking. All the settlement women needed each other. Irish wife Teresa Eldridge pointed out to newcomers that the settlers depended almost entirely on the Lummi for food and instructions on what to do with the dozens of unfamiliar local edibles. The indigenous wives learned to use store-bought ingredients and kitchen equipment to provide the bread and desserts the men enjoyed.[46]

Laich'wil'tach ("the unkillable ones") raids continued on the Salish Sea after the settlers arrived at Whatcom Falls. Leaving Fort Victoria for their winter longhouses in Tlingit territory or on Quadra Island, the raiders moved rapidly in their large war canoes, always seeking vulnerability, striking quickly and leaving swiftly. They could—and did—outrun the aging steamer *Massachusetts* the U.S. Navy leased for Puget

Sound patrol. Coast Salish villagers' defensive strategy had generally been to take on the invaders only when they organized overwhelming numbers of trained warriors for a trap or retaliation. Jenny's mother had lived through one of those battles, hidden in a tree stump. Without long-term experience, the settlers did not fully comprehend how lethal raiders could be, but Jenny and the other wives knew that they would bedevil the new community's life. The presence in town of the Lummi daughters linked the settlers and their people across the bay together in common interest.[47]

Jenny's cousin Whi'lano (David Crockett) had led the defense of the nearby small Pattle mine from an attack in May 1854, but the threat intensified. In a subsequent incident, Stikines from southeast Alaska pulled their canoes one thousand miles to retaliate against Olympia for the death of one of their young leaders there. While the Coast Salish preferred restitution, northern peoples usually demanded "an eye for an eye" and did not distinguish between the guilty and the innocent when seeking revenge. They did not need to go as far as Olympia to retaliate. Two Bellingham Bay men were found murdered and left adrift in their canoe. Sehome Mine manager E. C. Fitzhugh's pleas to the territorial government for assistance brought only a few muskets. The residence of some Northerners working at the mill and living within the community also spooked people. When the court indicted "Dirty Dan" Harris for selling weapons to the Northerners to attack the Lummi, the settlers realized they couldn't even trust all their own. The Lummi built more defensive works and hidden shelters at the peninsula, but the Wynns and other families across the bay were vulnerable if Lummi runners could not warn them in time to get everyone into the Whatcom blockhouse the men there had built.[48]

By fall 1855, the Treaty War had erupted in the southern Puget Sound area. Jenny had good cause to worry about her family and the relatives who might come under suspicion if settlers and Lummi lost their trust in one another. Into the uncertainty about what would happen to the mostly peaceful and cooperative relationships on Bellingham Bay, baby Marshall made his appearance two days after the 1856 New Year.[49]

Tom and other mine employees did not join the local militia company that was subject to orders to move south. Governor Isaac Stevens wanted the strategic mine guarded and producing coal for the warships cruising the Sound during the conflict. For Tom this may have worked out well, given Quaker reluctance to serve in the military and traditional support of indigenous demands for justice. When the local militia left for distant Snoqualmie Prairie, a small detachment remained behind with the employees to guard the families who slept every night in the Whatcom blockhouse and at the mine. The war never touched Whatcom County and the native residents and settlers remained at peace. They preserved their friendship and in-law relationships.[50]

After U.S. Army Captain George E. Pickett and his company arrived in 1856 everyone relaxed, thinking that any raiders would be deterred when they heard about the fort's guns and after "Dirty Dan" Harris was indicted. But if the Wynns thought the trouble was over, they were wrong. Less than a year later, raiders landed at fortified, guarded Sehome in the dead of night while people slept. They walked silently to Whatcom, broke into and stole from a cabin, then retreated to the canoes and left—all without waking anyone except the terrified burglary victim taken hostage for the walk back to the canoes. Frightened settlers began to argue and many talked of leaving. Then Jenny's grandfather, Songhees Chief Freezy, arrived to warn them that he had seen four hundred raiders on the Salish Sea. Captain Pickett's troops building the fort were in disarray, with many locked in the guardhouse for drinking, fighting, and insubordination (see chapter 4). They would not be as helpful as the town hoped. The Sehome men quickly built their own blockhouse since the one at Whatcom, which was armed with a cannon, was too far away for the Wynns and others to reach quickly in an overwhelming attack. Jenny, baby Marshall, and the other young wives and their children slept inside the cramped structure nightly, guarded by their men and a new cannon. Fitzhugh had only Tom and nine other men available to fight if the war canoes arrived again.[51]

The Lummi hosted a meeting of Coast Salish leaders from around the region to organize a common defense. Captain Pickett and Fitzhugh attended uninvited, though perhaps not unwelcome after it was determined that everyone had the same goal. Seven months later, Fitzhugh wrote that everyone felt more confident with the defensive improvements and his "great faith in the support" of the Lummi. By that time, the U.S. Boundary Commission's Army escort was in place up the coast near the Semiahmah village. The new Lummi preparations, the presence of the army with cannon in two locations, and a patrolling gunship discouraged new raider forays into American territory.[52]

By early 1858 the mine's shaft sloped 121 feet down from its crude opening. A bigger steam engine with water pumps required Tom's attention during its installation. At a small mine like Sehome's, the blacksmith's responsibilities included repairs, sharpening tools, and shoeing the mules. Tom's future seemed secure at Sehome instead of a mile away where Roeder's mill was floundering because of Whatcom Falls' unpredictable flow.[53]

Spring 1858, and the Fraser River gold rush brought a spectacularly different chaos to Jenny's neighborhood. It had already been a worrisome year. After a poor salmon run, the winter had been hard for Jenny's people. Her father Sea'nult died in March, possibly victim of another Puget Sound epidemic that raged through the Lummi and Samish in late winter. Mine manager E. C. Fitzhugh, now also the local Indian agent, had gathered people in several longhouses scattered among the bay settlements for food and medicine. His "white" rations had to supplement what little they had. Both Fitzhugh's and Lummi medicines were generally ineffective against the still-unidentified epidemic that killed dozens (see chapter 4).[54]

Steamers disgorged old California hands Solomon Allen (see chapter 3) and other hopefuls onto the Sehome Mine dock below Jenny's cabin shortly after the epidemic waned. All summer she watched thousands camp on the beach, occupy every empty sleeping space in homes, and wander her neighborhood, often drunk and belligerent. They waited for months for Fraser River water to drop and expose the gold-bearing sandbars. Dozens of businesses sprang up, some highly desirable to Jenny and other wives, and many most certainly not. Sehome Mine carpenter Nicholas Sheffer was "impressed." "For debauchery and immorality," he said. "I don't believe it was ever equaled on the American continent, if in the world."[55]

Historians have overlooked a possible contributor to the unsettled and often lawless atmosphere of the gold rush summer: two geographic events that might have rattled the newcomers, and possibly all the bay residents who had little access to current scientific information and culturally saw many events in a spiritual context. In April, just as the first wave of miners arrived, Mount Baker began to erupt. The light from the lava fountain was visible even on Vancouver Island at night and the region was shrouded in smoke most of the summer while the volcano continued to "belch." On June 2 the "unlooked for, untold and unusual visitor" Donati's Comet first showed itself "brandishing its crystal tresses" in the night skies and remained visible until at least October. With its tail spreading across more than a quarter of the sky, it often appeared to dip closer to the earth. In a century when people looked for divine omens foretelling disastrous days to come, these two events that coincided with the gold rush and its accompanying bedlam may have frightened people of both cultures.[56]

As soon as the first news of the gold strike arrived in early spring, Sehome Mine employees, Whatcom Mill hands, and Fort Bellingham soldiers began to desert. Before long, the only employees at the mine with Fitzhugh were Tom Wynn, mining engineer McKinney Tawes, carpenter Nick Sheffer, and office clerk/civil engineer John Tennant. Alone they could do little to get any coal out, but they kept busy with county jobs and others that required their skills, as well as guarding the mine families. In the face of the numbers and liquor arriving, the sheriff saw that the ramshackle shed of a county jail would get busier. Captain Pickett did not want the fort's guardhouse overrun with civilians. Tom got the contract to reinforce the crude jail with thirty pounds of iron the county bought for him.[57]

After the bulk of the Fraser-bound miners invaded in June, the proximity of Lummi longhouses and miner tents led to the first recorded violence against indigenous residents. Deep Lummi anger at the invasion of thousands of men who preyed upon their women and disrespected the men, coupled with the liquor-soaked atmosphere, led to volatility and violence between the two groups. It was a first. Miners murdered as many as ten native people.[58]

The stubborn residents around the mill and mine took care of each other that year in the face of the socially destructive invasion. They even used real estate to generate cash income for the community. Russell Peabody had his land claim surveyed, lots marked out, and officially called it "Whatcom." Tom Wynn bought a lot for fifty dollars and re-sold it to a gold rush newcomer eager for a business location. In twenty-four hours, he made a 450 percent profit![59]

As a couple, the Wynns found another cash opportunity. Ten thousand stranded miners had no organized transportation to the

Fraser River Canyon mines. With the Whatcom Trail shortcut to the river unfinished, the only route was by water. U.S. Boundary Survey personnel watched Salish shovel-nose river canoes, rafts, and rickety boats full of miners head for the Fraser delta, knowing many would die in the massive waves off the river's mouth. The craze to be among the first at the sandbars when the water receded opened an unlimited market for the larger, heavier saltwater canoes. Mine carpenter Sheffer started building small boats that brought whatever price he named from the gold-crazed buyers.[60]

The Wynns convinced some of Jenny's relatives at Lummi to go into business together. Their daughter said that Jenny was the link with family members who carved or bought saltwater canoes from others and delivered them to Sehome. Tom negotiated the sale to impatient prospectors. According to their daughter, they "did a land office business" for the outrageous price of $400 to $500 each (around $13,000 in 2017). It is not so clear what portion of the proceeds went to Jenny's family and other Lummi who worked tirelessly to produce the canoes quickly.[61]

The sale of so many canoes coincided with another poor salmon run. In some locations, they didn't come at all. Some Lummi had sold their own canoes, but ultimately needed more canoes that year to search out enough fish for winter reserves. Remembering the previous winter, the Indian agents called a meeting of elders and tried unsuccessfully to convince them to stop selling any canoes to the Wynns. The canoe profits gave the Wynns a solid financial base for their family and profited her Lummi family, but it came at the expense of people with less foresight and fewer connections to help them. Some people ended up completely dependent on resident agent Fitzhugh's ability to bring in supplies that winter. Hunger was widespread. The unforeseen consequences of the Wynn business clouded their reputation.[62]

As quickly as the miners and merchants had arrived, they left, taking the hastily built stores with them. They left only a single brick store building that became the community's rainproof center of life. Prices for Whatcom lots and everything else dropped precipitously. Jenny gave birth to her first daughter, Anna Maria ("Mariah") the following summer. She may have been assisted by Mary Bird Tawes, the Sehome midwife and spouse of the mine engineer, but a Lummi midwife would have been preferable. Jenny's life settled back around her husband's work at the mine and the attendant laundry problems of a blacksmith's wife with two youngsters. When the syndicate ownership leased the mine out for six years, Tom found himself with new bosses, and expanded operations that produced a company town with thirty-five employees, more saloons, gambling, and repeated violence.[63]

Sehome ne'er-do-well hotelier and gambler Sheriff Enoch May resigned in January 1860. New sheriff Fred Lane promptly had book-keeping trouble and angrily resigned a few months later. Jenny's husband—the Quiet Man, the Quaker—found himself appointed "Sheriff Wynn" in short order, and people knocked on her door day or night. Covering a roadless area that now is three counties, all transportation around the coastline and islands was by canoe. Tom had only Deputy William Kelly and a constable in the San Juans to help him. The situation meant that he—unpredictably and frequently—had to leave his wife, two babies, and regular job. After the army left for the 1859 "Pig War" on San Juan Island (the boundary dispute between the United States and Britain), Fort Bellingham's abandoned blockhouse had served as the county jail. Before Tom took office the County Commission declared it hopelessly decrepit as it had the previous jail, so he or a deputy were forced to canoe prisoners to Camp Pickett's guardhouse on San Juan Island. That relieved Tom of daily responsibility for prisoner upkeep and security, but Captain Pickett happily charged the county a handsome fee for the service.[64]

With its Quaker foundations, Pennsylvania had no death penalty. Both Quaker and Coast Salish traditions preferred apology and compensation to physical punishment. Unfortunately, Western frontier settlers loved hard labor, jail time, or hanging for miscreants who didn't simply disappear. If there was to be a hanging in Whatcom County, Sheriff Wynn would be in charge. People expected him to carry a gun and to use it if necessary. The office might not turn out to be a comfortable fit.

One event demonstrates Jenny and Tom's situation. His new office immediately thrust him into the middle of a court case, *Territory v. Oscar Olney*. The Sehome bartender was indicted for assault with intent to kill, and for waving a knife and pistol in the midst of a crowd. Prior to his trial, Olney was housed at Camp Pickett. Friends posted bond for the "crippled" defendant, whereupon Constable Gustav Graff snidely reported Olney "librated (sp)." After the District Court jury convicted him in Port Townsend, now-Territorial Justice E.C.

Fitzhugh remanded him to Tom's custody until sentencing in a county seat (Whatcom), which had no functional jail. Back in Whatcom, the county commissioners ordered their friend Tom to take Olney out to the Camp Pickett guardhouse to serve out whatever sentence Judge Fitzhugh imposed. The number of long canoe trips back and forth to the islands and the Port Townsend court, even if aided by a small sail, took a toll on the busy blacksmith.[65]

Records show that the county commissioners accepted Tom's resignation immediately after he returned to town with Fitzhugh's order and received the commission's order about incarceration. Tom may have known that Fitzhugh was planning a sentence of one day in jail for the serious crime. He may have refused to travel two days back out to the island with the prisoner, wait one day for Olney to serve his sentence, then travel two days home. Curiously, after Fitzhugh imposed the fine and one-day sentence on Olney, locals petitioned Governor McMullen (a Virginia legislature friend of Fitzhugh's) to help the veteran. No other case exists in the Third Territorial District Court records in which a governor paid the fine to get a convicted felon released. Tom resigned barely six weeks after his election to a full term, although the Commission made him serve until the December elections. Tom's reason, if not in protest to the Olney case, may have simply been that he found the job too frustrating and time-consuming for a busy blacksmith with a young family. In any case, the incident ended his interest in county government positions.[66]

Tom moved Jenny and the children south to the Grennan and Canney Mill on the north side of Camano Island for a new job not long after his resignation in 1860. They seem to have moved out of the county even while he was forced to remain in office, though Deputy Kelly was probably in actual charge at Whatcom. Tom started work at the Utsalady mill where other Whatcom County men went occasionally to earn extra money. Jenny had to leave her familiar small Sehome neighborhood where she had women friends of both cultures to join a mill community of several hundred people. At Sehome, she had been close to her own family but at Utsalady a two-day canoe journey separated Jenny and her Lummi-speaking children from them.[67]

Tom joined blacksmiths from England and Ireland at the large mill. Lawrence Grennan and his partners supplied spars of the finest quality and size for masts and yardarms to shipbuilders, merchant ships needing repair and European navies. The knot-free, 125-foot-long spars, three to four feet wide at the base, gained easy fame for their ability to withstand the tremendous stresses placed on the largest fully rigged ships sailing the world's fiercest waters. The giant vertical saw that handled two-hundred-foot-long logs needed a blacksmith's constant upkeep along with the iron rails, steam engine, and tool repairs.[68]

The Utsalady settlement's atmosphere was different from that of the struggling Bellingham Bay "towns." Part-owner Marshall Thompson and his Kikiallus (Lower Skagit) wife lived at her nearby village, while bachelors at the large mill lived in Bummer's Hall. The owners had recently built solid, single-family homes for the "mechanics" like Tom with families. Puget Sound steamers made regular stops and the mill owners built a school for the children, both of which represented improvements over post-gold-rush Sehome. Ships from around the world brought multinational crews that exposed Jenny and the children to many cultures and languages, encounters that were probably both positive and negative. The family stayed three years while a busy port town grew beside the prospering mill.

Jenny gave birth to her third child during stormy November 1862. They named the healthy little boy Thomas Benton Wynn, the newest descendant to hold Dr. Thomas Wynne's honored name.[69]

While Tom worried about what was happening in wartime Pennsylvania, Jenny's family concerns focused on the massive changes taking place at Lummi since the U.S. Senate ratified the Point Elliott Treaty in 1859. The new bureaucracy began to significantly impinge upon her relatives. The intermarried farmer-in-charge, C. C. Finkbonner, supervised the construction of "white"-style homes beside the longhouses, coined "New Lummi Village." The health and benefit of American indigenous peoples held little priority for a government at war. The treaty's agreed-upon "annuities" of tools, clothing, and foodstuffs were shoddy and skimpy, not at all what was promised. The government also interfered with Lummi leadership by starting a system of appointed chiefs whose certificate of appointment required them to spy on their own people. Lastly, the new boarding school at Tulalip Reservation began to (often forcibly) siphon off the smartest of the leaders' children, including Jenny's cousin (and future chief), teenaged Henry Kwina.[70]

The Wynns moved back to the Sehome Mine. After Tom's childhood friend, carpenter Henry Post, arrived in 1863, the two made plans for a common move and new beginning on farms near the Nooksack River. Tom's friend at the mine, John Tennant, had already married Jenny's cousin Clara, daughter of her uncle Tsi'lixw and Annie, a Duwamish woman. Tennant had taken the county's first agricultural land claim, on the Nooksack River close to where the cousins' extended family lived on the east side of the reservation. Without a definitive survey, it remained vague where a claim was permissible around the reservation's fringes. Tom decided to move to the fertile *Ske'laxen* prairie adjoining the Tennant prairie (*Si'lat'sis*) before all the choice land was grabbed by others. In fact, the Wynns joined the Tennants within reservation borders on *Chah'choo'sen* "island." Like Tennant, Tom assumed that the government would ultimately adjust the boundaries to allow them as "Old Settlers" with prominent Lummi wives to remain where they were. And if they didn't, Jenny might have allotment rights or he could claim that *Ske'laxen* had been a wedding gift from her father.[71]

Ske'laxen had been the home of a small group of Coast Salish who, a few years before whites colonized the bay, moved upstream toward the Nooksacks or were absorbed by the Lummi. Thirty years before that, they had some control over the Nooksack River's delta and part of the bay. Their rich, cultivated prairie that Tom Wynn coveted was the natural home of the nutritious blue camas lily bulbs, the *shugrack* (wild carrot), and probably other food plants. Open prairie attracted elk, deer, and other wildlife for hunting. Like *Si'lat'sis,* it was an agricultural gem with which Jenny and her family were familiar.[72]

The Wynn family officially settled on their claim in June 1863. Tennant noted in his journal that Tom "came up to work on his place" on a warm and fair Sunday the seventh. Jenny and the children may have canoed out from Sehome with him to see her cousin Clara's new baby and visit while the men walked over to the Wynn claim. Tennant, a professional surveyor, probably measured out about 160 acres for Tom, who also needed to prepare a temporary shelter.[73]

The 1862 homestead rules required at least one spouse to live on the claim for more than six months out of each of the five years leading to obtaining title. In practice, settlers usually kept homes in Whatcom or Sehome in addition to cabins or crude shelters on the claim. They documented their improvements in anticipation of the opening of a government land office in Olympia, though it was still ten years away. Nine months after Tom established his claim, the U.S. General Land Office published a warning for settlers to beware of any absence that could be construed as desertion. That kept claimants from leaving to fight in the Civil War. It also stressed that the claims were for agriculture, not for logging. To prevent that, a pre-emption claim filed in anticipation of the land office opening couldn't be sold for five years. Primary rights went into force as soon as the claimant moved onto the land, even if it was a tent occupied only half the time. This protected people like the Wynns from having to go to court to eject an interloper.[74]

Jenny's farm life thus began in a crude cedar cabin, if not in a tent. When Tom was not there working on the required improvements, he worked at one of the coal mines for cash until the farm could support his family. It is not known how much of the time Jenny and the children were at the claim, or if they were alone there any of the time. They may have slept at the Tennant cabin and walked over to the claim in the daytime.

It was probably at this time that Thomas T'ing and David Sco'tah moved to the Wynn farm. The men were *stseanaq*, part of the Northwest and Alaskan coastal indigenous bondage system. Unlike American race-based slavery, it was based only on loss of social status and personal history after capture in warfare or raids. Many were highly skilled and important members of the labor force of elite families. Like her cousin Clara Tennant's *stseanaq*, the men probably were a wedding gift from Jenny's father, though nothing indicates that they lived with the family while the Wynns were at Sehome or Utsalady. Most likely discomforting for a man from a Quaker abolitionist family that believed in equal treatment of everyone (and possibly operating an Underground Railroad safe house), nevertheless Tom Wynn showed respect for his wife's upper-class culture, but he also took advantage of it for his own profit until the end of the Civil War definitively ended all slavery in the United States.

The two men had different histories. Tom T'ing said he thought he might have been born in British Columbia, although descendants' research found that he was more likely Haida from southeast Alaska. Raiders took T'ing and his mother when he was a baby, if his clearly inaccurate census age was even within ten years of his actual age. According to Jenny, her father bought the boy at Victoria for a very large sum. David was older, about Tom Wynn's age. Lummi had given him the second name *Sco'tah*, "Crow" in English. In contrast to T'ing's history, David's parents were long ago British Columbia captives and he was born at Lummi. People remembered him as a "dwarf," but it had been a youthful accident that permanently bent David's back, according to Jenny's son Harry. The disabled man liked to tell the Wynn children (in Lummi dialect) the story of his adventurous escape and return from southern Puget Sound after he was sold to someone he didn't like. David must have repeated the tale many times to have it so clearly remembered by his young listeners.[75]

Twenty-one months after settlement, Tom was in a Salish canoe fighting the current past Treaty Rock to the slough at Tennant's with a load of Utsalady lumber. Jenny would soon have a more substantial cabin for her family to replace their temporary one. He sited her new home only a short walk northeast of Clara's. The cousins both had babies who would be fortunate to live close to family elders, and the women's proximity to each other prevented loneliness.[76]

Jenny and Tom's sweet-smelling fourteen-by-twenty-two-foot home was an improvement over the first cabin, especially with skilled Henry Post in charge of construction. The Wynn house was beamed with large cedar logs and covered with vertical planks. Windows flanked the center door under a steeply-pitched shake roof that hid the sleeping and storage attic. A lean-to expanded the house to four rooms.[77]

The Wynns had immediately started a market garden and large orchard with John Tennant's help plowing and seeding the first field. In the tradition of the Quaker "good neighborhood," Tom and friends built his potato house together so he could have a quick cash crop,

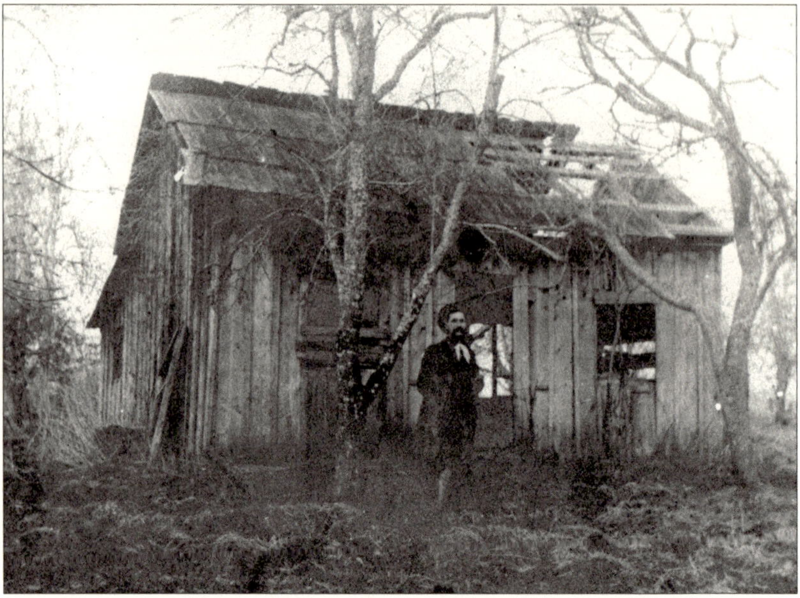

Ruins of Jenny and Thomas Wynn's house which replaced their initial cabin. *Percival Jeffcott Collection #19, Center for Pacific Northwest Studies. Western Washington University, Bellingham, WA.*

and he helped others in return. Jenny's knowledge of the cultivation of potatoes on *Ske'laxen* gave Tom an advantage. With help, he built a large barn, eighty-four by forty-six feet, second only to Tennant's and possibly with two floors so the crops could be stored above the animal shelter. Its size hints at the volume of wild Indian hay the men were harvesting from the *Noos'kwiem* and adjoining Lummi family lands.[78]

After the move to *Ske'laxen*, Jenny bore two more children before the land became officially theirs: Harry Post Wynn in 1866 and Julia in 1869, named for Jenny's half-sister. Tom left the family alone for long periods in the early years while he was away earning cash. Traditionally, Coast Salish women always spent time outside the company of men, working and socializing with each other. Jenny's marriage had brought her technologically advanced household items, but when Tom was away and she was mostly alone, her burden was large. Though they had Thomas T'ing, David Scotah, and Henry Post to rely on, it took years of backbreaking work to get beyond the break-even point.[79]

Despite the loss of the garden and some crops to the 1868 forest fire, by the 1870 agricultural census the farm's value had reached $1,000, half of Tennant's $2,000 but double that of some others. Perennial bachelor Henry Post had left the Sehome Mine and moved to adjoining land in 1867 when he and Tom formed a farming partnership. They also shared their farming, carpentry, and blacksmith tools with neighbors, which benefited the entire small river community. After seven years of work, the Wynns owned five dairy cows for their growing family, beef cattle, and two oxen for plowing. Tom sold potatoes, fruit, beans, and Indian hay from the delta. The census showed that Jenny's contribution was equally valuable. In the year before the census, she made two hundred pounds of butter and tended garden produce valued at $350, a very large sum for the time. Jenny began selling eggs and feathers in large amounts after Bernard and Catherine McDonough opened a reservation trading post where they also wholesaled farm commodities to the Seattle market. In poor crop years, a farm wife's butter and eggs provided crucial income to keep her family going until the next harvest.[80]

Universal emancipation in 1865 definitively ended the bondage prohibition that had been in the 1855 Point Elliott Treaty but was never enforced. It changed the relationship of Tom T'ing and David Sco'tah with the Wynns to wage-earning farm workers and adjunct family members with ties that grew with time. The large amount of wages paid out appearing in the 1870 census reflected that change. The men did not know the way "home" if they had wanted to go. Wynn and Tennant both had to address the residential, cultural, and emotional attachment problems for the two men now free.[81]

Wynn and Tennant (son of a prominent Arkansas abolitionist missionary) probably discussed how to explain the new situation. According to the children, Tom explained to Jenny that her culture's custom was not right—in fact, against the law—but that they couldn't just abandon the two propertyless men. The Wynns and Tennants found their own solution for the future of the people dependent on them and integrated into their family circles. According to the Wynn children, for the rest of their lives T'ing and David professed their loyalty and affection for Jenny, even without any obligation to her.[82]

Once free, T'ing married Julia, Clara Tennant's former *stseanaq*, and they moved into the original cedar Wynn cabin. He continued to work for the Wynns while he and Julia started a family and cared for the aging and disabled David Sco'tah. T'ing acted as the Wynns' negotiating agent for the produce they sold in Whatcom and in the 1880 census, he declared himself a farmer, while his boarder David still identified as a farm laborer. This may reflect T'ing's growing responsibilities and expertise as Tom Wynn helped the young husband and father transition into his new role as independent breadwinner who would soon have his own farm. Tom T'ing is still remembered at Lummi as one of St. Joachim Church's early bell ringers, calling residents to Mass or prayer services. Known from childhood only as T'ing, he may have chosen his baptismal name of "Thomas" to honor Tom Wynn.[83]

The small homely man David never married and lived with the T'ings and their children but stayed close to the Wynns, all of them becoming adopted family members. After the McDonough trading post opened in 1871, David worked there for many years.[84]

Jenny's contributions to the family's economy were typical, but her growing ability to smoke an exceptional ham led to a cottage industry unique to her. The Wynns owned forty pigs in 1870, more than anyone else on the river. The hogs happily spent their lives loose down in "the swamp" (the *Noos'kwiem*) until the men drove them up to the farmstead for final fattening and a cooperative butchering day. Tom canoed some of his fresh pork into town, but most of the meat went into bacon and hams, customarily salt-cured by western settlers. The initial process was laborious, covering the future hams with salt, letting it pull the liquid out for weeks on racks. The hams were then taken into the smokehouse where a maple or alder fire was intermittently kept burning under the hanging meat. Jenny built on what she already knew about smoking Lummi salmon and started smoking as many as thirty-five hams at a time. When the hams were ready, she hung them to cure for as long as two years. In the coming decades, her reputation and demand for her smoked hams grew in town and the surrounding area. According to Jenny's daughter Maria, the family rarely had any ham at home because they were "always sold as soon as they were cured."[85]

The infant river community grew slowly and cooperatively. Blacksmith Tom Wynn repaired his neighbors' tools and equipment, and took over his friend Jim Carr's grindstone after his death. Henry Post was a superb carpenter-builder. John Tennant brought his agricultural skills from Arkansas, which the urban-raised men didn't have. The close-knit group's ability to work together, handle most repairs, and get tools sharpened within the neighborhood was essential because a trip to town for an errand ate up at least one valuable day. Solomon Allen and his Nlaka'pamux wife Mary from the Fraser River Canyon (see chapter 3) moved away from town to the Nooksack's eastern mouth in 1866. They were followed by Reuben Bizer, formerly James Patterson's ranch partner upriver (see chapter 2), who brought his Nooksack wife Sally. In 1870, a couple moved onto *Chah'choo'sen* who were not intermarried: the former Sehome Mine engineer McKinney Tawes and his wife Mary. Others like them soon followed.[86]

Jenny

Jenny entered the thorny Lummi Reservation boundary issue in the early 1870s, which put her squarely between her family's culture and her husband's, but not as mediator. The issue was white settlement (including the Wynns, Tennants, and Allens) within the reservation borders and the 1873 re-survey of the entire reservation. Jenny Wynn, daughter of Sea'nult, became the face of rebellion.

Puget Sound tribes and men who wanted land had often drawn different conclusions about reservation boundaries after the treaties. The government paid "legitimate" pre-1855 treaty squatters to leave the territory's reservations shortly after ratification, but new squatters replaced them. At first, most of those settlers within the borders of many reservations were cross-cultural families like the Wynns, but soon all-white couples (like the Tawes) joined them along the indistinct boundaries.[87]

The government was familiar with this messy situation. Since colonial times, ignoring the squatters if at all possible was an unwritten policy as officials negotiated with tribes and established new reservations. A government reluctant to antagonize voters always redrew the boundaries to allow "Old Settlers" to remain. Americans long assumed that when a man married a native woman, he acquired access to her rights associated with tribal membership and a shortcut to acquisition of a desirable piece of land. John Tennant had probably told Tom about this pattern since his own parents had once benefited from it in northwest Arkansas.[88]

The Treaty of Point Elliott stated Lummi Reservation boundaries in general distances and directions from the conspicuous glacial rock named *No'yes'quen* ("tattletale"), which became known as "Treaty Rock." It rose in the delta of the Nooksack's east channel near Mary and Solomon Allen's claim. The Lummi clearly reserved *Chah'choo'sen* between the river mouths in its entirety. An 1859 township survey included only part of the reservation and failed to reconcile differing versions of the eastern boundary as it crossed and followed the ever-changing river's beds and sloughs that ended in the bay. The oversight had allowed the Wynns and the others to infringe on *Chah'choo'sen*. Not long after ratification, a commission arrived at Lummi and conferred with the treaty signers about the boundaries. Subsequently in 1860, Territorial Indian Agent Michael Simmons recommended redrawing the boundaries to conform to the national township model based on straight lines that had replaced the old landmark method. This would inevitably cut off most of *Chah'choo'sen's* wedge. Simmons' report also mentioned the fertility of the area that would be released from the reserved lands. He presumed there would be no objection to the convenient boundary changes when they were made.[89]

Nineteenth-century Euro-American men's desire for land when they headed west remained as visceral as when the first colonists arrived on the east coast. Settlement on *Chah'choo'sen* with their elite Lummi wives so close after ratification implies that Wynn and Tennant thought they might double their chances to own prime open prairie land. If the original eastern reservation border from Treaty Rock to Barrett Lake held, all settlers (including Wynn and Tennant) encroaching on the northeastern portion of *Chah'choo'sen* would be told to leave. However, Jenny and Clara might then be eligible for allotment of the same ground despite their non-tribal marriages. Being from a large influential Lummi family virtually assured them a preferential right to allotted trust land over people from one of the "outsider" groups, for example the Semiahmah, also assigned to the reservation.[90]

Jenny's son later stated that land was a factor in the union of his parents. The Wynn children firmly believed that Sea'nult gave his daughter and her husband hereditary tribal rights to *Ske'laxen* prairie when they married in 1855. Many accounts confirm that Jenny believed she had legal and moral rights to the homestead even if the subsequent deed put sole ownership in Tom's name.[91]

The reservation border issue continued to heat up, with unwanted white encroachment at Lummi a constant refrain in agency reports. In 1871 the Washington Superintendent of Indian Affairs reported that the Lummi were fully capable of farm management and wanted allotments, but he didn't retreat from Simmons' 1860 opinion that no one would object to a change to straight-line borders. He wanted a new survey using the township system and proposed selling the Swinomish Reservation and sending that group to Lummi. If ever implemented, this would have put five other groups in addition to the Lummi families in line for allotments, far too many to ever get a piece of land sufficient for profitable agriculture. New federal legislation supported the contemplated changes by taking away tribes' status as independent entities similar to states, a policy that had been in place since the George Washington presidency.[92]

This issue put Jenny and Tom in the middle between opposite positions regarding the boundaries and settlement. Regional Catholic missionary and current Tulalip Indian Agent Father Casimir Chirouse reported that he had to referee difficulties between Indians and the increasing numbers of whites invading the reservation edges. It came to a head when Congress ordered the 1873 official survey. The situation surrounding the new surveys troubled Chirouse. Congress wanted to reduce Lummi Reservation in size, alleging there were not enough Indians to fill it. A simple head count of the four groups assigned there would show this was patently false. The same year, the General Land Office branch in Olympia opened to receive patent applications.[93]

Jenny and Tom re-married on June 1, 1873, in a second ceremony presided over by neighbor and Justice of the Peace John Plaster (himself in a tribal custom marriage). Friends and children witnessed and celebrated the "official" union. Two months later on July 29, Tom became an official homestead owner at age fifty-four. Though Jenny's name never appeared on the official patent certificate with its large red seal, their marriage recorded with the county auditor guaranteed that the piece of Lummi territory on which the Wynns lived became legally the property of a Lummi woman and her family. No matter how the reservation land issue ended, the Wynns were safely in possession of their land. Jenny's widow rights and those of her children were secure.[94]

Tom and Jenny could have viewed the re-survey as nearly irrelevant. Other mixed families who had settled more recently along the river obtained at least a marriage license during that season when newcomers were pressuring the "Old Settlers" to regularize their tribal custom marriages. Many believed any county record would be sufficient paper evidence to legitimize their tribal custom marriages and possibly be necessary to secure possession of a homestead wrestled from forest, wetland, and prairie.[95]

The 1873 re-survey by executive order (much of it done by U.S. Deputy Surveyor John Tennant) pulled back the reservation's entire northern border and opened that prime arable land to white settlement. As well, it took away Lummi Island (and its resources) to reduce the reservation's size. The new sharp-lined eastern border cut off the northeast end of *Chah'choo'sen*, which put the Wynns and their neighbors firmly outside the reservation.

As the intent and results of the survey became clear, a rancorous meeting convened at the government-built "New Lummi Village" in September. The government representatives probably included Farmer-in-Charge John McGlinn, John Tennant, and Father Chirouse in his dual role as area Indian agent and Lummi's parish priest. His periodic visits to the village, centered around a large cross and flagpole, were usually filled with weddings, baptisms, Mass, and celebratory dinners. This time things did not go so well. A woman disrupted things. All evidence indicates that she was Jenny Wynn.

Reporting for the local weekly newspaper on the meeting held at the gathering place next to the McDonough trading post was an attendee called "MAC," almost certainly Catherine or Bernard McDonough. The headline read "Quieting a Native Lady, the Wife of a Quiet Citizen." Father Chirouse had spent the day settling disputes and "preaching" the advantages of (Euro-American) "civilization." He told the Lummi that it was to their advantage if the survey divided the reservation into small farms with a title for each head of household. "MAC" said the unnamed woman of the headline disrupted the "harmony" of Chirouse's visit when she rose and spoke. She told the assembly that Chirouse and Farmer-in-Charge McGlinn were lying when they said the survey was for the Lummi's benefit, when it actually benefited the whites. She created a disturbance when she was "too free with that unruly member called tongue," a phrase derived from an old English tract into a common catch-phrase for women talking too much and in unapproved ways. Chirouse sent her home. Speaking in the Lummi language, he told the men they were foolish to listen to her stories and that it was "not manly for any of them to quarrel with a woman." In other words, it was beneath the men to seriously debate the "native lady."[96]

This unusually loud confrontation between the respected priest and the outspoken Lummi woman—and the subject of her identity—has been the source of speculation for many years. The woman's angry intrusion into male deliberations shocked the settlers who read the newspaper, but giving advice and admonitions at council discussions was the traditional right of Coast Salish women. Years earlier U.S. Boundary Survey ethnologist George Gibbs called their "freedom of tongue highly edifying." The new authority structure disagreed. Men from both cultures had begun to strongly discourage female participation in deliberation and decision-making. The first farmer-in-charge, himself intermarried, had physically assaulted the wife of appointed Chief Whi'lano (David Crockett) when he thought she was "too vocal with her complaints." Coast Salish women exerting their leadership rights did not fit into the Euro-American, male-dominated political culture or long-standing beliefs about tribal leadership that dated to colonial times.[97]

Nineteenth century white male attitudes declared that a lady should stay out of the newspapers —"anonymous, silent and home." Men discussed the problem of controlling the "unruly female tongue." It should not be surprising that Father Chirouse reacted defensively when confronted and contradicted by a woman who wouldn't acquiesce to the unwritten rules of the society she had joined. Chirouse was also part of a church structure where women had no leadership role. Frontier partnership marriages propelled women into an expectation of strength and independence, but it wasn't enough to break through male attitudes. The "native lady" married to the "quiet citizen" was out of control.

The "native lady" caused such an uproar that "MAC" found it necessary to tell newspaper readers not to trifle themselves about the incident. The writer apparently felt it important to allay newcomers' fears of an uprising by people they didn't know well.

Several facts lead to the obvious conclusion that the "native lady" was Jenny Wynn. First, the adjective "quiet" was a euphemism for

Quakers, the "quiet people" and referred to their style of worship and their Quietism movement of recent years. Local readers already knew Tom Wynn was a Quaker and could recognize the reference.

Second, like Jenny, Tom grew up accustomed to female rights to leadership and expression. Did the writer also include the adjective "quiet" to slyly admonish Tom for his lack of control over his wife?

Third, Jenny was slowly detaching from the Catholic Church. Chirouse had baptized only two of the four children. Northwestern missionary priests were lenient about tribal custom marriages, but after Jenny's civil marriage to a Protestant, she lost the right to receive sacraments if Chirouse enforced rules. Such estrangement might lead to less verbal respect for the priest-agent's moral authority, the only one he retained over her. To call any priest a liar in public, at a place where he was respected and well-loved, was a bold move.[98]

Lastly, only Wynn and Tennant had important Lummi wives on the lower river, and Tennant was an unlikely candidate for the adjective "quiet," since he was an active politician and office holder. He was also in charge of the government's re-survey. "MAC" probably never identified the woman by name because she was both a customer and a commodity supplier for the trading post.

Though Jenny was nine months pregnant with her sixth baby, she fulfilled her leadership role. She stood to represent her family and her community, as well as what was morally and legally right, to the American authorities, even though her personal future was already secure. By that time Jenny's last brother Frank had died, which left only the sisters' uncles and husbands to negotiate with the bureaucracy for Sea'nult's family. Like her mother who had negotiated the rescue of captives, and Jenny herself when she had done her best to save little Harry during the forest fire, she found her courage. Because she had lived within the white community for nearly two decades, Jenny possessed knowledge of white intentions and white ways that could help her family and the Lummi defend against a new kind of outside threat. The innocent-sounding government goal to provide each nuclear family with their own farm would work against Coast Salish extended family closeness and culture. She apparently refused to retreat from her stand and the only way Chirouse could shut her up was to force her to leave rather than deal with the truth she told. Nothing says how she was made to go home, but some sort of intimidation seems implied, unless it was Tom's protective arm for his heavily pregnant wife.[99]

Jenny's rebellious outburst seems to have been one of the last examples of a Lummi *si'em* ("worthy people") woman, who understood her traditional property and speaking rights, publicly forcing her opinion upon the new power structure that excluded women. She had nothing to fear from the Church and no fear of losing the allotment to dampen her voice.

Less than a week after the stormy meeting, Jenny gave birth to Sallie, named for both Tom's maternal grandmother and his unmarried youngest sister. Jenny's final baby ended 17 years of childbearing. No accounts indicate any of her babies died. Father Chirouse baptized Sallie when she was seven months old. That day may have been the last time that Jenny actively participated in her church's sacraments.[100]

No clear aftereffects of the meeting at Lummi are readily attributable to the "native lady's" outburst, though her warnings contributed to a less trusting general atmosphere. Some months later, Chirouse wrote his Indian Department superiors that the recent survey had not produced satisfaction among the Lummi. During the winter following the meeting, "white disturbers" had told them that the government was planning to force them to stop logging and move out of their *illahee* (homeland) so whites could have it all. The Lummi had even been told that a government steamer was coming to take them away forcibly to stop their logging. This potential loss of resources and community resulted in a visit to the reservation agency office by armed Lummi men angrily demanding answers. Chirouse thought that only a fair land distribution and a permanent lawful title issued for each allotment would allay the perceived threats. He conceded that previous injustices had led the Lummi to have little confidence in American government pledges and he found it increasingly difficult to convince them that whites were their friends.[101]

Jenny and Tom

Newcomers who coveted only land and resources found the friendships and family ties between the 1850s settlers and native families irrelevant. They knew nothing of the existing relationships marked by respect and mutual support. They saw the first settlers' native in-laws only as obstructions to "improvement" of the county.

In what unknowingly became a bulwark against newcomers' efforts to make the small Nooksack River mixed community irrelevant, the year after the confrontation Jenny and Tom donated a piece of their prairie and their second cabin for the Wynn School. This second school outside of the Sehome-Whatcom area opened in the summer of 1874 enabling younger Wynns and others to sit in Miss Alice Eldridge's classroom instead of hiking miles into town to the Sehome School or canoeing down the dangerous river to the Allen School, which had opened the previous year (see chapter 3). Most of the initial fifteen students were mixed-blood, which made adjustment to school easier for the younger Wynns whose first language was their mother's. Harry said that he didn't speak English before age twelve, and though that may be a slight exaggeration, it implies that Tom had made no attempt to bully his wife and children into an all-English home as some others had done and he had almost certainly learned to speak rudimentary Lummi. In the coming summer terms, the mixed-blood students became a minority among the new homesteaders' children from the reservation land taken from the Lummi. The Wynns agreed that their children needed to learn to speak fluent English to become future participants in the wider Whatcom County community. Jenny sewed school clothes and traded her eggs for shoes and other children's clothing at the McDonough store. The Wynn School quickly became the river neighborhood's community center for adults as well as children. Sitting among the ferns on *Ske'laxen* prairie, it became the seed of what would become the community of Ferndale.[102]

The Wynn School's board hired Alice Eldridge for the first summer at the princely sum of $25 per month for the three-month term. Harry Wynn and his cousin Bayard Tennant seem to have been the major source of mischief for Miss Eldridge and her successors.[103]

Tom

Tom witnessed an echo of the local changes when he went home to Pennsylvania for the nation's one hundredth birthday. Twenty-three years had passed since he had sailed around Cape Horn bound to his western future. When word arrived that his parents were failing, he had the financial means and the people to support his family and farm so he could be gone a long time. Henry Post had moved into the

Wynn house by then, where he became a fixture at Jenny's dinner table for the next two decades. Tom took a sentimental sail home on the Cape Horn route, probably on a lumber ship, which by then was the only way to go by sail.

After Tom arrived, the Philadelphia Centennial International Exposition of 1876 opened on 450 acres of Dr. Thomas Wynne's original estate. With as many as ten million visitors, it was a spectacular extravaganza. The farmer-blacksmith from Washington Territory could see cutting-edge technology like Mr. Bell's telephone and Mr. Edison's new electric light in fourteen-acre Machinery Hall. Nine acres of agricultural exhibits in a flamboyant Gothic barn beckoned. He probably peered at George Washington's coat and the Statue of Liberty's arm.[104]

"Cultural" exhibits of a different sort also drew visitors. Tom found that his past life with the eastern folk among whom he stood, and his present with Jenny and his Lummi in-laws, collided in the way Northwest tribes were depicted. Americans who read about the current western Indian wars were interested in learning more about Native Americans. The exhibits sent the message that indigenous people and cultures belonged to the nation's receding past, and encouraged comparison to the technological advances Euro-Americans had made in the century of nationhood. The evolutionary sequence the fair presented reinforced the American notion of Manifest Destiny and racial superiority. The exhibits on Northwest tribes featured magnificent carved and painted canoes and totem poles, only to have spectators liken them to "hideous monsters...painted in crude colors." As a man of his time, Tom probably agreed with the presentation of white culture as superior based on technology alone. He may have felt differently, however, when faced with condescending attitudes about his wife's cultural heritage.[105]

Tom sold his interest in the family farm to his brother Delaney a week before their mother died in March. His father died in June. Tom's share of his parents' estate was said to be $10,000. (If his daughter remembered correctly, it would be nearly $234,000 in 2017.) Before he returned home, Tom bought a trunk full of dresses, "finery," and assorted gifts for Jenny and the children. Taking the transcontinental train, he was back in Whatcom County by July 11 to testify at a hearing. On the train with him was an expensive wagon, which, once hitched to the Wynns' four matching black horses, became the local funeral hearse.[106]

Over the years, the memories of the children and Jenny's family about Tom's visit to Philadelphia became increasingly muddled. It is clear that he left for a substantial amount of time that proved difficult for everyone—at least six months. Many nineteenth-century homesteaders and military families tolerated long separations, but in Jenny's culture a good husband and father would "never" leave his family alone for so long and her relatives felt she was disrespected.[107]

Jenny and Tom

Tom barely had time to absorb the death of his parents before he and Jenny buried Marshall, who died at twenty-one in April 1877. Their oldest child was apparently disabled his entire life, called by the newspaper simply an "invalid." His condition was never fully described but the Wynn accounts at McDonough's Store, as well as a notation in Henry Roeder's business diary, present some clues. Roeder noted that he was going to buy some Oil of Araganum for the four-year-old boy's back when he sailed south. Later the family frequently bought Hall's Balsam and Wistar's Balsam, patent concoctions sold for lung diseases of all kinds. Possible chronic physical problems might include spina bifida, cystic fibrosis, or severe asthma, among others.[108]

Two years before Marshall died, he bought twelve and a half acres on the Nooksack's riverbank at a sheriff's sale. It was near the location of Billy Clark's canoe ferry where the trail to Semiahmoo crossed the river, making the purchase a smart one. Days before Marshall died, he transferred the land to his little sisters Julia and Sallie, then eight and four. Now-Probate Judge John Tennant, who had lost his own first son, assisted in the property transfer. The gift would be a tangible remembrance of the girls' big brother, as well as an investment in their future. In a few years, it turned out to be a smarter idea than Marshall could have realized.[109]

Life on the farm continued in its seasonal routine, punctuated by school terms, balmy or abominable weather, and Tom's occasional duties on the school board, as an election judge, or estate administrator. The children's pet fawns frequently wandered into Jenny's kitchen, and sometimes bears and cougars harassed the livestock. The county fair called for a yearly family sail across the bay in the big Wynn canoe for a day of fun. The summer after Marshall died, Methodist camp meetings at Clark's ferry landing began, adding another respite from farm chores. Tom was reputed to be one of the men who backed out of conversion at the last minute in 1879, despite their friend (and new preacher) Tennant's fiery exhortation to repent.[110]

Tom continued to enthrall his children with tales of Dr. Wynne's ocean voyage, Margaret's stand against the British soldiers, and Elizabeth's Underground Railroad stop. David Sco'tah repeated the story about his escape. Jenny told her traditional Lummi stories.

At age sixty, Tom opened a full-service blacksmith shop for the infant towns of East and West Ferndale. He had already bought more land, and continued to build the family's economy with his Quaker value of industriousness, probably supplemented by his inheritance. The newspaper called his new smithy (apparently on his daughters' land at East Ferndale) "first class." He'd been doing work for his neighbors for years, but this expansion was badly needed. The county was punching rough roads through the woods in all four directions from the ferry landing. With the recent removal of the "Big Jam" that blocked navigation, a small local steamer ran upriver to the new towns. The growing population at the facing townsites and new homesteaders needed implements and small parts fabricated, horses shod, tools sharpened, and wheels repaired. Tom had the money to invest in the additional tools, bellows, and raw iron for a full-service general smithy.[111]

The Wynns soon bought eighty more acres, but they also had a more pressing need for extra income. Jenny and Tom's son Harry and his cousin Bayard Tennant attended H.B. Stewart's private academy a short morning walk away in East Ferndale. Thomas B. was a boarding student at the Alden Academy in Anacortes, the closest thing the region had for a college prep school. In addition to Tom's inherited money, farming, and the smithy, other funding sources to keep the boys in private schools may have been the profitable sale of his 1856 Whatcom lot and Jenny's continued sale of feathers to McDonough's wholesale operation.[112]

Along with the Wynn School land donation and Tom's service on the school board, the priority that Jenny and Tom put on their children's educational needs signaled a turning point in Wynn family identity.

Tom T'ing and David Sco'tah

Ten years after the reservation meeting, the government prepared to allot eighty-acre parcels to eligible heads-of-household at Lummi, though there was not enough land for all. David Sco'tah and Tom T'ing both received allotments, despite being non-tribal members and from the lowest priority group when the limited number of grants were made. How did this happen?

It is helpful to look at who could exert influence with the Indian agent and Jenny's first cousin Chief Henry Kwina, who consulted on the allotments. According to Jenny's daughter and others, she did some "wire pulling" for Sco'tah and T'ing. Chief Kwina exerted great personal influence among the Lummi as Tsi'lixw's son with traditional rights to leadership, as well as being the government-appointed chief. Another cousin, Hillaire Crockett, was a subchief and the appointed tribal judge. At that time, a Lummi chief could adopt a Canadian Indian without government interference, and then vouch for him to get an allotment. Accounts say that Crockett adopted Tom T'ing, who then received eighty of the less desirable inland acres. U.S.-born David Sco'tah received eighty acres between Jenny's sister Mary and one of Clara Tennant's brothers, and may also have been adopted. Probably because of Jenny and her relatives' efforts, both David and the T'ing family moved to the reservation and spent the remainder of their lives on their own land.[113]

Jenny and Tom

September 19, 1885, brought a horrific disruption to Jenny and Tom's pastoral community and their family's life: murder.

Julia Wynn, who was sixteen when the murder occurred, later in life called James Guildy (then age forty), "the sort of man women instinctively avoided." She and other local teenage girls repeatedly rebuffed his advances. Her sister Maria and her husband, Australian Thomas Oxford, lived on their homestead two miles north of the Wynns. Guildy's insulting remarks about the Wynn-Oxford clan resulted in Oxford's threat to "thrash" him. The man also defamed Julia's friend Inda Mayfield, daughter of Ferndale's doctor. After Inda's brother did indeed beat up Guildy, the man vowed revenge against both families and Ferndale in general, and left. When he resurfaced, he fatally shot Inda's father and critically wounded her brother before he vanished into the fields and woods. The Wynns, Oxfords, and their neighbors kept apprehensive watch while a large posse pursued the fugitive (motivated by a substantial "Dead or Alive" reward).[114]

Julia stayed with her pregnant sister and her four children while Oxford joined the search. After three days, Julia opened her eyes in the middle of the night to find her bedroom lit by flames. Home for some sleep, Oxford yelled that the barn was on fire. He ran to save their cow and calf, and was mystified to find them tethered away from the unstoppable blaze. Arson was obvious. At first light, the posse searched the Oxford farm and found Guildy napping against a tree, rifle across his lap. Surprised, he shot at the posse before they "riddled" him with bullets and buckshot. John Tennant said a few prayers over the body which they hastily buried where Guildy died.

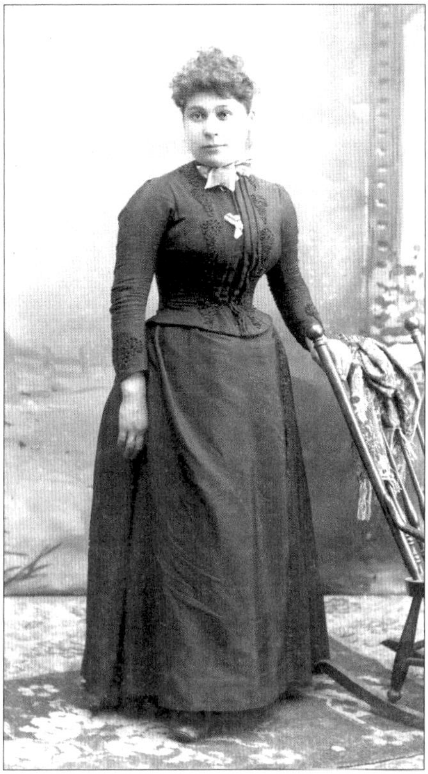

Julia Wynn. *Dobbs & Fleming, photographers. #1971.0059.000061. Courtesy of Whatcom Museum, Bellingham, WA.*

Even as Jenny's reservation family dealt with a disastrous flood that wiped out the new village, Tom was planning another house for his wife of thirty-three years—one that would be a visible sign of their success. Their fourth house was in Gothic Revival style, decades later called a "vintage landmark" by a historic building assessor. As he had for two previous Wynn homes, Henry Post took charge of construction for the big farmhouse that faced the main road to the river crossing. When finished, Jenny's house was beautiful, utilitarian, and large enough to accommodate her children and grandchildren, as well as Post.[115]

The railroad came to consolidated Ferndale. In March 1890, Jenny and Tom granted a one hundred foot right-of-way across the southwest corner of the farm, with the provision that they could remove the fruit trees and reclaim the 2.65 acres if the line were ever abandoned. Months later, railroad officials and the Wynns still argued about a critical right-of-way across the land Marshall had given Sallie and Julia planned for the approach to the Nooksack River bridge. The parties finally decided to let a jury determine the compensation. After Tom hired an excellent law firm, the jury found for the Wynns, and compensated the young girls handsomely.[116]

Despite the intrusion, legal wrangling, and loss of land, Jenny and Tom lived in the middle of the most exciting period the bay area's breathless residents had experienced since the gold rush. The route crossed Maria and Tom Oxford's land, too, and she remembered everyone watching the new track's progress as explosives destroyed timber, surveyors laid a route, and men prepared the roadbed. The construction train headed north, its "gandy dancers" laying track at a quick 1.5 miles per day from an endless belt suspended from the front of an engine that rode the finished tracks. It passed from their horizon to horizon in little more than a day. Twelve days after the inaugural train festivities, heavy rain dislodged a log jam, which then took out the

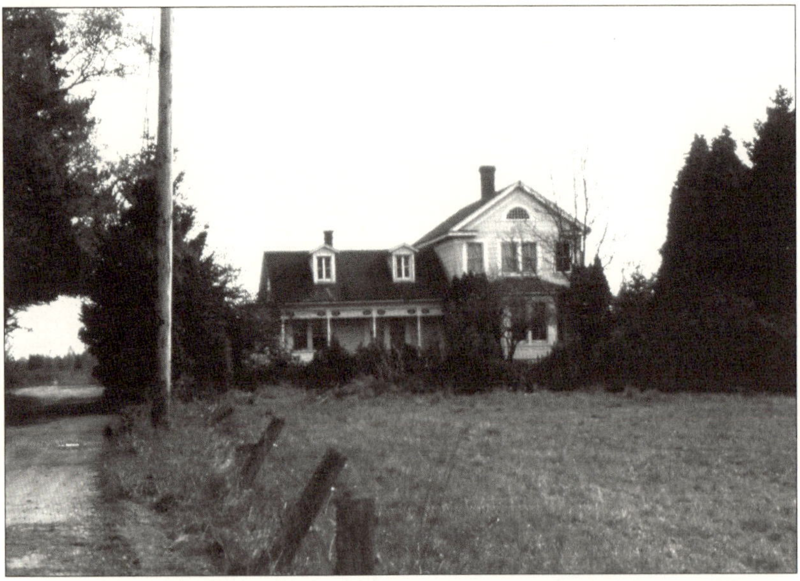

Jenny and Thomas Wynn home. *Michael Sullivan Collection slide #127. Courtesy of Center for Pacific Northwest Studies, Western Washington University, Bellingham, WA.*

impressive new bridge over the river anchored on the Wynn girls' land. The subsequent use of three hundred pounds of explosives to destroy the jam broke nearly every pane of glass within a mile, likely including Jenny's and Maria's.[117]

Railroad officials encouraged Ferndale farmers to send their spare produce into Bellingham via the daily train. Tom Wynn told his family: "Shucks, I don't believe we could sell a carrot a day in Bellingham." His pessimism was short-sighted. He sold all the produce the family could send to town.[118]

The century's last decade brought unexpected events good and bad to the Wynn family. First, Jenny told them that she wanted to return to the Catholic Church, so Julia asked Father J. B. Boulet at St. Joachim's on the reservation to meet with her mother. The rest of the family was not interested in joining Jenny, including the children Father Chirouse had baptized as babies. The Wynn children remained Protestant with their father. If, as rumored, Jenny and Tom were among the couples who participated with the Tennants in a mass Methodist wedding at a camp meeting in the 1870s, that would make the Catholic ceremony Jenny asked for her fourth wedding. Tom agreed to her wish and Father Boulet "ratified" their marriage on May 31, 1891. Because they already had (at least) a civil marriage, they only needed a sacramental blessing upon their union. Perhaps with tongue firmly in his cheek, Boulet recorded that he made the non-Catholic partner sign his formal assurance that any new babies would be raised as Catholics. Tom was seventy-two and Jenny was in her fifties. The children attended the ceremony and enjoyed the wedding cake Maria made for her parents. The following summer, Jenny made her First Communion, which completed the return to her parents' Catholicism.[119]

Painful events called for Tom's assistance in Pennsylvania three years later. Unmarried Sarah, age sixty-two, and widowed Ruth, sixty eight, wanted their big brother to help sort out their finances. Delaney, Hannah, and Sarah had continued to live together after their parents died, as adult unmarried Quaker siblings often did. When Tom received the plea for help, Hannah had died unmarried and a colt had recently kicked and killed seventy-six-year-old Delaney. Tom's two married sisters were both dead.[120]

At seventy-five, Tom took a winter train across the country for a final visit home. Jenny and the clan were probably deeply worried about the elderly man. His eyesight was poor and one eye wandered. His lifelong bushy Quaker beard and sideburns were gray with age. A winter train east was brutal, a "long, rough journey" in cold dirty cars. Outside temperatures dropped as low as seventy degrees below zero when the train passed through Montana mountain valleys in howling winds. The Wynn sons with Henry Post were fully capable of running the farm and caring for the women, but Tom completed a long-distance real estate transaction in February and was still at Wynnstay with his siblings in October.[121]

With everyone else who owned shares in the historic farm gone, Tom helped his sisters sell the land, minus house and yard, which was directly in the path of suburban growth. Knowing he would not see his sisters again when they said their goodbyes, Tom took the train for home just in time for the Rockies' cold fall weather.[122]

The Wynnestay estate house that Dr. Wynne started in 1690 passed from Tom's uncle Samuel's family a few years later. It remains the oldest inhabited home in Philadelphia, to which Wynne descendants pilgrimage.

Tom Wynn died two years later, on the evening of November 11, 1896, surrounded by his family. Rev. Walter Crockett of the Christian Church, and one of Whidbey Island's first pioneers, presided over the funeral. In a tradition common to both spouses' cultures, someone sat with Tom's body the night before the funeral. The sad congregation of family and friends was very large despite a November storm.[123]

Tom's death shared the newspaper's front page with the election of President William McKinley. The *Reveille* article called the Wynn farm one of the county's best, particularly extolling the "splendid farm house" Tom had built.[124]

Both Bellingham newspapers dismissed Jenny in a way they never would have done to a non-Lummi spouse after forty-one years of marriage. Both the *Reveille* and *The Blade* chose not to use her name, instead calling her "a daughter of the Lummi." One editor managed to say she was left a mourning widow and mother, and added that one of her daughters was married to a leading Ferndale citizen.

Jenny's youngest, Sallie, married two weeks after Tom's funeral. Both unifying family events hid cracks in the children's relationships that soon emerged and caused Jenny three years of problems with both money and children. Tom had left no will, despite his own experience when his parents died without one.[125]

After Jenny waived her legal right to be executor in favor of her son Thomas B., his estimate of the estate's worth was so low that Maria decided he had left some farm valuation and personal property out. She claimed that her brothers owed their father substantial sums dating to their lease of the farm. They had also failed to pay the taxes as promised, leaving their parents vulnerable to foreclosure. The brothers produced a fifteen-year-old deed that showed both Tom and Jenny had signed over the land for $1.00, although it was never filed with the county auditor. A new executor, railroad construction engineer M. L. Stangroom, took over after Maria forced her brother to resign. The arguments got more contentious until the siblings couldn't even agree on who owned the horse tack. Maria besieged Stangroom with accusations of gross misconduct by her brothers.[126]

Stangroom received no cooperation from anyone. Jenny and her younger daughters refused to hand over any personal property and her sons wouldn't concede the land and machinery to his authority. He couldn't even get Jenny to hand over a ten-dollar cider press. The exasperated probate judge suggested they might want to take it all to Superior Court. Stangroom filed suit against the estate and named everyone but Maria as defendants. The one point everyone seemed to agree on was that the household goods were Jenny's community property. She wasn't being uncooperative, she was just keeping what was hers. The brothers didn't want any of the household items or cash, just the farmland and machinery.[127]

From Wynnstay in Pennsylvania, Tom's sister Sarah and a niece gave depositions about Tom's final visit. He told them he wanted Thomas B. to inherit the gold watch in contention. Because the timepiece's future seems to have been as important as that of more valuable assets, it may have once been owned by Tom's father or grandfather. No further conflict over the watch surfaced, but everything else was still in question.[128]

After the Wynns saw the empaneled jury, they apparently reconsidered whether they really wanted the conflict heard in open court and subject to local gossip via newspaper reports. Their attorneys returned from lunch to announce a compromise and family request for dismissal. The lengthy written compromise allowed everyone to vent their claims and arguments, confirmed the deed, and split the homestead between the sons. Jenny and the others agreed to give Maria fifteen acres, and the brothers bought her share of the personal property.[129]

The *Reveille*'s editor took front page space to proclaim that "the legal fight among the heirs over the Wynn estate at Ferndale was stopped." Neither the paper nor the case file hinted at what went on behind the closed doors at the lunch hour meeting, but there may have been another player helping to move the case ahead so Jenny and her children could stop fighting. His name was Henry Post.[130]

De facto family member Post made out his own will four days after the Wynn family signed the compromise, and months after it was accepted by the court. He died of tuberculosis three weeks later in the middle of the night, a year after Tom's death, in the house he built for the family he had joined decades ago. Jenny had taken responsibility for the sick old man's everyday needs for over thirty years, giving up her privacy for their friend. Probably an unwilling bystander to the rancor among people he loved, Post may have talked to them about what he might do with his adjoining homestead.[131]

Henry Post's will contained some surprises. For one thing, the bachelor had a son in Philadelphia, born after Tom left for the West. When the Wynn brothers supplied Post's personal information for the death return, they had to say he was "single as far as known." He had apparently never said he was a widower. They at least suspected there might be a deserted wife in Pennsylvania, or that Post came west because he had fathered an illegitimate son. He left just the required minimum of one dollar to his son and primary legal heir, W. H. Post. Henry's only asset was his 160 acres next to the Wynns, which he bequeathed to his namesake Harry Post Wynn and to Julia. He required that when she married, her share would revert to Harry. Out of simple love and gratitude, Post provided for the only unmarried Wynn children, while at the same time he kept his farm intact and owned by the young man who carried his name. Already terminally ill, if Post voiced this plan to the family he loved when he saw the interminable estate argument going public, it may have triggered the compromise. Everyone in the family would be taken care of by inheritance or by marriage, and he followed through.[132]

When Stangroom was ready to distribute the estate a year later, the court declared all assets to be community property, but state law allowed

Jenny only a third of funds from their dividends Tom had inherited. After her long marriage, she had been forced to wait three years after Tom's death before the household goods and just part of their bank savings were officially hers. It was enough to support herself.[133]

The estate conflict never permanently broke the close family ties. Nor did it change the Wynn children's choice to live close together, repeating a pattern among both Lummi and their Pennsylvania Quaker relatives.

Jenny

Jenny remained busy after Tom and Henry Post's deaths. Harry and Julia lived with her until they married, and Thomas B.'s family was in the older house. The Wynns' tiny first cedar plank "house," once occupied by the T'ing family, still stood with its walnut tree to remind the family how far they'd come. The T'ings visited frequently, as did her friend from Sehome days, Caroline Kavanaugh of Skagit County.[134]

Jenny attended St. Joachim's on the reservation and stayed close to her Lummi family and friends. Her aged mother went blind, but lived until about 1910. A new chapter opened for Jenny after her sister Mary Wea'cheloot's death. Five days before she died, Mary signed a legal county will witnessed by Chief Kwina and two other cousins, an unusual if not unique document for a reservation resident of that period. She took disposition of her allotment outside of federal inheritance rules and avoided the equal subdivision between all heirs that was official policy. By then familiar with how probate court worked, Jenny petitioned the court to admit her sister's will.[135]

Though Mary listed three of her four sisters as relatives in the will, she bequeathed the entire allotment to her "beloved sister" Jenny, her caregiver during her final illness. The allotment lay on the east side of the reservation near St. Joachim's, just south of the allotments of the will's witnesses. Thus Mary transferred a tribal trust land allotment to Jenny, a woman who had married out of the Lummi Nation to a non-Indian, and who had physically (if not emotionally) lived in white society for over forty years. At the same time, Mary had also transferred the land to an enrolled Lummi woman who, by widowhood, was no longer married to a non-Indian and had the right to live at Lummi. It appears to be the first such confusing allotment inheritance situation involving an intermarried woman.[136]

At the end of October 1898, during the Wynn estate battle, Jenny took possession of Mary's eighty acres that lay close to her sisters and cousins. She started spending more time with family at the reservation. The year her mother is believed to have died, Jenny was "boarding" at Mary and Henry Kwina's house when the census taker arrived in June 1910. The Kwinas were famous for the warmth of their open-armed hospitality that welcomed everyone in want of a good meal to their big table, as well as children and adults who needed to stay for a while.[137]

Julia Wynn Smith believed that her parents had never ceased living in separate worlds outside the walls of their home. Fearless in some situations, Jenny never fully adapted to life in white culture. Her language difficulties particularly bothered her, and she feared ridicule by outsiders. This was perhaps a well-founded concern after cross-cultural marriages were no longer socially acceptable to the new majority of white residents. Jenny built a small house on her reservation land. She could return to her most authentic self when she wanted, yet be only a few miles from her children and grandchildren. By then Thomas B., Harry, Julia, and Sallie all lived cozily on the Wynn-Post homesteads with their families, and Maria was just a few miles north. Jenny's new home would allow her to live within the cluster of her cousins and sisters on their allotments, be free to participate in cultural gatherings, and be near St. Joachim's.[138]

At the same time that Jenny built her little house, her younger sister Harriet caused serious interpersonal trouble at the reservation. Jenny was appalled and ashamed of this breach of honor. In her humiliation and anger, she thought there was no other choice but to apologize for her family and cancel her plans to spend the rest of her life at Lummi. She abruptly left the reservation after the summer of 1912 and moved in permanently with Julia, whose kind husband Walter Smith doggedly practiced Lummi dialect so he could better converse with his mother-in-law.[139]

In the last years, Jenny spent her days surrounded by her sons, daughters, and the twenty-six grandchildren living within sight of each other. They fondly remembered her sitting in the rocking chair, knitting "with considerable deftness" though she had lost much of her eyesight like her mother before her. She rocked and told them stories of her parents, her uncle Chow'it'sut, and her Lummi girlhood. One grandson remembered teasing Jenny for not speaking English more often, and she would just "pepper [him] with more Salish." Overcoming the embarrassment of the earlier incident with her sister, Jenny visited her Lummi relatives when her children could take her there. Acting in the charitable ways her birth family's heritage expected, she carried "great quantities" of food and other supplies to share with those having hard times.[140]

When Jenny died September 23, 1916, she left a last sock partially knitted, which Julia lovingly saved. After the Catholic funeral at St. Joachim's, the family buried her beside Tom at Ferndale's cemetery. She was memorialized in stone only as "Mother." Their son Marshall lies next to them.[141]

The Bellingham press ignored Jenny's passing altogether.

Jenny tried to reward her daughter Julia's care with the gift of her reservation allotment, but her late sister Mary Wea'cheloot's Canadian stepchildren contested the transfer and were given equal shares by the government. Fifty years later 1,350 people, including Jenny's descendants, shared unwieldy ownership of the eighty acres.[142]

How did the people of Whatcom County see Jenny Wynn in the early twentieth century? Eleven years before her death, a local newspaper writer combined distorted stories of Tom, Jenny, David Sco'tah, and Tom T'ing into a romanticized and disrespectful story for children that bore little resemblance to Jenny's true story. It is easy to imagine the disgust and anger it probably caused within the Wynn family, who were not consulted. The children were already struggling with their identities and local biases.[143]

Ten years after Jenny's death, Lottie Roeder Roth's voluminous history of Whatcom County was published. Roth and her ghostwriter (newspaper editor Frank Teck) characterized Jenny's life in this way: "Wynn was one of the pioneers who had taken unto himself a Lummi maiden as his wife, a woman who proved herself as fine a helpmate as any woman of Caucasian blood could have been." Though they condescendingly praised Jenny in the common way of the time, the pair did not use Jenny's name or seek detailed information about her. In the biographical volume whose entries used information supplied by the book's subscription buyers, the authors were unable to bring themselves to say that the mother of three prominent Ferndale citizens was Lummi. True to the period when intermarriages had become socially unacceptable to newcomers despite their role in Whatcom County's establishment, Roth's history referred to Jenny as "a native of this state." The phrase continues to leave readers with a different interpretation than its real meaning.[144]

The Wynn Family

Jenny and Tom's focus on education would bear fruit as the years passed in a way they could not have imagined.

The siblings never quit living in a cluster, just like Jenny's and Tom's families. Younger generations described Jenny's children as a tough lot, the women particularly described as "hard"—strong, outspoken, and stubborn. The ladies were also tender—avid flower gardeners and excellent homemakers all three, skills learned from their mother. Jenny's children told her grandchildren Lummi stories learned at her knee.[145]

Unlike many other children of cross-cultural marriages, the Wynn siblings uniformly married "white." Fully immersed in that society, they experienced bigotry from both sides of their heritage. This may have led to the inconsistent and conflicted answers about "color" (ethnicity) they put on official documents. Sometimes it seemed just easier to turn their backs on Jenny's family and culture to get ahead in white society, a common response.

However, two of the children tried to use their Lummi heritage to their own financial advantage. Though the Oxfords owned a homestead, Maria cited her mother's Lummi enrollment to apply for an Indian allotment after World War I. Thomas B. also applied, but both were denied under a new rule that stipulated tribal children were ineligible if they "lived white." Demonstrating the sometimes conflicting circumstances they found themselves in, Maria's son told his own children painful memories of being refused entry into Ferndale taverns because he was Lummi, and yet was also ridiculed by his Lummi cousins for being too white. His daughter (Jenny's great-granddaughter) and her husband were both teachers and another became a professional singer who worked across the West.[146]

Thomas Benton Wynn carried Dr. Thomas Wynne's name forward another generation among the "Wynns of the West." After he left Alden Academy's classical education, he spent a year at the University of Washington before teaching back at home. He spent eleven years as the local justice of the peace, and was active in civic organizations. In Wynn tradition, he and his wife Ida named one son Thomas Delaney Wynn. Thomas B.'s family showed ambivalence toward their mixed heritage in a more formal way than had Maria's family. All of his children's birth certificates noted that they were fully white. By 1898 Thomas B. was active in, and served as an officer of, the Old Settlers Association, unlike nearly all other biracial offspring. He served as an officer a number of times, culminating in being the honored "Old Settler" presented with the silver loving cup in 1935 at the group's fortieth picnic. Two thousand attendees at the weekend gathering witnessed the presentation. Four of Thomas B.'s six children became teachers.[147]

Harry Post Wynn attended secondary school in Whatcom and Acme Business School in Seattle before he taught school back at home and married local teacher Blanche Getchell. He served as township assessor for eighteen years and on the local school board. He and Blanche had two boys, one of whom, Noel, became both a teacher and the family genealogist whose familial pride led him to put the "e" back in his surname. One of Harry's grandsons also became a teacher.[148]

Thomas and Harry also served the farmers who were without their own harvesting machinery and took their thresher to all corners of the county.

While Maria and Thomas B. left their mother's people and culture behind, Harry took a different path. While they had tried to use their Indianness to obtain an allotment, Harry enrolled in the Lummi Tribe and instead of seeking land, sought service. During the 1920s, the Lummi and other Puget Sound tribes began to assert their claims against the government's broken promises by forming their first pan-tribal political organization, the Northwest Federation of Indians. Each tribe chose official representatives at a general meeting of tribal members. In 1925

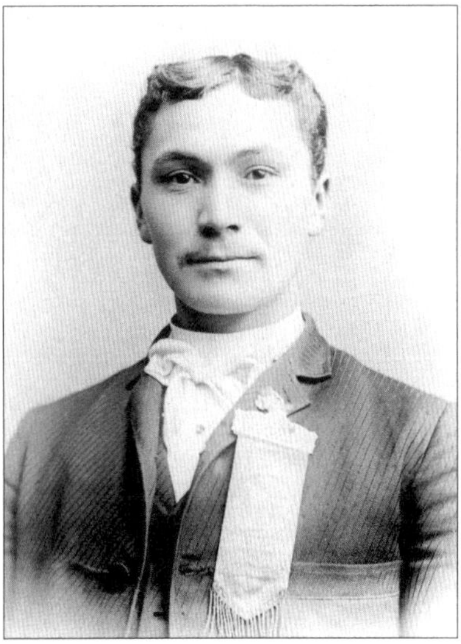

Harry Wynn, wearing his International Order of Odd Fellows badge. *E. A. Hegg, photographer. #1971.59.63. Whatcom Museum, Bellingham, WA.*

Harry Post Wynn and several cousins were among those unanimously designated Lummi "headmen" to represent the tribe's interests for the oncoming federal lawsuit. Lummi Nation members recognized his descent from Sea'nult and accepted him as Jenny's son.[149]

Tom and Jenny sent their teenaged daughter Julia into Whatcom to board with Superintendent of Schools Nellie Coupe, a legendary teacher. Julia experienced newcomers' prejudices that had been absent in the biracial neighborhood of the Nooksack River farms. "Some of my boyfriends' mothers were free with remarks of disapproval as to my suitability as a prospective daughter-in-law. My feelings were badly hurt and I cherished resentment against these mothers all of my life although time has largely erased this feeling," she said later.[150]

Julia married her father's hired hand Walter Smith before they bought part of the old Post homestead she'd temporarily inherited, and built a poultry and egg business while raising four children. She assisted local historian Howard Buswell for many years before her death at ninety-one, and confessed to him that her own link to the reservation was broken. Perhaps the most regretfully conflicted sibling, she knew who her Lummi cousins were but associated with them only casually when they met in town. Even so, Buswell noticed that she still spoke Lummi dialect and voiced a full knowledge of social rank and a snobbishness about reservation politics and marriages that betrayed her maternal history.[151]

Sallie (born Sarah) was the child born days after Father Chirouse ejected her mother from the 1873 mass meeting and who married Frank Vandemark shortly after her father's death. The pair lived on the north end of the Wynn homestead. She also displayed ambivalence about her heritage and what place her family would occupy in white society. On records, she inconsistently defined herself as "Indian-white" or just "white." Sallie's daughter became the private secretary for a State Supreme Court Justice and her son Jesse bought her brother Harry's farm and passed it on down to the fourth generation. Many years later, Lummi Nation endorsed Jenny's Vandemark great-great-grandson for State Representative in an election and though he did not win, he never forgot the gift from his distant family. Vandemark descendants became teachers also.[152]

Jenny and Tom's descendants slowly discarded their Lummi identity. It remained a proud memory, but not a culture in which later generations participated. The Wynns reared a family who incorporated an astonishing legacy from their parents into their lives for generations to come. They gave service to their community, most visibly as teachers.

Mixed-race children of the frontier West are often portrayed as misfits ignored by their father's relatives. As happened with the children of some other local intermarriages, Tom Wynn's death did not sever the bond between his children and their Pennsylvania family. Sallie's son visited his great-aunt Sarah and cousins at Wynnstay while in the military during World War I. When Sarah died in 1921, she left one quarter of her substantial estate to Tom's five children, still called the "Wynns of the West." Some cousins on both sides stayed in touch for at least another generation. In 2009 the Pennsylvania and Washington Wynn(e)s re-established their ties.[153]

At Lummi Reservation, descendants of Jenny's relatives preserve her memory. Her personal Coast Salish name endures among them and they remember how some whites made her feel inadequate. After a fire at Julia's house, a few possessions survived to remind the Wynns of their founding mother: what is believed to be her three-legged iron Dutch oven and a Salish basket. The sock Jenny was knitting when she died was lost in the fire along with photographs. Among Jenny's descendants, her memory remains vivid, thanks to the stories left by her children, who take pride in continuing to be a family of educators descended from a woman and man who, with few missteps, modeled the finest values of two cultures to their children. In 2009 a grateful former student established the Wynn Memorial Scholarship to honor Vivian Wynn, head of the Math Department at Ferndale High School, and granddaughter of Jenny Wynn.[154]

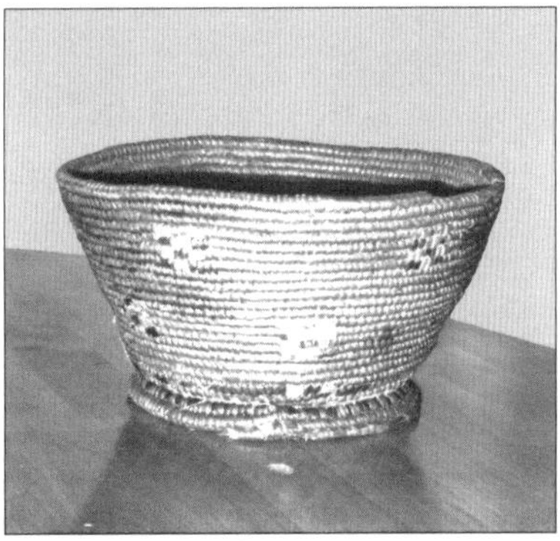

Coast Salish basket, believed to be Jenny Wynn's, inherited by her great-granddaughter Echo Oxford Dorr. *Candace Wellman, photographer. Courtesy of the late Echo Oxford Dorr.*

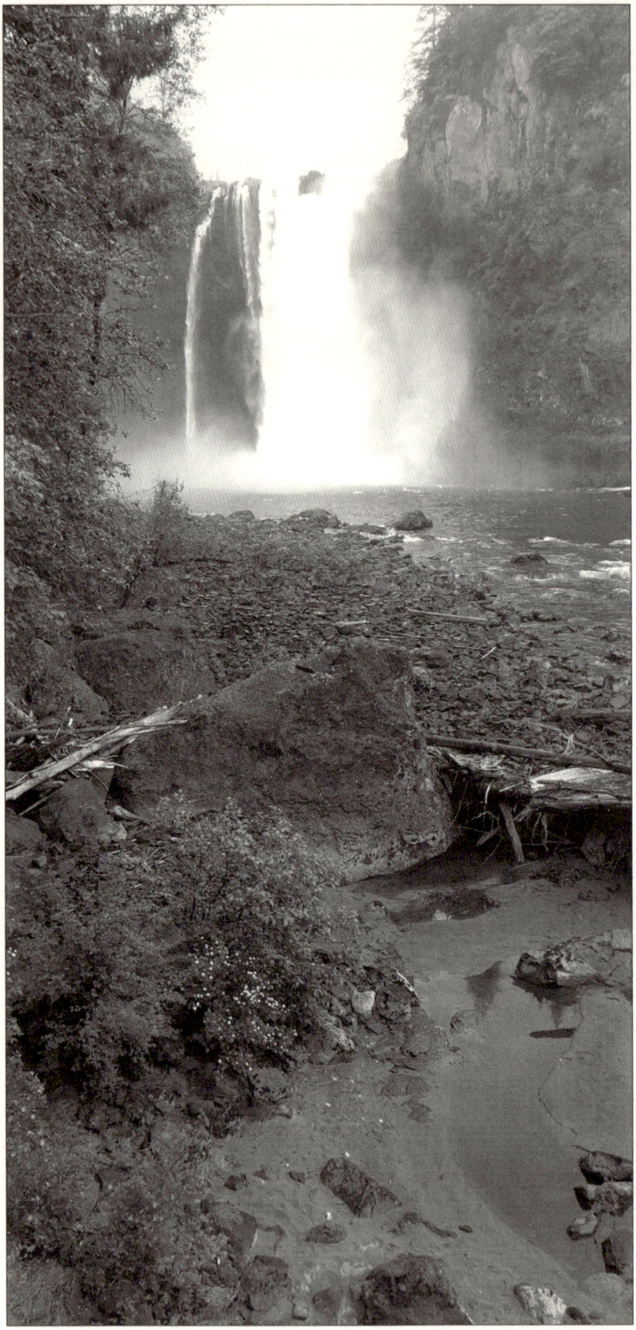

Snoqualmie Falls (268 feet high) in the Valley of the Moon, birthplace of Elizabeth Patterson. *Courtesy of Patricia Johnson, photographer.*

Chapter 2

Elizabeth, Daughter of the Moon

Bellingham's 1925 Tulip Time grand parade was at hand. Fraternal groups, bands, and flower-bedecked floats from Seattle and Canada would proceed down Cornwall Avenue behind the Tulip Queen. Two avid readers and prominent pioneer daughters, Dolly and Nellie Patterson, probably saw local newspaper articles about parade plans with a mixture of pride, bemusement, and even offense.[1]

Organizers announced that in the spirit of the year's focus on early residents, Indians would be a central feature and join the last known surviving veteran of Captain George Pickett's Fort Bellingham command. Lummi men would represent their forebears, who supplemented Pickett's soldiers to protect Bellingham Bay. Behind a Salish canoe carrying locals representing Henry Roeder and Russell Peabody's arrival on the bay would be the float depicting the 1855 Treaty of Point Elliott. Lummi men portraying Chow'it'sut, Snoqualmie chief Patkanim, and other Coast Salish leaders would re-enact the moment they signed away millions of acres to the American government. Swinomish and Lummi men would march with the float and be applauded by thousands.[2]

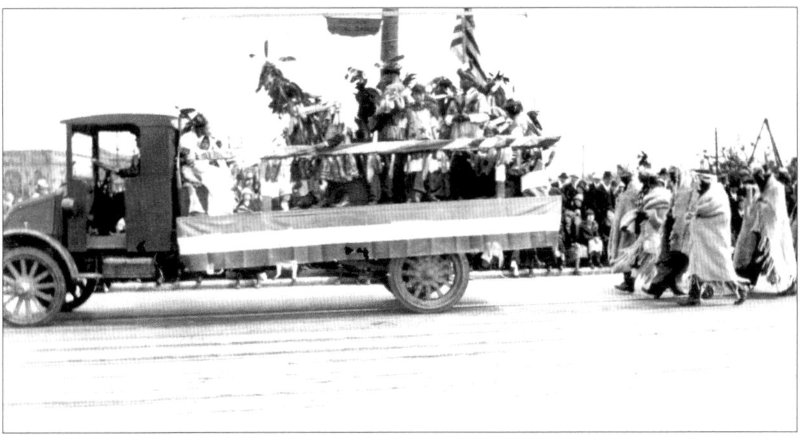

1925 Tulip Time Parade float portrayal of treaty-signers, including Patkanim, father of Elizabeth Patterson. *#1970.64.3. Courtesy of Whatcom Museum, Bellingham, WA.*

On parade day, another float showcased the Alaskan Haida winner of a Seattle Indian beauty contest, adorned with a Plains Indian headdress. Her float's banner proclaimed her "The Real American Queen." Symptomatic of the town's ambivalence toward their indigenous neighbors, organizers did not invite any young Nooksack or Lummi women to join her.[3]

Neither did anyone invite Dolly and Nellie to join the parade, despite the fact that their late mother, Elizabeth Patterson, was the daughter of treaty-signer Chief Patkanim. By 1925 few people from Bellingham or Lynden knew the two women were his grandchildren or that the treaty moment portrayed was a history-changing event in their own family's past.

Elizabeth

The town of Lynden, Washington, claims Ohio's Phoebe Judson as its founding mother, but before her another woman whose family played integral roles in the early history of Washington Territory made her home on the banks of the Nooksack River. There she gave birth in her log cabin to two little girls who were the reason for Lynden's founding.

To read local accounts of Elizabeth Patkanim and James Patterson's time on the future town's site is to come away with the impression that "Lizzie" had no identity beyond that of an overworked, timid young wife and mother. The Patterson daughters' foster mother (Phoebe Judson) first described her as "a very superior woman" of high Snoqualmie birth, but that accurate recollection was lost with the passage of years. By the time Judson wrote her 1925 memoir, the aged author described Elizabeth as a Snohomish girl purchased from the chief to work on her husband's dairy operation. The second version endured in local history, and could not have been more wrong.[4]

The Pattersons' personal histories are emblematic of how people from alien cultures living together related within marriage, friendship, business, and armed conflict. Theirs involved a complexity much different from what anyone in Whatcom County realized.

By one account, Elizabeth's grandfather Twees'hri was from *Suquamish* on the Kitsap Peninsula, the home of her father's cousin Sealth ("Chief Seattle"). Another account said that he was born a Nez Perce in eastern Washington and migrated to the Snoqualmie River valley where he married the daughter of *Sno-qual-bixu* (Snoqualmie) leader Shushem. Twees'hri's name became "Putcadub" in Lushootseed language and rendered by whites as "Patkanim." Elizabeth's father (the second Patkanim) was thus either a fusion of Coast Salish and Plateau cultures, or of the Coast Salish saltwater Suquamish and the upriver Snoqualmie sub-cultures.[5]

The marriages of Elizabeth's father and his many siblings produced a wide net of familial relationships with other western Washington villages as well as the peoples across the Cascades. They consolidated the Kanim family's political and economic power in a single generation and many names resonate in Washington State history of the post-treaty conflict. Elizabeth's uncle Qualawort led villages on the Snohomish River north of the Snoqualmies. Her uncle "Lake John" led an important upriver Duwamish village on a major cross-Cascade trade route. Snatelum, a Skagit leader on Whidbey Island, was a cousin. Elizabeth's aunt Why'it married Wyamoch, son of the primary Nisqually leader of the villages around the Hudson's Bay Company's (HBC) Fort Nisqually. The Kanim clan's military reach extended farther when one of Wyamoch's sisters married Leschi, the Nisqually war chief. This made him Patkanim's brother-in-law by Coast Salish custom. Another Kanim brother moved to Upper Yakama territory and joined Chief Owhi's family, thus relating Patkanim to Owhi's son Qualchan and even to Kanasket, Chief of the Klickitat (1850s rebellion leaders). Those men reinforced their own cross-mountain ties by marrying Puget Sound women who were probably related in some way to the Kanims. The familial complex extended to leaders Nelson and Kitsap of the Muckleshoot and Chief Kamiakin of the Lower Yakama. Everyone reinforced their ties at Fort Nisqually, the year-round trading center where they regularly encountered each other.[6]

Settlers who met the native leaders greatly underestimated the importance of these family relationships should hostilities ever break out.

By the decade of Elizabeth Patkanim's birth, her father was arguably the most powerful indigenous leader in western Washington. With the Kanims' relationships and growing military power, they nearly controlled all three main Cascade mountain passes critical to trade. At Snoqualmie the kinsmen developed a highly organized government and Patkanim rose to paramount power, supported by brothers leading affiliated villages. A tiered system of family, longhouse, village, and district ending at High Chief Patkanim was so structured that her father had been approved by all and represented everyone's concerns. Kanim marriages, alliances, and adoption of elements from both larger cultures gave the family control

Map 3: The Upper Nooksack Country

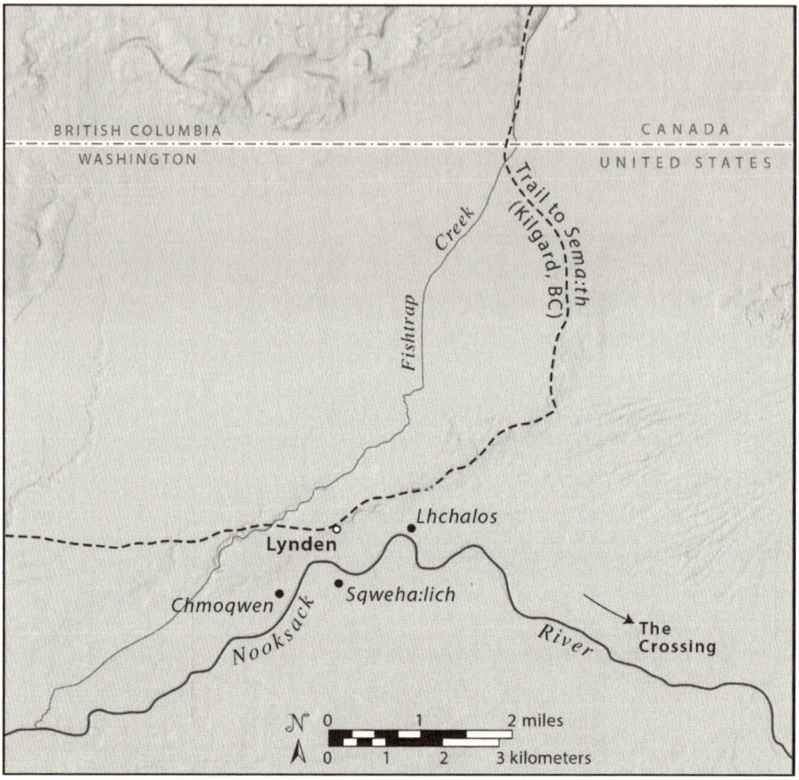

The Upper Nooksack Country is where Elizabeth Patterson spent her married life. The trail from Lynden north went to the village near today's Kilgard, BC, where she died. James Patterson's cattle coming from Whatcom had to be driven east to The Crossing at the village of Popohomey to ford the river and then west to the ranch where Lynden is today. *Map by Chelsea Feeney*

of the transition points between coastal and plateau culture groups. Like a Plateau chief, Patkanim authoritatively controlled a distinct territory, unlike the overlapping family jurisdictions of the saltwater Coast Salish. He possessed enough military, economic, and personal power as a diplomat and warrior to call upon allied tribes nearly without argument. According to descendants, other leaders elected him "Protector of Puget Sound," which allowed him to call up thousands of warriors, most of whom trained at the "military school" run by a Kanim brother on Whidbey Island. Also the leading shaman (spiritual leader and doctor) at Snoqualmie, Elizabeth's father held all the authority positions.[7]

Elizabeth was born about 1843 at *Tohlt'w* (Tolt) to a Nisqually wife of Patkanim, one of five wives of Coast Salish and Yakama origins, not an unusual arrangement for a wealthy leader. Her political and social connections at birth spanning both sides of the Cascades were unmatched. The large family longhouse sat on the bluff above the small Tolt River's confluence with the Snoqualmie. Elizabeth joined older siblings Bob, William, Julia, and Margaret, and Susie was born when Elizabeth was about five. At the time of her birth, Patkanim was at the height of his power and her people took pride in the title other groups gave to them—the "extraordinary people."[8]

Elizabeth's world in the Cascade foothills east of today's Seattle centered upon their most sacred place, *SqwEd,* breathtaking Snoqualmie Falls. The Snoqualmie have always believed that Heaven and Earth meet at the site of creation, the waterfall between upper and lower valleys. Mists from the 268-foot-high cataract carry prayers, hopes, and dreams up to Creator. For perhaps 8,000 years, Elizabeth's people lived in fourteen villages on terraces and prairies along the river's three forks. The falls where they buried their dead were always central to their culture, beliefs, and spirituality.

The other significant feature of Elizabeth's world, *Kelbts* (Mt. Si), rose above the river drainage. Oral history says that in long ago myth time, a rope swing between sky and peak once provided an escape from the sky world for two kidnapped women who had been made the wives of star men. One brought back her son who became *Snoqualm,* the Moon, who changed myth time people into animals, plants, and landforms. He changed the fish weir site of the kidnapping into the waterfall. The women's people became the "Children of the Moon."[9]

Patkanim's immediate jurisdiction was the Lower Band's thirty-eight houses from *Tohlt'w* to the confluence with the Skykomish River. His band controlled the salmon and steelhead runs below the falls, while his brother Sanawa's Upper Band controlled the river and mountain lakes' trout harvest above the falls. Snoqualmie women and girls cultivated rich prairies born of river floods in both areas.

Elizabeth's village was also the site of the *Halalt* ("the capital of the people") longhouse, an important symbol of unity where political and diplomatic business took place. Carvers recorded major decisions, social events, and conquests on the *Halalt* walls. It was also the educational center for carvers, flint makers, and weapon makers because the Kanims controlled the flint trade with the Yakama. *Tolht'w* was a village like no other.

The Snoqualmie were safe far up their river from the *Laich'wil'tach* raiders in their massive canoes. The salmon runs passing the villages, and first access to trade goods coming from the east, allowed them to stay in their longhouses more than coastal families whose salmon harvest often took them away from home. Still, Elizabeth's family harvested seafood on Whidbey and Camano Islands, and took mountain goats and huckleberries from Cascade peaks and meadows.

The annual summer trip east across Snoqualmie Pass highlighted Elizabeth's year. Thousands of relatives, friends, and acquaintances made their way to *Che-ho-lan* ("Valley of the White Chalk"), the vast council grounds in the broad Kittitas Valley just over the mountains at today's Ellensburg. Patkanim's relative by marriage Owhi controlled that valley and hosted the gathering of family and allies. Yakama families came from their own valley over the steep arid hills south of the six-mile-wide campground. Some groups came from as far away as Idaho and British Columbia. The men hunted and women socialized while they prepared meals. Children played. Everyone brought something to trade: horses from the east, shells and clams from the west, beaver and bear skins from the north, baskets and blankets from the south. In addition to the games, horse races, music, and generally colorful atmosphere, Elizabeth encountered material goods she'd never seen before: tiny dentalium shells from Alaska, copper bracelets, and buffalo robes brought from the Great Plains by men who had traveled the continent's interconnecting trade routes. Families settled disputes and renewed ties. The two most powerful tribes, the Yakama and Snoqualmie, strengthened their alliance and arranged marriages.

It was to Patkanim's advantage that Julia, Margaret, Elizabeth, and Susie be married to ranking non-Snoqualmie men with complementary assets. In the same way, coastal families sought marriages with upriver families to gain access to the wooly white hair of mountain goats, upcountry foodstuffs, and medicinal plants. Plateau families also wanted access to the salt water resources of the Snoqualmie and other Coast Salish. Surprisingly, Patkanim did not marry his eldest daughters to ranking men from either group. Both girls married lower status, nonnative men with little personal influence, but with access to the economic resources, cash jobs, and assets of the HBC, which was the armed power until the American army arrived. It had weaponry to force peace between quarreling parties, a different type of asset that might be useful to Patkanim.

Elizabeth's much older sister Julia wed HBC employee Thomas Glasgow, one of the first Americans living north of the Columbia River, probably around 1847 to 1848. The marriage enabled her to live near her Nisqually mother's family and Patkanim's sister Why'it at Fort Nisqually's employee village. The Kanim family frequented the fort, and when they traveled nearby major trails they could visit Julia. Having both his daughter and sister in the heart of Nisqually territory also provided Chief Patkanim ideal sources of useful information about both fort and village.[10]

From the beginning, Glasgow was a violent abuser and troublemaker who entangled Julia in events that Patkanim could not have predicted, and that echoed in Elizabeth's life twenty years later.

In 1848 Glasgow and A. B. Rabbeson sought to become the first white settlers on Whidbey Island, where resources were overseen by several Coast Salish groups, including the Snoqualmie. The men chose the large prairie near Penn's Cove, where the Patkanim family joined his cousin Snatelum's people every summer. Snatelum exerted enormous influence within Skagit territory and was both a war chief and a converted Catholic religious leader. The presence of his cousin's daughter Julia with Glasgow and Rabbeson was probably key to the temporary patience shown by Snatelum.[11]

The men's settlement on shared territory soon became problematic, perhaps because of Glasgow's abusive demeanor toward Elizabeth's sister Julia and other indigenous people. The men's depredations on the prairie they considered wilderness, rather than administered and cultivated agricultural land, also created tension. The growing understanding of American land hunger, and that others would follow, spurred increasing irritation.

Patkanim hosted a council at Penn's Cove in August 1848, the site of the warrior school. It was attended by some 8,000 people, many already on the island for the seafood harvest. The men vigorously debated white invasion and whether to drive out the settlers before they multiplied. When a factional fight loomed, Julia advised her husband to hide. Her father advocated getting rid of the settlers, but leaders from the northern Coast Salish villages argued that settlers provided additional protection against the *Laich'wil'tach* raiders. Julia took Glasgow and Rabbeson to the council where she translated deliberations into Chinook Jargon for them. Rabbeson became so alarmed by the hostility towards them that he immediately left the island.

Snatelum's opposition to driving out the whites seemed to prevail, but shortly after the council ended he began to organize reprisals for the depredations. Julia brought Patkanim's warning to Glasgow that he was in mortal danger. Historians have dismissed the message bearer as an anonymous young woman and ignored her status as Patkanim's own daughter and Glasgow's wife. The couple moved back to Fort Nisqually.[12]

It is possible that Julia's presence as a Nisqually daughter kept her American husband safe when he behaved without regard for Nisqually rights or dignity. After quarreling over his disturbance of graves, he kicked to death a relative of influential female leader Mother Steilacoom. HBC Factor William Tolmie knew the consequences for the Nisqually if they killed an American, and he told Glasgow to respect Coast Salish custom and make reparations to atone for his crime.[13]

Julia finally left her drunken abuser and escaped to Snatelum's village. At this point, Julia's life and the future of her younger sister Elizabeth displayed parallels. Snoqualmie women did not desert their children except under the most extreme conditions, usually because they expected to die. In a situation that Elizabeth would repeat, Julia left her three small children, two daughters and a son, with Glasgow. Indigenous women had no legal right to children born to white fathers, and Glasgow may have made that point. After remarriage, he dispersed Julia's daughters to the neighbors. Olympia's wealthy African American restaurateur Rebecca Howard and her husband adopted little Frank after Glasgow abused him and a new wife until locals drove him out of the town.[14]

In the midst of Julia's problems at Fort Nisqually, Patkanim and his family became involved in an 1849 altercation there. The result was the execution of two of his brothers and repercussions that reached the territory's post-treaty armed conflict six years later. Patkanim was furious when he heard that his sister, Why'it, was being brutally abused by her husband, although her marriage was supposed to seal a reconciliation with Chief La-ha-let's family. Patkanim arrived with thirty Snoqualmie warriors and his brother's Skykomish men.[15]

Dr. Tolmie of the HBC invited Patkanim into the fort for dinner and an explanation. Outside, a general row broke out at La-ha-let's longhouse and Nisqually families ran for the fort. American Leander Wallace was caught outside and accidentally shot and killed, as was one of Patkanim's men.

The homicide of an American resulted in the U.S. Army's critical decision to handle any future violence north of the Columbia. Patkanim apologized for Wallace's death in the melee, but it was out of Tolmie's hands. The Oregon Superintendent of Indian Affairs arrived and offered a large reward for six Snoqualmie suspects. Patkanim brought in his brothers Kusass and Qualawort. When female village leader Mother Steilacoom's Nisqually son also died of his wounds, they were charged with his death as well.

Kanim family members camped all winter by the fort to see what American justice would be. The executions of Elizabeth's uncles were the first ones in Washington and left enduring bitterness between all parties. By exacting retribution instead of reparations, the government thwarted the traditional system for restoring peace.

The American government's ability to put force behind its decisions was clear. The following year, when Isaac Ebey and his family settled on Whidbey Island not far from Glasgow's aborted claim, no one drove him out. Patkanim began to ally himself with the new power structure. Some historians wrote that the government took Patkanim to San Francisco to cement in his mind the magnitude of American power, and that what he saw led him to side with whites from then on. However, it was William Steve who returned from San Francisco and told Patkanim what he had learned. Steve became Patkanim's translator and aide who helped his leader better understand American motivations and culture. Some influential whites remained skeptical of Patkanim's true feelings, one calling him the standard stereotypes of "shrewd, designing, cunning and crafty." Patkanim was probably determined to protect his own leadership, his people, and his surviving brothers. No others could be sacrificed in opposition to the new authorities.[16]

Shortly after the tumultuous family events of the late 1840s, Patkanim married his second daughter Margaret to Scotsman John McPhail, the HBC's head shepherd who appeared to have few assets to offer. However, the successful marriage put her in Fort Nisqually's employee village, around company management conversations, and McPhail did seasonal hiring. Fort protocol expected Margaret to learn the ways of a white Victorian housewife and behave like wives of other management employees, adding familiarity with another part of the alien culture to the Kanim family's knowledge.[17]

In the five years following the disturbing events on Whidbey and at Fort Nisqually, the lives of young Elizabeth and other Kanims reverted to long-established patterns, even as white presence increased. Patkanim's behavior during the early 1850s reflected a long pattern of indigenous survival by accommodation to the invasive culture and authorities. For example, Patkanim (and presumably his family) converted to Catholicism at least by the early 1850s and he owned one of the painted wood "Catholic ladders," which taught the Bible in picture form. He befriended the missionary Oblate priests who settled at Olympia, which gave him a conduit to the territorial governor. Elizabeth's father worked with ethnologist George Gibbs to write a Snoqualmie dialect vocabulary. He and his brother Sanawa guided expeditions to evaluate the Cascade pass trails for expanded commercial and military use. He and Sealth cultivated friendships with influential Seattle settlers. They helped identify suspects in a retaliation killing of a white man on Whidbey Island.[18]

In return, Territorial Governor Isaac Stevens "appointed" the two men "head chiefs" and told them if their people behaved he would take care of them, but if they didn't maintain the peace, arms would be used against them. Stevens pressured the cousins to select official sub-chiefs, something bound to cause strains among their own people. Elizabeth's father also warned authorities about the growing dissatisfaction among the eastern Washington tribes. He may not have realized how his growing involvement in territorial and tribal politics would endanger his family.[19]

January 1855 brought a major event in the life of adolescent Elizabeth and the Snoqualmie. Her family journeyed to Mukilteo on Puget Sound for treaty negotiations with Governor Stevens. Taking winter camping supplies, they arrived at windy and frigid Point Elliott (south of the Snohomish River's mouth) as soon as the treaty grounds opened and tents were available. Being first on the site made Patkanim the senior man to welcome later arrivals. It might have been a pleasant gathering in the summer, but January weather can be miserably cold and wet. Still, people played games, socialized, and danced as they waited while officials customized a standard treaty form after obtaining agreement on the site of a central reserve at Tulalip.[20]

In addition to Patkanim and Sealth, Governor Stevens and the head Indian Agent designated two other men as paramount chiefs: Goliah of Penn's Cove on Whidbey and Chow'it'sut of Lummi (Jenny Wynn's uncle, chapter 1). Most important to Stevens, all four had maintained friendly contact with the whites. He placed Patkanim over the Snohomish and Stillaguamish village residents and empowered him to sign away their lands, though he had no cultural right to do so. Elizabeth's father, like so many others, had no experience signing paper documents, understanding their nuanced significance, or grasping the concept of "legal" ownership and permanent alienation of vast territories.

Stevens' specific goals had the backing of army guns. Patkanim's strategy seems to have been to try to retain everything the Kanims and Snoqualmies already had. His people and others prayed to the new Christian God during the negotiations and before signing. The treaty would change their lives forever.

Elizabeth's younger sister Susie remembered their father doing most of the negotiating. Patkanim's priority was food resources and he wanted to reserve the salmon, deer, elk, bears, beavers, clams, dry trees, and the cedars. Said Bill Kanim, Patkamin's nephew, "Gov. Stevens agreed to let him have all that he asked." Most especially, Elizabeth's father claimed *Tohlt'w* and its salmon river. Recalled Kanim, "He didn't want to let it go. Said his house was right there and it was the house of all these people."[21]

Kanim family children clearly remembered Patkanim's impassioned speech at the treaty negotiations. Patkanim declared that the Snoqualmies' "hearts are with the whites." The family believed that

Stevens told Patkanim his grandchildren would still have the land plus money from Washington, DC, but that he must not steal from or kill white men that came. Soon, events would show that Patkanim took his pledge very, very seriously.[22]

Patkanim and the others signed away Coast Salish lands all the way to Canada in return for promises and the lands they reserved. He signed as the "Chief of the Sno-qual-moo, Snohomish and other tribes." His brothers signed as sub-chiefs. A witness described the setting for the signing as within sight of large poles hung with loops of rope, and the army guns. "So Indians were scared, they thought that if they didn't do what Governor Stevens wanted he would hang them all."[23]

Elizabeth's father and the others pledged permanent peace with the whites in the 1855 treaty, and to turn in offenders for trial, something Patkanim had already done with terrible consequences for his brothers. This time, he made the promise for people other than just his own. His influence, power, and life were on the line for the Americans' truthfulness about reparations, support personnel, and the reservations.

Winter winds blew across the treaty grounds as Patkanim's family and the other Snoqualmie packed their belongings to return to their valley and wait to see if officials kept the promises. Patkanim's request to stay in their home valley would be quickly ignored. After the 1859 ratification of the treaty by the U.S. Senate, they would be told to abandon their sacred waterfall and move to Tulalip Reservation in Snohomish territory.

Within months Patkanim heard about increasing hostility to treaties signed east of the Cascades as well as west. He secretly went to his friend Arthur Denny, one of Seattle's founding fathers, to discuss events. Perhaps he was already afraid of retaliation for his commitment to the whites. If armed hostilities broke out and spread through the passes and down the rivers, they would inevitably engulf Elizabeth's family when the army responded.[24]

In the fall, rebellious Klickitats (under Patkanim's relative) joined like-minded warriors from the Sound. Nisqually war chief Leschi and his brother (Patkanim's in-laws), still offended by Stevens' treatment of leaders at treaty negotiations, brought warriors in on the side of their mother's rebellious Klickitat people. Nine Americans died near present-day Kent in Muckleshoot territory, which brought in the troops from Fort Steilacoom. The commander suspected Patkanim of complicity after hearing that he had shadowed the pursuing troops, and ordered the Kanims arrested and kept hostage in irons aboard the U.S. Navy ship *Decatur.* Viewed by the Snoqualmie as the most powerful "settler headman," Arthur Denny vouched for his friend. He got permission for Patkanim to peacefully bring in his family without arrest and guaranteed their conduct. The friendship strategy paid off.[25]

Elizabeth's father was forced to make decisions about the pledges he'd made and how to balance those with his loyalty to the larger group under invasion. This inevitably also meant family, given the web of chiefly marriages that tied leaders to counterparts in eastern Washington. Denny thought the army's careful investigation of the accusations against Patkanim, and the just outcome, were what convinced the chief to offer his services on the side of the government, and to entrust his family's welfare to officials. The government intended for Elizabeth and the rest of her family to spend the remainder of the conflict at Whidbey Island's Holmes Harbor. They organized internment and protection for those who stayed out of the hostilities, but what were really concentration camps also gave the military easy oversight of people they did not trust. In effect, Elizabeth and others would be hostages to ensure her father's continued loyalty to white goals.[26]

Patkanim's wives and children, other families, and elders from downriver gathered and waited on the beach for an escort. Patkanim's second-in-command Quesam and others who remained upriver were angry about the situation.[27]

Elizabeth's family arrived within the deadline, bringing a cargo of mountain sheep skins, venison, hides, and possibly horses. Patkanim presented them to the *Decatur*'s captain, who saw visible proof of Snoqualmie cooperation and friendship. More likely, it was Patkanim's military diplomacy. He did not fail to notice the ordnance and troop numbers on board and on shore.[28]

He sent a messenger upriver to tell his remaining people that all would be well if they came down. His disaffected, but loyal, brothers brought 250 people in seventy canoes downriver to go to Holmes Harbor. The bad news was that 150 men had gone into the mountains to join the Klickitats with whom there were family alliances. Snoqualmie unity under Patkanim's domination had disintegrated.[29]

Patkanim used Father Pascal Ricard as an intermediary to offer his services as guide and interpreter, plus a hundred warriors. The legislature hastily passed a resolution to employ Indians in the war.[30]

When Patkanim returned from his first assignment carrying dispatches, he found problems at Holmes Harbor. The internees told him the agents (including Sehome coal mine manager-turned military aide E. C. Fitzhugh) neglected their promise to furnish provisions to his people. Patkanim requested and got eight bushels of potatoes immediately, and another week, the agents handed out 342 pounds of inappropriate hard bread and twenty more bushels of potatoes. Patkanim's people "complained bitterly of their treatment."[31]

On January 26, 1856, the *Decatur* opened fire on Seattle where warriors (many under the command of Patkanim's in-law Owhi from Kittitas) had taken up positions behind the shabby buildings clustered around Henry Yesler's mill, after they burned homesteads and threatened settlers. Shooting ensued while families ran for the blockhouse or boarded the *Decatur*, including many native families of settlers. After the "Battle of Seattle," the Americans realized how much help they needed. A week later, Elizabeth and the rest of the family watched her father and the first fifty-five armed Snoqualmies canoe out of Holmes Harbor to form their own military unit while their families stayed "interned." They kept Patkanim's commitment, despite later reports that seven hundred "internees" had been poisoned (possibly by spoiled food), and their bodies burned.[32]

Elizabeth's father could be brutal. He executed Klickitats found at Snoqualmie Falls trying to recruit stragglers, and delivered their heads to Olympia. He chased down his kinsman Leschi and a murderous ten-hour fight erupted after they threatened to take each other's heads. Offered a bounty for participants in the Battle of Seattle, Patkanim turned in many heads, possibly including some of his own slaves, to obtain the money before the authorities canceled the bounty in distaste.[33]

In the early spring of 1856, the north Sound's militia company (including most Bellingham Bay men) and Patkanim's warriors were ordered to protect Snoqualmie Pass and build several small blockhouses along the trail. Patkanim and the company commander developed an acrimonious relationship. He was accused of making the man "wait on his pleasure."[34]

The military's plan to build three forts above and below Snoqualmie Falls signaled to Patkanim that whites were establishing a permanent presence in the Valley of the Moon. The militia quartered at Snoqualmie to build the river forts included Patkanim's unit, which enabled them to watch over the pass as they always had. By the time the militia started construction of the small fortified cabins on the fertile prairies, hostilities had nearly ceased. Leschi, the kinsman Patkanim had fought so hard, fled to the Yakamas. The Whatcom County men spent the final months of the Treaty War pleasantly lounging around the forts and fishing.

By autumn 1856, Leschi was in custody awaiting a trial that ultimately led to his execution. Patkanim was struggling to trust promises the white government had made to him two years earlier. For the appointed chiefs, the question was also personal: What would happen to their families if they were wrong? What would the future hold for Elizabeth Patkanim and her family in their Valley of the Moon?

James Alexander Patterson

James A. Patterson's path to the Northwest was enmeshed within a family who eventually had one son living in the White House while another lived in a log cabin on the Nooksack River.

Patterson's grandfather and family left Virginia for the Appalachian frontier shortly after his Continental Army service ended. They settled among the Scots-Irish immigrants in East Tennessee whose self-reliance, clannish loyalties, and fearlessness gave the region a flavor much different from the southern culture of the rest of Tennessee. James Patterson's family adopted their ways.[35]

The Pattersons helped found Tennessee's second town, Greeneville. James' grandfather became one of the first magistrates. His son Andrew's wife Susanna Trotter gave birth to James Alexander Patterson on March 15, 1811, six months after the wedding. He was the first of Susanna's ten boys and two girls. Andrew began a twenty-four-year tenure as county clerk. A young lawyer named Andrew Jackson practiced at the courthouse and the county clerk's friendship with Andrew Johnson, another future American president, grew close. James' father simultaneously operated a paper mill.[36]

Northwesterners perceived James Patterson as an educated and rather aristocratic Southerner, and his parents did appreciate the value of education, helping found a local school taught by a former college president. Their son David went on to a law and government career and the rest of the children were similarly literate.[37]

The labor of a family with ten strapping boys enabled them to prosper and relocate for a new venture in South Carolina. The southern tribes were being driven from their lands, and people speculated on new industries. Indications are that the family and three slaves moved en masse, leaving sixteen-year-old David to watch their home and mill while he studied. James may have married a woman named Polly Barnes before they left, but she disappeared from all records after her marriage and may have died. Six years later, James and his family were operating a second paper mill in former Cherokee territory.[38]

The Pattersons decided to move to Independence, Missouri, where Susanna's uncle lived, when James was 31. Seven sons and two daughters migrated, by then a physically mature labor force wedded to each other's futures. Lawyer David stayed in Tennessee and Joseph lived in Georgia with his own family.[39]

The Pattersons moved during a national depression, but some things made Independence, Missouri, attractive in 1842. Livestock and traders' pack trains to Santa Fe were the primary economies, but new trails to the Far West were opening markets for Missouri cattle and sheep. American Durham Shorthorn cattle proved to be much superior to both Spanish and the nearly wild (and almost inedible) Texas longhorns. To the Pattersons, the depression meant low costs to build a herd. Missouri had recently passed inspection laws to improve livestock quality, and the federal government opened up more land for preemption claims. The Pattersons and thousands of other Southerners headed for Missouri.

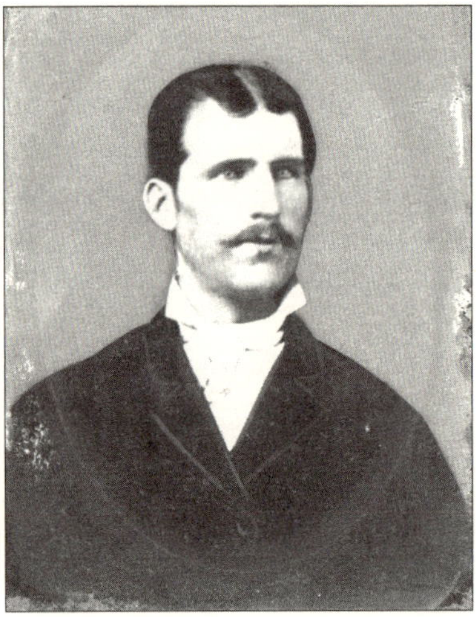

James Alexander Patterson. Tintype, 1850s. *Courtesy of the Nellie Patterson McDonald Photograph Collection.*

Fewer than seven hundred people lived in the Pattersons' new town on the Missouri River 460 riverboat miles northwest of St. Louis. Residents capitalized on their geographic advantage for frontier travelers who wanted to go as far as possible by water before taking to the overland trails. Land not in crops grew abundant bluegrass for grazing.

For the first time, James Patterson encountered what historian Anne Hyde called "composite communities," where all sorts of people lived on the leading edge of western settlement. Independence was home to many indigenous wives and their nonnative husbands, and James probably worked with many of their sons. Settlements in the vicinity of what would become Kansas City were born from the fur trade's intermarriages, and there were similar villages all along the Missouri River. Santa Fe, New Mexico, was also a hub of cross-cultural marriages with Mexican and indigenous women. The Pattersons became friends with Kit Carson, who was working the Santa Fe Trail and happily married to an Arapaho woman. Like other husbands in this book, James Patterson found that there were more types of marriages than the ones he had known in Tennessee and South Carolina.[40]

Two decades earlier, when Mexico legalized informal trade with Missouri at the northern end of the Santa Fe Trail, it resulted in America's first boomtown at Independence. The wagon trains that replaced pack trains moved goods almost eight hundred miles and by the 1840s, local merchants had extended their range five hundred miles into Mexico. By the time James' family was ready to enter the trade, the U.S. Army was escorting caravans for the six-week trip south and the return when wagons were loaded with furs and Mexican gold and trailing herds of Mexican mules.[41]

The Patterson brothers were ready to haul freight to Santa Fe. It was unlike any type of travel they had known. They had to keep the rigs at least ninety feet apart for the entire distance, which could stretch one train for three miles along the trail.[42]

The Pattersons arrived in Missouri at just the right time to take advantage of other fresh opportunities. The ground-breaking 1843 "Great Migration" wagon train to Oregon left from Independence. Outfitting emigrants brought handsome profits to Independence entrepreneurs. The Pattersons excelled in the livestock business within their first five years. James was now a cattleman.

Hints of James Patterson's western future began two years after he arrived. The Independence traders had to cancel their caravan when Mexico closed the trail temporarily. Record floods and a killer tornado destroyed the town's river landing in June, sending wagon train business to new towns further west. Kit Carson and John C. Fremont arrived to report the good prospects at the end of the new California Trail and at John Sutter's fort. The Pattersons celebrated the election of the second brother William to the Missouri legislature and his new Land Office job, only to mourn his death before he could serve in either post. It was unsettling.

Once again, Nathaniel became the family scout, setting in motion new opportunities. When war with Mexico loomed and the Santa Fe traffic slowed in 1846, he worked for a wagon train headed to Sutter's Fort, accompanied by the ill-fated Donner-Reed party which split off.[43]

Sutter's Fort was a trading post and fortified defense outpost, by then a center for new California arrivals to resupply, get medical help, and find temporary lodging. Cattleman Nathaniel joined the large crew. When the U.S. Army took possession and garrisoned the fort during the Mexican War, he joined up with John C. Fremont's volunteers and carried mail from Monterey to San Francisco, giving him wider familiarity with California's terrain.[44]

When he arrived in California, the market for quality beef was not yet profitable. But by 1849, gold rush miners wanted tasty beef for dinner and Americans saw the opportunity to supply better cattle than the tough Mexican steers. At Independence, outfitters like the Pattersons had a new customer—the forty-niner in a hurry. The first 30,000 left in April, racing west, not knowing if any supplies would be available on the route. They left a fortune with Independence businessmen, but cholera had come upriver with them. Some 250 residents were lost, including James' parents who were among the first to die.[45]

After the youngest Patterson brother also died, the remaining siblings decided to explore a move to California where Nathaniel had developed numerous contacts. James and Benjamin either left with a herd soon after the senior Pattersons died in May, or they were already out on the trail. A. J., Daniel, Martha (now married), and teenaged Belle stayed behind in Missouri for the time being. The California town of Stockton attracted professional freighters and drovers on the major routes to the southern mines. After Benjamin died there, James and Nathaniel went home, freighted the Kansas City-Salt Lake City route that supplied the new Mormon city, and established a feed store and livery operation back at Stockton.[46]

After Nathaniel married back in Independence in 1851, he brought the other siblings west. They took 30,000 sheep with them, an astounding sight still remembered by an overlander seventy years later. The profits probably financed the land purchase for the Pattersons' sheep operation near Modesto in an area still called "Patterson Pass."[47]

James and his brothers became major livestock dealers. They returned home at least one more time, but by 1854 were permanent Californians. A. J. and Nathaniel accumulated large landholdings while raising sheep and cattle in a fertile valley on the east shore of San Francisco Bay. The brothers became town fathers of Livermore and Oakdale.[48]

In Tennessee, David practiced law. With Andrew Johnson's support, President Franklin Pierce appointed him to the federal court circuit in Tennessee, although he had requested Washington Territory. There is no record of what first turned James Patterson's eye toward the Northwest, but it could have been correspondence with David that brought the growing area to his attention.[49]

Elizabeth

After the Treaty War, Elizabeth's sisters and family remained generally where they had been before the conflict. Treated by authorities as hostiles during the war, her sister Margaret and her Scots husband now lived safely at their land claim on former HBC land. Snatelum still sheltered their sister Julia. The rest of the family (including teenaged Elizabeth and little Susie) returned to life near their sacred waterfall and the graves of their ancestors in the Valley of the Moon.[50]

Trouble started immediately when some former militia members and a few others attempted to settle on Snoqualmie agricultural prairies. They tried to drive Elizabeth's family and relatives away, and would not heed Patkanim's orders to leave. The Snoqualmie did not want to move to Tulalip Reservation until the Senate ratified the treaty and paid them for their land. The whites did not like to hear that.[51]

Controversial events also separated the Kanims and other Snoqualmie leaders from those on Puget Sound. Personal and political resentments grew, some common to all and some entirely individual. Patkanim's in-law Leschi was unjustly convicted and executed in

February 1858. This contradicted Patkanim's earlier belief that the American justice system would search out the truth. Someone murdered Leschi's brother Quimuth (father-in-law of a Fort Steilacoom lieutenant) inside the governor's office and no one was charged. Lastly, the Snohomish did not like the continuance of Patkanim's appointed leadership over them. By the 1858 Fraser River gold rush, Territorial Indian Agent Michael Simmons reported that he didn't think the feuding saltwater and river tribes could live peaceably together at the proposed reservations.[52]

Simmons knew that the Snoqualmie harbored hostile feelings against authorities after their internment. Patkanim's brother had gone to him to protest the ruinous alcohol being brought to the Snoqualmies by the invading settlers. The Steilacoom newspaper carried a report from the Yakima River that their writer had seen an Indian runner taking word to Owhi from Patkanim that he was ready to go to war against the whites. Unstated was how they determined who the runner was, or his purpose, but if the report was true it took place only shortly before Patkanim's mysterious death.[53]

On November 26, 1858, the Olympia newspaper announced the deaths "in the last few months" of Patkanim and the Point Elliott Treaty interpreter, Snohomish leader John Taylor. The editor reminded readers that both had led companies of allied tribes in the recent war before revealing the true feelings of many who had only tolerated Patkanim's personal risk as a necessary evil. "It is well enough, perhaps, that Pat Kanim is out of the way. We never had a particle of confidence in his profession of friendship."

Controversy remains over exactly how Elizabeth's father died. Historians, descendants, and writers have speculated about murder without solid evidence that would point to a suspect. According to his daughter Susie, Patkanim sickened and died in Seattle, possibly at the longhouse of distant relative Suquardle ("Duwamish Curley") near his son-in-law Henry Yesler's mill. Descendants today say the men were murdered at the mouth of the Snohomish River and hastily buried. The Snoqualmie later moved Patkamin's remains to the Tulalip Reservation Cemetery.

The newspaper article announcing his death did not even have a date. That Susie Kanim said he became sick implies that the cause could have been simply illness, but Patkanim's complex life lent itself to suspicions.[54]

The Snoqualmie tried to avoid the move to Tulalip as long as possible, but after "the big Indians" died, whites tore down Elizabeth's family longhouse at *Tohlt'w* and others, burned villages, and drove Patkanim's people away from their prairie fields. Unwilling to stay at Tulalip, they returned and doggedly found ways to survive at home in the Valley of the Moon. Elizabeth's people regrouped into three villages (including *Tohlt'w*), built new longhouses, and continued their culture while making adjustments to compete with the settlers. They navigated their way through the permanent invasion as best they could to survive. Ratification of the treaty in 1859 inevitably brought even more people who coveted their prairies.[55]

James

With his parents' deaths, James Patterson became the de facto head of family and though he might be expected to be the responsible brother, that didn't happen. He may have been the family's black sheep, invited to take his cattle dealing and hard drinking elsewhere. James seems to have left his family behind in February 1856, after visiting his sister Belle and her husband Tyler Heiskell, a prominent state representative and sheep rancher.[56]

James' whereabouts between that visit and when he appeared at *Tohlt'w* in 1859 are unclear, though there are some hints. A "James A. Patterson" was appointed out of San Francisco to the post of Indian Agent for the new Klamath Indian Reservation on June 10, 1856. Agent Patterson's conduct was abominable: repudiating agreements, and spending much of his time in Crescent City's saloons. After he passed out two days in a row, his superiors replaced him in mid-May 1857. If that was James, he may have prospected or worked with cattle in Oregon until he appeared in Washington in 1859. His future ranching partner, Ohio native and prospector Reuben Bizer, met him during that period.[57]

By that time James, in his late forties, was calling himself "Colonel" Patterson, despite no evidence that he ever served in the army or militia. Inflating his identity even included a specious claim to West Point attendance. A lifelong habit of lying may partially explain why he left California. Along with drinking, it may have caused problems for his brothers who wanted to be respected town fathers and businessmen in the booming economy of the new state.[58]

The Northwest's burgeoning cattle industry in the late 1850s would have been an attraction if Patterson was looking for new opportunities. He may well have moved north first to Oregon's Willamette Valley, the livestock nursery for the Northwest, where he had old Missouri friends. Northwest army forts were major consumers of beef. Second, the Fraser River gold rush opened up new markets. By the end of the 1858 summer, the Steilacoom newspaper claimed that beef was one of the scarcest items in the Canadian gold fields, and the movement of miners further north to the Cariboo fields was yet to come. When it was available, beef already commanded unheard-of prices and some had to be imported from Hawaii.[59]

Men drove cattle from Oregon City in the Willamette Valley to the Columbia River, ferried them upstream to The Dalles, then north to British Columbia. Young Ben Snipes and others (perhaps including Patterson) moved from the Willamette to The Dalles and started to build huge herds and develop the eastern trails to the British Columbia mines and Puget Sound.

In 1859 Patterson participated in a pioneering cattle drive of stock from eastern Washington over Snoqualmie Pass to Puget Sound's population centers. Patterson is credited for cutting the new trail that ended at the Upper Duwamish village (today's Renton), the travel and trade crossroads between lake and river people. A butcher owned a large cattle ranch near the intertribal meeting grounds at Kittitas to supply his Seattle and Steilacoom markets. He or another Puget Sound cattle dealer probably organized the cattle drive that Patterson and Reuben Bizer are said to have gone on. At that time the partners brought their first herd to overwinter on Snoqualmie Prairie, and they set up quarters in an abandoned militia fort near Elizabeth's home at *Tohlt'w*.[60]

Precedent for allowing Patterson to stay the winter was set the spring before Patkanim died—before the heaviest American invasion of the prairies. Cattleman Jeremiah Borst settled in the upper valley at abandoned Ft. Alden with Snoqualmie permission. Unlike his brother Patkanim, Sanawa made known his openness to white settlement in his district if he could keep his village and a prairie, since he didn't want to move to Tulalip Reservation. At age twenty-eight,

Borst enhanced his acceptability by marrying into the Kanim family. After his first wife died, he married Elizabeth's cousin Mina, who was also a granddaughter of Twees'hri. Years later, after Mina's death, he married Kate Kanim, the daughter of Patkanim's brother Lake John. The marriages helped Sanawa's Upper Snoqualmie stay in place years longer than Patkanim's Lower Snoqualmie, who continually battled white incursion and were weakened by his death.[61]

Jeremiah Borst was a gentle, honest, and helpful man with a temperament more acceptable to the Snoqualmie than the aggressive attitudes of former militia men trying to stay in the valley. The spot he chose displayed remarkable foresight because it soon became the first rest stop for men driving herds from eastern Washington over an expanded trail through Snoqualmie Pass. As well, it provided the final pasturage for livestock headed the other way.

Borst and Patterson had already crossed paths, through business or prior acquaintance when Borst lived in Sacramento near the Pattersons. Patterson and Bizer settled on what became known as Griffin Prairie, not far from *Tohlt'w* and its stubborn families holding onto their territory. The Snoqualmie didn't drive them away, perhaps because they didn't plant crops and thus didn't appear to be permanent, or because new Kanim family member Jeremiah Borst vouched for them. James may have first seen teenaged Elizabeth at that time, though accounts place their marriage later.[62]

In the year after the men started their operation, the market for beef and dairy products continued to increase beyond gold field possibilities because housewives in growing towns could not produce their own butter and cheese. The Sound country produced only one-sixteenth of the butter consumed and imported the rest, most of which arrived rancid. It was clear that more local commercial dairies were needed.[63]

Patterson and Bizer heard from someone (possibly Whatcom's Captain Henry Roeder) about the attractive prairies along the Nooksack River. The pair visited the upper river's prairies and by early June 1860 pastured some cattle on the one across the river from *Sqweha:lich* Nooksack village. The Nooksacks' main trail to the Fraser River began nearby and the men may have only rested there, but then realized the riverside prairie was ideal for a permanent operation where they could winter cattle headed north to the booming Cariboo gold fields. By August, optimistic prospectors and pack trains left the Olympia area for the mines, including Patterson's friend Holden Judson, owner of an Olympia store and safe where James kept his cash (and later to be an important part of Elizabeth's life). Being first with a cattle ranch many days closer to the Cariboo than the Dalles route to the Okanagan Valley in British Columbia would be an advantage.[64]

Sqweha:lich prairie was perfect for the distribution of beef or cattle on the hoof north, to the army on San Juan Island, the Boundary Commission headquarters at Semiahmoo, or even to the crew out cutting and marking the border. There was a ready pool of labor and guides for the trails north who lived in the nearby Nooksack villages. Cattle could be driven upstream to The Crossing at *Popehomey* (today's Everson) and then down the Fraser gold rush-built Whatcom Trail to the bay settlements.

The *Chmoqwem* plank houses rose on the low bluff slightly above the marshy prairie the men wanted. A bit upstream sat the small village of *Lhchalos,* along with the Nooksacks' tree burial site. The land they wanted was not wilderness. It was in the middle of a large Nooksack community and on its agricultural prairies. The contemplated squatter claim was also going to be on land the Nooksacks never released because they did not attend the treaty negotiations in the face of deep winter ice on the river.

The nearly two-mile-long riverside prairie stretched about four hundred yards back from the riverbank and commanded an almost unobstructed view of the great white volcano of Mount Baker that felt touchable in the right light. Patterson had no interest in the mountain or the forests of epically proportioned cedar and fir. His interest lay solely in the grass-rich prairie and its river frontage where canoes could land. Nooksack women grew abundant crops of potatoes, *shugrak* (Indian carrots), and camas root on their prairies. By trading the excess at Fort Langley, the tribe had been able to acquire weapons, implements, and British-made clothing. Now, leaders saw that their prairies attracted men who wanted to displace the crops and deer-hunting habitat. Even if the adjacent prairies had been open to settlers, the two men were eligible only for 160 acres each and they wanted more, so they unilaterally occupied four hundred acres and decided to make the stopover place a permanent cattle ranch.[65]

When Elizabeth came to Patterson's ranch, much about the Nooksacks' territory and lifestyle would be familiar. They harvested salt water foods at Bellingham Bay, but emphasized upriver resources. Like the Snoqualmie, their closest ties were along the Cascade foothills to groups linked by river systems. An inland trail connected them to villages as far south as the Snoqualmie, but it was snow-free only about three months of the year. Another trail led north to the Nooksack villages across the new U.S.-Canada border, HBC Fort Langley, and the Fraser River. Many Nooksacks spoke Elizabeth's Lushootseed language with the Upper Skagits and other villages south of them who supplied many brides.[66]

The Nooksacks had zealously guarded their territory along the upper river's three forks since the American settlements on the bay started. They immediately resented Patterson and Bizer's cattle invasion. The foreign animals trampled the prairie and its crops, and consumed the grass browsed by deer and elk. Soon after the cattle arrived, the Nooksacks made their displeasure known by stealing a steer. Patterson filed a formal complaint for damages with the territory. The Nooksack message may have been twofold: the drovers should leave and stop destroying agricultural land, and all food resources in their territory were shared resources.[67]

The retaliatory action of taking an animal which had no place in the Nooksack diet had a history of which the two men may not have been fully aware. In his extra position as local Indian agent, Sehome Mine manager E. C. Fitzhugh had traveled upriver to see how the Nooksacks were faring two years after the treaty. He found three "bands" unified under a strong overall leader, Humptalem, who lived at *Kiskewell* (The Forks). The old man considered himself a friend of the whites passing through as long as they didn't stay. Fitzhugh understood the Nooksacks' valuation of their prairies. He firmly believed that without treaty agreements, the Nooksacks were "determined not to have their lands taken from them."[68]

The "Battle of the Blockhouse" had taken place only about a year before Patterson and Bizer arrived with their cattle, and relations with the bay community may have remained touchy. A conflict arose over the arrest of a Nooksack wanted for an intertribal murder. Men on both sides died before Deputy Sheriff/Assistant Indian Agent John Tennant brokered a solution. The Nooksack people lost their trust in settlers. Taking one of the invaders' steers and butchering the useless animal sent a clear message that settling without permission would not go well.[69]

For Patterson and Bizer, the practical solution was a simple one: marry one of the partners into an influential Nooksack family to obtain cooperation as a family member. The union would not necessarily be strange to the Nooksacks, since cross-cultural marriages had begun as soon as trade and employment north at Fort Langley began over thirty years before. One Nooksack woman, Annie, had married merchant Charles Richards of Whatcom and lived in town.

Bizer married Matilda (Mary/Martha) George, daughter of Nooksack headman George Olusius who controlled *Popehomey* (The Crossing) from his nearby village of *Kwanech.* The ford on the upper river was the only crossing for animals en route north, and pack trains supplying the U.S. Boundary Survey Commission regularly used it, as would any animals being driven by the partners up the Whatcom Trail from the bay. The Bizer marriage also provided a connection at *Sqweha:lich* because Matilda's sister was the wife of headman Jim Selhameten ("Lynden Jim"), who also led the subsidiary villages on the same prairie the partners coveted. Patterson and Bizer may have met Matilda's parents earlier when the couple worked for "Captain" Henry Roeder on his large scow that took livestock, freight, and people up and down the Sound. Both Olusius and Selhameten spoke many languages and dialects used in surrounding directions, including the Snoqualmies' Lushootseed. They could help interpret with several groups and George Olusius spoke English from also visiting California.[70]

Olusius' willingness to marry his daughter to Bizer implies a reality-based Nooksack interest in acquiring a mediator with authorities as well as cash jobs. They faced a growing invasion as more and more whites used the Nooksacks' canoe ferry at The Crossing, as well as a white-owned intermittent one. The Nooksacks did not appreciate the determination of their troublesome visitors. Olusius could call upon a son-in-law to assist with situations like the one that had ended with the "Battle of the Blockhouse." That incident's leader, Telliskanim, was the same man who took Patterson's steer a year later. Without participation at the treaty, the Nooksacks could claim no governmental protection from settlers appropriating village and resource sites. Armed resistance a year before had brought in the army. If the appropriation of their land continued, they would have to move to Lummi Reservation where they would be linguistic and cultural outsiders. White in-laws could be helpful.[71]

With Bizer's marriage, the men apparently got permission to settle on the prairie that extended for a mile west of *Chmoqwem*, the largest traditional village, and upstream on the prairie was the smaller village of *Lhchalos* that was the source of the Nooksacks' language name, *Lhechelesem*. Taking over the land with its proven fertility and abundant grass, the Americans soon displaced the people of *Chmoqwem* and *Lhchalos*. However, to say "forced" or "drove away" may be too strong. It is unlikely that such an event could have been executed by two men in the face of armed opposition. Most of the prairie's families moved to *Momeqwem*, miles away near the international boundary. Traditional villages were rarely "forever" places.[72]

Patterson's damage claim for the steer appropriation dragged on for at least a year and seems to have come to nothing after the Civil War diverted governmental attention and funds from such a small matter. Or, he could have dropped the complaint out of consideration for his new neighbors and adjunct family members. Bizer's marriage solidified Matilda's family claims to the sharing of food and economic resources by the partners.[73]

Patterson continued to build his herd on the new ranch. In late 1861 Henry Roeder noted in his diary that he was ready to load Patterson's cattle on his scow *General Harney* at Olympia, but James was too drunk to bring his herd in. Roeder waited several days until he could load twenty-nine head and a pony. Excessive drinking and alcoholism was ever-present among early Washingtonians, and the irritation that Roeder expressed did not harm their relationship. Patterson and Bizer drove their cattle out the widened Whatcom Trail from the Sehome dock to The Crossing, through the shallow water to the north side of the river, and then miles back downstream to what had become known as "The Patterson Ranch."[74]

Elizabeth and James

James Patterson had more on his mind in the next few years than his business or starting a home. His Unionist home county in Tennessee became an island in the midst of the Confederacy. Union supporters included his brother, Judge David Patterson. By then he was the son-in-law of United States Vice President Andrew Johnson, their father's friend. East Tennessee changed hands many times and Confederate forces repeatedly arrested David and charged him with sabotage and other war crimes, but always released him. News about James' brother made its way to the Washington Territory newspapers, though editors showed no awareness that any local connection existed.[75]

Family sources say Elizabeth and James married in 1862, so they may have wed only after he built a better cabin and outbuildings at the Nooksack prairie for his final move north. It's also possible that he married her as early as 1860 to obtain permission to live on the Snoqualmie prairie so close to her village. If so, he left her with family until he moved the entire operation to the Nooksack ranch. According to the census, the partners were not living in Whatcom County at the time when Patterson filed his stolen steer complaint, so they probably continued operations at both locations for some time.[76]

Elizabeth in 1860 was about 17, pretty and intelligent according to those who knew her, and judging from her daughters' appearances at the same age. She would have spoken at least one additional language, probably the Yakama of her extended family. As an elite young woman, she probably wove blankets and cedar baskets and could decorate buckskin dresses with colorful trims from Yakama country. There was no girl in the Puget Sound area who was better connected to the territory's influential native men and women. What she did not have at the time was a father to negotiate her marriage. The remaining Kanim elders probably agreed that the tall, handsome, educated Patterson might provide cash jobs and some protection against unwanted white settlers. If both Jeremiah Borst and Patterson's wives were Snoqualmie, it might help their families resist a forced move to Tulalip Reservation or at least help them continue to access their salmon fishery and other resources. For Patterson's part, the Kanim clan provided employees, important knowledge, and access to the route over the mountains with contacts on the other side.[77]

Like the Coast Salish on the saltwater, Snoqualmie tribal custom marriage explicitly affirmed ongoing family relationships and placed obligations on the husband to value his wife's contribution to the new economic unit. Elizabeth was supposed to own the products of her own labor. James probably had no language skills outside of Chinook Jargon, and if no one explained in English, he probably did not understand the traditional obligations he pledged to the Kanim family. He came from a slave-owning family and state, in which people of color were economic assets, not partners. He was at the least a hard drinker and may have been one of the white husbands who generated the stereotype of a man who purchased a servant. Ironically, his wealthy young Snoqualmie bride was herself used to servants laboring for her family.[78]

Patterson first appeared in John Tennant's journal in June 1862, when he stopped in at the only other farm on the river. Not only was Tennant his closest neighbor though far downstream, he was also experienced with cattle drives. Even then, six months went by before Patterson appeared again to deliver a sack of butter. Most likely, Patterson and Bizer kept two operations going for some time, beef only at Snoqualmie where Elizabeth was, and building the infrastructure for a dairy at *Sqweha:lich*. Bizer's wife was available there to churn butter, normally a woman's job.[79]

The partners, almost certainly with the help of Nooksack in-laws and employees, built their ranch buildings at the top of the gentle rise overlooking the grazing area and river landing. Patterson never filed a preemption claim, which would have reduced the four hundred acres he wanted down to 160. Without competition, he was free to use a larger area with no messy ownership agreements. Like others, the partners probably built an Appalachian high-sided "cow pen" to shelter and protect the dairy cows from ever-present wolves, bears, and cougars. They built a milk house and probably a small barn for hay, as well as the usual chicken coop, root cellar, and hog pen. The ranch's small orchard and garden were never intended to produce market crops, nor was it Patterson's intention to sell eggs.[80]

Dan McClanahan arrived in 1862, married Jim Selhameten's sister Nina, and claimed land two miles upriver. This reinforced the in-law relationships with the Nooksack beyond Bizer's marriage to Selhameten's sister-in-law. The men entered a partnership which could have been necessary if Patterson needed money to expand. Bizer's participation in the ranch started to fade about that time out of disinterest or frustration with Patterson. His wife may have become ill at that time also, since she died in 1864. A few years later, Bizer and his second Nooksack wife Sally moved downriver to farm near her brother Albert Descanum, Tennant's brother-in-law.[81]

In the early 1860s, Henry Roeder bought "Beaver Pass House" in British Columbia near the end of the Cariboo Trail, and began to drive cattle five hundred miles to the gold fields. Such a "house" was a stop on the trail for men and animals alike. It included some pasture, a restaurant-saloon, and barracks-style sleeping rooms, but a bath was probably the biggest attraction. Roeder had no experience driving, selling, or caring for cattle, and his association with Patterson grew closer. Washington cattle were the closest livestock and British Columbia Governor James Douglas wanted no obstacles to keep the Americans from driving them to the mines. That Ben Snipes and other herd owners from The Dalles had to drive their cattle hundreds of extra miles put Roeder in a position to compete. The first steers that arrived in the Cariboo each year sold for ten times as much as their owners paid for them.[82]

Once the gold rush was on, British authorities spent two years widening the narrow trail along the Fraser Canyon's walls to an eighteen-foot-wide wagon road. Patterson could see that his ranch's location close to the border was even better for making his fortune than when he first decided to start the ranch. The route taken by Roeder in trying it out had been the old HBC trail on the bluffs above the river. The new one would cut time substantially.[83]

When Elizabeth clambered out of the canoe on the banks of the Nooksack River, she entered a complex environment into which the ranch was inserted. Vine maples and other brush grew in the peat marsh between prairie and river. Evergreens towered on a second rise behind the cabin that awaited her up the path. In the first two miles upriver were the Nooksack burial tree site, ancient pit house depressions, a small lake, and *Lhchalos*. Jim Selhameten operated his fish trap on an excellent salmon stream behind the ranch. His longhouse and smaller dwellings sat across the river at *Sqweha:lich*, which then gave its name to what would be the new American settlement. *Kweq'Smanit* (Mount Baker's summit) was a towering backdrop to all, and intermittently reminded residents of its power with smoke, steam clouds, flames, and earthquakes the entire time the Pattersons lived at *Sqweha:lich.*[84]

Elizabeth's small home was not the most carefully planned building on the ranch. About twelve by sixteen feet, it was roughly assembled with hewn timbers in notched-log fashion and bore great resemblance to Tennessee mountain cabins. Her door faced the river under an overhanging porch with crudely hewn posts. The cabin's location proved unlucky when the river flooded and water entered. The stick-

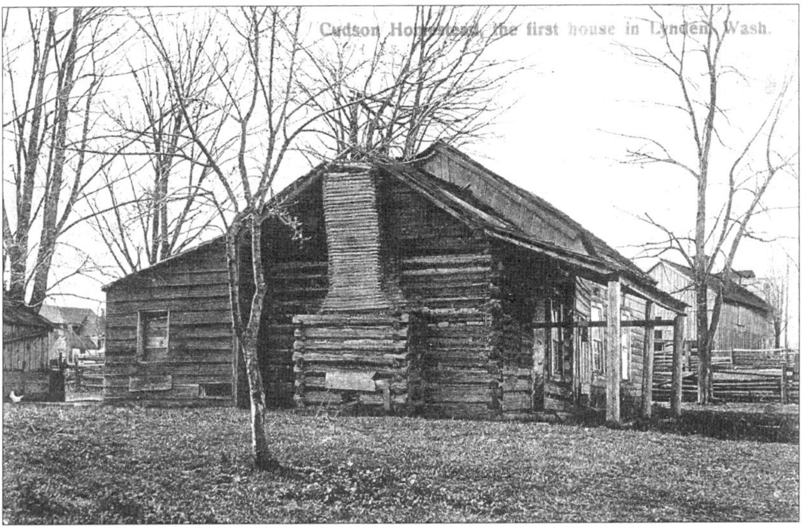

Elizabeth and James Patterson's cabin on a postcard in the early 1900s. Visible is the clay and stick chimney common to early cabins. The door and overhanging roof faced the river landing and *Sqwe:halich* village. The barn in the background is believed to be an enlargement of the original Patterson barn. "Judson" was misspelled on the postcard by the publisher. *Image #B14 courtesy of Lynden Pioneer Museum, Lynden, WA.*

and-clay chimney's primitive off-plumb construction looked fragile, but the fireplace was strong enough to provide heat and a cooking source for many years. Elizabeth probably covered her dirt floor with rush or cedar mats she made, brought along, or got from Nooksack women. Patterson added a windowed lean-to kitchen on the back, which left more of the cabin free, perhaps after Dolly was born. Elizabeth used the shallow back overhang to keep firewood and other supplies dry and cool. It was nothing like her father's longhouse.[85]

Ordinarily, Elizabeth's elite family would have sent servants to do menial chores and discouraged her new in-laws from treating her as their servant, but the treaty outlawed slavery and her father was dead. She and the Kanims had little idea of the kind of physical labor to come in her future. With the death of Chief Patkanim, the disarray at Snoqualmie, and Elizabeth's distance from home, there was little chance that her family could help in any meaningful way if she was treated badly by her new husband. Both her sisters Margaret McPhail and Julia Glasgow died in the early 1860s, severing more ties that could have aided Elizabeth.[86]

Elizabeth did not live in social and linguistic isolation as many believe. Upper Skagit women and other Nooksack wives spoke Lushootseed and exerted great influence over village activities. Patkanim's family was Catholic, as were the Nooksacks at the time. The well-known woman Nooksack canoe captain Sally had a shaman brother from Skagit country who sometimes lived at Snoqualmie during his travels. Because of Elizabeth's far-reaching upriver connections, it is certain that once she introduced herself, the Nooksacks knew exactly who she was and her rank. Ex-Whatcom militiamen who had been stationed in Elizabeth's valley would know the name Patkanim and some may have even met her.[87]

Elizabeth was fortunate to have Matilda Bizer and others who spoke her language, understood her ways, and might be supportive when she was alone on the ranch. Dan McClanahan's marriage to Jim Selhameten's sister Nina placed another young Nooksack woman on the north bank of the river. All the same, in Elizabeth's culture the prolonged absence of a husband, as she experienced once James started his cattle drives, was neglectful and abusive.

Unfortunately for Elizabeth, she lived on a dairy ranch where there was no respite from twice-daily milking. Producing commercial butter and cheese would give the couple a steady income from town customers who were eager to buy fresh dairy products. The Nooksacks lost interest in sharing Patterson's products after sampling the rustled cow in 1860. They called consumption of milk and butter a "very foolish thing" because they thought it too "dirty and unhealthful to use."[88]

The milk house typified the complexity of the job Elizabeth was supposed to share. It was the most elaborate and elegantly constructed structure on the ranch, built to the latest technological standards. A good milk house kept butter and milk cool without using immersion in cool water, and in the winter kept the milk and cream from freezing. Patterson's milk house had dirt-filled double walls overlaid with more dirt for insulation and covered with white muslin. It had to provide conditions under which the milk and utensils could be kept absolutely clean. The quality of milk and butter in the 1800s varied with dairy worker experience and the milk's freshness, but the crucial factor was the atmosphere and cleanliness of the building. The whole process was exacting.[89]

Elizabeth had to learn how to milk cows, a miserable job for most women. It required her to rise before dawn every day of the week, even if she had additional help. There was no help for kicking cows, freezing winter days, summer heat, splashing manure, flies, or a switching tail. Patience and a calm soothing manner had to be summoned twice a day, every day.[90]

Elizabeth and helpers had to observe detailed rules to churn and get saleable butter. Cow, milker, and equipment had to be scrupulously clean. The butter maker had to be aware of current temperatures and the cream's shelf life before it turned sour. The cream had to be away from other foods, and she could not churn in the milk house. There were rules for when to skim the cream off and how to stir. The cream had to be kept at an even temperature with light and air but no drafts. If the butter was to be shipped a long way, it had to be brined in a barrel, buttermilk washed away, and laboriously shaped into molds. Matilda Bizer and Nina McClanahan probably helped with this "women's work."[91]

Elizabeth, used to free time to pursue more valuable and artistic work than menial chores, now led the life of a servant. Phoebe Judson wrote that Patterson treated his wife like property with little consideration and often left her alone to milk twenty cows, year after year. A Snoqualmie elite woman who was supposed to own the products of her labor, and expected her husband to honor her contributions, had married a Tennessean who was culturally and mentally unprepared to treat an indigenous wife with respect.[92]

Sunday was visiting day for farm families and kept as free from chores as possible, but at a dairy the milking routine went on. The Tennant family often visited at the Patterson home and sometimes John or all of them stayed overnight in bad weather rather than risk the river. Such visits broke the routine, but for Elizabeth at the only "white" settlement on the upper river, it meant she had to be prepared to serve extra meals and host overnight guests without notice.[93]

Elizabeth gave birth to Dolly Caroline on February 27, 1863. The *Eliza Andersen* had recently arrived from the Fraser River carrying news from the Cariboo gold fields mired in snow and below-freezing temperatures. Supplies for overwintering miners were very low, sending prices high, and men were heading for the mines despite the continued cold. The new father prepared to leave with a herd.[94]

To make the most money, cattlemen wanted to leave as soon as conditions permitted. Thousands of miners had decimated wild game populations early on, and there was no cattle industry in British Columbia. Thinking they would leave immediately, Patterson and McClanahan bought supplies from Whatcom merchant Charles Richards. When they didn't leave and didn't pay the bill, he sued them to get payment. The dispute ended when Richards discovered that Patterson had $600 in the store safe, more than enough to pay the bill. James still didn't leave, though Roeder set out in May on his second expedition. By then, the men had a loose alliance. The roadblock to their departure may have been President Lincoln's new wartime embargo on any livestock leaving the United States. He finally lifted it in August in view of the meat scarcity in the Cariboo and the prospect of a large illegal beef industry developing. The cattle drives were free to resume. Patterson, Bizer, and their Nooksack drovers would compete for a place on the Cariboo Road and sales with the big players driving large herds from east of the mountains.[95]

Roeder's diary description of his own 1862 drive was probably similar to Patterson's trip the next summer: rock slides, bad grass, swamps, cold, sickness, lost horses, deep mud, rain, no feed, hundreds of rivers and creeks to cross and recross, and lost cows which had to be recovered no matter how long it took to find them. Roeder's herd crossed one creek thirty times.

James left Elizabeth with a six-month-old baby and a heavy load of farm work. Now she was alone with Dolly at night, listening to wolves and coyotes in the darkness. Occasionally, cougars roared. Even in the daytime, the predators boldly approached the cabin and cow pen looking for easy pickings. For at least one break, she left the ranch with the Catholic Nooksacks to attend one of Father Chirouse's festive visits to Lummi when he baptized Dolly.[96]

For Roeder, ranching on-site at his Beaver Pass House soon made sense. Cattle could be overwintered for the best prices when miners returned in the spring, or sold to boomtown residents. His 160 acres lay halfway between the two new towns along the final stretch of the Cariboo Trail and was the destination for the Patterson herd. It was the only full-service roadhouse within a hundred miles. Income rolled in from keeping and feeding stagecoach horses, selling food, drinks and lodging on the floor as well as supplying cattle to the slaughterhouses in Barkerville. He and Charles Roberts (deserting husband of Whatcom's midwife) started putting in a dairy; the cows came from Patterson.[97]

By 1864 James Patterson's business had become both his dairy and the annual cattle drive, but it proved to be the high-water mark for both the gold fields and beef prices. The next years took on a pattern. James bought steers in the south Sound. Sometimes Roeder acted as his agent, buying cows for the dairy and transporting steers and cows to Whatcom. If Patterson found a way to take brined and molded butter produced over the cold months hundreds of miles to Barkerville, it commanded prices as high as three dollars a pound, equal to about fifty dollars today. However, the market dropped after Canadian dairy cows were imported into the Cariboo to Canadian-owned roadhouse ranches.[98]

The Cariboo gold rush was realistically over by 1865 and Patterson's beef market underwent monumental change. Cariboo area ranches grew so large that they reversed the south-to-north supply line and sent cattle south to butchers. Prices fell precipitously and then the B.C. government passed a stiff import tariff on all imported cattle. It is unclear when Patterson made his last trip north before enlarging the home ranch that year into a bigger commercial dairy. The ranch now produced more beef and lamb (or mutton) for the local market as well, after John Tennant helped him build a slaughterhouse.[99]

The Civil War's end brought peace to Patterson's own family. Tennessee elected his brother David to the U.S. Senate. He moved with his family into the White House when his father-in-law became president after the Lincoln assassination. Martha Johnson Patterson served as White House hostess for the entire Reconstruction-era administration because her mother was always "indisposed." All the while, David's eldest brother and family lived in a twelve-by-sixteen-foot cabin on the Nooksack River.[100]

Elizabeth gave birth to Nellie on March 28, 1866. She and James built what was the happy home remembered by Dolly and Nellie as adults. The two dark-haired girls loved life in the snug cabin with everything two little girls needed. Moss chinking between the logs kept howling November winds out and the clay fireplace kept the small space warm.

Their father worked nearby, clearing his land with the help of the Nooksack men and driving the oxen, Jake and Ben. Elizabeth roasted bear meat, venison, fish, and fowl in the fireplace, and her garden and orchard supplied vegetables and fruit. If Elizabeth hadn't done much sewing before, she now made warm winter clothing for her family. Life on the north bank with loving parents and other children to play with held everything Dolly and Nelly needed.[101]

Whenever James returned from a cattle drive to Sumass Lake and other places, he told Elizabeth and the little girls stories of his adventures. Occasionally, the four Pattersons went to Sehome by canoe after they stopped at Clara and John Tennant's home overnight. The trips gave the girls a chance to experience all the community activity and the wonders of Sutcliffe Baxter's general store at the Sehome Mine. The trips were welcome respites for Elizabeth and she could shop for things unavailable upriver.[102]

One memorable day in 1866, Tennant strolled up from the landing with three other men on their way to attempt the first climb of Mount Baker, even though the volcano was smoking, steaming, and occasionally flaming. When the day turned foul, the group stayed overnight and Elizabeth made their last hot home-cooked meal before two weeks of trail food. After a failed attempt, the party stopped for a visit and meal on the way home. Two years later, there was a repeat visit before Tennant and three others successfully summited. Tennant brought his family back upriver a few months later to spend Christmas week with the Pattersons. He had gone on an Arkansas-California cattle drive in his youth, and the friends probably traded many adventure tales of trail and mountain around the crackling fire and over whiskeys.[103]

Elizabeth and James' marriage ended in 1869, the same year his brother left the U.S. Senate and White House, having served a president that resentful Southerners saw as white trash. Little attention has been paid by those who told of the marriage's end to the "how" and "why," or to the identity of the young man "Ned" who aided Elizabeth's flight from the little cabin.

Phoebe Judson wrote her version of the events that ultimately brought her own family from Whidbey Island to *Sqweha:lich.* When the "severe taskmaster" (as she called James) had left his wife alone during cattle drives she had only Ned, a young Nooksack employee who lived at the nearly deserted *Lhchalos*, to help her with the heavy work if Dan McClanahan was not available. Elizabeth was still young and pretty in her twenties, and James later told Judson that Ned was good-looking and smart.[104]

Loneliness haunted all homestead women. Elizabeth was not the only woman of any ethnicity whose husband saw his wife as a work horse, according to historian Susan Butruille. Most western pioneers just wanted their wives to take charge of garden and house, do what they were told, keep quiet, and not make a lot of demands. When a wife expressed her feelings about her situation, it often led to being called a "shrew" or "scold." Butruille wrote that these predominant conditions often resulted in "silence, absences, divorce, manipulation, violence, and even murder."[105]

American society's norms in the nineteenth century West expected that physically abused wives would suffer in stoic silence. Victims usually told their troubles to friends in the most veiled ways. For a woman like Phoebe Judson, "severe taskmaster" was a subtle way to avoid saying "abusive" and "domineering." It is clear that Patterson's daughters deeply loved him, but for their mother things seem much different. Unlike Elizabeth's aunt Why'it at Fort Nisqually, no family received word to come to her defense because the new government's legal system did not tolerate the Coast Salish way of dealing with husbands who mistreated their wives.

Ned, the young man Judson described so briefly in her memoir, was much more than just a Nooksack employee. He was Ned Salasoten, Nooksack village-born and about eight years older than Elizabeth. The fathers of Ned and Jim Selhameten were brothers, which made him the first cousin of both Jim and of Nina McClanahan, almost a sibling relationship in their culture. Ned's Sumass mother's second husband was Nooksack. As a young man, Ned lived ten miles north of The Crossing at *Sema:th* (now Kilgard, British Columbia). He was a skilled carpenter when he went to work for James Patterson and moved to *Lhchalos* next to the prairie.[106]

Judson based her version of the 1869 events on what James Patterson told her and some conjecture: "The burden of life under the colonel's stern sway became unbearable, and yielding to Ned's pleadings, one night while the colonel was at home to look after the little girls, she crept out in the darkness, and joining Ned, who was waiting for her, together they fled to the Sumass country." In the morning, Judson wrote, James listened (apparently from his bed) for his wife doing her chores. "Lizzie, Lizzie," he called, but heard only silence. The little girls called their mother. No answer. James soon realized that his "willing slave," (i.e. a woman who loved him) had left. "His grief and dismay were great," Judson observed, probably evident from his emotional account of that day. He apparently guessed or heard from the Nooksacks where the pair had gone. He sent messages pleading for her to return to her bereft little girls, but in Judson's words, "the bitterness of the bondage was too great for even her mother love to draw her back again."[107]

In Judson's version, Patterson finally realized that despite his entreaties, Elizabeth had no intention of returning to do all the work and she was beyond his reach to force her compliance. He was mad. He vowed that she would never see her girls again.

This picture of Elizabeth's abandonment of her daughters has been interpreted to mean that she and Ned were having an affair and she left her little girls behind as no respectable and loving mother ever would. Perhaps while her abusive husband was gone for months, she did find solace in Ned, but the situation was far more complex than that. James probably was not truthful with the Judsons about the level of marital discord and maltreatment that preceded the tragic events.

The problems in the Patterson marriage were not entirely private. On one overnight Sunday visit downriver at the Tennant home, Elizabeth and the girls did not go home with James on Monday. Uncharacteristically expressive, John Tennant entered the following in his journal that day: "Colonel went home—alone—I made currant jelly." His dash in the entry told everything. He did not mention when Elizabeth started for home.[108]

Coast Salish communities supported abused wives who left their husbands. Ned's people allowed for leaving the children with their father if desertion was necessary, and he may have told her that. Elizabeth, like her sister Julia Glasgow, lacked legal standing in family matters. No territorial wives had rights to children. Even if Elizabeth had a civil marriage, she would have had no claim to custody of her half-white children in a split. Fathers and courts saw such children as needing to be saved from a life in their mother's village without the "advantages of civilization." Had she taken the girls, her husband could have petitioned British authorities to help retrieve them. In Washington Territory just a few years before, an HBC husband died and the judge forced his prominent Nisqually wife to leave her children with a guardian and go home. Subsequently, the judge ruled that she had abandoned them. Because she had returned to Indian ways, "their custody and education should not be safely entrusted to her." It is possible that Patterson had already told Elizabeth that she had no chance of keeping the girls if she left, and so she quietly left her babies behind rather than expose them to a vicious and ultimately fruitless battle.[109]

The other factor in Elizabeth's decisive (and to many today, shocking) behavior was quite different. Snoqualmie mothers did not leave their children behind unless they expected to die. Even her sister Julia may have thought she was going to die, as she did three years after deserting Glasgow. Ned's pleadings with Elizabeth to leave may have had less to do with romance, and more to do with saving his friend's life. She was dying of tuberculosis and there was a renowned First Nations doctor at *Sema:th,* his father.[110]

In truth, an epidemic existed among the small group of mixed families at Patterson's prairie. The common perception is that indigenous people caught tuberculosis in crowded longhouses or boarding school dormitories, but there was another source. Bovine tuberculosis was contracted from infected cows and their raw milk. Among the few people who lived around the ranch's dairy herd, at least four people are known to have died of the disease within a ten-year period: Elizabeth, Nina McClanahan, and her husband Dan; their daughter Nora suffered from it into the 1880s before she died. The cause undocumented, Matilda Bizer had died in 1865 and Reuben's second wife Sally died in 1874, as did another intermarried husband at the prairie, Hawaiian worker Joe Emmerling. Perhaps Nooksack tribal employees at the ranch died too, but no one linked their deaths to the dairy. It was a very unusual cluster of early adult deaths in an unusually healthy climate for that age group. Only James Patterson and Reuben Bizer would walk away unscathed.[111]

Called "the white plague," tuberculosis was contagious, incurable, and fatal. Some died quickly and some lingered for years, like little Nora McClanahan. Her mother Nina died less than a month after giving birth and apparently infected her. Bovine tuberculosis was common among those who milked cows, when a cough into a milk bucket could expose everyone who drank the raw milk. Milkers' hands cross-contaminated cows. The onset was slow and insidious with weight loss, fever, lack of energy, and an infectious cough. Once advanced, contagious bloody sputum from the lungs signaled oncoming death.[112]

Elizabeth could not foresee what her departure would ultimately mean for her daughters, but she probably saved their lives. Dolly and Nellie lived into their eighties and their adult lives became their mother's legacy.

The shock of Elizabeth's flight became an unavoidable crisis for James. Their daughters, ages three and six, cried for their mother and needed meals, baths, constant supervision, and their aging father's attention. He had his own ranch chores and cows demanding to be milked twice a day. Nearly all of his business was the most schedule-intensive and perfectionist form of agriculture. His products also needed to be delivered to town. Winter was coming on and he was struggling to change his business from the dying Canadian beef trade to one that met local needs in a variety of ways. It was probably obvious within a week that he needed a foster mother if the girls were not to live with the McClanahans or Emmerlings in their cabins, where tuberculosis may have already shown its presence. The half-Nooksack children of the departed Whatcom merchant Charles Richards were living with Jim Selhameten in his village, but Patterson wanted his bright little daughters to be educated and live life within the white community. Dolly and Nellie spoke their mother's language better than English, given their father's frequent absences, and needed immersion in English to be ready for adulthood in the changed society.[113]

James discussed his situation with Henry and Elizabeth Roeder in Whatcom. They argued that Phoebe Judson on Whidbey Island was an obvious choice for fostering, if she was willing to take on the job after recently losing her own infant. Phoebe was Elizabeth Roeder's best friend from their Ohio days and James had known the Judsons for many years, starting when he used their Olympia meat market's safe for his money. They fell for his line about being "Colonel" Patterson, impressed by his good looks, education, wide travels, and good stories, and he visited them frequently. He may have met Jack Judson during that time, the indigenous boy they adopted at ten after his parents died and he was in precarious circumstances. Phoebe had raised Jack to adulthood and presently had only three children at home. She and Holden had still not found a location where they were happy and successful. Phoebe might be open to raising two little girls in need of a mother on a piece of prime farmland.[114]

Patterson seems to have cared for the girls at the ranch briefly, probably with Nina McClanahan or Catherine Emmerling helping. At the same time, his business was in financial trouble as more cattle came over the Cascades to market and more farmers sold butter and milk. Alcoholism and inattention may have also contributed to the situation. He contemplated moving on if he could settle the girls permanently. He took the girls to stay with the Judsons to see if it worked out.

On Christmas Eve 1869, the coal mine store filed suit against him for his unpaid balance. They believed that he was going to leave without paying and won attachment of five of his cows. Soon, they filed a second suit for a loan note they owned, originally an Olympia debt for steamer transportation. Though the coal company alleged that he might have already left the territory, he was only in Seattle, probably trying to sell some of the herd to stabilize his finances. The court attached twenty-one more head.[115]

In a few short months life, both personal and professional, closed in on Patterson. He appealed seizure and got the sheriff's sale of his cows postponed while he tried to pay off his debts. He mortgaged thirty-five head and got the others released with the condition that he would turn them over if he lost the lawsuits. Patterson could earn money from his cows' production and the county didn't have to find someone to milk them twice a day. Probably anticipating the end of his dairy ranch days, Patterson did not go to the courthouse and register his brand when the county started the book the same month, unlike all the others on the river. In the end, the lawsuits were settled in his favor.[116]

James had still not heard from Elizabeth by February. After he got his cattle back, he went to Whidbey Island to see the girls. He observed how they fit into the Judson family circle and signed a set of unusual documents with Phoebe and her husband on March 3 and 4, 1870. First, he and Phoebe (alone) signed a "conditional deed" for her care of the girls in return for his ranch. Elizabeth's daughters would live in their own home with their foster mother, instead of on Whidbey. Phoebe legally agreed to "rear, maintain, educate and take care of [Dolly and Nellie] and treat them with affection and in all respects as

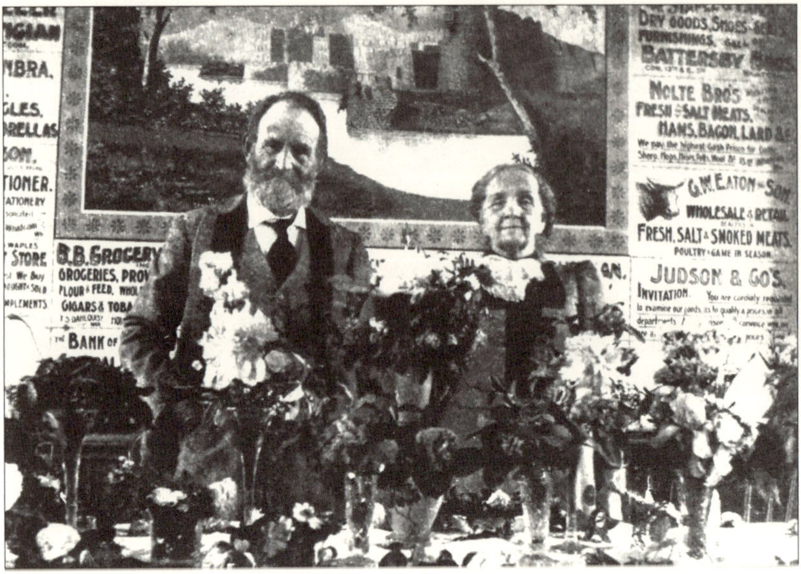

Holden and Phoebe Judson, foster parents of Dolly and Nellie Patterson, at a wedding anniversary celebration in the late 1890s. *Image #F57 courtesy of Lynden Pioneer Museum, Lynden, WA.*

she would her own children" until age eighteen. This unique detailed language is unlike any other guardianship filed in territorial Whatcom County or six other counties in the region. The agreement required Phoebe to move to the ranch as soon as possible, and if she failed to perform her duties satisfactorily, that would void the agreement. The children and the ranch (though never legally owned or even claimed by Patterson) would revert to James.[117]

In the document, Dolly and Nellie's father reserved the right to make his home on the ranch with them for the rest of his life, whenever he desired, "not interfering with the convenience or comfort" of the Judson family. That is, he would board there on mutually agreeable terms. This lesser-known provision enabled a father who loved his children to return at any time and share dinner and home with his girls, but without jerking them away from a woman they would grow to love as their mama. Holden was curiously absent from the first agreement, but Patterson's purpose was to designate a loving new mother for his children, not to find a new father. In addition, if the Judsons should ever divorce or if Holden died, Phoebe would be able to stay on the farm with sole custody of the girls and no legal entanglements with the guardianship laws.

An agreement/lease with Holden and subsequent revision specified the future of the dairy operation. The Judsons could file a patent after the government survey but they would have to relinquish the ranch if they left within the lease and an extension's time limits. Most oddly, the papers directly contradicted the agreement with Phoebe for James' lifetime rights to live at the ranch. It specified that he would have no right to occupancy after the end of the second lease. Perhaps Holden was afraid that they would end up with a permanent, aging, demanding guest.[118]

On March 18, 1870, the little steamer *Mary Woodruff* pulled up to the Sehome wharf. A new phase in the lives of both the girls and the Judsons began. Dollie and Nellie looked down from the rail at the smiling faces of their friends Jim Selhameten and the river's best canoe captain Sally and her husband Job. Patterson had sent three Nooksack canoes to greet and transport the party and their belongings on the arduous journey upriver. Phoebe noticed only a few bedraggled houses left in Whatcom after the gold rush, and that "most of those belonged to the Indians," probably meaning the three longhouses along the shore. The group spent the night with Reuben and Sally Bizer after the grueling portage around the mile-long log jam on the lower river.[119]

After the two-day river journey, Elizabeth's daughters saw "home" in front of the hovering mountain. Having lived in a decent house on Whidbey Island (possibly Ferry House), the Judsons saw the shabby cabin and log dairy buildings that they had agreed to make into their new home. Holden had farmed, but the operation of a commercial dairy was a daunting task for anyone inexperienced. Despite that, James officially turned over his ranch the day they arrived. After eleven days of reunion with his daughters and exhaustive hours spent teaching Holden Judson the operation, he canoed downriver to visit the Tennants. James probably needed comfort and counsel, in addition to other business there or in town. A week later, he bought four pigs from Tennant for the home and ranch that were no longer his. It was the last time Tennant would ever mention the man who had treated the daughter of Chief Patkanim so abominably that she had run away.[120]

Phoebe Judson believed that James Patterson never ceased to regret his part in bringing such loss and sorrow to his children's lives. He stayed at the ranch intermittently as he transitioned his dairy and his daughters to the care of the Judsons. He may have stayed in the old Bizer cabin, empty since Reuben moved downriver. Or James may have slept in Elizabeth's cabin to be with the girls. He appointed County Auditor John Briggs, perhaps a regular cowhide customer and friend, to handle his remaining stock and dairy interests. By September, he had left.[121]

James Alexander Patterson had just turned fifty-nine. He was an aging, hard-drinking cattleman with little time left to build a new life. His daughters would spend their childhood in their own home, in the capable and loving hands of Phoebe Judson, and surrounded by the memories of the mother they missed. They were his only legacy left behind in Whatcom County. He never legally owned any real estate or held office there, seemingly the only literate settler who had not served. He didn't completely cut his local ties and popped back into town from time to time to do business and visit his daughters. There is no evidence that he ever tried to find or contact Elizabeth again.[122]

On behalf of Patterson, John Briggs sold portions of the herd during the two years after his departure, particularly when the regional cattle market crashed in the onset of a general depression. James spent the next few years back in California, possibly dealing cattle again. There, his brothers had become town patriarchs.[123]

The new blended family settled into Dolly and Nellie's memory-filled cabin. In the early months, Phoebe's fear of Indians based on experiences traveling west twenty years earlier persisted. She hoped that the presence of the girls would keep her family safe, but she didn't trust the Nooksacks and carried a gun upstairs with her to bed. Soon, her need to be with other women overcame her suspicions, since her friend Elizabeth Roeder was two days away. The tall canoe captain Sally went from only a transporter of goods and people to become Phoebe's comfort, companion, and "most intimate neighbor." The two sat in Jim's longhouse across the river or on the cabin porch, knitting, and watching their children play together. Chinook Jargon and the common language of mothers was enough.[124]

It wasn't long before the Judsons completed an addition with a sleeping loft to the cabin to relieve the overcrowded home. They converted the original cabin into the kitchen and dining room and added a fine brick fireplace in the new part to supplement the rustic old stick and clay one. No one heard from Elizabeth, and since James had told the girls they would never see her again, "they mourned as one without hope."[125]

Elizabeth lived on for some time, but it is unclear from Judson's book and speeches just how long. She was only ten miles north in *Sema:th* and Nooksacks traveling the trails to villages across the border took word to her that her daughters had returned to the cabin. She walked the trail (probably escorted by Ned) to the ranch secretly and left bits of her clothing on bushes for the little girls to find. Once she knew James had moved on and she had nothing to fear, she journeyed to Jim Selhameten's longhouse where she was probably greeted as family given her friendship with his sister Nina. She sent a message to Phoebe asking if she could visit her daughters. Phoebe believed that it would help the desolate and hopeless little girls to see their mother, despite what their father had said. According to Judson, the little girls were "wild with delight" at the prospect of seeing their mother.[126]

As Judson told it, early in the morning, Dolly and Nellie stood quietly at the cabin window, staring wide-eyed at the path from the riverbank. "I see her. I know it's Mama, she has on her red shawl," said one according to Judson. Very, very slowly Elizabeth Patkanim Patterson walked up the slope, her solitary red silhouette a contrast with the greens of the foliage. She entered her home that was now the territory of another woman. Mother and daughters stared at each other for a long moment before she gathered them into her arms, speaking *Lushootseed* words of endearment. The girls snuggled and laughed and played with the loose braids hanging down their mother's back. The trio stayed close together all day long. Phoebe no doubt cooked a noon meal for the obviously fragile mother to eat with her babies.

When it came time to leave at the end of the day, Elizabeth gave her girls the universal mother's admonitions at such a time of separation. She may have told them that she would return, even knowing she was probably too ill, but the girls were crying. Phoebe didn't understand the words, but she didn't have to. Every mother would be trying to ease their anxieties when she left them with the other woman. Wise enough to understand the mother-child bond that did not need to be completely broken just because the father was angry, Phoebe hoped there would be another visit, but word came that Elizabeth died shortly after that day.

Nellie's loss of her mother seemed to affect the little girl's personality and she developed a special empathy for young animals also crying for their mothers. Most telling about the trauma of abandonment was an incident in which Nellie found a mother hen trying to withdraw from her maturing chicks. For several nights, the little girl stayed out after bedtime and held the hen on the nest so her chicks could snuggle under her wings. She tearfully scolded the mother hen for not caring for her babies. In adulthood, Nellie would adopt and foster other children in need of a loving mother.[127]

Patterson's choice of the Judsons could not have been wiser. They proved to be genuine family and community builders as soon as they moved to the ranch. Only three years later, Dan McClanahan became another tuberculosis fatality. The probate judge had to decide where the four children should go since Nina had no legal standing and was already ill from the disease. He appointed Holden guardian and the eldest three, all eight and under, joined the Judson home. Nina returned to live with her youngest child in her brother's longhouse across the river. When she died too, Jim Selhameten carried his disease-free little nephew to Phoebe. In a probate guardianship agreement, Holden pledged to treat all four as his own until they reached age eighteen. He received control of the McClanahan homestead and cattle profits, as long as he returned the same number of animals to the adult children.[128]

Within four years after Nina's death, the Judson household included Phoebe's elderly mother, three of their own children, and six foster children ages seven to seventeen. The census listed all the children as "adopted," not "boarders" as many foster families did. They crowded together in the cramped original cabin and its addition, perhaps supplemented by some of the cats and dogs the children loved. In the mid-1880s, a family scandal brought Phoebe's four nieces and nephews to the Judson's newer, larger house.[129]

James

James Patterson arrived back in Whatcom from San Francisco on October 21, 1876, five years after his last recorded appearance. The *Bellingham Bay Mail* announced the visit of "the first pioneer on the

Nooksack above Mr. Tennant." The sixty-five-year-old took advantage of his right to visit his daughters and stay on the ranch. The newspaper noted in early December that Patterson had been in California, but had taken up a claim near his old location. There is no documented record for this claim which the elderly man may have only contemplated as an estate to be left for the girls. This plan fell through and he soon left again, perhaps after Christmas.[130]

The next year, Dolly and Nellie (fourteen and eleven) may have shared the holiday with their father again when he returned for several months. Patterson was still dealing cattle, and sold thirty-one head from the ranch, which further reduced Holden Judson's obligation to care for them. Patterson's whereabouts the next two years are unclear. He may have gone to The Dalles, the undisputed center of the Northwest cattle trade and crowded with men like himself. The town remained the hub for cattle headed to the Sound through Snoqualmie Pass, floated downriver to Portland, or driven east and south to Salt Lake City to meet the railroad bound for eastern markets. By the late 1870s, men like Patterson, Ben Snipes, Jack Splawn, and buyers from the East talked the same language at the Umatilla House and in the many saloons. Cattle king Snipes, Patterson's early competitor for the Cariboo trade, had 125,000 cattle grazing in eastern Washington's Columbia Basin. The Dalles was a town where Elizabeth's former husband could have found both employment and friends.[131]

If James didn't use The Dalles for a base as he went back and forth to the ranch after his California sojourn, he may have been in the Willamette Valley. Summer 1880 found him at age sixty-eight living at Forest Grove with Ben Catching, a church-going farmer of the same age. His land lay in a district populated by cattle raisers and dairy farmers which was the original Northwest center of breeding herd foundation cattle. Phoebe Judson's siblings lived there and possibly other contacts, but Patterson and Catching probably had known each other for decades. Catching's late wife was also from Greeneville, Tennessee, and the couple lived in Independence, Missouri, when the Patterson clan arrived. The widowed Catching's household when James boarded was a blend of single and married sons and small grandchildren. The census listed Patterson as a "farmer," perhaps an elderly hired hand.[132]

Wherever Patterson's wanderings took him, six years after his Oregon residence he was back in The Dalles where the town had boomed once more, but as a center for the construction crews extending the transcontinental railroad extension to its terminus in Tacoma. When construction ended, it became clear that The Dalles would no longer be the regional cattle shipping hub. Long cattle drives were unnecessary if livestock could be loaded onto rail cars. The Dalles, an indigenous trade hub for centuries before it was an Oregon Trail terminus or cattle industry center, rapidly declined into just another small agricultural town. James Patterson was in his final decline as well.

James Alexander Patterson, age seventy-five, died May 20, 1886, at the county hospital in The Dalles. People had seen him around town until a week before he died alone in a place without family. In his last years, he had continued to tell convincing tall tales about his past, perhaps after a few too many whiskeys at the Umatilla House. In a short article about his passing, the newspaper editor said he had learned that "the old gentleman" was a California pioneer who was "the first secretary of state after its admission in the union in 1849." Early pioneer yes, secretary of state absolutely not. There was nothing about cattle, dairy farming, or his daughters in Whatcom County. The editor noted that Fresno papers near his brothers' towns should copy. Unless his brothers and sisters heard the news and had his body shipped to California, James Patterson lies in an unmarked grave in Oregon.[133]

Dolly and Nellie

Phoebe Judson is celebrated as the "Mother of Lynden" for several reasons. She used her home nursing skills for decades to help both settler and Nooksack women. She mothered the two groups into a community by turning her orchard into a worship site for both in order to bring a Methodist missionary there regularly. After the Judsons obtained title to the Patterson ranch, they turned much of it into the new town of Lynden and nudged its development along with donated lots for things they thought a new community needed. Most of all, county residents fondly honored her with the title because of the ten foster children she raised in addition to her own four. If he never visited, locals may have been unaware of Jack Judson, the eleventh, until she wrote her memoir.

The friendship between the Judsons and James Selhameten grew over the years and he helped the settlers in the growing town frequently, including armed protection. Residents came to call him "Lynden Jim"

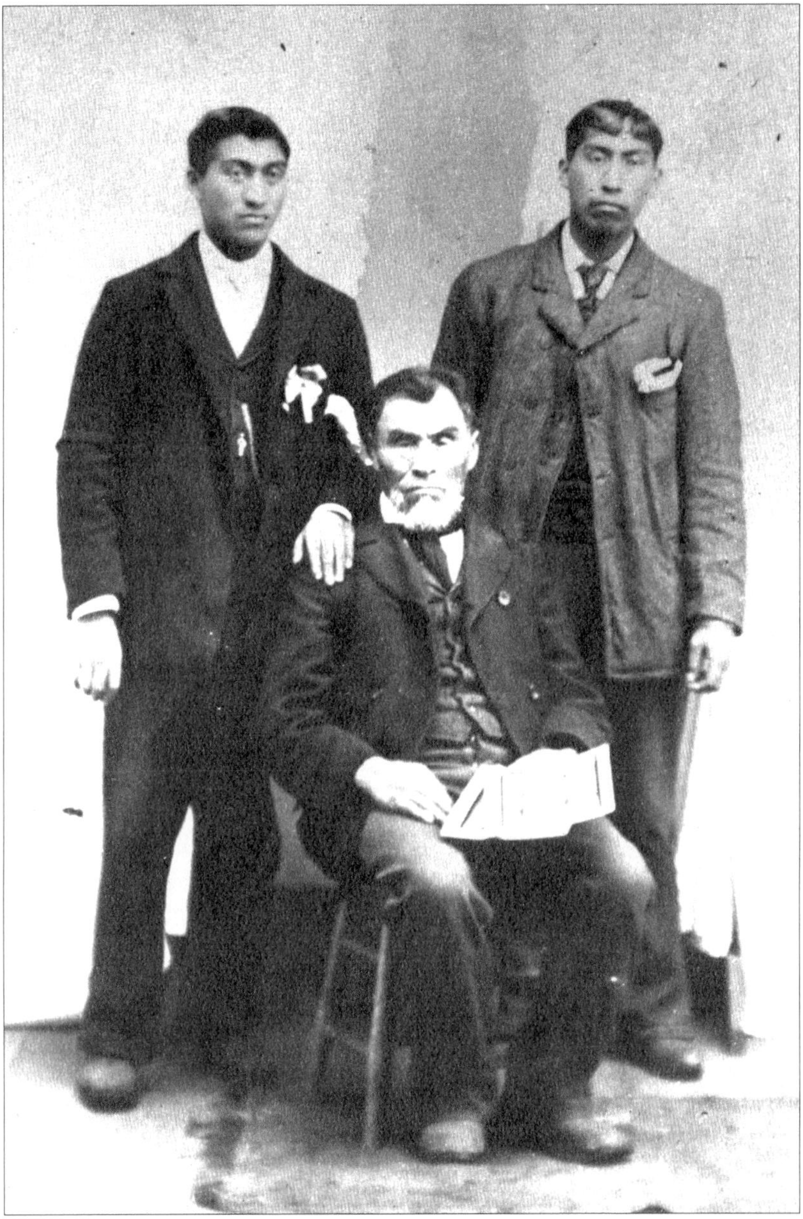

James Selhameten Yelewqaynem, "Lynden Jim," headman at *Sqweha:lich* with his nephews. He was a mentor and friend to the Patterson girls and other local children. Robert Emmett Hawley dedicated his own memoirs to "Chief Jim Yelokanim," the "Old Friend and Instructor in the Lore of the Nooksack Tribe." *Percival Jeffcott Collection #1349. Center for Pacific Northwest Studies, Western Washington University. Bellingham, WA.*

as most people know him today. As the McClanahan children's uncle, he was a personal friend and mentor for them, Dolly and Nellie, and other settlers' children who knew and loved him.[134]

Holden Judson may have been the quieter foster parent, but he proved a powerful role model for the children who did chores beside him. He signed a petition in the 1870s that successfully halted newcomers' efforts to send Jim Selhameten and all the Nooksack to Lummi Reservation. Under a new federal homestead provision for Indians he, with John Tennant and also intermarried James Bertrand, assisted Lynden Jim and other Nooksack family heads to file on land that kept major villages and fishing sites in Nooksack hands. Judson started the Lynden post office, operated a store, was his town's first mayor, and served as a county commissioner. He even built an opera house for Lynden's social occasions and entertainment.[135]

Elizabeth Patkanim Patterson's daughters grew up within a community-minded home where people were cared for and who cared for others. Dolly and Nellie, the only robustly healthy girls, took "attentive care" of Phoebe's mother, of Nora McClanahan, who lived into her teens with tuberculosis, and of frail Mary Judson who had a heart ailment.[136]

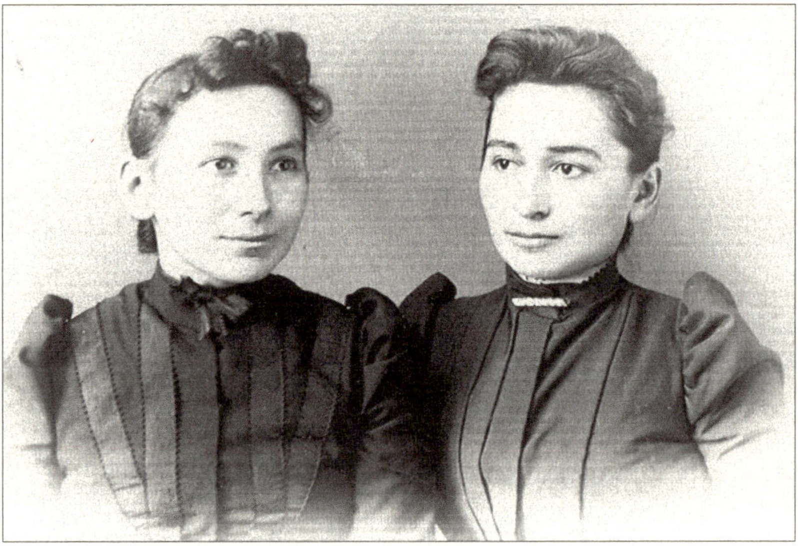

Dolly and Nellie Patterson as teenagers. *Courtesy of the Nellie Patterson McDonald Photograph Collection.*

As loving as she was, Phoebe still had the American sense of cultural superiority. She once referred to the girls as her "little half-breeds," and wrote of her feelings that children of intermarriages were doomed to discrimination and unhappiness. The girls grew up identifying with white culture but stayed connected to their friends across the river. They spoke Chinook Jargon like most of the children and may have used their Lushootseed at *Sqweha:lich* as long as they could remember it.[137]

Education was a concern from the beginning. The nearest school did not start for several years after the Judson family arrived and was far downriver on Thomas and Jenny Wynn's land. Phoebe taught her household's children along with several Nooksack students until Grace O'Neil settled with her family north of the Judsons and started a small school across the Fish Creek bridge for all the children.

Dolly

One day in 1881, twenty-nine-year-old Miles Rittenberg of Shenango Falls, New York, stepped off the small river steamer *Gem*. He was the crew foreman for Judson's construction of Lynden's first "industrial" building. The large log structure would produce hoop poles. He boarded at the Judsons' and met eighteen-year-old Dolly with her large almond eyes reminiscent of Patkanim's. She played the organ and sang soprano during evening sing-a-longs that included their boarders. A mutual interest in music brought musician Miles and Dolly together. When the crew left, Miles stayed behind to marry Dolly and live with her in a snug cabin on their own homestead. Miles turned the empty hoop-pole building into a cooperage, Lynden's first permanent industry. He brought his love of music to the small community and enriched its culture by teaching and organizing a cornet band.[138]

Phoebe delivered Dolly's two boys and two girls. Following her example, the Rittenbergs took in foster children. Despite her busy home life, Dolly developed her own business as the well-paid town dressmaker until she was at least in her sixties. A proudly presented project was the wedding dress she sewed for the granddaughter of her friend Lynden Jim.[139]

Elizabeth's eldest daughter survived her husband until 1943, when she died at age eighty, recognized by the local paper as the oldest living settler born in the county. One of Dolly's own daughters followed

Phoebe Judson into midwifery, and many descendants still live in the county and other Washington cities. Their research has restored family knowledge of the importance of Elizabeth's father.[140]

Nellie

Nellie Patterson had a different experience from her sister because she did not marry early and lived at home during the Judsons' most prosperous years. Nellie's eighteenth birthday ended the agreement between the late James Patterson and Phoebe Judson, though she continued to live with them. Phoebe and Holden had fulfilled all their promises, the land was theirs, and they had turned much of it into a town. Phoebe had brought both sisters to adulthood safely and in good health. They were young women who were loved and who knew how to love others.

The Judsons demonstrated their love and integrity by putting a real estate foundation under the young women. A month before Nellie's twenty-first birthday, the Judsons did what was only right for Elizabeth's daughters whose childhood home they possessed. They signed over five Lynden city lots to each of them. This gave the girls a place to build their own homes, open a business, sell, or give away.[141]

Nellie still helped care for the family invalids, but at twenty-two she enrolled in Lynden's Northwest Normal School where she was the only biracial student. Two years earlier, Professor J. R. Bradley had established the first institution to train teachers in the territory. Joining his brother, he was enthusiastic about the town that did not tolerate liquor and billiards, so the Judsons donated land for a suitable two-story building. In 1891 petite, dark-haired Nellie, who so resembled her dashing father, was photographed with Bradley and the other twenty graduating students.[142]

Sometime after graduation, an Everett family hired Nellie to be their disabled child's nanny. Having grown up helping with Mary Judson's bad heart and Nora McClanahan's tuberculosis, Nellie's nurturing personality and education were attractive qualifications for the job.[143]

James McDonald arrived in Lynden with enough money to build Everson's first lumber mill at the shallow river ford once known as *Popehomey* —The Crossing. He and his brother then built the Clipper Shingle Mill in the isolated South Fork Valley of the Nooksack, followed by two more. At age thirty-one, Nellie married the handsome lanky Scot from Ontario.[144]

When a Clipper village neighbor died after childbirth, Nellie and James informally adopted the infant and raised him as John Sypien McDonald with their only child Ivan. Until she died, Nellie emulated Phoebe as her sister did, taking in many foster children for extended periods. The McDonalds sent Ivan to Gonzaga University for a time before he and John ultimately joined the forest industry.[145]

For three decades the McDonald mills at Clipper, Acme, and several other locations in the county provided employment for hundreds of families, including many McDonalds and Rittenbergs. At Clipper the community of employee families resided on Nellie and James' land. Nellie continued her lifelong passion for reading by organizing the Clipper Reading Circle for the isolated women. As many as twenty gathered in her home to discuss readings for possibly four decades, documented by occasional photos.[146]

Always overlooking the activity in Nellie's home was an oval-framed portrait of her handsome father, with his blue eyes, mustache, and black hair in a dashing wave over his brow. The picture may have hung in the Patterson cabin of her childhood and reminded her of how her life started many years before. It held a place in her home equal to that of the portraits of James' parents.[147]

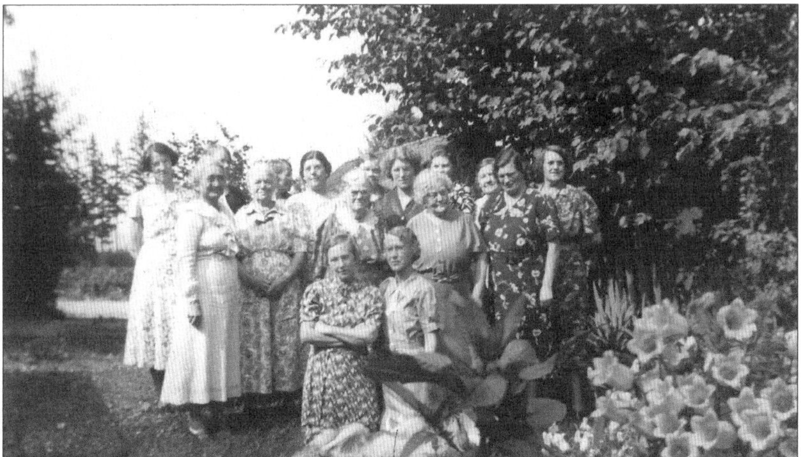

Clipper Reading Circle. Nellie Patterson McDonald standing left in middle row. The club met for at least forty years after Nellie Patterson McDonald founded it to enrich the lives of wives and mothers living in the Clipper logging community. *Courtesy of the Nellie Patterson McDonald Collection.*

Nellie never cut her childhood ties to Nooksack friends, some of whom worked at the mills the McDonalds owned. She attended their traditional funerals, if not other events. She passed along values to children she had absorbed from her indigenous mother and the lessons from Lynden Jim. Like Phoebe Judson, her Nooksack childhood mentor had set an example for taking those ill or in need into his home. He had become the first Nooksack Methodist convert and added Christian teachings to his own spirituality. He taught the girls and other children about respect for the birds and animals that give their lives for food. Nellie then taught her own sons and grandsons that "you don't shoot a second bird until the first one is eaten."[148]

Once the original Patterson cabin burned after the turn of the century, the physical reminder of Elizabeth and James Patterson's marriage was gone. The California Pattersons never seem to have contacted the girls, though they may have known they existed from correspondence with James when his daughters were born. In 1921 Nellie cut all physical ties to her birthplace when she sold her Lynden lots to one of the new Dutch majority's churches.[149]

By summer 1938, both Miles Rittenberg and James McDonald had died. At the well-attended Forty-third Pioneers Picnic, Dolly and Nellie shared honors as the latest recipients of the Old Settlers Cup on which their names were engraved. No mention was made of their noble Snoqualmie mother's existence in the *Bellingham Herald* feature interview with the elderly widows. Another article emphasized their births in the 1860s, but again failed to mention the woman who gave them life but lost her own too soon. It wasn't popular to mention that some of the oldest residents were from cross-cultural marriages. The event chairman emphasized that no one else even came close to them in longevity in Whatcom County.[150]

Nellie died March 1, 1953, a few weeks shy of her eighty-seventh birthday. The *Herald* wrote a much longer article about her than it had for her businessman husband when he died three decades earlier.[151]

Ned

And what of Ned Salasoten, the young man from *Sema:th* who convinced Elizabeth to leave her family and walk the trail north to his village where there was an indigenous doctor? Friend or lover, he was probably with Elizabeth when she died and buried her in Canada far from her family.

He became Chief Ned of the First Nations Kilgard Band (*Sema:th*) in British Columbia, and for many decades was politically influential on both sides of the border. He hosted large-scale events at his longhouse and fed crowds of workers on the reserve's major projects. Chief Ned spent his life committed to the defense of First Nations civil and land rights in the face of the white invasion. He continued to share traditional life with his cousin, Lynden Jim Selhameten.[152]

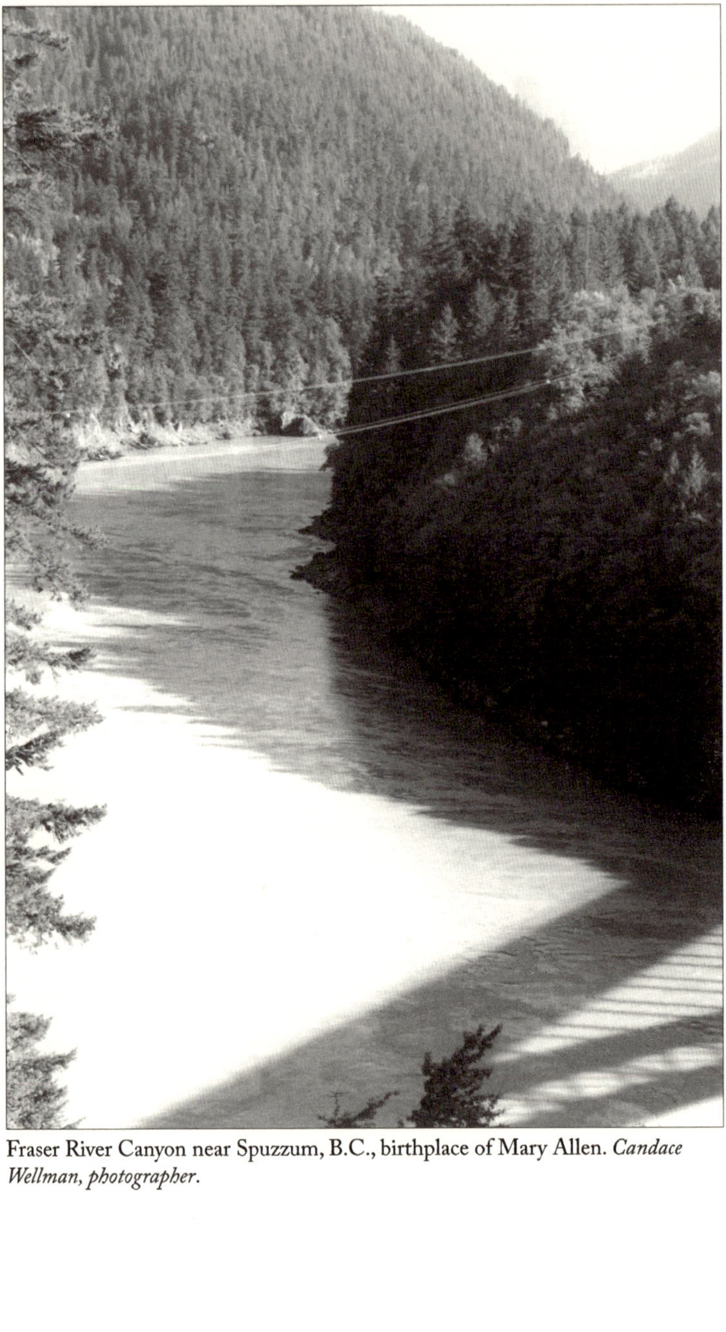

Fraser River Canyon near Spuzzum, B.C., birthplace of Mary Allen. *Candace Wellman, photographer.*

CHAPTER 3

Mary, From the Rapids

ALL DAY LONG, the sweaty crowd in the imposing new sandstone courthouse grew. They spilled out of the second floor courtroom into the hallway and down the grand staircase. By the time the clerk called the final witness of the day, the lucky standees filled the center aisle and formed two great hollow squares around the seated audience. Those outside the courtroom strained to hear.

A slender brown-eyed boy wound his way through the perspiring mass to the witness stand, watched over by his parents Mary and Solomon Allen. The next day, the *Fairhaven Herald* would describe the youngest witness as "bright" and "cute." Though only twelve years old, Jimmie Allen was the pivotal witness in a murder case that infuriated the county's white residents and galvanized Lummi Nation. No one had ever seen the Lummi people fill a courtroom in support of one of their own before. Neither had anyone ever seen a Lummi defended by an expensive and eloquent Seattle lawyer like Samuel Piles, very soon to be U.S. Senator Piles. On young Allen's testimony rested the life of George Swe'lus, the first cousin of his family's friends Jenny Wynn, Clara Tennant, and Chief Henry Kwina.

It was March 1892, and most Whatcom County newcomers knew nothing about Jimmie's family history, or that of the defendant. But to Lummi Nation and the "Old Settlers" he was the son of Mary Allen, an Nlaka'pamux (aka Thompson River First Nation, Knife, or Couteau) from British Columbia. His father Solomon Allen was one of the 1858 Fraser River gold miners who returned with his family and settled at the mouth of the eastern fork of the Nooksack River. Eleven years earlier, Jimmie's parents had platted the new village of Marietta across from Lummi Reservation. His mother and father occupied the cultural middle ground of Whatcom County that for thirty years had enabled them to be friends of both Coast Salish and settler communities. The prosecution and the defense might trust the biracial boy's version of events.[1]

Mary

Mary's history differed markedly from that of Jenny Wynn and other Coast Salish wives who had been her neighbors along the Nooksack River since the 1860s. She was Interior Salish, an Nlaka'pamux (ln'thla'ka'p'mech) woman from the steep-walled Fraser River Canyon in British Columbia. Unlike Coast Salish women who identified themselves by home village and both parents, Mary carried her father's name, "Kowpelst," as a surname, which clerks in the county auditor's office often corrupted into "Copals" if they didn't just call her "Mary, an Indian" (or once inexplicably, "Mary O'Padesty").[2]

Kowpelst was the political chief of the canyon's lower villages centered at *Spuzzum*, the southernmost one about ten miles north of the Hudson's Bay Company's Fort Yale. *Spuzzum* marked an informal boundary between the canyon village residents who spoke *Nle'kepmx*, and the Coast Salish Sto:lo peoples who spoke *Halkomelem*. Most villagers on both sides spoke at least two languages because they traveled the region and married both north and south into neighboring villages.[3]

Perhaps more than any other woman in this book, Mary's life and identity were tied to her *Spuzzum* home's geography.

The Nlaka'pamux way of life in the thirty-mile-long canyon bridged the Coast Salish salmon-based culture, downriver and west, with the hunting and horse-based interior Plateau First Nations to the east. *Spuzzum*'s history in a narrow canyon between the Cascades and the Rockies spanned some 3,500 years during which the Nlaka'pamux adopted lifeways common to both of the larger cultures. During Mary's childhood, her riverside village was a meeting place of lifeways, language systems, and even religions.[4]

Some elements of Mary's culture developed from the Fraser River Canyon's geography itself. *Spuzzum*'s location on the river's southbound path to the bend at Fort Hope allowed marriage and trade with upstream and downstream villages to influence it, while the difficulty of traversing the steep canyon walls and the turbulent river generally isolated Nlaka'pamux villages from more distant people.

After the Thompson River joins the Fraser where the upriver Nlaka'pamux lived (at today's Lytton) north of *Spuzzum*, the combined rivers squeeze into the constricted channel barely one hundred feet wide that is completely impassable to upriver travel. British explorer

Simon Fraser in 1808 called it "the gates of Hell" from which it became "Hell's Gate." The river below rises and falls as much as one hundred feet in times of great runoff as it flows through the rapids and on to the great bend at Fort Hope.

The sheer granite walls that enclose the river's rapids south of Hell's Gate were particularly close around *Spuzzum*. Deadly whirlpools spanned the cataract in times of high water. The maelstrom terminated in an eddy at the canyon's end which the Nlaka'pamux called "Always Horns" for the animal carcasses and unlucky humans the river deposited there to endlessly circulate. When Europeans arrived, they called it "Dead Man's Eddy." The repellent sight warned outsiders what happened to those who ignored the river's warnings and challenged its power without proper knowledge and spiritual power. The Nlaka'pamux men who canoed the river possessed generations of knowledge about its ways, but still faced ever-present peril in the terrifying river as they pushed or pulled the *cukwtm* (paddles) of their craft and took responsibility for the passengers they carried.

Mary's childhood world lay beneath those canyon walls towering 1,500 feet above her, where snow lay on the loftiest hilltops nearly all year. Stars and constellations visible between the cliffs and hills supplied her people with a rich artistic, storytelling, and spiritual heritage. The rocks, lakes, and other formations along the river and atop the cliffs told their story from the time of the Transformer Beings and surrounded them with the possibility of encounters with both human and spiritual beings. The Nlaka'pamux treasured the red ochre paintings on rocks in secluded mysterious places done by generations of youth and others on spiritual quests. They carried knowledge elder Annie York called "a university" for those who followed. Every trout pond, root meadow, berry ground, trail resting spot, salmon fishery, and work site had a name. Each name was drawn from that place's traits, activities, resources, spiritual qualities, historical event, or location. Wilderness did not exist for Mary, only neighborhood.[5]

Two villages lay on either side of Spuzzum Creek's mouth. Mary's home *Spuzzum* ("Little Flat") occupied the southside bench just above the Fraser's high-water mark. *Shwimp* lay on the north side of the creek's mouth and was the location of the villages' common cemetery with its unusual dresser-drawer burial boxes. Sandbars, accessible above the green-brown water only in the summer's driest period, dotted the river. When the Europeans made their first visit to the canyon, one of the densest non-agricultural populations in the world lived in the villages that were sited every mile or two along the terrace-like benches above the river. All along Simon Fraser's route were drying racks used every summer to wind-dry the world's largest salmon runs, a method still used today. By Mary's time, *Spuzzum* and other lower canyon villages had built rock-walled fortifications on benches high above the villages for protection against Northern raiders who might brave the rapids. They were already willing to travel far up the more placid river below Fort Yale to steal their salmon and people.[6]

Canyon seasons also generated different lifeways from the Coast Salish. To Mary, deep winter December and January was the "going in" time, when her family moved into one of the snug winter homes anchored deep in the soil (*kikwillies*) and scattered around *Spuzzum*. Arctic winds screaming down the canyon replaced the constant warm spring and summer breezes that swept up the heated canyon walls from the water and dried the salmon catch. Two steep trails led up Broadback Mountain behind *Spuzzum* and *Shwimp*. In the warm months, their mountain supplied berries, game, and vegetables. In times of famine, villagers searched out kinnikinnick leaves there to chew and suppress their hunger.

Mary's Kowpelst family's prestige in British Columbia history, as well as among the Lower Canyon people, began with her grandfather Pa'lek nearly four decades before her birth.

In June 1808 British explorer Simon Fraser's canoes entered the Upper Canyon from inland, the first Europeans to experience the terror the river gifted to strangers. Knowledge of Europeans, their metal ware, smallpox, and Christianity had made their way to the Canyon people earlier via native travelers, but this was their first personal contact. They called the men *xwelitem*, "strangers." Word of the *xwelitem* came from cousins upstream and Pa'lek, *Spuzzum*'s young leader, met with the party. He both welcomed and assessed their intentions before he guided Fraser's frightened party downriver. They felt at the mercy of the "awful tide," with all hands working to keep the canoes from crashing into the canyon walls on one side and being engulfed by the waves on the other.[7]

Where rapids were impassable, Mary's grandfather guided Fraser's party along the narrow trails impressed into the canyon walls. For hundreds of years they had been used by Nlaka'pamux people going to other villages and fishing stations. When the sheer walls outstripped the Brits' abilities to climb to the woven ladders and webbing that stretched along the steepest rock faces one hundred feet above the rapids, Pa'lek and his men pulled them up. The river's enormous whirlpools defied experience and British equipment. The physical skill of the Nlaka'pamux and the sign language they used to communicate across the cataract astounded the visitors who owed their lives to the men.[8]

When Fraser arrived with Pa'lek at *Spuzzum*, people greeted him as a guest who might also be a supernatural being with dangerous powers. Villagers treated the British explorers to a roast salmon, berry, and onion dinner before they departed. The memory of Pa'lek's courage and courtesy, guiding and making friends with the strangers to protect his people, entered both their narrative history and the expedition's journals. That encounter endures in both written and Nlaka'pamux oral history today. Mary's grandfather lived at least until about 1881, the most respected leader "for land, law, and prayer," a man who demonstrated strength and leadership during contact with the *xwelitem* again and again. All of the families at *Spuzzum* today descend from Pa'lek.[9]

After Simon Fraser's visit, life continued much as it had, even though the British and their merchandise began to move through the canyon regularly by a network of trails and waterways connecting fur trade forts. The world's largest salmon runs that supported Mary's family and the other people of *Spuzzum* continued undiminished. They still used hundreds of plants and trees for food, medicine, building materials, and other needs while they also traded for British merchandise. The British had no desire to colonize the Fraser River Canyon. That was an advantage because the densely populated canyon could not support a large influx, though it only became obvious later in 1858.

Judging by later records and her own accounts, Mary was born about 1845 to Kowpelst and his wife, said to be Chilliwack from Sto:lo country downriver. When she was a small child, cultural disruption in *Spuzzum* increased after a new fur brigade trail passed through the village. The HBC use of horses on the trade routes sped up the dissemination of disease. A ship-born measles epidemic spread to *Spuzzum* from the distant mouth of the Columbia River. Young Mary survived, but many, many others did not.[10]

Four months after the new trail was broken, Mary and her family watched as three fur brigades arrived in a mile-long train of four hundred horses and fifty men. The company built a small depot right at *Spuzzum*, which became the first permanent presence of European culture in the Lower Canyon. Tensions rose with the invasion, and people died. The villagers erected new palisades for protection because they anticipated that the safe houses hidden among the cedars and firs on the high benches might not always be enough.

Mary's childhood passed in this combination of traditional life and growing *xwelitem* cultural disturbance. With the trouble they brought, the meaning of *xwelitem* began to take on a new implication: "the hungry ones." A few *Spuzzum* and *Shwimp* women married packers and most people added Chinook Jargon to their other languages. Mary's father traded a compressed stack of marten pelts for what his family believed to be his people's first gun. Still, the Nlaka'pamux did not come under much pressure to change their culture, with the exception of religion.[11]

In the same way that *Spuzzum* was a boundary between languages, it also marked the division between Anglican missionary activity above and Catholic below. French HBC employees brought Catholicism, and their British bosses brought Anglicanism. Both clergy were ambitious to make converts and advance colonialism. Mary's family was at different times affiliated with both churches. Catholic records indicate "Mary Susan" was first baptized "Marie Suzanne" by a priest before Anglicanism dominated her village. At least by the late 1850s, the family had joined the Anglican Church. Mary's people absorbed Christianity as an addition to their spiritual world view, not a replacement.[12]

In this atmosphere of progressive cultural invasion, Mary presumably still followed the traditional life of all young girls with a few exceptions. A girl's day began with bathing, using soaps and shampoos made from wild strawberries and other scented plants. The long hair of girls like Mary was washed and decorated every day.

If the Kowpelst family was like other elites, dressing for the day could take two hours and was an important social and spiritual activity that began with prayer. Wealthy people owned a large wardrobe and any particular day's garments reflected their status and age, as well as the weather and what they planned to do. Decoration on the buckskin clothing provided a visual representation of the person's visions, guardians, and experiences, as well as personal taste. Cedar and willow bark clothing items combined with the buckskin. People added tattoos, painted face and body designs, different hair styles, and jewelry. The colors they chose for paint or beading carried symbolic expression. The daily choices spanned what Leslie Tepper called "a rich visual vocabulary of personal adornment." Mary and all the Nlaka'pamux were encouraged to develop individuality expressed through their outward appearance. *Spuzzum* people added British clothing, cotton cloth, and glass beads to their wardrobes, too, as soon as Forts Kamloops and Yale were built.[13]

The Kowpelst family's yearly cycle began in the fall with hunting, followed by the retreat to warm winter pit houses that sheltered as many as thirty extended family members who climbed down the ladder from the entrance at the top of its conical wooden roof. After a dinner of the foods the family had worked hard to preserve, around a central fire Mary listened to children's songs that imitated crickets and birds, along with special prayers and stories just for them.

Starting in the spring, families lived in smaller two-sided frame structures covered with mats or bark constructed in the shade near mountain springs or fishing sites. For many months, life for the women of Mary's family focused on plants and their fruiting seasons, in addition to the successive salmon runs. Family activities took place around the riverside drying racks in the undying breezes and warm sun reflected off the sunbaked cliffs. Salmon filets cured coppery and luminous in about ten days, with a concentrated salmon flavor unlike that of the smoked salmon of the Coast Salish. Work lasted long into the night, but Mary's family and others eagerly anticipated the season's sociability. Using rocks as sundials and watching celestial movements, specialists timed summer solstice celebrations similar to those of Plateau culture tribes.

The salmon harvest was critical no matter how enjoyable it seemed. In their tradition, dietary restrictions based on age and fertility divisions applied to everyone. Dried salmon was the only food allowable for everyone at any time, under any conditions, which made its abundance essential for winter survival. Like the coastal people, the First Salmon Ceremony was solemnly observed to assure that.

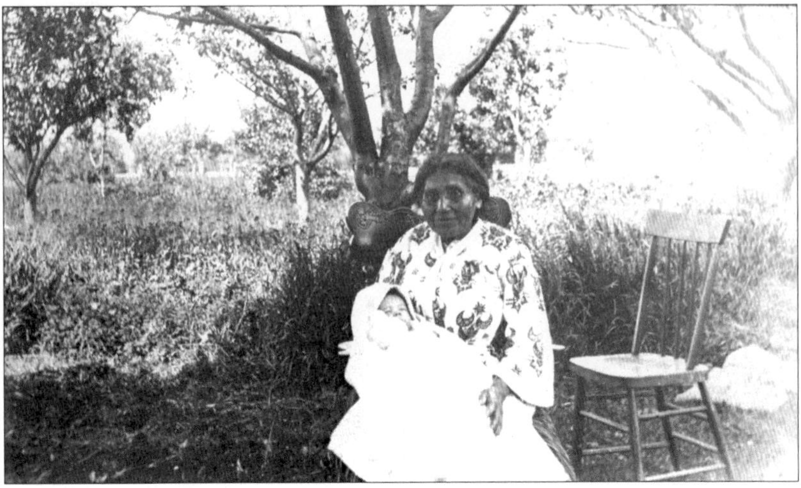

Mary Allen in a traditional Nlaka'pamux jacket with cultural symbols, probably a customary gift made by her male Nlaka'pamux family members. *Howard Buswell Collection #27. Center for Pacific Northwest Studies, Western Washington University. Bellingham, WA.*

As Mary approached puberty, her training intensified for all the skills she would need: animal skin preparation, weaving, basketry, child care, medicines, and food gathering and preparation. She had much to learn, for example, poisonous plants to avoid and the emergency foods to seek only when lost or in famine times. Mary later became a midwife, so she may have been trained at that time. Grandmothers often began taking the girls away to a pit house for short education periods as early as age nine. During a puberty seclusion and training for adulthood that could last four months, Mary and other girls sought contact with a guardian spirit guide who would help them through life crises and bad health. As a typical girl, Mary would have lived in a *tipi* built by putting four small fir trees in a square and tying them together at the tops, then covering the floor with soft branches. Mary probably wore a waist-length covering of fir boughs, constructed much as the *tipi* was, for the first days of her training. During the seclusion months, girls trained in individual skills and exercised vigorously. Evenings were for rituals, dancing, and songs around a fire. It was a special time.[14]

By the time teenaged Mary met Solomon Allen in 1858, she was probably spending more time on her appearance to attract a suitable husband. If she hadn't completed her puberty training, she wouldn't have been eligible for marriage. Her clothing changed to more adult items like decorated leggings and dresses with a collection of moccasins and caps for different looks. Male relatives gifted young women with painted vision images or designs from the girl's isolation experiences on buckskin garments. Over fifty years later, Mary dressed for a photograph in her Nlaka'pamux jacket that bore painted symbols of the moon, stars, and other traditional designs.

Solomon Allen

Solomon Allen's story began with a river, too. At the end of the War of 1812, his father William left Tennessee on the water trail that led to the Illinois frontier. He wanted land of his own that wasn't worn out, with soil that was not so rocky, and best of all was only two dollars an acre. With the British policies regarding Indian lands gone, and indigenous tribes overrun and defeated, he joined a throng of veterans and others who headed for America's first western frontier. His flatboat trip to the old French capital of Kaskaskia was a "grim slog, a lengthy, tedious, expensive, and often dangerous undertaking" with bad accommodations, unfamiliar food, and untrustworthy traveling companions over weeks or months as one river led to another. Within six years after William's leap into the unknown, one fifth of the American population lived in the Northwest Territory.[15]

Perhaps to his surprise, Solomon's father met mostly intermarried French-Indian families in Kaskaskia, where French settlers and indigenous people had lived peacefully for a long time. He found the rest of southern Illinois nearly empty of indigenous people after the Illinois tribes signed treaties and most moved across the Mississippi. William and the other migrants came predominantly from the back-country South like James Patterson's family (chapter 2). Like Patterson's Tennessee family, they brought with them the same distinctive subculture: prideful independence, toughness, a belief in retaliation, and frequent family violence. They passed the traits to their children, including Solomon. They built their cabins and houses in wooded gullies that resembled home and where they felt safe from the wide open vulnerability of the prairies where bison herds still roamed.[16]

Southern Illinois' new settlers just wanted the remaining indigenous population gone from the rolling hills and they didn't care where they went. The legislature offered a fifty dollar bounty to anyone killing or capturing a "depredating Indian." Occasional raids by those who refused to move justified racism and the theft of Indian land. Squatting and using "public" land before it was legally available for sale in Illinois nearly always resulted in the government leaving squatters alone, as it would throughout the West and in Whatcom County.[17]

Despite their anti-Indian attitudes, settlers like Allen had to confront the mixed-race place that was Randolph County, where Kaskaskia was the only commercial, shipping, religious, and governmental hub. The town's architecture looked French and its Catholic residents spoke mostly French. Men and women wore foreign-looking clothing unlike the newcomers' rough dress. The American takeover of French territory with the Louisiana Purchase and the subsequent loss of status as a capital city started Kaskaskia on a slow slide to obscurity, though it retained a national claim to fame after the Marquis de Lafayette visited in 1825. For many years, the French town continued to be the "big city" for Solomon Allen's family and other settlers scattered along the Kaskaskia River (called "Okaw" by locals). In 1829 Illinois passed a law forbidding any intermarriage with Indians, and that further destroyed the French cultural island.[18]

As more accessible northern Illinois on the Great Lakes developed, southern Illinois turned into a static backwater where residents were reluctant to change their traditional methods and practices in every arena. Such a place would, in twenty years, be the perfect breeding ground for young men who wanted out. Like father, like son.

William hadn't lived on the prairie long before he married Georgia-born Tabitha Vermillion when he was twenty-two and she was only fifteen. This was not unusual on the frontier, as it would not be later in the Pacific Northwest. Sturdy wives had to work the same long hours as their husbands and they raised sons like Solomon to expect the same from a future wife.[19]

Three children born to Tabitha and William Allen died before Solomon was born December 2, 1827, followed by another three children. Unlike most who wanted to live down in the protected gullies, William had settled on a six-mile-long north to south ridge slightly elevated from the prairies and the highest place in the new county. An Indian village had once been located just below the north end and burial mounds reminded Ralls Ridge families of the people they had displaced. Clashes with remaining indigenous people were rare with so many mixed families at Kaskaskia where everyone did business, but Solomon and other Ralls Ridge children heard mostly negative stereotypes that entered the county's narrative history. Most of the family of the Allens' neighbor Robert McMahon had been killed on another prairie by Indians years before they arrived, and he spent the rest of his life in hatred, telling lurid tales to children and adults alike. Local hero John Moredock prided himself on being a professional Indian killer.[20]

Soon a small ferry on the "Okaw" a few miles away from their farm enabled the Allens to ship their crops down to Kaskaskia and the Mississippi River. Randolph County developed into the castor oil capital of the world after most farmers added castor bean fields to their corn and cotton, probably including the Allens. Foul-tasting castor oil was a basic medicine for the home nurse. Ingested, it was a powerful laxative whose end results were thought to cure most ailments, plus worms. It also went on the skin in an attempt to cure warts. It is reasonable to assume that Solomon was a reluctant recipient.

For Solomon's generation, the land of their Southern fathers' dreams was not an idyllic place. Social changes and political tensions about what the region was to become led some people to leave. For example, Catholic institutions underpinned the originally-French Randolph County, but new residents were more often Protestant. Irish and German immigrants brought new customs to the mostly backcountry Southern population. The slavery question in part of a northern state heavily populated by Southerners added long-term political issues.

Some residents moved west after major river floods inundated their farms and towns. The 1844 Mississippi River flood nearly destroyed Kaskaskia and it never recovered. Major health issues tipped the balance for some people. When cholera came full force to Randolph County three years after the floods, it primarily carried away children who died in as little as four hours.

In the midst of those events, when Solomon Allen was nineteen, President James K. Polk declared war on Mexico. It was the young nation's first conflict to be fought on foreign soil and 50,000 volunteers were needed to supplement the 8,000-man regular army. Polk requested four volunteer regiments from Illinois and got fourteen. Solomon and other boys from southern Illinois enthusiastically joined up, more for glory and adventure than patriotic anger at a foe about whom they knew little. Five weeks into the war, dark-haired, dark-eyed, and five-feet-nine-inches tall, Solomon signed up for one year at eight dollars per month. Doctors looked for "habitual drunkard" or "deserter" branded into his teenaged flesh during his physical exam. Extreme bad breath and lack of front teeth would have also led to a quick embarrassing return to boredom on the farm. He mustered in the same June day in 1846 with his own musket, some clothes, and a sleeping blanket. Recruiters put him and the other local boys in the same company of the 2nd Regiment of Foot Volunteers, commanded by Colonel (and future governor) William Bissell.[21]

Gun and cannon fire weren't the biggest threat Solomon would face. Few of the Illinois farm boys thought about their lack of exposure to many infectious diseases and they knew little about camp sanitation. Even the mumps and measles could be fatal to someone without childhood immunity and already impaired by camp dysentery. About 13,000 men died in the war, and only 2,000 of those deaths were battle-related. Volunteers fell ill in the camps at twice the rate of the regulars, but the Army obligated doctors to treat the regulars first, leaving most of the new enlistees like Solomon to suffer. One Ohio volunteer called the Illinois regiments "the most sickly, enfeebled set of men I ever saw. They ought all to be sent home for their health." Sometimes the Illinois regiments didn't have enough healthy men to conduct drills.[22]

Private Solomon Allen became one of those "enfeebled" soldiers when he caught a cold and then the measles on board his transport ship. His regiment was headed to Port Lavaca, Texas, where he would train and leave for Mexico. Colonel Bissell and the surgeon sent him home on August 7. He'd been a soldier in the U.S. Army for all of six weeks.[23]

Solomon not only missed out on his friends' heroics in Mexico, but he had to watch their glorification and listen to their war stories when they got home. Enlisted men soon won town and county offices, and higher offices went to men in command. Being sent home early would affect Solomon's personal future as long as he lived in Randolph County.

Cholera struck southern Illinois again in 1849, and yet again in 1851, along with another major flood of the Mississippi River region.

The post-war atmosphere and the California gold rush enticements probably pushed Solomon to seek a new life elsewhere in 1852. Like thousands before him, the decision to go west meant a physical and emotional break with both home and past, very like his father's forty years earlier. Once he left home, Solomon Allen never saw his parents or siblings again, a truth most of the westbound migrants faced. Both his parents were dead within a dozen years.[24]

In 1852, Solomon made his way to Council Bluffs, Iowa, a major launch point for overlanders from Illinois because it was further west than Independence, Missouri, where James Patterson and his family had built their business (see chapter 2). He became just one of 10,000 emigrants planning to make their way over the Oregon Trail that year. By then, people went west prepared to start businesses and provide trade services as well as farm. The lonely track had become a thoroughfare, with ferries, bridges, and supply stations. For a long way out from Council Bluffs, farms and towns dotted the Great Plains. Allen's very life and the six-month journey's success depended on his choice of animals and supplies, plus cash to re-supply. Like most others, he probably bought his horse(s) and supplies from the sometimes unscrupulous outfitters eager to take his money.[25]

Solomon Allen's sons said he was one of the single men who worked their passage driving stock or handling pack animals. A farm boy with no land to sell to finance the trip probably did not have enough money to see him across the continent and have a "grubstake" when he arrived. However, he was young and strong and had carpentry skills, valuable when wagons and their wheels broke down. That year the trail experienced its rainiest season ever. The endless rain meant rivers were more dangerous to cross and many people drowned in the attempt. Everything stayed damp and making fires and keeping food dry while cooking became a major task.

Solomon left no stories about his contacts with Native Americans on the trail, but it is almost certain that he had some. Although western settlers told many violent contact tales in preference to more mundane happenings, it is also true that the tribes through whose lands the emigrants passed often saved lives. Conflicts were few until over a decade later. Indians worked at ferry crossings, acted as interpreters, guides, teachers of plant lore, sellers of horses, and even cattle guards.

Far more Indians were killed by emigrants than the reverse. Perhaps the very absence of "exciting" Indian stories meant that Solomon experienced those positive contacts.

Allen's sons believed that after Solomon arrived in The Dalles, he decided to take advantage of the Oregon Donation Claim Act in Oregon's Willamette Valley. Some evidence suggests that he may have staked a claim near Albany but didn't register it. He said he planted some oats before he left for California the next spring to seek gold, leaving his cabin and claim unattended four hundred miles away.[26]

Oregonians discovered Northern California's Yreka gold fields in the summer of 1850 and quietly built a rough road south across the steep Siskiyou Range to the valley of the Shasta River. By spring 1851 word had leaked out and miners arrived from all directions. Solomon seems to have gone there two years later, when about six hundred men laid out the haphazard town of Yreka to serve the miners. Some of the multi-nation men learned to live with one another in the gold fields and town, but American prospectors attacked newly arrived Chinese and Mexican miners. They also attacked local Modoc and Pitt River Indians whom they saw only as obstacles. Their behavior only repeated what had happened all over California and would go with miners to Mary Kowpelst's Fraser River Canyon. Solomon Allen and the others worked all week and left Sunday for housekeeping, resting, gambling, fights, and very little praying.

Solomon gave his version of events that followed. He kept at his prospecting and amassed $100,000, though that much in the mid-1850s by a single man was likely a gross exaggeration of the truth. He told his sons that he missed a ship for home by four hours in 1857. Frustrated and worried about security, he buried his money under a shack's floor for safekeeping, but others found his hiding place and stole his fortune. So he said.[27]

Solomon's plans changed, his triumphal return home delayed. He headed back to Oregon and discovered that the squatter's claim he'd left behind had been usurped by someone else as abandoned. That person had officially registered it. As a landless farmer in the rapidly filling Willamette Valley during a national depression, the thirty-one-year-old was out of luck. And then in 1858, an attractive escape from his problems presented itself.[28]

Just when the California gold rush was effectively over for the solo miner, the Fraser River gold rush was on in British Columbia. Gold nuggets lurked in more than three dozen sand bars that seasonally emerged along forty-five miles of the turbulent river. The Nlaka'pamux families had discovered the gold and been trading it to the HBC for some time, but word only reached California in March 1858. British Columbia Governor James Douglas thought that a small gold rush would boost the colony's fledgling economy, so he had sent samples south and advertised for miners he planned to license. The Nlaka'pamux rightfully saw the gold as their own asset, lying as it did within their territory. Outsiders traditionally needed permission to access economic resources in the Fraser Canyon and paid for the privilege. One of the major resource administrators of those gold-bearing sandbars (including the one at *Spuzzum*), was Mary's father Kowpelst, the political "chief for the land." Douglas naively cautioned interested American prospectors that they would have to respect First Nations miners and families in the canyon.

Leaving their *kikwillie* in the month called *Nxu'it* ("coming out"), teenaged Mary and her family faced an invasion of tens of thousands of *xwelitem* bent on taking the gold. They were heedless of their disruption of critical salmon harvest seasons or the everyday lives of First Nations canyon residents. Large numbers of miners started to arrive in April, first using the HBC trails from the Okanagan Valley of British Columbia and Fort Yale to *Spuzzum*. They named the sandbars and organized associated companies to govern themselves. The men camped among villages and families, including a large number at *Spuzzum*. They took game, animal fodder, and firewood. Mary and her people watched as the *xwelitem* consumed everything in their path, now truly "the hungry ones," never satisfied.

Men and animals arrived weekly, but spring runoff brought higher and higher water levels. The increasing numbers without an early claim who were waiting for more bars to emerge had nothing to do but plunder and disturb. Charles Wilson of the British Boundary Commission wrote in his diary "where there is so much young blood and no female population there are sometimes fierce scenes enacted and the bowie knife and revolver which every man wears are in constant requisition."

The all-male miner society assumed the superiority of their own culture and envisioned Nlaka'pamux women as primitive, dangerous, and sexually available. Life for teenaged Mary and other women rapidly became a nightmarish daily battle to avoid assault or death while finding a way to do their seasonal work.[29]

Future Whatcom County settler Marc Stangroom wrote to a friend in California: "The idea of a lot of California miners treating Indians with judgment at any time or with justice when they think themselves strong enough to impose on them is simply absurd." He knew that Douglas' directive about respect would stop nothing. The armed miners felt no remorse about displacing or destroying any indigenous people who got in their way, just as they had previously done to at least 50,000 Indians in California.[30]

The Nlaka'pamux families like Mary's found ways to profit from the unwanted invaders. They continued to mine, sold food, worked as guides, operated canoe ferries, and maintained the trails. Mary's father and other men excelled in their knowledge and skill with canoes in the ever-changing currents, and after the river fell enough to be passable, arrogant prospectors unwilling to pay them often joined the flotsam in Dead Man's Eddy. Many First Nations men, women, and children walked the canyon trail from the hastily built "business" center of Yale, carrying backpacks as heavy as one hundred pounds to earn cash. The tragic result of their valuable work was that miners saw Mary's extended family members as no more than pack animals.[31]

Strong leaders would be required to fight or accommodate the invasion in ways that would prevent annihilation. Though Kowpelst had inherited his position from his father, to keep his authority at *Spuzzum* and its neighboring villages he had to demonstrate leadership, strength, and wisdom while respecting the "collective thought" of his community. Every decision based on the unspoken rules tested his authority and risked a loss of support. Before the gold rush crisis, people were more autonomous, free to disagree, and leave if they couldn't come to agreement. Now, their survival depended on acting as one. Mary's wise, experienced grandfather Pa'lek was always behind Kowpelst advising and watching as the canyon moved perilously toward widespread armed confrontation.[32]

The presence of the large number of heavily armed Americans disturbed Governor Douglas enough to visit. He met with Kowpelst to discuss the thirty white miners who were harassing the eighty indigenous miners at nearby Hill's Bar and taking their gold. He arrived just as Mary's father was standing on a stump talking to his people who were now armed with their HBC muskets after a miner had struck him on the head with a shovel. Kowpelst and his people knew the true value of their gold and had been taking over an ounce apiece each day. At first, the miners and Nlaka'pamux men had cooperated on the half-mile long, sixty-foot-wide bar that lay just over the informal boundary with Sto:lo territory. However, liquor had disturbed the mutual peace.[33]

If Mary's people chose violence, the miners would be trapped in the middle of the river. The miners anticipated the worst and prepared. However, Kowpelst was a pacifist who advocated a moderate approach. Douglas convinced him to abandon Hill's Bar and its gold, and in a canny political move he appointed Kowpelst an official magistrate. That position would put both a mediator and a government representative on the river. Douglas later praised his "great influence, resolution, and energy of character" as the only visible presence of the colonial authorities delegated to handle all problems. It may have been one of the few times when the goals of the British government and the First Nations people coincided.[34]

Solomon Allen, now thirty-one, took passage from Portland on the sidewheel steamer *Sea Bird* only a few weeks before the meeting at Hill's Bar, and probably was on the sailing that arrived at Sehome on May 11. Also on the *Sea Bird* was Ezra Meeker with twenty head of cattle bound for beef-hungry miners. Solomon always told his family that he had worked for the future Puyallup hop magnate. If he did, this was the most likely period. It looked possible to drive cattle across Whatcom County's prairies and use old brigade trails to Fort Langley that crossed two river fords, though it had not been tried. Working a cattle drive would enable Solomon to carry supplies and earn grubstake money. Many miners did not heed the well-publicized advice to bring provisions, and those still in the canyon by winter found themselves in rags and starving 150 miles from Whatcom.[35]

Solomon found a river on the rise like none he'd ever seen. One miner who arrived weeks earlier said that a quarter of the canoes attempting to go up to the bars were lost in the rapids. Solomon made it to somewhere near *Spuzzum*, probably via the 1847 HBC trail high on the bluffs if he was on Meeker's cattle drive. Having arrived relatively early, he found a place to wash gold where he didn't have to wait for August's low water. And he quickly found a lot of it, despite the rising river.[36]

Having lost his first fortune in California, Solomon filled his leather pokes with the precious new riches painstakingly won from the sand. For the first wave of miners who arrived before the water was at its highest, the bars around *Spuzzum* were very lucrative, especially Hill's Bar where Kowpelst's people and the miners worked different ends until he agreed to leave it. Given the time frame of events, it is unlikely that Solomon amassed the $150,000 in gold that he claimed, even at more than the average rate of one hundred dollars a day. The amount probably increased along with Solomon's years of tale-telling. He didn't have any war stories to tell his children, but he did have gold rush stories.[37]

The fortune in his poke was vulnerable to another theft. Solomon needed to go downriver to the assayer's office in the hastily erected "town" of Yale. By June some 5,000 impatient miners were encamped at the boomtown below the canyon's entrance, and that made walking around with a full poke dangerous.

Mary and Solomon

Unlike the stubborn fools trying to get downriver to Yale alone, Solomon chose to go with the experts. His son John described the Kowpelst family as Solomon's "friends" at the time of the incident that changed his life and that of Mary, though he may not have known the teenaged girl. He could have met them still mining at Hill's Bar, if he camped near *Spuzzum*, or if he had paid to go downriver with them before.

Solomon told different versions of who was in the heavily loaded canoe, probably because he was unsure of the relationships. In general, the passengers were Mary, other children, and several adults from her family along with their belongings.[38]

As the canoe moved swiftly along, it was seized by a sudden cross-current. Rapids threw the craft against a rock despite the canoe pullers' efforts. It shattered and threw everyone into the icy water. The usual result was that a splintered canoe would upend and disappear straight down, reappearing in pieces miles away. Its passengers would contribute to the body count at Dead Man's Eddy. Few people ever survived such an accident.[39]

In that moment, Solomon Allen acted differently from the miners who treated the Nlaka'pamux as less than human. Not only did he manage to get himself to shore in his boots and heavy clothing, but he grabbed Mary and swam to shore with her. They were the only survivors. Mary lost her family members. Solomon's poke went to the bottom, another fortune lost.

He had already cheated death four times: in the Mexican War, on the journey west, in California's mining camps, and now in the canoe disaster. It's reasonable to conclude that he took stock of his life past, present, and future.

American parents generally taught their sons to see marriage at the center of a moral adult life, even as they used women they perceived to be social inferiors. Solomon Allen and others existed in the Fraser Canyon in "utter loneliness in a sea of men," yearning for a home. Some aging veteran miners like Solomon began to see the positive qualities of indigenous women that had nothing to do with sexuality.[40]

The rescue opened the door to a life uncluttered by youthful dreams of going home a rich man. Kowpelst and other family wanted to arrange a marriage with Mary's savior. That was not completely unusual since Nlaka'pamux women had married HBC men and lived from Fort Colvile to the Willamette Valley's communities of retired fur traders. Considering Solomon's age and the number of second chances he'd had, perhaps he saw it as prudent to throw in his lot with the place he found himself, find land, settle down, and raise a family in a new community where possibilities for success might be unlimited.

Mary and Solomon married "in the custom of the country" ("tribal custom" in the U.S.) not long after the accident. As he later rationalized the large disparity in their ages to his children, he sought to take the teenager under his wing after she lost so many family members—to be a "guardian" of sorts. Then, thinking much of the young and attractive Mary, he decided to marry her. She later told a friend that she was afraid of the older man, but Kowpelst and Solomon had made arrangements and her father said to go live with the miner after he received the marriage gifts. Mary's status required a sizable gift from the groom, as well as other obligations. Traditionally, the gift included blankets, weapons, and other useful items to compensate her parents for the loss of her company and economic contribution. Later, those who told the story valued Solomon's gifts at $600. By 2017, the value would be over $17,000, making his contribution a substantial amount for Solomon to have to recoup after his loss, unless he already had some cash on deposit in Yale's vaults.[41]

Perhaps Solomon saw this arrangement as similar to his parents' age difference when they married. Unlike twenty-first century standards, the large disparity was typical for that period in British Columbia, intermarriage or not. North American men considered girls as young as fourteen eligible throughout the nineteenth century and girls did not stay single long in the gender-imbalanced Canadian colony. Most marriages contained a patriarchal element. Marriage licenses were only issued in Victoria far away on Vancouver Island and clergy were not in the canyon regularly, so no authority discouraged either the age disparities or tribal custom marriages along the Fraser. Though Mary had been baptized by that time, it was expected by everyone that she would follow Nlaka'pamux marriage customs.[42]

Kowpelst probably saw the situation differently from Solomon. He was trying to manage the increasingly acrimonious coexistence in the canyon, as leaders farther upriver began to talk of war. Guarding the life of teenage girls got harder and harder for the families. Many were raped, others terrorized. Without law enforcement on site, miners had come to see violence against the women as a lark and a man's sense of decency was the only deterrent. When a woman was raped or killed, Mary's people were not above brutal retaliation that ended with a headless body floating in Dead Man's Eddy as a warning to be respectful. Instead it pushed the miners to desire eradication of all local First Nations people. Miners wanted only "good Indians" who would not resist the white invasion, and they killed many. Perhaps Kowpelst saw Solomon as one *xwelitem* who displayed proof of good character. He displayed the physical strength and courage that would be Mary's protection, in addition to a solid work ethic that would give her family more access to material goods.[43]

More importantly, Allen might help with miners and white authorities in Kowpelst's efforts to find a peaceable solution to the crisis in the canyon. Everyone would be safer. And, in Nlaka'pamux culture, if Mary and Solomon split up she need not be embarrassed because "everyone" knew that sometimes there was no compatibility.[44]

Though intermarriages in the canyon helped with one problem, they created another within the dangerous period. *Spuzzum* parents had good reason to fear that their daughters might leave both the place and culture. "Going over to the whites" they called it. That was in Mary's future, as it was for the daughter of war proponent, upriver leader Cunamitsa. Chinese miners in the canyon tended to permanently settle with their Nkla'pamux wives' people but there were no guarantees for parents.

As the intermarriages proliferated at *Spuzzum* and other villages, the marriage obligation system broke down. Even if the couple stayed in the community (as the Allens and John Warner with Cunamitsa's daughter did before all moved to Whatcom County), the white husband's own family was unavailable to provide traditional support for the new couple. Some husbands ignored their obligations to wives and families, like pack trainer Cataline Caux, whose wife was Mary's relative. His relationship with his *Spuzzum* family was so spotty that finally, he knew his children only by distant sight.[45]

As the summer wore on, violence increased in the deteriorating atmosphere while mining and indigenous fishing activities clashed. Thousands of tents occupied level areas required for drying racks. After driving First Nations people from the sandbars, miners sluiced and ruined them, diminishing the critical salmon harvest. By August, at least five hundred miners from a dozen countries were camping at *Spuzzum*. They trespassed on homes and destroyed property. People died violently. Nlaka'pamux anger grew. Families tried to keep their distance from the miners but it must have been a frightening situation whenever Mary's father or Solomon were absent. Large-scale armed conflict was nearly inevitable.

Thousands of American miners up and down the canyon, who had once caused havoc around Bellingham Bay, began to coalesce into virtual armies. Governor Douglas feared they might try to annex the colony to Washington Territory. American H. M. Snyder independently negotiated illegal treaties with Kowpelst and others. The "Whatcom Company," on the other hand, set out to drive Mary's people away by burning villages and ruining fishing sites. The smell of burning salmon sheds drifted along the river. This kind of conflict was unfamiliar to the Nlaka'pamux who were used to raids, ambushes, and retaliation.

Gaining influence over a wider area by strategic marriages in the way that Pa'lek had done had always been preferable to conquest.

The August "Battle of Boston Bar" ignited the "Canyon War." The miners burned three villages near *Spuzzum* and killed five chiefs plus thirty-one other men. More terrifying for Mary, former Texas Ranger "Captain" Charles Rouse and his men took her father hostage. They dragged Kowpelst through Yale, and threatened to lynch him before they delivered her father to the HBC's Ovid Allard at Fort Yale. Gov. Douglas hurried from Victoria and met with Kowpelst at the fort. He was furious that an appointed magistrate (indigenous man or not), should be so disrespected and in the process insult the colony government. Farther upriver, Kowpelst's cousin Chief David Spintlum of Lytton worked to dissuade the other chiefs of the Upper Canyon and Plateau allies from all-out war.[46]

By early September, Douglas tamped down the conflict, aided by lower river levels that enabled thousands of idle men to start mining. He declared the Fraser Canyon open for settlement, giving legal acceptance to Yale and white-owned ferries. A few months later, former Sehome coal miner Thomas York opened a cable ferry at *Spuzzum* for the HBC's river crossing after he also married a daughter of war chief Cunamitsa from today's "Spence's Bridge." Solomon Allen certainly knew York at his ferry and heard about the long-term prospects of the Bellingham Bay communities he had passed through in the spring.[47]

Violence again flared among starving and bored miners that winter, but the ringleaders left for the new Cariboo gold field upriver as the Fraser bars played out. By spring, most of the *xwelitem* had gone except for mining diehards, a few intermarried Chinese, and men like Allen, Warner, and York who had also established permanent ties by marriage. Kowpelst, Cunamitsa, and Spintlum, the three most prominent leaders, by then had daughters married to whites who stayed near their in-laws. As the Cariboo field proved rich, the rest of the miners left, except the intermarried ones.[48]

By summer 1859 Mary was pregnant. She gave birth to Fred the following April at *Spuzzum* where she would have been assisted by a midwife and her family women. Evidently the Allens and their infant moved over the newly-marked international border to Whatcom County by June 1860, when Solomon told the census taker he was a carpenter. Three other men lived with them, so Mary had joined the other wives taking in boarders for scarce and crucial cash. The few dozen voters knew Solomon well enough by election day to award him a part-time, cash job as the county coroner. The office required no special skill other than the ability to discern a gunshot wound from a knife wound from a drowning. It apparently was not to his taste, either the odious tasks or the wait to be paid by the case, and he resigned after only a few months.

The move to Whatcom County may have been a strategic one for the Allens. Solomon certainly observed that life in the canyon had permanently changed. The construction of the improved wagon road to the Cariboo by the Royal Engineers for the movement north of pack trains, cattle drives, and miners hundreds of miles was destroying critical areas of the canyon. Pandemonium reigned again as the heavy traffic disrupted life in new and permanent ways. Solomon apparently decided that he didn't want to work on the road or mine anymore, and so relocated back to the United States, where he knew that good land was available. One can assume that it was an emotionally wrenching time for Mary, who had already lost family members to the river.

After Mary, Solomon, and the baby moved away, her family was subjected to new attacks on their way of life. A smallpox epidemic two years later killed one-third of the B.C. First Nations people and might have killed the Allens and baby Fred had they stayed. By the next year, all the potato terraces along the river were in the hands of whites armed with claim papers. The *Spuzzum* community ended up restricted to a small flat area on the creek. They still had access to their cemetery on the *Shwimp* side, but no longer had any rights to the mountains, fishing sites, or winter house locations that had been theirs for over three thousand years. In the 1870s, the railroad took whatever land the settlers had not.

British colonial policy world-wide tried to make aboriginal people European-like through a combination of agriculture, education, and Christianity. Kowpelst's (literally "white hat") calling shifted from being the land chief and administrator of a large resource and resident area, to that of the *Spuzzum* people's interpreter and intermediary with whites and their bureaucracy. He grew conflicted. In 1871, he said "The White Man came and took the country and us." The following year, speaking at a new *Spuzzum* church site, he paid an ironic tribute to the power of British tactics. He proclaimed that the Indians had reconciled to the whites' presence because they had also brought Christianity.[49]

Far from the Fraser Canyon's cultural devastation, Mary learned to live within the new society, although she was spared the forced nature of what happened to *Spuzzum*'s families. Years later, she still remembered her stressful early days of marriage. Solomon wanted her to do things his way. She had to learn to sit in a chair though she was more comfortable sitting and working on the floor. He bought all the cooking tools white wives used, including the ultimate in pioneer housewife desirables—an expensive cast iron stove with boiling plates and oven. With this wonder, she could have hot water all day and could roast and boil at the same time. Mary was caught between her expertise with rock-lined pits and fire cooking, and the unfamiliar equipment and tools that took years of adjustment. Some people said that she never mastered them and Solomon continued to do much of the kitchen work. However, in her later years she taught at least one neighbor to barbeque, a technique that harkened back to her youth.[50]

After a short time in Whatcom, the Allens moved to the Sehome Mine community, just down the mud street from Abner Dunn's popular saloon and male refuge. Mary cooked and washed coal-dust-saturated clothing for three boarders who slept rolled in their blankets on the floor. Her earnings contributed to the couple's savings and ability to buy food and goods they couldn't trade for or grow themselves. Solomon's carpentry job at the mine was important, while major upgrades and expansion continued, but water leaks that formed a combustible mixture with the sulphur in the coal seams still plagued the tunnels.

Mary Allen was yet a teenager, far from home. Other indigenous Sehome and Whatcom wives spoke languages unrelated to Nlaka'pamux, but there was Chinook Jargon and some spoke Halkomelem, Mary's second language. The carousing, arguing, fighting miners constantly reminded her of the violent times in *Spuzzum*, especially if her boarders were some of them and disrespected her. Sometimes the loneliness and frustrations of learning to live in her new community, with a husband who could behave just like the others, became overwhelming. In those moments, she would run down the hill to the beach where she hid in the bushes to cry until Solomon found her and took her home.[51]

In late summer 1861, Henry Roeder hired Solomon to (illegally) cut and haul hay with a crew of Lummi men and others on reservation land. He quit after a week, but he had seen the fertile soils, grass prairie, timber of manageable size and variety, and convenient location. Solomon also had a source of information on the area's possibilities. One of Mary's boarders was Frank Mahoney—California forty-niner, San Francisco Vigilantes member, county commissioner, and former sergeant in the short-lived militia. He took a squatter claim on the Nooksack River delta after the 1855–56 Treaty War and ignored the reservation's boundaries. After the 1859 treaty ratification, the government paid him to leave, but instead he married a native woman (probably Lummi) and stayed for two more years. Mahoney harvested wild hay for the coal mine mules and rented grazing land to others before the government forced him to leave. He then moved into the Allen home, apparently after abandoning his wife, or after her death.[52]

Mary's traumatic adolescence during the Canyon War left her permanently fearful of violence, but she didn't know that Mahoney would bring it into her sheltering home where she tended a baby. On a May Saturday in 1862, mine employees partied at Abner Dunn's saloon. About 7:00 p.m., Mary's husband, Mahoney, Dunn, and others headed for the Allen home to eat her dinner and counter the effects of the liquor. Inside her small house, a drunken political argument escalated to grappling. Friends pulled Dunn and Mahoney apart. When Sheriff William Kelly happened by, he saw Mahoney in the street banging stones together and muttering that the quarrel was not over. Kelly told him to go back inside and eat dinner.[53]

After dinner, Solomon and the others returned to Dunn's where they continued to drink. The group returned to the Allen home where Mary and little Fred remained. The men were planning to sing and thought that would help put the pair's argument to rest. It did not. Civil War politics intruded and the Kentuckian Dunn called Massachusetts Yankee Mahoney a "damned Black Republican." Now that the previously minuscule Republican Party controlled the territory's government, tempers flared easily among the shut-out Southerners, especially over the slavery issue. When Dunn called Mahoney out with that insult, he implied that the Yankee supported the end of Southern culture.

Solomon was ready for bed after a couple of drunken melodies. Dunn left to walk home in the dark, but returned after Mahoney threw rocks at him from behind a stump. After Dunn left again, Solomon heard a gunshot about a hundred feet from the Allen picket fence. Soon Mahoney appeared at the door with a chest wound. Solomon raised the alarm and men came running to carry Mahoney into the house where they placed him on his blankets in the candlelight. Mary was probably the chief nurse through the night until James McCluskey arrived to canoe Mahoney to the army's Dr. Robert Orr Craig on San Juan Island. Mahoney left for Alaska after he recovered, eyewitnesses left for the Cariboo gold fields, and barkeep Dunn never went on trial. The incident only escalated Mary's fears about violent men unaccountable for their actions.

Henry Roeder took advantage of Canadian business possibilities in the new gold rush and started herding cattle for hungry miners up the Cariboo Trail that passed *Spuzzum* (see chapter 2). He hired Solomon to sell beef from his cattle pastured in the Nooksack delta on the squatter claim abandoned by Alexander McLean when he left for the Cariboo. When the General Land Office issued rules about preemption settlers who abandoned their claims, McLean's land opened for a new claimant, echoing Solomon's loss of his Oregon claim. Solomon knew the land and wanted the bay frontage, prairie, timber, and a deep slough. The channel, widened by John Tennant and James Carr, accessed both the main river channel and the bay. The Allen family could immediately move into McLean's existing cabin once they cleaned it up. Besides Fred, it now included infant William, named for Solomon's father. Solomon officially declared an April 1, 1863, move before anyone else could take McLean's claim. In the little cedar cabin, Mary gave birth to John C. Allen on June 4, 1864, possibly assisted by Nellie Carr. The Sto:lo teenager from the lower Fraser River spoke Halkomelem, had similar childbirthing customs, and may have already had the midwifery skills she regularly used later. Though she never became a midwife the other nearby woman, Lummi Clara Tennant, may have also assisted because it is difficult to think of Mary giving birth with only Solomon to help, though not impossible.[54]

The Allen land claim also included some things important to the Lummi. On the property, *E'lik* ridge was the location of the hide-out *Com'com'in* to which Jenny Wynn's Lummi family retreated from raids (see chapter 1). The claim contained valuable Lummi butter clam beds, and a spring salmon fishery was offshore. They could easily see Treaty Rock in the water, from which Lummi Reservation's boundaries were measured.[55]

Solomon started his own cattle herd with John Tennant's help. He, Tennant, and Carr cooperated extensively as they worked to clear and develop their pre-emption land claims. They shared skills, implements, and labor for building, harvesting, butchering, and herding. For example, Solomon helped build Tom and Jenny Wynn's cabin when they moved out from Sehome (see chapter 1). All four of the indigenous wives gained a social network for women's work, company, health, and learning the alien homemaker skills. In the first years at the Nooksack, Mary lost William at two years of age, and in 1865 her first little girl died when she was only eleven days old. Without her own family to support her in grief, she had to lean on her husband and new friends.[56]

In the coming years, Solomon frequently left the young mother, often pregnant, and always with small children, to cope with farm chores alone or with the help of hired men from Lummi. He went hunting or for jury duty in Port Townsend for as much as two weeks, and did carpentry jobs valuable to bay residents that kept his skills sharp. (When the new townsite of "East Ferndale" developed some years later, he helped build the first hotel and store). Mary told her friend Edith Graham that she was usually happiest when Solomon was gone. He was a "hard man," she said, her gentle euphemism for abusive and authoritarian. He was probably typical of many American men of his century who saw dominance as his right. He may have felt, like some others, that she was bought and paid for so he had the right to force compliance. He also came from southern Illinois where Southern backcountry settlers brought that value with them as well as condoned family violence as an acceptable part of life. Edith thought Mary did not have a very happy marriage with a man of whom she was afraid. Mary's determined tolerance for the flawed father of her children perhaps was to be expected from a chief's daughter who had already been exposed to many violent events.[57]

Mary Allen built a reputation for strength and bravery that lasted long after her lifetime, though she always feared the sound of quarreling men. People took note of her actions during the monster forest fire of 1868 that left the blue sky unseen for six weeks and caused birds to fall from the smoke-filled sky. The Wynns and other neighbors helped each other fight the unstoppable fire. Solomon was gone and Mary faced the flames alone when the wildfire came to their farm, burning through the alders in the river bottoms. Retreating to the beach, she built a raft by laying driftwood across two canoes in the native way. She took her little children, food, and blankets onto her raft, and pushed it away from shore. They stayed a safe distance out until the fire passed a day later, and she even found a way to build a small cook fire on the raft. Mary and the children watched as bears, deer, livestock, and other animals large and small gathered peacefully on the shore before the ashes and embers drove them into the water also. When Mary finally returned to shore, she found her house miraculously spared.[58]

Edith Graham told a story to local historian and Allen family friend Howard Buswell that demonstrated Mary's physical strength. Her friends called it "Mary's deer story." Meat was an expensive necessity to buy or to raise, precious in time, effort, and money for a growing family. Free meat was even more precious. Solomon was gone the day Mary saw a buck deer run past her house and into the water. Mary went after it. She grabbed an axe, ran to the shore, jumped into a canoe, and paddled after the deer until it tired. She came alongside the exhausted animal who lay its head on the canoe's side, apparently thinking it was a refuge. Mary dispatched the deer with the axe, but had no rope to secure it. Neither could she lift the dead weight into the canoe. She removed her apron, and fastening it around the horns, she towed the carcass home to her family.[59]

If Mary ever wanted to leave Solomon, she was in a poor position to return home, despite her culture's acceptance of divorce. She was without quick communication or transportation and she was often pregnant. By 1879 the Allens had five boys and one girl ranging in age from infancy to nineteen. David had come along in 1869, the twins Samuel and Mary Jane in April 1874. Only nine months after their birth, Daniel was born and died in January 1875, perhaps the result of a pregnancy that began too soon after the twins' birth. She gave birth to her final child at age thirty-four. James Elias, named for two of Solomon's brothers, arrived in October 1879. Since her father was by then known as Chief "James" Kowpelst, the name honored men of both distant families.[60]

Another enduring anecdote demonstrates the growth of Mary's personal courage with the passing years amid her growing brood of lively children. If it is true, Solomon considered leaving them at one time. The story goes that she led him to the orchard and pointed to the ground. She told him that was where he would go if he tried to leave his family. He stayed.[61]

Carpenter Solomon built a thirty-by-eighteen-foot frame house for Mary and the children in 1869, the year their third son David was born. However, the farm's value was only one quarter the value of neighbor John Tennant's in 1870, and he had only improved five acres, much of it in orchard. There was also a barn, probably small and built of logs as the agricultural census taker assigned it little value.[62]

The lack of cleared land in 1870 and a comparatively small barn indicates that the Allens' income from field crops was substantially lower than that of Tennant and Wynn. Their small herd led to lower production—fifty pounds of butter compared with the Tennants' eight hundred. Solomon and Mary's total farm income that year was $950, with market produce accounting for $800, and Mary may have been largely responsible for the butter. Generally, farm wives bore great responsibility for gardens where a smaller clearing could be intensively farmed in vegetables. The Allens' large proportion of income that was market garden may indicate that Solomon spent a large amount of his time there also, in addition to caring for Roeder's cattle in the winter, carpentry jobs, and working for wages occasionally for his neighbors or Roeder.[63]

During the next decade, Solomon only cleared another seven acres. He added sheep and wool production, but did not plant field crops, so his income rapidly fell even farther behind that of their longtime neighbors, though he sometimes hired extra help. This was unusual for a man raised on an Illinois farm, but nothing indicates what held his farming operation back so far, except perhaps a focus on other types of jobs. He had to mortgage half the farm in 1877.[64]

While Mary and Solomon struggled in the late 1870s, he tried a new direction for the farm. Bernard and Catherine McDonough lost their reservation trader's license in 1879 and had to leave Lummi Reservation. To start over close to their Lummi customers and serve the Nooksack River neighborhood, the Irish Civil War veteran paid the Allens one hundred dollars for four acres in the northwest corner of their homestead. The McDonoughs built a house, a bigger store, and a ninety-foot-long crib dock on the waterfront. Small Puget Sound steamers used it as well as the McDonoughs' own magnificent forty-foot Quileute cedar canoe from the Olympic Peninula. The growing complex became a convenient terminal for Nooksack River farmers to wholesale their commodities for the Seattle market, as well as to buy their own everyday supplies. Mary and other women sold McDonough significant quantities of feathers, cranberries, eggs, butter, and chickens to augment family income. In addition to potatoes, hay, and apples, Solomon started selling cedar shingles and hauling wood for McDonough. Clara Tennant's brother-in-law Albert Descanum and Lummi men started up a canoe delivery service and water taxi from the riverbank for people going to the islands, La Conner, or upriver. Postmistress Catherine McDonough moved the "Lummi"

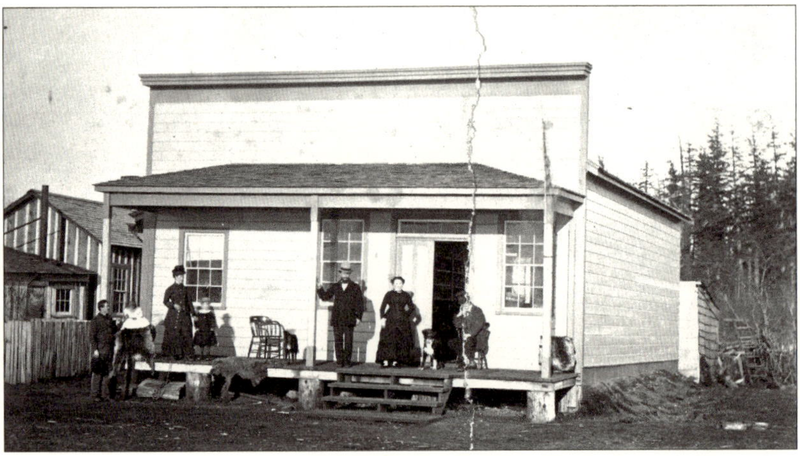

The McDonough Store located on the Allen land. Catherine and Bernard McDonough believed to be on either side of the door. *Howard Buswell Collection #439, Center for Pacific Northwest Studies. Western Washington University, Bellingham, WA.*

Post Office with her which brought more regular visitors. The Lummi and local settlers started holding large-scale holiday celebrations at McDonough's and a small chapel supplemented the reservation's St. Joachim Catholic Church. The Allen homestead became much more than a farm after the sale of the four acres. That part was moving toward becoming a community. People now called it "Lummi."[65]

As Mary matured, her stature in the community on the river grew, particularly for her midwifery skills. She became neighbor Nellie Carr Lane's midwife before Nellie became one herself on Lummi Island. Nellie may have also preferred Mary since she almost certainly spoke Nellie's Halkomelem, the language spoken just south of *Spuzzum.*[66]

Other women, native and nonnative alike, sought Mary out to deliver their babies, for even though pioneer midwives usually had no formal training, nineteenth century women far from home preferred them over male doctors. Fetching a doctor from town took many hours and extra cash they often did not have. Women like Mary worked for pay and they worked for free. Across the continent, women respected folk medicines handed down from mother to daughter, which led to respect for indigenous women's knowledge. A native midwife was usually in demand anywhere women lived in isolated and cross-cultural areas. To indigenous women, childbirth was a natural process that didn't have to be accompanied by fear, and that alone supported frightened young women far from their own mothers. Mary probably used the Nlaka'pamux methods learned from her elders, by which a woman gave birth on her side holding a rope while the midwife rubbed her abdomen gently and gave her warm water to drink. After the birth, the midwife gave the mother tea she had made from berries or cedar.[67]

As more settlers moved into the river neighborhood, Mary gained a reputation for generosity, a gregarious personality, and disregard for social intimidation. A childhood friend of her son Sam said years later: "Mrs. Allen was a likeable person. She had a keen and pleasing nature. You couldn't get mad at her...She was always friendly with everybody."[68]

When the river community was still young, indigenous wives looked forward to Sundays and holidays when families canoed the river to visit one another. In later years, Mary attended neighborhood "teas" hosted by settler wives and sometimes visited overnight at their homes. She welcomed others who had been to McDonough's Store to her modest home for a few hours rest before they made the long hike home, and some stayed for dinner and sleep. When William Baer arrived from Solomon's Illinois home town (by then called Red Bud) to find a homestead, he stayed in the lively Allen home for several weeks.[69]

In Illinois, Solomon grew up near the Catholic families of Kaskaskia, and Mary's family had been both Catholic and Anglican at different times. When they asked Father Casimir Chirouse to baptize eighteen-month-old David on one of his Lummi visits, the sacramental record listed him as "the natural son of Solomon Allen and Indian Mary du Fort Yale." Chirouse did not consider their marriage an official one by church standards, but that did not preclude baptizing their non-Catholic son. The Oblate Fathers, experienced with the "country marriages" of the HBC, had not pressured spouses in tribal custom marriages to get a church wedding, but they married couples of any religion, or baptized their children when asked.[70]

In the early 1870s the county's growing Protestant majority and their ministers began to exert pressure on tribal custom couples to marry "officially." The Allens were one couple whose paperless marriage was not considered legitimate or respectable by the new settlers.

The newcomers, and some earlier settlers, used property inheritance, religious, and most of all, "social propriety" arguments, to compel the "Old Settlers" to regularize their marriages with civil or religious ceremonies. Like others who felt insulted, Mary and Solomon capitulated and their bayside home became the site of their second wedding on September 17, 1873. The officiant, Probate Judge John Plaster, had legally married his Samish wife only two weeks before, but witness John Tennant didn't regularize his marriage to Clara for another three years. Like Jenny and Tom Wynn's re-marriage, the Allen wedding may have been an excuse for another neighborhood all-night party of food and dancing with Tennant on the fiddle.[71]

Four years later, the new local priest Father Jean Boulet baptized Mary's eight-month-old twins "Marie" (Mary Jane) and Samuel at the Allen home. Solomon may have had a spiritual awakening in the years

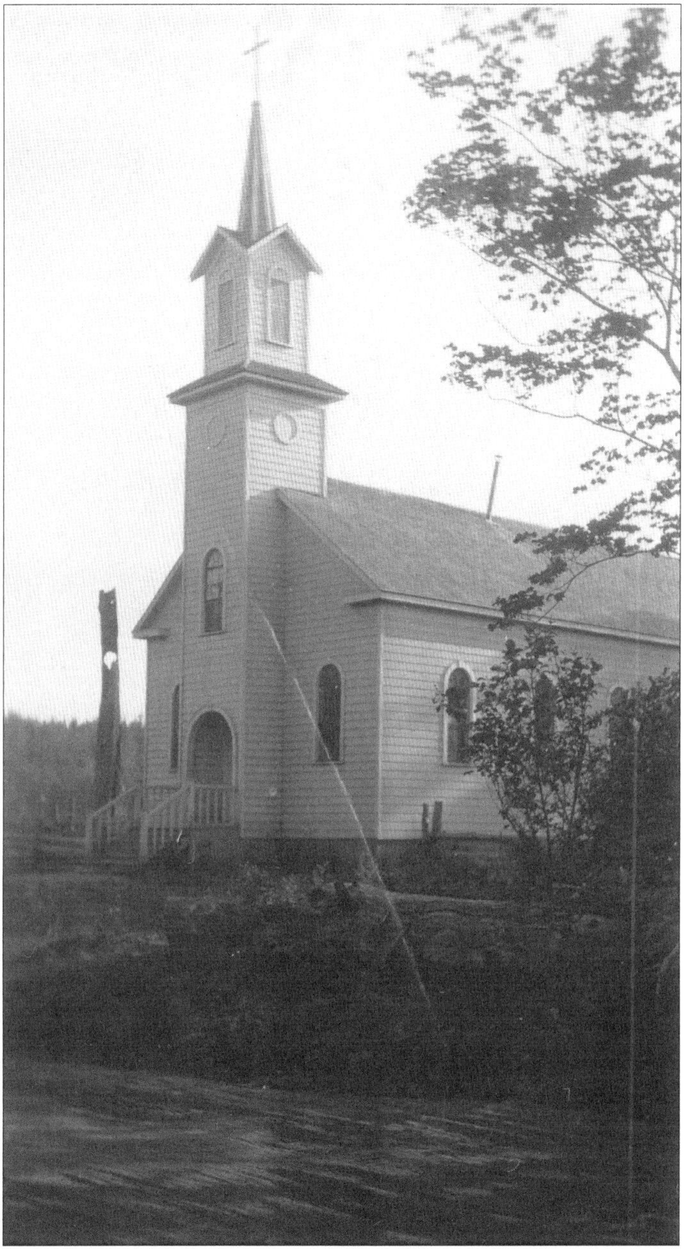

St. Joachim Catholic Church, Lummi Reservation. The lumber was transported by Solomon Allen and his sons to the reservation where they worked on the construction. *Howard Buswell Collection #229. Center for Pacific Northwest Studies. Western Washington University, Bellingham, WA.*

following the twins' birth and baptism. Father Boulet baptized him at St. Joachim's in 1880. He "conditionally" baptized Mary, indicating that she had been previously baptized, but he had no record in his hands. She used her original baptismal name "Suzanne" for her confirmation, a favorite of the Kowpelst family. Irish Catholic Bernard McDonough stood as godfather for both of the adults. Father Boulet noted that "the parties at the same time renewing their consent of marriage long ago made before a justice of the peace in the presence of B. N. McDonough."[72]

Mary had now wed Solomon three times!

Thereafter, the Catholic Church became an important focus of their lives. The Allen family regularly appeared in sacramental records and witnessed for others. Solomon and the boys helped build a new St. Joachim's (still standing). They bought and rafted the lumber from a mill in Whatcom to the reservation for the construction project. It took a second trip to get the cargo safely delivered after the first load was lost in the bay's stormy waves.[73]

After the birth of James Elias in 1879, life with four boys and the twins was strenuous and expensive. More than other customers at the McDonough Store, Mary and Solomon bought large quantities of bacon (country ham), and oatmeal. Invoices hint that the boys habitually lost their straw hats and the frequency of boot purchases point to six pairs of rapidly growing feet. Mary's fabric purchases ran to practical denim, unbleached calico, and gingham for children's pants, shirts, and dresses. However, she also bought good Castile soap, even scented bars, perhaps to reward herself for being the harried mother of five boys.[74]

Fred, the oldest boy, walked five miles along the beach to the little white Sehome School for several years, but was able to study near home after Solomon spearheaded a new school district and built the first school outside of town. The tiny building, made of shakes and timbers cut on the spot, was partially floored with driftwood, and the beach served as an outhouse. Solomon and the other director-fathers hired teacher William Fouts of Olympia and he moved his family into the vacant Whatcom house built for Capt. George Pickett when he was Fort Bellingham's commander. The Allen boys studied in clear view of Fouts' wooden switch. The next year upriver settlers started the Wynn School for their children. When funds ran low to operate the Allen School, the boys walked to the Sehome School rather than make the more dangerous walk up the riverbank.[75]

The Allen school district re-organized. The three eldest Allen boys helped the school fathers build a new log school close to the river's mouth. Hardly an ideal location, wetlands surrounded it on three sides and most students fell into the muck at least once. Four Allen boys, Mary Jane, and a few others studied in a classroom with only one window and plank desks nailed to the walls because that was what the parents could afford. Florence Boone, a well-educated, half-Skagit young mother from Lummi Reservation, taught. She had a warm personality and didn't believe in using a switch on the children.[76]

Health problems began for both Mary and Solomon when he was in his fifties and she was about thirty-five, still with a toddler. The timing of the couple's physical decline was a potential disaster for a not-too-prosperous farm family with children. It may also have played some part in Solomon's religious conversion and devotion to the church from that time on. Solomon described his illness as an aftereffect of his Mexican War measles, but others called it chronic bronchitis, or consumption (tuberculosis). Mary began to suffer from a chronic back disorder. Even so, she continued to serve the community as their midwife and contributed goods to sell to McDonough. John missed a lot of school to help at home because Fred had married by then and started his own family, which eventually grew to include eleven children.[77]

To their regular purchase of castor oil (that dreaded supplement, wart remover, and laxative produced back in Solomon's home county), the Allens added Hall's Balsam, German Syrup, and Susman Salve. Hall's Balsam was the established patent medicine for lung ailments, also used by the Wynns for their son Marshall (see chapter 1). The salve may have been for Mary's back. However, German Syrup was a morphine derivative used at that time as a cough suppressor and painkiller, and its regular use would have resulted in addiction for either Solomon or Mary within a short time.[78]

Chronic health problems may have been what led Solomon to think of turning their homestead into a town. It was to be a move that brought Mary and her family a different financial underpinning. It cannot be assumed that she contributed to the plan, but it is an equally poor idea to assume that strong-willed Mary did not.

John Tennant surveyed the road improvement and worked on the township plat with Solomon. They laid out sixty lots in four blocks fronting the bay south of the McDonough complex. After the farmers had manipulated the river to get rid of century-old log jams, a deep water channel was no longer nearby, but the slough still gave adequate river access. La Conner's *Puget Sound Mail* printed a small article about the new enterprise and with the usual boosterism, proclaimed that it would doubtless become the "commercial metropolis of the Nooksack."[79]

After a year and a half of preparation, Mary and Solomon signed their plat in mid-1883, when their youngest child was only four. Tennant suggested they name the town after their only daughter with "etta" added for sound, which perhaps inadvertently would also recognize Mary Allen as the years passed. Solomon advertised his lots: sixty-two dollars for water frontage and fifty for back lots. He advised anyone starting a business to consider Marietta before seeking to locate anywhere else because of the metropolis he was so sure it would become. The Allens made sure that their sons who wanted to live on the homeplace all received lots for their own houses.[80]

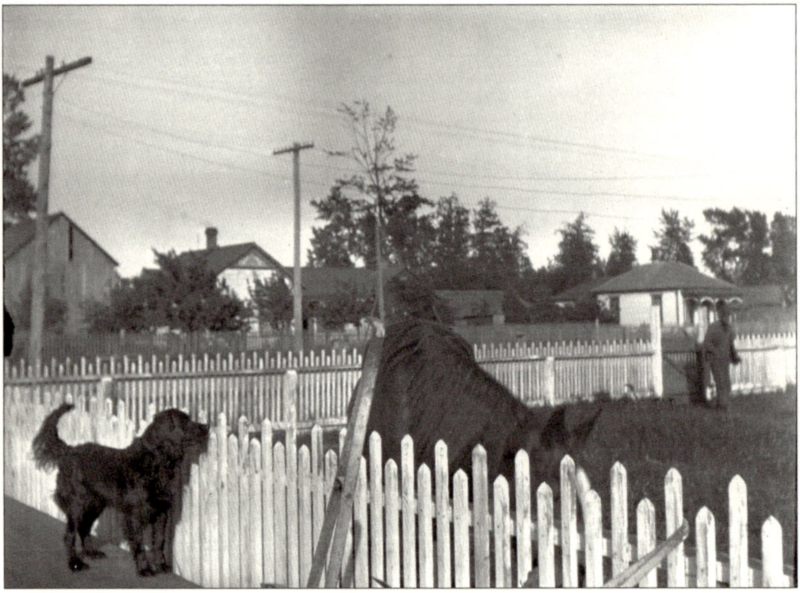

Marietta, Washington, founded by Mary and Solomon Allen. *Howard Buswell Collection #298, Center for Pacific Northwest Studies. Western Washington Univesity, Bellingham, WA.*

Mary's only daughter, Mary Jane, died in February of 1887, at the age of twelve from an unrecorded cause. Her grieving mother prominently displayed a picture of her beloved daughter until Mary passed away herself. The place name Marietta remains her memorial.[81]

As the years passed, many lot buyers took out mortgages from the Allens and the annual interest payments brought in additional income. The little community grew, with its own hotel and stage service within the first six years. Logging mills and camps in the surrounding area identified their location as Marietta. The population became mostly fishermen, loggers, and a small group of S'Klallam Indians from the Olympic Peninsula's north coast, but with too much chronically wet ground, it never became a "commercial metropolis."[82]

Aging and ailing Solomon adopted the look of Marietta's founder and "proprietor." He sported a silk top hat atop his wavy silver hair during his frequent visits to Whatcom. He and Mary were surrounded by activity and grandchildren, but earned very little income after most lots were sold and paid for. After the War Department denied Solomon's application for a military pension increase from $3.50 per month, they needed some support while Jim was still in school. The Allens had already used much of their townsite sale income to send John and Dave to business school in Illinois, and they helped their parents out.[83]

Perhaps because serious violence was rare along the lower river and in town, each new incident was more frightening for Mary. After her violence-filled youth at *Spuzzum*, the Mahoney incident in Sehome, and perhaps Solomon's own behavior, her fear of male violence continued to grow with the years. She once hid in the bushes along their crude road and waited for Solomon's return, based solely on the rumor of a fight.

Mary continued to be especially sensitive to community violence. In 1879 Ferndale-area neighbors worked and socialized during a butchering day at Fanny and Tom Barrett's lake when newcomer Sam Brown stabbed Peter Gallagher to death in a jealous rage. Brown escaped after a posse's feeble effort to find him, and his wife disappeared after selling the homestead. Five years later the Mayfield murder at nearby Ferndale that so terrorized the Wynn family (see chapter 2) and the entire lower river area took place. It is understandable if Mary, with six children, saw evidence that her fears were justifiable.[84]

Given Mary's abhorrence of violence, she was probably horrified when the Allens became part of a headline murder case that put the aging couple and their son squarely in the public eye for nearly five months. It was scarcely three weeks after Whatcom's 1891 New Year's Eve "Red Men's Ball," when the all-white lodge membership and their wives dressed up as Indians and "honored" indigenous people even as they hoped for their disappearance. Within three weeks, the celebrants and others would call for the lynching of a local Lummi man from the most prominent extended family.[85]

On January 21, 1892, popular elderly Civil War veteran and inebriate Moses Younkin was found beaten and dying off the bayside railroad track just after it crossed Little Squalicum Creek at the north limit of Whatcom. Twelve-year-old Jimmie Allen was walking along the tracks toward town in the late afternoon winter twilight when he saw the assault happening in the distance. Frightened by what he saw, he turned and ran back home. Younkin died of the beating that night and based on first reports, the authorities went after George Swe'lus ("Swiloos" in the case file) and his visiting nephew. Jimmie was the only eyewitness at the inquest. Very quickly, many town residents called for a lynching and in the midst of the threatening and chaotic atmosphere, Swe'lus escaped. The Allens waited for cooperating

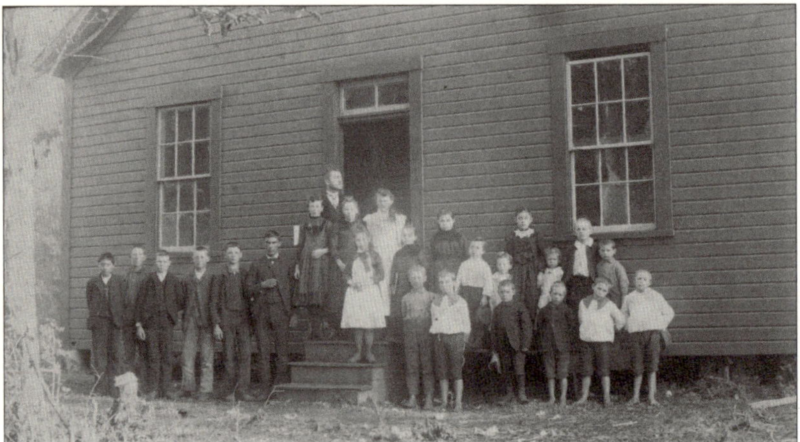

Jimmie Allen at left. His brother Sam sixth from left. Marietta School, 1889, a few years before Jimmie witnessed the Moses Younkin murder in January 1892. *Howard Buswell Collection #832, Center for Pacific Northwest Studies. Western Washington University, Bellingham, WA.*

Lummi authorities and the county sheriff to bring in the accused man. Living near the reservation, Mary and Solomon probably watched over their youngest child closely.[86]

Swe'lus, age forty-two and disabled from a bear attack, was the first cousin of Chief Henry Kwina and prominent intermarried women Clara Tennant (see *Peace Weavers* chapter 4) and Jennie Wynn (see chapter 1). The large family collected defense funds at Lummi and at Nooksack villages where residents had their own lynching murder to resent. They hired Seattle's Samuel Piles, a talented trial lawyer and former prosecutor whose future would include election to the U.S. Senate and an ambassadorial post. Piles would oppose the local prosecutor and an assistant who were no match for his reputation.[87]

Finding a jury took much longer than usual. It was necessary for the sheriff to comb the county hinterlands for male voters who didn't read the newspapers and didn't talk to other people very often. The court quickly dismissed Solomon Allen from the initial list of eligible jurors.

Jimmie occupied the center of local attention, and newspaper headlines about him appeared regularly until after he testified. Despite the notoriety, the boy maintained his near-perfect school grades and classroom behavior at the newer Marietta School. One newspaper reported that on the witness stand, he "spoke clearly, his lips always parted with a pleasant smile when talking" as he testified. In a situation with many inconsistencies between witnesses, both sides trusted the boy.[88]

Had Jimmie's mother been a Lummi instead of indigenous Canadian, his testimony would probably have been considered suspect by the enraged white community who believed Swe'lus to be guilty beyond any doubt before the trial even started. Had his mother and father both been whites, the Lummi community probably would never have trusted Jimmie to be truthful. As it was, Mary Allen's personal history was the underpinning of the position he occupied, a threat to neither side because of his dual ethnicity. Or conversely, a threat to both sides. His teacher George Brown called him "a very truthful boy" in the newspaper.

After Piles masterfully presented the final defense argument, the jury that had been so difficult to assemble quickly returned a verdict of "not guilty." As soon as Swe'lus was released, Lummi men waiting outside helped him escape the "wild" mob and reach British Columbia. Jimmie's teacher (the man who had described Jimmie as very truthful) assembled a posse to chase down and lynch Swe'lus, but they failed to locate him. Townspeople, frustrated that the justice system actually worked for both whites and Indians, barred members of the jury from their businesses for weeks.[89]

Brown, also the Marietta correspondent for the *Daily Reveille*, continued to write anti-Lummi diatribes even as he adopted the role of local intellectual. The incongruity of the teacher's attitudes toward the Lummi and toward the half-Indian children he taught did not seem apparent to Brown.[90]

On January 21 the next year Solomon, with a shaky "X" instead of his usual signature, deeded to Mary what he named her community property: the remaining forty-nine acres of the homestead and the town lots. Two days later, he died at age sixty-eight from his lung disease. The marriage born in the unforgiving waters of the Fraser River had lasted thirty-six and a half years.[91]

At Solomon's large funeral in the church he had helped build, Father Boulet praised the devout man he had baptized as a "greatly respected gentleman" who had given to others generously. The family buried him on his farm close to the children's graves but moved them to Bayview Cemetery in Bellingham a few years later when floods threatened.[92]

Mary

Mary's father Kowpelst died the same year as Solomon. She had maintained contact with her own family down the years but would grieve far from home. Throughout the century, the major political leaders at *Spuzzum* had been Pa'lek, then Kowpelst his son, and now the tradition of authority continued when Mary's nephew James Paul Xixne was elected chief. He served until 1926. The government noted later that Xixne and Kowpelst had held an "unwavering determination" to achieve recognition and resolution of their land claims. After Xixne's death, Kowpelst's great-grandson Henry James continued the family's leadership in the lower canyon.[93]

After eighteen months of financial struggle, Mary applied for a Widow's Service Pension with the assistance of son John's wife. Minnie wrote that her in-laws had depended on their married children's support since 1891 and Mary's assets were worth very little. Age fifty-one and suffering with back problems, Mary was incapable of earning any income, according to her own statement. Nothing happened despite two years of repeated submissions. Again, Minnie wrote the government that not only did Mary lack money for necessities, she had sold most of the rest of her land and was threatened with the loss of the remainder for overdue property taxes. Minnie called her "honest and deserving as any in the land." She believed that if the pension on which Mary pinned all her hopes was not granted, the blow would kill her.[94]

Mary submitted another application four years after her husband's death, but the War Department never granted the pension based on Solomon's few weeks of military service, even if he believed he had suffered long-lasting effects. She lived for some years in a small house behind John and Minnie's new home before she moved in with Sam and his family, and spent her remaining days surrounded by grandchildren. Old friends like William Baer, the Illinois houseguest, invited her to his family gatherings and she made friends among newer neighbors, like the young boy (and future historian) Howard Buswell.

This "remarkable woman" as Buswell called her, died of old age January 3, 1913, at about seventy-four. She had lived on her homestead for nearly fifty years. Father Boulet conducted her funeral before she was buried near Solomon and Mary Jane at Bellingham's Bayview Cemetery, though the boys never marked her grave with a stone.[95]

The Allen Sons

Mary's five sons scattered before long. She had often told other people that she wanted her boys to emulate and adopt their father's culture, not her own. Perhaps she thought that was best for their futures, but her belief sadly exemplifies how indigenous wives and their knowledge and contributions were being discounted and disrespected by that time. Her sons did as she advised in large measure, though not consistently. A tribute to her strength of character, they incorporated her qualities into their lives as well, and they kept the connection to her *Spuzzum* family alive.

Part of Mary's reservations about keeping her culture alive in her sons may have come from the fact that while she was socially accepted by many whites, they did not consider the Allen boys worthy marriage partners for their daughters, as one who sympathized observed. Studying the children of British Columbia intermarriages, historian Sylvia Van Kirk concluded that sons lived a more public life which exposed them to stereotypes that emphasized deficiencies instead of strengths. This worked against them in the marriage market, and may have been present in Whatcom County also, if not everywhere.[96]

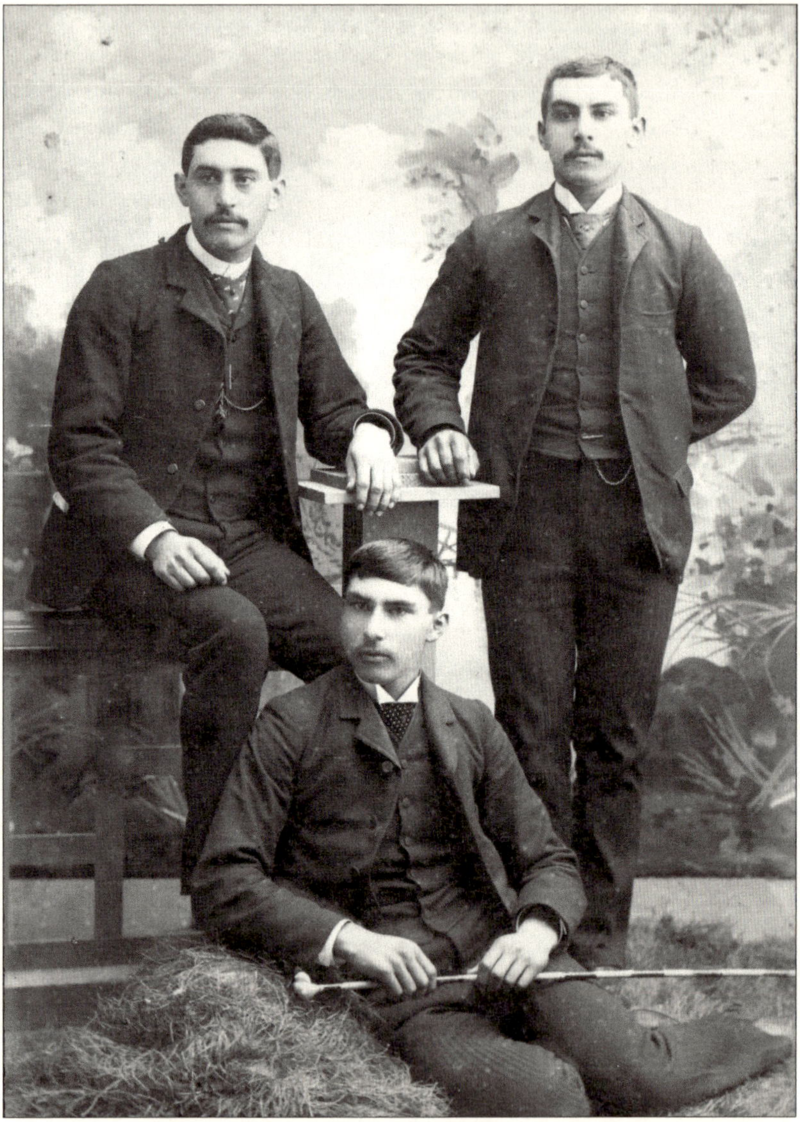

Three of Mary and Solomon Allen's sons: John, Fred, and Sam. *Howard Buswell Collection # 292, Center for Pacific Northwest Studies. Western Washington University, Bellingham, WA.*

As it happened, Mary's sons had a variety of marriage experiences. Fred, the eldest, married Mary Eva Boulon, daughter of a Skykomish intermarriage that had ended badly when her mother died and her logger-gold miner father disappeared. She and Fred had eleven children, but six died before adulthood. The family left Marietta for Ketchikan, Alaska, after Fred was denied the post of Lummi Island postmaster on the excuse of inadequate education. He commercially fished out of Ketchikan, an echo of his Nlaka'pamux ancestry. Some years later, they moved back to Washington to farm in Snohomish County. Fred's son Solomon went to *Spuzzum* where Mary's nephew (his cousin) had become chief and he worked there among his mother's family for some time before he joined the U.S. Army in World War I. Fred and Mary Eva's grandson Frank Allen and his mother Esther Ross became prominent Indian rights activists for the Stillaguamish Tribe in its ultimately successful quest for federal recognition in 1976.[97]

Mary and Solomon sent their tall and handsome sons John and Dave to their father's home state for more education when they were twenty-six and twenty-one, probably financed with the town site lot sales. Evidence and John's later jobs suggest that they attended Brown's Business College ("the only high-grade business college in southern Illinois") in Centralia, where they had a photo taken for their parents. The school's location was no coincidence because it was very near Solomon's family at Red Bud and they established contact. In later years, rumors claimed Mary and Solomon sent their sons to Illinois to "pass" for French in order to marry white women. Mary's sons were in an ethnically diverse area that still had many French-Indian families and Solomon may have recalled that Catholic boarding schools in St. Louis had long catered to intermarried fur trade families. However, with the exception of the birth certificates of John's children, there is no evidence that the brothers tried to conceal their indigenous roots from their cousins with whom they became friends or from the people of Illinois.[98]

John met Minnie Hatterscheit during his time in Illinois, the "very educated, sophisticated" daughter of German immigrants. She traveled to Washington to meet the Allens before Father Boulet married them in November 1892, three years before Solomon's death. John farmed his part of the remaining Allen land, and Minnie began to teach piano lessons, in addition to taking in boarders as Mary had once done. As the widowed Mary aged, the other sons signed off on a land gift from Mary to John and Minnie so they could build a nice home in front of the smaller one where she lived. It is evident from stories, photos, and Minnie's letters that she was devoted to her mother-in-law during the years Mary lived beside her. The couple had two children, delivered by Mary. They named their daughter Mary Cecelia, after her grandmother.[99]

After Mary's death in 1913, John and his family followed Jim to Petersburg, the center of Alaska's fishing industry and where Fred fished, one hundred miles north of Ketchikan. They arrived in the midst of a boom just as the isolated settlement became an official town and John soon became one of its most prominent residents. At a time when Petersburg's "prominent" citizens included "Greasy Bob" and "Salvation Charlie," a man with a formal business education who wanted to help build a community was very welcome. Within a few months John was appointed Deputy U.S. Marshal, praised by the local paper as a man who would do his duty "fearlessly and without discrimination." This could be a daunting job in a town whose main saloon was known as the "Bucket of Blood."[100]

Following her husband, Minnie gave her heart to a town built on pilings over muskeg and tides. Despite Petersburg's 110 inches of rain and three feet of snow a year, Minnie wrote and published loving poems and songs about it. She composed the town song "Happy Petersburg" and her classic "Humpback Salmon," which are still sometimes sung one hundred years later.[101]

When John and Minnie's son Charles Herbert froze to death on a winter camping trip in 1916, the entire town closed down for the funeral. They buried their son down the Wrangell Narrows at their home "Green Rocks" on Kupreanof Island. Shortly after, John was appointed U.S. Commissioner for the Petersburg region. He was the only judge and federal administrator for a large area of islands and mainland reachable only by boat (reminiscent of his grandfather Kowpelst's appointment). After a Seattle education, their daughter Mary Cecelia returned and taught music, dance, and art to the culture-starved locals. She played piano for their silent films, operated their ice cream parlor, and was a licensed gas boat skipper. She became a professional photographer whose photos graced postcards with vivid images that were mailed out by residents and travelers. Over the years, John served as town clerk and postmaster, as well as operated a fox farm and guided Easterners on bear hunts. Living in Tlingit country, the family made no secret of their pride in Nlaka'pamux ancestry, even if the couple had registered the children as "white" back in Whatcom County.[102]

Dave's future was quite different. While a student in Illinois, he met Ella Quinn, the daughter of an Irish immigrant grocer. Unlike Minnie, she did not meet Mary before the wedding because they married in Illinois, with cousin Howdy Allen from Red Bud serving as Dave's witness. They took the train west, and their baby boy was born ten months later at Marietta, with a licensed doctor attending and precisely registered as "white ¾ and Indian ¼." A persistent local rumor said that Ella was shocked when she met Mary because Dave had not told her his mother was Nkla'pamux. Unhappy about that, she insisted on moving back to Illinois "to get away from the Indians." True or not, the young couple did move back to the Midwest after the birth of their first baby. Dave found work as a carpenter in St. Louis where he put to good use the skills he had learned from Solomon. Though they never returned to live in Washington, Dave visited when his mother died, and two of his daughters later moved to Seattle.[103]

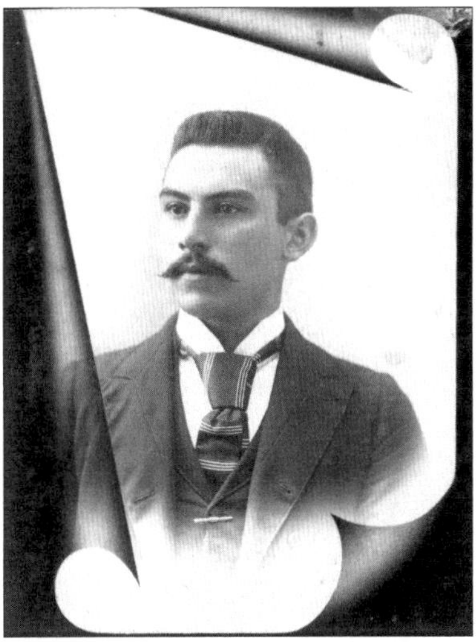

Dave Allen, son of Mary and Solomon Allen. *Howard Buswell Collection #291, Center for Pacific Northwest Studies. Western Washington University, Bellingham, WA.*

The birth of the twins Sam and Mary Jane was very unusual for that century. The growth and activities of the little Allen twins were likely a popular topic along the Nooksack and well-known in town, too. Mary Jane's death at twelve made Sam just another one of the brothers. He walked to high school in Whatcom every morning, but there was no money to send him to Illinois after Solomon died. He married Edith LeBeau in Everett, and settled at the home place where they started a family and he became a commercial gillnetter (the second son to follow the Kowpelst family tradition). Mary moved in with them later and helped with the children, even telling the 1910 census taker that was her occupation. Sam and Edith struggled financially after Mary's death. John sent barrels of cod down from Alaska to help feed the family, and Sam's son Alva lived with John and Minnie in Petersburg to attend school for some time. With John's help, the whole family finally moved to Alaska and settled in Petersburg.[104]

Like Fred's son, one of Sam's children went "back" to Mary's Fraser Canyon home where her extended family members lived. Lytton's St. George's School for Nlaka'pamux children opened upstream from *Spuzzum* in 1901. Sam and Edith sent their fourteen-year-old daughter Corinne down to the school from Alaska. After Canadian laws regarding intermarriages passed in 1876, Mary had lost her First Nations status by her legal marriage to Solomon but Corinne was still admitted for the free education. Perhaps it happened through the influence of her father's first cousin Chief Paul Xixne, or because the school was new and needed girls with some good prior education. Corinne lived for a time amidst her grandmother's family and culture and was exposed to acculturation methods as harsh as those in the U.S. They were abusive and unnecessary for the Alaskan girl.[105]

Corinne returned home when her family had a crisis with her younger brother after he broke into his uncle John's post office with some other boys and took a substantial amount of money. Sam and his family endured a newspaper editorial that called his son's crime "a warning to parents to watch their boys and guide them a little." Shortly after Corinne arrived home, she suffered a nervous breakdown or a stroke. Confined to her home, the "universally liked" girl with the "sunny disposition" "wasted away" over the following weeks and died at the Juneau hospital after being transported unconscious by boat one hundred miles for help.[106]

Long years later, Sam retired back to Washington after his wife died and lived near his brother Fred in Oso, Snohomish County.

And what of James Elias Allen, the little boy with perfect school attendance and a ninety-eight grade average, whose testimony saved the life of George Swe'lus?

After high school in town, he worked as a mill hand until he was twenty-four when the U.S. Forest Service sent him to Alaska. Jim arrived in the rough settlement of Petersburg about 1903 and influenced John and Minnie to see the potential there and follow. Ranger Jim Allen supervised timber claims and issued logging and pile driving permits. He soon was known by everyone for a hundred miles around as his boat made its way among the green islands and the waving black and white fins of humpback whales.[107]

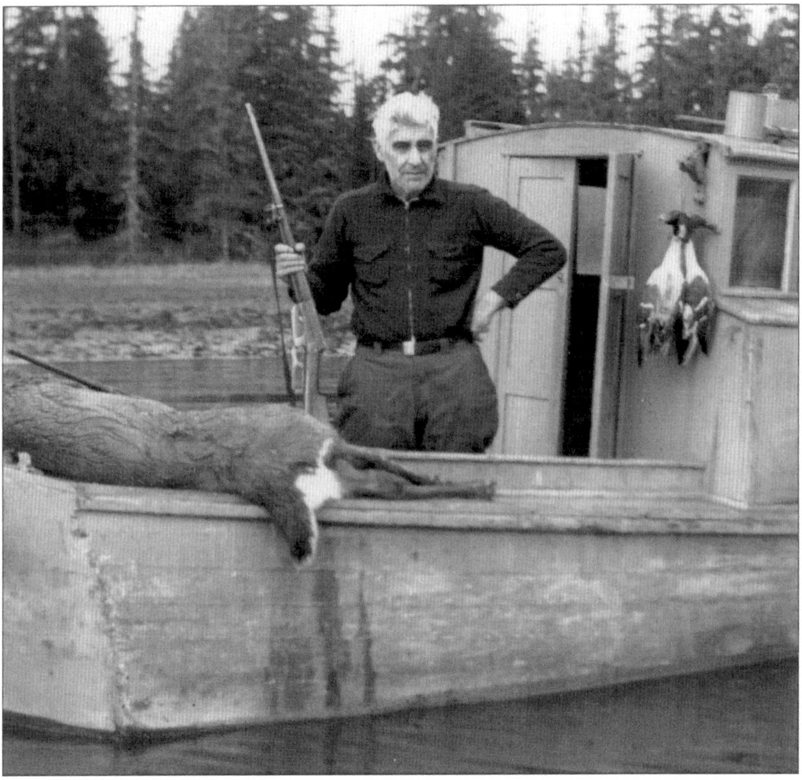

Jim Allen, son of Mary and Solomon Allen. *Howard Buswell Collection #1703. Cropped from a larger original. Center for Pacific Northwest Studies, Western Washington University, Bellingham, WA.*

The Preuschoff brothers arrived in 1909 and built the most successful logging business in southeast Alaska. When their sister Marie joined them, she quickly fell for the good-looking local forest ranger and the pair boated to Ketchikan to have a Catholic Church wedding. They never had any children of their own but became the much-loved aunt and uncle to children on both sides. Jim continued making his rounds on the *Ranger 2* until the 1930s, often ferrying locals from one tiny settlement to another as he went about his duties. Like John on Kupreanof Island, Jim and Marie owned an Arctic fox farm on Grief Island until the Depression destroyed the market for fur coats. Jim became one of the earliest members of the Arctic Brotherhood, a lodge formed for camaraderie of those who braved the conditions of pioneering the North. Jim and Marie also supported independent fishermen against Bellingham-based Alaska Packers who were taking all the fish with their deadly efficient traps, just as they decimated the fish runs in Whatcom County.[108]

Jim never left Petersburg and died there in 1946.[109]

Solomon and Mary Kowpelst Allen have scores of descendants today from Alaska to Washington. Those men and women take pride in their ancestors who grasped hands in the Fraser's rapids and lived to found a family and a town before their sons contributed to the development of Southeast Alaska.

Today, the once thriving logging hamlet of Marietta has been largely washed away by the changing course of the Nooksack River and the bay's tides. Only a few decayed buildings remain.

CHAPTER 4

Mrs. Pickett, The Commander's Wife

TWO HANDSOME YOUNG MEN tentatively shook hands in San Francisco on a spring day in 1885. Both had thick shocks of dark brown hair and even darker eyes, and both were deeply loved by their families. In every other way, they could not have been more different. Though they were both carriers of family legacies, one was the future of his family's military tradition. The other was the blossoming of a gift of artistic talent from the mother he never knew.

George Edward Pickett Jr.'s father was the legendary Confederate hero of the Battle of Gettysburg. Everyone expected him to enter the army and his mother wanted him to marry into another prominent Confederate family. This West Coast trip freed him from her smothering domination and the personally stifling atmosphere of Virginia where his name could both help and hinder.[1]

The other was James Tilton Pickett, half-indigenous son of the general's cross-cultural marriage, and a serious artist who was studying

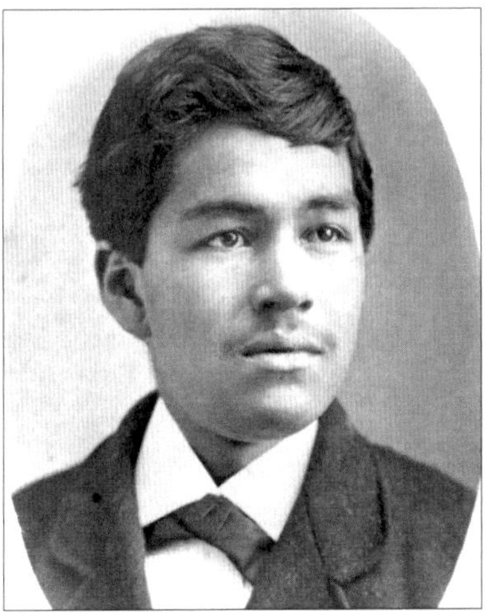

James Tilton Pickett, son of U.S. Army Captain and Mrs. George E. Pickett. *#X.4839. Whatcom Museum, Bellingham, WA.*

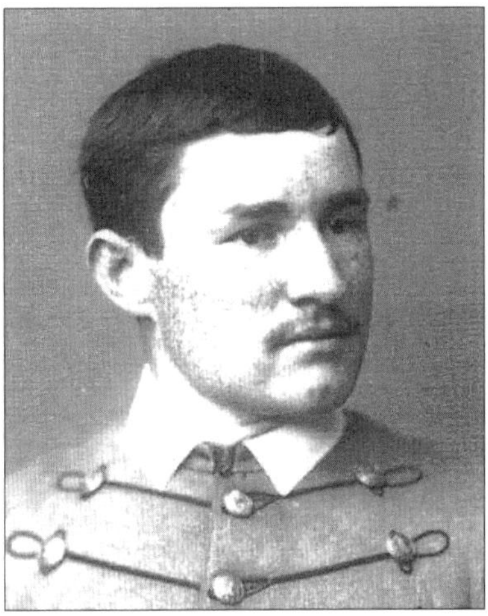

George Edward Pickett Jr., son of Confederate General George E. Pickett and his third wife, Sallie Ann Corbell Pickett. *Courtesy of the Pickett Society.*

at the first professional art school west of the Mississippi. He looked forward to meeting his younger half-brother, the other son of a father James knew only through letters written before the general died a decade earlier. He had never met another blood relative after his dimly remembered father left Washington Territory.

George Jr. knew about James too, but since his father died when he was eleven, he may not have known the full truth. His mother concocted a Southern woman's acceptable explanation for the presence of a mixed-blood child in her late husband's life. She told everyone that a "Lummi chief" gave his baby son to then-Captain Pickett in gratitude for his mercy after the defeat of thousands of Lummi warriors. Being a polite man, she lied, her future husband adopted the boy. People believed her.[2]

The artist and the "First Family of Virginia" scion, separated by seven years of age, geography, and mutually foreign lifestyles, crossed their personal divide. The meeting did not go well, but perhaps not for the reason James thought.

Both men were probably stunned when they stood face-to-face. George could not deny what James always knew. There was no adoption. They were brothers. It was almost like looking into a mirror.

George's eyes told him that James was his half-brother left behind when Captain Pickett joined the Confederacy. It was clear that his mother fabricated the explanation for her continued interest in a stepson across the continent.

George's reaction when confronted with his older brother's "Indianness" deeply hurt the sensitive artist. James saw only racial arrogance and overbearing Southern snobbery.[3]

The young man dreamed of joining his family in Virginia one day, as his father once promised. After the meeting, he realized his dreams had always been just that, and his hopes for a relationship with George died. James never saw his brother again.

The Second Mrs. Pickett

The indigenous second wife of Confederate General George E. Pickett and her family is both Washington's most well-known cross-cultural marriage story and yet the story most inaccurately told. It has long needed a new examination. Confederate historians and others long buried or abbreviated the story of General Pickett's non-white second wife because it seems to be a piece of uncomfortable racial history. A century of national Civil War historians and Northwest writings about the couple repeated assumptions and used erroneous sources. As late as 2013, a *Wall Street Journal* article called Mrs. Pickett a "mistress" and "Lummi lover."[4]

The popular legend tells of a young Haida "princess" named "Morning Mist" who meets the dashing widowed army officer and they marry by tribal and civil ceremonies (or don't marry at all). She dies shortly after their son's birth, leaving behind only her red leather trunk. When Captain Pickett leaves for the war, he boards their son Jimmie with "a Collins family" and the boy grows up a lonely biracial misfit unable to find his place in the world. He dies early and poor at a shabby Portland, Oregon, boarding house, clinging to his mother's trunk, "the Gettysburg sword," and a few other mementos of his father. So goes the myth that includes romance and tragedy to fit biased white cultural beliefs and assumptions. The second Mrs. Pickett was an individual, not a myth, and clues about her life exist. Her son's life bore no resemblance to the myth.[5]

The most egregious conversion of myth into popular "fact" was the name "Morning Mist." In 1937 Archie Binns used a fanciful version of the Pickett story as a prologue to an unrelated novel and invented the name. Other authors repeated it as fact. Neither James Pickett, his foster parents, nor any of Mrs. Pickett's friends ever shared her personal name with others. Mrs. Pickett's good friend Cecelia Kennerly (later Toby), an intermarried Coast Salish woman, told her son George Kennerly (aka Kinley) that people always used the respectful term "Mrs. Pickett" for the fort commander's wife. That would be customary protocol for military and local people alike at any post. This chapter does likewise.[6]

William Walter (the second foster father), James Tilton Pickett, and reliable witnesses agreed on one thing: Mrs. Pickett was a "Northern Indian," from "Russian Alaska," the peoples who lived far north of the Coast Salish on the islands and inlets of southeast Alaska. Walter said she was Haida. His information came from his wife Catherine, the foster mother, who got hers from George Pickett. Like Mrs. Pickett's name, her geographic origin also needed careful reexamination.[7]

The nineteenth century Kaigani Haida lived on the southern parts of Alaska's Prince of Wales Island, north of their homeland Haida Gwaii (Queen Charlotte Islands) while the Tlingit lived on the mountainous mainland and nearby islands around today's Sitka, Alaska.

Both groups paddled over five hundred miles south to work and trade at Fort Victoria starting in the 1840s after the sea otter trade had declined dramatically. They were less warlike than the *Laich'wil'tach* raiders, though they were not above doing some raiding occasionally before returning home for the winter. In the mid-1850s, a number of Tlingit and Haida Hudson's Bay Company (HBC) wives lived on San Juan Island, and several "Northern" wives (specific group left undefined) lived in Whatcom. Northern men worked at the Roeder mill and had served in the local militia during the 1855–56 Treaty War just before Pickett arrived. Haida men worked for the HBC at Semiahmoo (*Semiamah* territory) north of Whatcom, but no official or unofficial accounts said Tlingits were there. The Haida families were with their men at Semiahmoo and it was probably there that the Picketts first met. The historical assumption that Mrs. Pickett was a socially isolated oddity among local Coast Salish wives is false. Her parents probably still lived at Semiahmoo, perhaps with other siblings, and one witness said she had a sister on San Juan Island.[8]

One problem with establishing that Mrs. Pickett was Haida from "Russian Alaska" is that the Russians generally kept to the mainland and close-by islands of southeast Alaska, having more influence and trade with the Tlingit. The Haida further west across rough waters traded less with the Russian colonizers and met any efforts at control with armed hostility. They traded more with the HBC and Americans sailing farther from shore. Terminology in accounts differ just enough to make final determination of Mrs. Pickett's origin impossible without new information from Alaska. William Walter and Jimmie Pickett, from their geographic and time distance, may not have understood those subtle differences in using the term "Russian Alaska." Nevertheless, it is most logical to go with what the people closest to the information said.

Mrs. Pickett's homeland, or at the least that of her parents, was geographically very different from that of the Coast Salish, though it had some cultural similarities. The retreat of Ice Age glaciers that formed the islands and steep-walled fjords of Haida Gwaii and southeast Alaska birthed a culture whose origins go back at least 13,000 years, according to recent research. Centuries of isolation on the islands produced a language unrelated to others. Her people were nurtured by the richness of what the sea and mountains provided in a fog and mist-laden land where rainfall is measured in feet not inches. Salmon anchored both Tlingit and Coast Salish culture, but for the Haida, it supplemented the halibut, their most important fish. Found on the continental shelf, the giant flatfish could weigh six hundred pounds and be eight feet long, yielding a large amount of succulent protein per fish. Both Haida and Tlingit prized seals, shellfish, river salmon, and black cod. They harvested auklets and murrelets as well as great flocks of migrating waterfowl flying to and from Coast Salish territory. It is still the land of the "ghost bear," a white subspecies of black bear found nowhere else, a sacred spirit.

Like the Coast Salish, Mrs. Pickett's people made giant cedars their basic material resource. The Haida lived enveloped by art in their everyday environment, and in their family's history remembered in tangible form. Haida and Tlingit produced the monumental painted full-round carved poles, robes, masks, bentwood boxes, embellished baskets, and other goods most Americans think represent all Northwestern native cultures. Unlike the Coast Salish who generally solved conflict without violence, the Haida (and Tlingit) were historically more warlike when angered. The Haida had numerous events and people, as well as their family totemic animals and crests, to honor in the poles that formed a manmade "forest" on the beach in front of their cedar longhouses. Tlingit also carved and erected them in front of their houses. Both peoples embellished and carved the interiors of their large houses, as well as the objects within them, with meaningful symbols and representations. From a single tree, Haida men carved a sixty-foot-long yellow cedar canoe that could carry seventy warriors or eight tons of cargo on the open ocean. These enabled pre-contact Haida to dominate the Tlingit and other neighboring groups by trade and force before the European strangers' gunships arrived. Their canoes were traded south to Coast Salish territory and were the reason why uninformed Northwest settlers who saw Northern raiders in painted and carved ocean canoes thought they must be "Hyders." By the 1850s, the primary *Laich'wil'tach* raiders were the Tlingit. Some southern Kwakwaka'wakw (Kwakiutl) from the Quadra Island neighborhood continued to raid after their disastrous defeats by the united Salish in the 1830s and 1840s, but they were no longer the predators they had once been.[9]

Northern women made intricately detailed skin and woven tunics and capes decorated with mountain goat and sea otter fur. The dense otter fur brought Russian, American, and British traders shortly after the Spanish made first white contact in 1774. The first traders were astounded to see such large buildings, beautiful clothing, advanced sculptures fifty feet high, and embellished household goods produced by people they saw only as fishers and hunters. By the time Mrs. Pickett was born, however, the sea otter pelt trade was in steep decline after hunters decimated the animal's numbers. This led to the Haida and Tlingit traveling south in the 1840s after Fort Victoria was built to broaden their economic base, a possible reason why Mrs. Pickett's family was at Semiahmoo. Though some Haida participated in raiding, the families at Semiahmoo lived and worked there peacefully.[10]

Like the Coast Salish, Haida and Tlingit lived in extended family longhouses. Lineage and rank was (and is) supremely important to both, and Mrs. Pickett would have been seen as a reincarnation of an ancestor. Parents preferred girls to boys because women perpetuated lineages traced through mothers. Both societies divided families into two overarching groups: Tlingit, raven and wolf; Haida, eagle and raven. From childhood, Mrs. Pickett would have identified with her mother's line and known that she would marry someone from the opposite group. Genealogical subgroups represented by totemic animals were a major basis of the decorative arts.

Like the Coast Salish among whom Mrs. Pickett would live, her family had the same lifeway of following a seasonal calendar of food acquisition in the warmer, drier months, and ceremonies in the rainy interior months of fall and winter. Like the Coast Salish, women were in charge of all things to do with food, and used many of the same methods the Coast Salish women used to cook and preserve, including making and using woven watertight cedar baskets. By her time, Haida and Tlingit had adopted potatoes from the Europeans and women grew them on small plots as they did in Coast Salish territory, but agriculture contributed a very small part of food production.

As a girl, Mrs. Pickett's activities were much like those of Coast Salish girls if her family was in Alaska or if they continued their customs at Semiahmoo. She learned what she would need to know as a wife and mother, as well as basket-weaving and garment construction and decoration. She had taboos to follow, especially at puberty, that her people believed could affect future events in her life or that of the group. Children listened to stories around the central fire, highlighted by the intricate carved and painted masks whose moving parts both frightened and delighted. In the summer, wealthy families held celebratory potlatches and gave away goods collected for years. Like Coast Salish custom, couples sealed their arranged marriages with an exchange of goods and services.

If Mrs. Pickett did indeed come from the Kaigani Haida on Prince of Wales Island, an early traveler noted that they were known for their "intelligence and good-will." Others noted the beauty and strength of the women there. After Russian settlement, many Southeast Alaska indigenous women married the newcomers, and labrets (piercings of the lower lip) went out of fashion. Intermarriage would not have been unfamiliar to the teenager or her parents at Semiahmoo.[11]

The young woman's future husband arrived at the Sehome Mine dock in August 1856. Captain George Pickett had a legendary paternal family history that included warfare, like hers did. However, he also had an entirely different maternal family history that has been clearly ignored by historians as a contributor to his dominant emotional makeup.

George Edward Pickett

The Huguenot (French Protestant) Pickett patriarch fled to England in 1586. His son didn't find England to his liking and sailed for the Virginia tobacco colony thirty-nine years later. Instantly, the Picketts became a "First Family of Virginia," although they never reached the heights of those with land-based wealth. It was William, George Edward Pickett's great-grandfather, whose family earned the moniker "The Fighting Picketts of Fauquier County" when thirteen members fought in the Revolutionary War. They included a young drummer boy, the first George.[12]

In adulthood, the drummer became known as "The Colonel." A Richmond lawyer and businessman, he built the Pickett fortune, starting with a rich wife. Pickett, Pollard & Johnston's varied business included wholesaling Thomas Jefferson's tobacco. When he bought "Turkey Island Plantation," he established closer ties with the great colonial families of the James River estates and took another social step up.[13]

Historians focused on the Picketts' fabled military heritage as the central factor in future captain and General George Edward Pickett's personality. They assumed that his love of music, acting, and nonconformist dress were simply rebellion. Just as likely it was the influence of his maternal grandmother Elizabeth McCaw Johnston's family. The

McCaw men became doctors for generations until they were the most prominent medical family in Richmond.[14]

Richmond's infamous theater fire tragedy on the day after Christmas in 1811 enshrined George E. Pickett's maternal family in city history. His great-uncle Dr. James D. McCaw, trapped upstairs in the inferno, threw a dozen women, trapped by their full skirts and a collapsed staircase, out a window into the arms of an enslaved blacksmith, Gilbert Hunt. McCaw jumped as the flames exploded and was permanently disabled when he struck the brick street. The final toll of seventy-two dead, including the governor, shook the nation. From that day forward, McCaw and Hunt have been two of Richmond's most acclaimed heroes. It was an example of selfless bravery and service that was not lost on George as he grew up in Richmond.[15]

George's mother Mary Johnston was the daughter of Colonel Pickett's business partner and Elizabeth McCaw. Mary wed Robert Pickett after he inherited Turkey Island, but they never achieved the prosperity of his father and never owned their own home in town. George's Grandmother Pickett's large brick home on "Quality Row," where Supreme Court Chief Justice John Marshall and the lieutenant governor were neighbors, provided a base for family business and social engagements.[16]

The birth of the future Confederate general on January 16, 1825, was followed by his parents' loss of six infants. Siblings Virginia and Charles were eight and fifteen years younger than their brother. The surviving three remained close the rest of their lives.[17]

George's youth had one similarity to that of his future Pacific Northwest wife: the seasons organized his life. He spent summers at Turkey Island where the city boy turned into a country boy, though one pampered by the family slaves. There were picnics, dances, weddings, and dinners with the James River families. Formal Richmond was a different world, where the Picketts paid more attention to theater and music, and George loved singing and dancing. Culturally a very Southern place, both beautiful and seamy, Richmond was also intimately tied to the North by its commerce. Slaves being sold at market, country folk in town to shop, and visiting Yankees made Richmond a social and economic intersection that exposed George to diverse ideas.[18]

With the competing influences of the McCaw-Johnston medicine-arts family culture and the Pickett military-business one, young George's personality grew increasingly complex. According to biographer Leslie Gordon, he grew into a talkative, boisterous young man with a ready laugh and good voice, the kind of personality traits that would endear him to residents of Bellingham Bay. The Southern manhood traits admired and indulged by his family were entwined with a rebellious nature and lack of self-reliance, sometimes "indolence." However, the boy also charmed everyone he met.[19]

George's scholarly father Robert Pickett had neither a business nor military mind and unexpectedly chose for his son Richmond's first public school—the excellent Lancastrian School whose methods were based on those of an English Quaker. The other students were mostly poor children who paid no tuition. The city's elite children had tutors or went to small exclusive schools, but the Picketts paid tuition to expose George to a better school and children who lived very different lives.[20]

At college prep Richmond Academy, George excelled in art but not academics. He seemingly had no interest in learning to run a business or plantation.[21]

Robert inherited the family business during a serious economic depression, but he proved a poor businessman and an equally poor gentleman farmer. When another depression struck in 1837, the Johnston in-laws bailed Robert and Mary out of debt in order to keep Turkey Island in the family. However, they put her younger brother, new lawyer Andrew Johnston, in control of their finances. George's parents could no longer afford his school and he left.[22]

At fifteen his lovable, undisciplined personality had not changed, so his parents sent him to study law with Andrew, who had moved to "frontier" Quincy, Illinois. George had to find an acceptable career to keep his social status and everyone hoped that his uncle's mentoring would work. Within two years of his own arrival, Andrew was town treasurer and had founded the *Quincy Whig* newspaper with its instant political influence. Andrew was often erroneously called Abraham Lincoln's law partner, leading to Lincoln getting George into West Point, but it was not true. Andrew did become friends with Lincoln, however, and was the first to publish his poems.[23]

Once in Illinois, George spent considerable time hunting, riding, and acting in a local play, and little time studying. He seemed unable to absorb how uncertain his future was. Frequent lectures via family letters had little effect on the teenager's efforts or ambition.[24]

To elite Southerners the law, medicine, and the military were the only acceptable professions. Since George made no progress toward a law career and was academically unsuited for medicine, his father turned to West Point. The academy accepted 93 percent of recommended applicants who passed the easy exams, and turned out self-reliant and disciplined men. Andrew Johnston worked his connections with former Lincoln partner Congressman John T. Stuart who agreed to nominate George. He entered West Point and found himself living four to a small room, fetching his own well water, and occasionally cooking. It was hardly the lifestyle to which he was accustomed.[25]

George found an identity and disciplined structure to balance his personality. He graduated last in the class of 1846, but half of those who entered with him never graduated at all. He was not physically imposing and his disdain for regulation appearance was odd, but his winning personality still prevailed. Sent straight to the Mexican War, he earned honors for heroism, strengthened bonds forged at West Point, and served under senior officers who might help him advance later. Training had largely (though not completely) transformed the recklessness and impulsivity that so exasperated his parents into courage and fearlessness that echoed both sides of his family.[26]

After the war, George's regiment moved to miserable frontier duty at Fort Gates on the Leon River in central Texas in the desolate Southwest. They guarded passing emigrants, gold miners, and far-flung settlers against the indigenous tribes who fought guerilla-style to protect their families and ignored standard military tactics. Miserable weather and boredom reigned. Fort Gates was said to be the army's worst assignment.[27]

When the war hero went home on leave, he courted Sally Harrison Steward Minge, member of a far more well-connected Virginia family than his. Her grandmother was both President William Henry Harrison's sister and a governor's daughter. Her father and grandfathers were Richmond medical colleagues of the McCaws. George had no doubt known Sally for a long time, though she was five years younger, because her aunt was his uncle's wife. James River plantation parents encouraged courtships between their offspring to keep the land within a small group of elite people. Elite Pacific Northwest indigenous families were similarly focused on economic alliances when their children married.[28]

In December 1850, George left Fort Gates for a wedding rendezvous with sweet-faced, dark-haired Sally at her sister's plantation near Franklin, Louisiana. Sally soon found herself pregnant. They left for Texas early enough to spare her the horrendous experience of traveling far in an army wagon in late pregnancy. The primitive conditions at the isolated fort when the twenty-two-year-old went into labor meant that she had only other wives and an army "sawbones" to help. George had already witnessed his mother losing six infants. On November 13, Sally and their baby died in childbirth.[29]

George paid a tragic price for taking his bride to Texas so they could be together. He escorted the alcohol-preserved bodies in a lead-lined casket on a months-long trip home and buried them in Richmond. He was inconsolable.[30]

For the next three years, George and his unit moved from one desolate Texas fort to another. He wrote to his family of continued depression and pain. Without his knowledge, in January 1854 his father, armed with introduction letters, asked Secretary of War Jefferson Davis to place his son in the new Ninth Infantry. After Robert Pickett's second plea and more recommendations, Davis appointed George to his first command. He would join other Mexican War veterans in Washington Territory's lush environment with friendly residents. It was a new beginning far from the heartache pursuing him across Texas.[31]

After five months of Treaty War duty at Fort Steilacoom, Captain Pickett and his men landed at Bellingham Bay, charged with building a fort to protect local settlers, the Lummi, and other nearby villages from the Northern raiders. Perhaps even more important, they were to guard Sehome Mine, the only American coaling station north of San Francisco. It was only forty years after the War of 1812 and there was also an unresolved border in the San Juans. Americans were not yet confident that the nation would remain friends with Britain, whose

Nanaimo, British Columbia, coal mine was the only other fuel source for the navy in the northern Pacific.[32]

When Company D arrived on August 21, Pickett saw scattered cabins, no streets, and only the mine's saloon and store for businesses. Stumps and snags and gigantic evergreens surrounded and rose above them. No "town," but still better than Texas. The people's pleas for help had finally been answered and they joyously greeted the bluecoats who instantly became the most popular people on the bay. Dr. Robert Orr Craig brought the first medical presence and the company laundresses increased the miniscule Euro-American female population. Mine manager Edmund (E. C.) Fitzhugh was probably more thrilled than anyone because he now had a fellow member of the Virginia aristocracy available with whom he could gamble, smoke, talk about old times in "Virginny," and enjoy a brandy.[33]

After the enthusiastic welcome, Pickett got off to a rocky start with the settlers when the topographical engineer Lt. George H. Mendell picked a prairie for the fort site. It hovered above the bay three miles north of Whatcom and had a twenty-mile view. However, it was the popular midwife Maria Roberts' land claim and she refused to budge when Pickett declared it government property. Seven months pregnant, she retreated under protest to a temporary cabin on her damp beach. After she and her husband Charles hired a lawyer to fight the seizure, Pickett started an effort to get them compensated for their loss.[34]

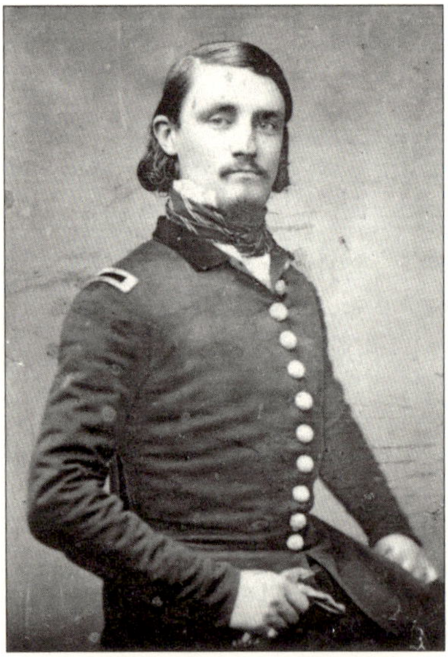

Captain George Edward Pickett, U.S. Army 9th Regiment at the time of his service in Washington Territory. Note his continuing habit of not wearing a completely official uniform. *#1994.46.1. Whatcom Museum, Bellingham, WA.*

Pickett's willingness to seek justice for the Roberts family and his "demeanor and numerous acts of gratuitous kindness" won over the settlers. He did drink too much, but so did most, if not all, of the men. Pickett hired Fitzhugh's Samish-S'Klallam brothers-in-law and Lummi leader Tsi'lixw's teenage son Henry Kwina as runners, which forged bonds with both indigenous families.[35]

While the soldiers built the fort, the usual grumbles and desertions began, as well as a burglary of the post sutler's house by two of his men. Officer trouble started after a lieutenant fresh from West Point arrived to replace Lt. Hugh Fleming. An Ohio Yankee, James Forsyth didn't like Mississippian Robert H. Davis, who had no military experience but was appointed first lieutenant by his uncle, the Secretary of War Jefferson Davis. Despite these irritants, after a year the stockade and essential buildings (including green-shuttered officers' quarters) were done and the garden planted. Russell Peabody had also built a "town home" on his own land claim for Pickett's use to tie the "genial" commander closely to the settlement.[36]

Captain and Mrs. Pickett

The young Haida woman who became Mrs. Pickett met her future husband twenty miles north of the fort at Semiahmoo sometime in his first seven months of command, unless her family had traveled to Whatcom. George may have been hunting, or scouting for the future headquarters of the U.S. Boundary Survey Commission and its army escort. The large principal Semiahmah village and burial ground had always been on the large spit that separated what became known as Drayton Harbor from Semiahmoo Bay. After decimating epidemics and raids, about 250 people, remnants of the smaller *Snokomish* and the Semiahmah, had consolidated in three longhouses on the banks of a small river mouth. Defensive forts were nearby. The Northerner HBC families lived not far away, from where ten Haida men had been recruited for the local militia as mercenaries.[37]

George Pickett received notice of his father's death a few months after his arrival. His grief and lonely observation of so many others living in the warmth of cross-cultural families may have led the thirty-one-year-old widower to notice the attractive teenager. Said to be a leader's daughter, like Sally Minge she was dark haired and dark eyed. One Boundary Survey officer at Camp Semiahmoo later noted that the Haida women were all "very good-looking [with] fine features."[38]

The pretty teenager presented another attraction that may have carried weight. She was from the region that produced the seasonal raiders. It would be hard for Pickett not to see an alliance with her Northern family strategically. Any army officer in the Puget Sound region that married has been found to have wed a leader-class woman. Pickett's word as an in-law might carry more weight in case of trouble and help preserve the safety of the settlers.

Pickett had been to dinner at the Victoria, British Columbia, home of Governor Sir James Douglas, his half-Cree wife Lady Amelia, and their entrancing daughters, all of whom spoke the French Pickett enjoyed. The Virginian was probably surprised when he first arrived in the Northwest to see prominent men with non-white wives, but soon adapted to the new society. The "custom of the country" couples he met in Victoria and at Bellingham Bay had carried interracial relationships into normalcy and respectability, particularly if the wife was of her own people's upper class, and even if the tribal custom marriage did not have "paper" legality. Officers at Fort Steilacoom and other posts had married indigenous women by tribal custom, including future-general Phil Sheridan's union with a Grande Ronde tribal chief's daughter. Lt. August Kautz married an equally important Nisqually woman. Pickett could not avoid noticing that companionship was easily available only with the young indigenous women. The community had no eligible Euro-American women.[39]

George Pickett was not like many elite southern men with secret liaisons in conflict with their public moral code. He was an emotional, sentimental, and lonely man who had lost a young wife and baby. Any elite indigenous woman who would match Pickett's status was chaperoned until marriage and would meet his ingrained southern standard for virtue. His wife-to-be may have shared Christianity with Pickett also, since missionaries had been converting her people for decades. Witnesses said he wanted a legal marriage, and that Justice of the Peace Russell Peabody married them after the tribal custom gift exchange ceremony. However, in 1857 it was illegal for Washington Territory clergy or civil officials to officiate at an intermarriage, so Peabody would not have written the illegal ceremony down. Even if he had, county marriage records do not exist after early 1855 until 1869. It is clear that historian Lelah Edson's 1904 interview with William Walter convinced her that the pair had been legally married, and Jim Pickett told a friend that his father had "met a native woman and married her."[40]

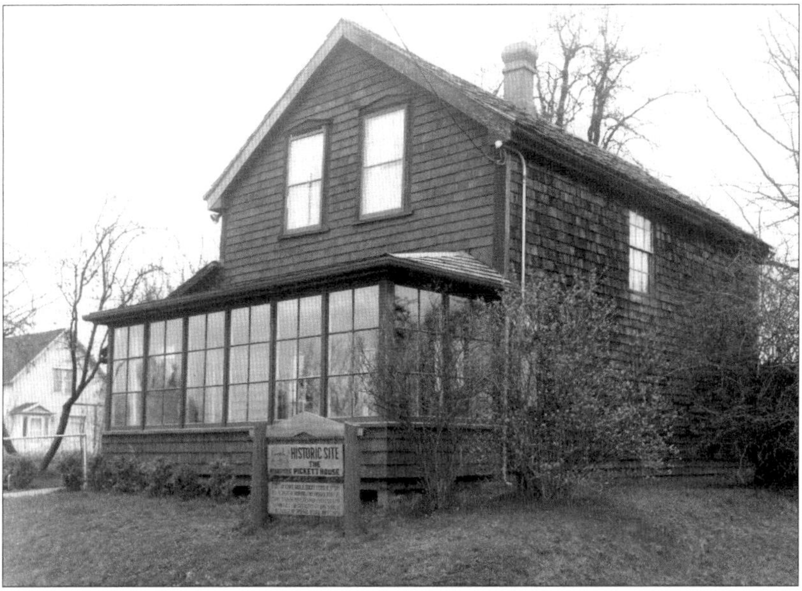

The home of Captain and Mrs. George Pickett, Bellingham, Washington. The home, Washington's oldest on its original foundation, is now a museum and national historic site. The house, surrounded by a low stockade, and with its own small blockhouse for sanctuary, was originally painted white. A subsequent owner added the glassed-in porch. Called the "Head House" at the time, the home for the fort commander was owned and built by Russell Peabody soon after Pickett arrived in 1856. *#1985.0070.000003. Whatcom Museum, Bellingham, WA.*

With Pickett's example before them, it wasn't long before his lieutenants married young indigenous women from the Swinomish village on a slough south of Bellingham Bay. A local account said that he required the men to also have a civil ceremony, but without written records, this cannot be verified. Nicholas Sheffer, the mine carpenter, saw the three couples and noted that all were "taking kindly to their surroundings." After the U.S. Boundary Commission arrived and built Camp Semiahmoo, several of their officers followed suit, including Smithsonian Institution naturalist and army surgeon Dr. Caleb Kennerly, whose Semiamah wife Cecelia was Mrs. Pickett's friend.[41]

Peabody cannily retained ownership of the Pickett house to sell after the captain moved on, but with the captain living there, Whatcom looked established, the military would pay more attention to what was happening in town, and George was available to socialize.

He rode his horse out to the fort daily. The whitewashed house built with Roeder Mill cedar boards came complete with paned windows, pocket doors, a dining room, a fireplace for heat and cooking, and a small barn in back for his horse. A protective stockade surrounding the house kept wandering pigs out and a small blockhouse sanctuary was ready in case of raider attack on the commander. Sometimes visiting military superiors or territorial officials climbed the ladder to sleep overnight under the roof. Considering that everyone else still lived in cabins and had been sleeping in the militia's blockhouse for months, it was the best home in town.[42]

Into her new hillside home, Mrs. Pickett brought her small red leather trunk bound in brass and painted with an elaborate white floral design. The artistically sophisticated and quality-conscious Haida wanted the finest British goods in trade for their sea otter pelts, and the exquisite green or red Chinese camphorwood tea chests from the HBC were very popular. It is her only personal possession to survive.[43]

Mrs. Pickett could stand at her door and look over the fence and across the deep green bay to Lummi Island and the sunsets beyond. Scattered on the slope before her were the town blockhouse, mill, the cabins, and Tsi'lixw's longhouse near the salmon creek. The only store was a mile away at Sehome. George probably thought little about leaving his wife home for extended periods or formal social occasions (as was the habit of army officers for many events), but she was not alone with Russell Peabody's Sumass wife nearby, the other Northern wives, and women at the longhouse. While George was gone, it is likely that other wives of both cultures taught her to keep house and cook for an American male who liked his bread and pie. She and George's first wife Sally were probably similar in their inexperience with caring for such a husband without servants.[44]

By April 1857, Mrs. Pickett was pregnant. That same month, the *Laich'wil'tach* raiders struck deep into the settlements one night and left behind threats to kill Captain Pickett (see chapter 1). From then on, her husband had family safety concerns as well as his military mission to consider while the raiders remained a problem.[45]

Even during Mrs. Pickett's late pregnancy, George continued to host evening and overnight guests at their home. Just weeks before the baby arrived, his friend Ben Stark (owner of half of Portland's townsite) came for a visit. In usual military custom at frontier forts, Mrs. Pickett did not cook the more elaborate meals held in Whatcom's only "dining room" for visiting politicos and superior officers. A fort cook would prepare the meal or George entertained at the fort.[46]

On Christmas Day with the baby imminent, Pickett held a commander's holiday feast (complemented by territorial politics) at the fort. His guests included Territorial Governor (and Virginian) Fayette McMullen, Territorial Secretary Charles Mason, and Territorial Surveyor General James Tilton. No women were reported to have attended. The weather was terrible with alternating snow, rain, and dangerous gales and it is unlikely that the very pregnant Mrs. Pickett went anywhere that day, though female friends may have looked in on her.[47]

During the days that followed, Pickett's attention swung between the birth he looked forward to—as much as feared it—and a squabble between settlers and the military after he jailed San Juan Island settler Edward French for harboring deserters on Christmas Eve. Acting Sheriff Robert H. Davis bailed French out of the guardhouse even though he had assaulted a soldier trying to apprehend the deserters. Davis had been Pickett's first lieutenant until he resigned in a rage when his commander stopped an "honor" duel between Davis and the mine manager Fitzhugh. It was a messy and awkward situation.[48]

George abandoned those concerns when his young wife gave birth on New Year's Eve. It is not difficult to imagine his fears that the terrible day when Sally and the baby died would be repeated. During his youth he had seen his mother's six infants die, too. Settlers knew that petite native wives of white men sometimes had unusually large babies that complicated the birth, and some died. Midwives Maria Roberts and/or Mary Tawes likely attended his wife, and perhaps he asked the fort's Dr. Craig to look in. Dr. Caleb Kennerly was one of the most highly trained surgeons in the nation, but he was twenty miles away over stormy waters at Camp Semiahmoo and did not come to town that day. Mrs. Pickett could also have demanded a native midwife.[49]

George named his dark-haired newborn son "James Tilton Pickett," after the territorial surveyor general, the boy's new godfather. The two men may have been friends since the Mexican War when both young lieutenants carried their regimental colors over the walls of Chapultepec. Tilton was raising an orphaned biracial slave child,

Charles Mitchell, in his home. He claimed that he planned to free him after he was educated and had a trade. Pickett may have thought that this situation gave Tilton special knowledge and advice to offer.[50]

Unlike at Fort Gates, birth conditions for little Jimmie Pickett's mother were good. She had nutritious food and other women who knew about childbirth and infants. However, the soulful-eyed little boy could not have been born at a more dangerous time for the odds of his survival and that of his mother.

After the 1857 salmon run failed and raiders stole other food supplies, a winter "starving time" threatened the independent Lummi and Samish people. E. C. Fitzhugh (now also the local Indian agent) convinced (or coerced) them to gather in the three longhouses at Whatcom and Sehome so he could distribute food and medicine. The flour and "white" foods supplied did not provide good nutrition or disease resistance. One of those longhouses was directly downhill from the Pickett home and full of vulnerable people.[51]

Influenza, part of a worldwide epidemic, had caused sporadic Coast Salish deaths at the bay since October, and by January it raged across Puget Sound. Fitzhugh was the son of a small town's highly-educated only doctor and likely had absorbed some rudimentary knowledge of illnesses and treatments. He thought influenza's final stage was causing the increasing number of local childhood deaths. Yet, some other symptoms made him think it was an odd type of whooping cough that was spreading to every child. Elders suffered more severe symptoms that included paralysis and dryness of the tongue so bad the patient could scarcely talk. Fitzhugh and his assistant visited and took medicine to the sick "continually." Craig and Kennerly, the army doctors, may have advised at least, if not helped. Despite the ration distribution and efforts at care, Fitzhugh was deeply concerned about the death toll to come as 1858 began.[52]

At the same time another unfamiliar disease appeared and spread across the Salish Sea that winter. Robert Fay, the Whidbey Island agent labeled it a fatal rheumatism variant which first paralyzed a patient's limbs. Victims suffered intensely from the pain, lingered long enough to become emaciated, and died. He knew of few who recovered.[53]

No reports mentioned any epidemic among the settlers, but large numbers of afflicted people lay sick in Tsi'lixw's longhouse down the hill from the Pickett house. Nursing mothers and infants were among the most vulnerable to winter-spring epidemics. Once active, either the whooping cough or the fatal rheumatism could kill within a few days.

A great mystery surrounds how and when Mrs. Pickett died because no one recorded her death date or exact cause, which led writers to use "at," "soon," or "shortly" after childbirth. Lelah Edson, the only one who talked to William Walter, the foster father, wrote that the new mother died "some months" after Jimmie's birth. That suggests that Walter told Edson she did not die a short time after childbirth as so many have written. One account said that Pickett sent for his "personal physician" who could not arrive in time to save the young mother. That could have been Dr. Craig, Dr. Kennerly, or Dr. John Kellogg on Whidbey Island. In March, Fitzhugh reported that twenty-seven people had died in the past seventy-five days. Captain Pickett's April 17 application for bereavement leave suggests that his wife died in late March or early April from one of the epidemics. Perhaps Jimmie's birth had left her among the most vulnerable.[54]

Several miles around the shoreline crescent from Whatcom jutted the low promontory settlers called "Dead Man's Point," the informal cemetery where tradition says Mrs. Pickett was buried. Mourners made cedar slab markers that split and deteriorated in a few years. Ferns and vines quickly obliterated individual graves.[55]

It is not difficult to imagine the sad flotilla of red and black Salish canoes and army whaleboats that carried mourners and the wooden casket, built by one of the local or army carpenters. Frontier funerals were always a community event that supported grieving families living far from the comfort of relatives. Pickett, officers, and soldiers from the fort, Lummi friends, perhaps Mrs. Pickett's family from Semiahmoo, and most of the settlement's people almost certainly gathered on the point. Once again, George said goodbye to a vibrant young wife dead after the birth of their child.

Mrs. Pickett is the first indigenous wife known to have been interred in the local "white" cemetery. It showed his respect and set an example. At that time, the burial location for native wives was controversial in some Puget Sound settlements. The Alaskan and Coast

Salish native preference for an upper-class person would be a tree burial, but settlers were never able to accept a custom so alien to their Christian belief in ground burial. And some simply had racial prejudices about who belonged in cemeteries. George Pickett gave his infant son's mother the best resting place he could. It looked back across the water at their hillside home, and from their doorway he could look across the bay at her place among the ferns.

What is certain is that Mrs. Pickett left behind a healthy infant son who did not succumb to any of the fatal diseases surrounding him in his first months of life. James Tilton Pickett was her legacy, destined to be a special child and living reminder of her. In his own life story rests his mother's legacy for the Pacific Northwest.

George and Jimmie

George needed to find suitable care for his infant at once. Almost universally, white fathers wanted their motherless biracial children raised within the world they considered more civilized and hygienic, although few excluded a relationship with the indigenous mother's family. That Pickett would send his only child to Semiahmoo to the boy's native grandparents for a long period (as the myth says) is improbable. More likely the baby stayed with a fort or town nursing mother. Whatever the circumstances, Jimmie was well cared for in the months after his mother died.[56]

George's mid-April request for bereavement leave was approved by his immediate superior Colonel Silas Casey, but confirmation from departmental headquarters did not arrive for a month. By then the fort commander had other concerns besides childcare. News of the Fraser River gold rush broke in California on March 9, and a trickle of miners become an invasion. Pickett had experience with Forty-niners on the trail in Texas and knew the problems they brought. By July Private William Royle wrote home that miners on the beach were "gambling, robbing and murdering one another all the time day and night." It would be a raucous summer, unsafe for women and children. Pickett planned his leave anyway, apparently confident in his baby's caregivers and the supervision of his godfather James Tilton who was in town frequently.[57]

George made another move before leaving for home. Army officers often found money-making ventures at frontier posts to increase their income, especially real estate. When Russell Peabody carved up his land claim into lots, Pickett spent one hundred dollars for one directly across the "street" from the slapdash court house uphill from his house. Peabody reserved the first lots for his half-Sumass children and Pickett seems to have followed his example. Although he sold two speculative parcels bought in partnership with Lt. George Mendell, he never sold the hillside one, and taxes were paid for decades.[58]

On June 1, 1858, George left Jimmie with caretakers, and they permanently vacated the house they had shared with the young mother. The widower left town for his long bereavement leave the same day aboard the steam sidewheeler *Pacific*, emptied of gold miners and mail.[59]

Pickett disembarked in New York City in July and checked into the Metropolitan Hotel before writing home that he would arrive soon. Dr. Blair Burwell, his sister Virginia (Jenny) Pickett's fiancé, heard the news from George's aunt and wrote to Jenny and her mother at the Rockbridge Baths, a summer retreat in the Blue Ridge Mountains for wealthy Richmond families. Jenny fretted that George had never come home to find the house empty of their father's presence. She asked Blair to keep her brother company, which he did. Unaware of George's terrible loss, the Pickett women lingered at the resort.[60]

In the single description discovered of George Pickett's demeanor after his wife's death, Burwell wrote Jenny that her brother "looks sometimes lonesome and weary." He told her it might be just the sudden lack of "excitement and bustle which he has been so long accustomed to in a new country" that was making him depressed, but George remained "generous and affectionate" to his friends. Either Burwell was under the impression that Fort Bellingham was a very exciting place, or he just wanted to give Jenny an acceptable explanation. In another letter, Burwell observed that George seemed to want the company of his still-absent mother and sister rather than go on any excursions.[61]

It seems that Pickett's depression was hard for his family to understand during the months he spent with them before he left in December, unable to stay for Christmas. After all, he had not been home since Sally and their baby died. Pickett probably did not tell his family that he had lost a second wife, at least during the early days of his visit. It was illegal in Virginia to marry across the color line, so to reveal it would be a serious decision for him. Even if the family considered his wife only a "mistress," it would not be considered proper news for the Southern ladies.

If Pickett thought he would spend more time with his toddler son after his return on January 14, 1859, it was not to be. George had but a few months to be a father. On June 15 San Juan Island American settler Lyman Cutlar shot a British settler's wandering pig that was eating his potatoes. No one had yet determined which nation owned the island, so American and British squatters shared the space with no clear civil authority in case of trouble. And when one man valued his potato crop and the other valued his pig, and there was a dead pig, that was trouble.[62]

Suddenly-patriotic American settlers sent Pickett a plea to keep the British from arresting Cutlar and evicting all of them. He landed six weeks after the pig's demise with sixty-four men and munitions, and from that point forward, his contradictory personality affected events. He posted rash and belligerent notices about the supremacy of American law, forcing the appalled British government to send in the world's most powerful navy. Over the coming months, a faceoff involving some two thousand men developed. Over a pig. Senior officers on both sides were furious.[63]

Two strong personality elements ruled George Pickett's actions during his time as the commander in an international conflict: bravery and belligerent impulsivity. Like other southerners, he was too quick to take personal offense over perceived disrespect when objectivity was needed. Superiors removed the irritating and undiplomatic Pickett from command as soon as another 9th Infantry company arrived. He spent most of the next four months on court martial duty, including an ugly case from his own unit when his first lieutenant threatened him. He served as Judge Advocate for a second court martial of Fort Townsend's "martinet" commander.[64]

After forces peacefully withdrew to opposite ends of the island, George had a second chance at command of Camp Pickett, but was ordered to take his company back to Fort Bellingham. He did not accompany his men's move back to Whatcom. He was absent on a very personal errand, first to Fort Vancouver and the dates suggest an additional destination.

The military context of George Pickett's fatherhood made it no longer feasible to keep his boy close. He might be called back to the island with no warning and Northern raiders occasionally still threatened. He sought a more suitable foster home for his son and he had contacts in James Tilton, the boy's godfather, and Hugh Goldsborough, George's informal banker and a settler of the Big Skookum Bay area (Hammersley Inlet) west of Olympia. George took his son to Aaron and Catherine Collins there between the end of November and the first days of December 1859. He had orders to resume command by December 5.[65]

In every decade of western expansion, frontier families were broken by illness, death, violence, desertion, and sometimes divorce. No social safety net existed other than the charity of others. Single parents often could not care for their children. Thus was born an informal system in which generous couples fostered children in need, and sometimes not-so-generous couples sought only unpaid farm help. In Washington Territory, the custom morphed into a way to care for children whose indigenous mothers died, or whose fathers wanted their offspring educated in a white home.[66]

When George took his baby to Collins Point, neighbor William Walter saw their arrival. He watched as the local steam scow *Capitol* dropped anchor in front of the beach. Crewmen lowered a rowboat, and two men (most likely Tilton and Pickett) climbed down. The crew lowered the red Chinese trunk, followed by the small bundle that was Jimmie. Two weeks later, George began to funnel his annual hundred dollar payments for his son's care through Tilton in Olympia (nearly $3,000 in 2018). It was a typical sum paid by other fathers.[67]

Within a few months superiors gave Pickett another chance to command San Juan Island's forces after firing his replacement. It affirmed the wisdom of getting Jimmie settled "permanently." While at Fort Bellingham, Pickett maintained communication with Catherine and Aaron Collins about his toddler's well-being through Tilton and a network of friends traveling up and down the Sound. On the island, fewer civilian channels existed to help him keep up correspondence with the equally isolated foster parents.[68]

The somnolent life at Camp Pickett would have been idyllic except for the encampment's barren surroundings, constant wind, and daily drills. However, the nation was moving toward civil war by small steps that

George read about in two-month-old newspapers. Letters from home included news of his mother's death. Again he grieved alone.[69]

During the winter of 1860–61, army officers all over the West read delayed news about the political conflict. Southern officers did not want to believe that Americans would ever support coercive action against their region, but they felt insulted by Lincoln's election. When British commander George Bazalgette rode over to visit Pickett on February 1, he found that the captain and Lt. James Forsyth had been arguing politics constantly. During his visit, the pair decided to call a truce and not discuss national politics again. They determined to focus on what they had in common: a lack of pay for six months and the uncertainty of what would become of them if the nation descended into civil war.[70]

The army had been George Pickett's home and identity for eighteen years. Former soldier and island settler Christopher Rosler frequently heard him declare that if the army left him on the West Coast he would not join the Confederacy, but he would not fight against Virginia. Pickett went to Fort Steilacoom for another court martial that month, which could have included time to visit Jimmie, though no account remains.[71]

Pickett wrote to his Uncle Andrew, now back in Richmond. He was trying to get leave, even as other Southern officers left. Andrew Johnston believed that George would absolutely come home if Virginia seceded (which it did on April 17) but George did not go immediately. He was loyal to the U.S. Army, but it was Jimmie who was his emotional anchor to the Northwest. He had already lost two wives and one baby. Could he really abandon his three-year-old as Lt. Forsyth was about to do to his daughter and Swinomish wife? Or was he to behave more like the Confederate president's nephew, Robert H. Davis, who elected to stay with Caroline and their son on their land claim for the time being.[72]

The Olympia paper published the weeks-old news that 15,000 federal troops were headed to Virginia where local militia was massing. George also found his cousin Henry Heth's name among the U.S. Army officers headed home.[73]

On June 18 a steamer brought an order telling George to close Camp Pickett and take his troops to San Francisco. Two days later an April order from President Lincoln arrived demanding that all officers take their oath of allegiance again, and that Captain Pickett report back when all had done so. To a man who had devoted his entire adult life to the army and served in isolated frontier posts where he lost both wives, the demand must have been devastating and infuriating. It cemented his decision to resign even before he heard that all West Coast officers would be recalled. Ultimately, of more than 1,100 U.S. Army officers, 270 would soon reach the same decision.[74]

Jimmie Pickett's father submitted his resignation on June 25, 1861. By then officers would resign, be dismissed, or declared absent without leave rather than being listed as deserters during the six-month grace period given them. He asked Hugh Goldsborough to release one hundred dollars of his savings to pay Catherine Collins for an additional year of Jimmie's care. After the resignation was accepted, he waited for his replacement company commander.[75]

When George left on July 25, he waved and yelled a final "Goodbye, Boys!" at former soldier David Tuck and his friends sitting on the beach. At Fort Steilacoom he turned over his weapons and the uniforms he had so proudly worn. He was lucky to depart with an official leave of absence to go home to "see about his parents' estate," though everyone knew it was a cover. He took a final ride to Olympia on his horse to leave support money with Tilton and talk about his son's future. George told Tilton that his sister Virginia would "look out" for his boy, should he die. Jenny must have known about her nephew by then, or else Pickett planned to tell her when he reached home. He trusted his sister with the future of his only child and heir, his second wife's living reminder.[76]

Pickett did not make a final visit to Jimmie at Collins Point, a twenty-mile canoe voyage from Olympia. Indicative of Pickett's feelings was the message relayed through Tilton that he felt badly and hoped to return "someday." George sent Jimmie some gifts, his well-worn brown leather Bible, and his commission. He wanted to leave something of himself behind in case he was killed in action. Pickett probably also feared that the six-month grace period given the resigning officers would be rescinded before he reached Virginia, and so he also left the incriminating leave papers behind. His Bible contained Jimmie's birthdate and a lock of the child's red-brown hair, probably cut at the time George sent him to the Collins home. Contrary to legend, Pickett never added an admonition that Jimmie should love his mother always.[77]

Many writers have suggested that Pickett didn't make a last visit to his son because he didn't care about his mixed-race child all that much. It is difficult to agree with this view because Pickett was a sentimental and emotional man who was losing his only child, perhaps forever. He had lost two wives, an infant, and both parents in nine years. More likely, he cared too much to face his precious son and say goodbye, and was (as Tilton said) truly "unable" to make the visit.

Tilton invented a story for Catherine Collins that the now ex-captain was going to travel overland and had only thirty days to get home without arrest as a combatant. The ruse would not put Catherine (and perhaps Tilton) in a position to be questioned about Pickett's movements by the authorities.[78]

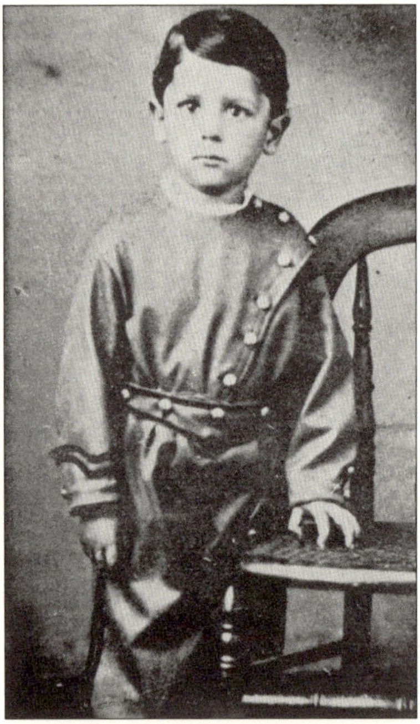

James ("Jimmie") Tilton Pickett, about age 4. Dressed in the reproduction army uniform made by many women for soldiers to carry. It was probably sewn from the nankeen fabric his godfather Territorial Surveyor General James Tilton brought to Jimmie's foster mother Catherine Collins. *#X.2879. Whatcom Museum, Bellingham, WA.*

In reality, George Pickett caught a steamer at Portland, easily able to afford the $250 first-class ticket with his unspent wages and real estate profits. When he transferred to the *Sonora* in San Francisco without the tell-tale leave papers, he took additional precautions against arrest. He traveled under his Whatcom friend Edward Eldridge's name. Eldridge probably knew about Pickett's plan to do so, may have even offered his name since it wasn't his birth name either. Pickett traveled with Sam Barron, formerly of the *Massachusetts* that patrolled Puget Sound under lease by the navy, whose father was now a Confederate commodore. Also on board was Pickett's former lieutenant, Hugh Fleming, who did not betray his fellow officer.[79]

Tilton forwarded the news of Pickett's safe departure to

Catherine Collins, with the promise that he would relay news about Jimmie back to George. James Tilton took seriously his duty to see that Catherine had what she needed to care for his godson, and he seems to have viewed her salary as just the starting point for paid expenses. Shortly after the future general left, Tilton sent her fifty dollars for Jimmie (almost certainly Pickett's money), along with shoes, pencils, children's books, and fabric for the growing boy. He didn't say that Pickett had shopped for any of it in Olympia, but he may have.[80]

The yards of nankeen, thread, and buttons that Tilton sent along are most interesting. Nankeen was a hard-wearing pale grayish-yellow cotton, not a good color choice for a little boy playing in the damp woods and mud, but it was ideal for sewing a miniature Confederate uniform. Many women across the South made similar uniforms for small boys. There was no standard Confederate uniform at the war's start, so Catherine put the buttons and military sleeve trim where she wanted them and depended on the fabric color to convey her intent. She took Jimmie to Olympia where a formal photograph was taken of the solemn little boy and sent to his father to carry into war.[81]

When Pickett landed in New York on September 17, a stranger slipped him money and a note written in Chinook Jargon from a former Northwest colleague. His identity is still unknown, though some think it was Rufus Ingalls who went on to be Quartermaster of the U.S. Army. Via a circuitous route home, Jimmie's father made his way toward a destiny that did not include the Pacific Northwest. Seventy-five years later, his grandson visited Bellingham and told the community: "My grandfather loved his men but he could not fight against his own people."[82]

General George Pickett

Brigadier General George Pickett was seriously wounded only a few miles from the Turkey Island plantation just four months after he left Whatcom. After recuperation, he became "Major General Pickett" with an all-Virginian division. His staff included many cousins, his brother Charles, and Jenny's husband, Dr. Blair Burwell. In Richmond another cousin, Dr. James B. McCaw, established the Confederacy's largest hospital where George's former parents-in-law, Dr. and Mrs. Minge, served throughout the war.[83]

The personal charm, impetuosity, bravery, and judgmental errors that led to Pickett's ups and downs in Mexico and Washington Territory came to full expression in the war. It was Pickett's rallying cry (echoing his youthful drama interest) which brought thousands into formation for the ill-fated "Pickett's Charge" at the Battle of Gettysburg: "Up men, and to your posts! Don't forget today that you are from Old Virginny!" Of 9,000 men in his division, he had only 896 combatants by the end of the day. All but one of his officers who walked into the field with the men were slaughtered. He lost all of his brigade commanders, dead, wounded, or captured.[84]

Pickett never seemed to recover his emotional balance after watching the Gettysburg carnage from horseback. He earned the derisive title "carpet knight" when he sank into near-obsession courting Sallie Ann Corbell before they married two months later. His Northwest reputation as a caring commander dissolved into that of a martinet and incompetent. It sank to its lowest point when he presided over the hanging of twenty-two home guards from the small town of Kinston, North Carolina, who had joined the Union army. In Washington Territory, the once admiring Steilacoom newspaper editor called him an "incarnate fiend" who deserved to be hung.[85]

A fellow officer soon described Pickett as "an old and broken man." As the war came to an end, General Pickett, his Sehome friend and now-Captain Fitzhugh nursing a head wound, and his division's remaining hundred men walked toward Appomattox Courthouse where his former Northwest comrades Rufus Ingalls, James Forsyth, and the Union army waited.[86]

The transition from combatant to civilian was sudden and final. The former general and his family men, dressed in their last dirty uniforms, turned their horses toward Richmond. Jimmie's photograph was probably still in George's pocket.[87]

Before Tilton moved to Georgia after the war, he asked Aaron Collins for a letter from seven-year-old Jimmie to his father. He didn't mention that it might help Pickett's depression when they visited. Through Tilton, Pickett had managed all through the war years to make the annual payments to Catherine and inquire after his son, apparently working his personal connections to the Northwest.[88]

Tilton told Collins that he planned to advise Pickett to leave Jimmie with them "always." Pickett was penniless with a new family to support. The best solution for everyone was to allow Catherine and Aaron to become Jimmie's permanent parents. Payments for Jimmie's care ceased that month, but his foster parents made no attempt to sever the father-son ties. Though the boy was not yet eight, Catherine ensured that he continued to recognize his father and stepmother's roles in his life. George Pickett never quit writing to his son.[89]

The former general and accused war criminal received amnesty with the other Confederates on Christmas 1868 and resumed civilian life with Sallie, free from the threat of prosecution for the Kinston hangings. The Pickett brothers tried to farm Turkey Island's rich bottomland, but had no money for labor, implements, or even subsistence, and the big house was in ashes. By then, he was obsessed with the health of his wife and new baby, as he wrote to Ben Stark in Portland. It was the almost inevitable result of his many losses. He turned down unacceptable job offers, including one from pre-Civil War army acquaintance, President Ulysses Grant. He went to work supervising insurance agents in three states, but found trying to sell insurance to equally penniless former Confederates demoralizing. David, his firstborn with Sallie, died in 1873, a tragic pattern repeated.[90]

In Norfolk, Virginia, on business in July 1875, suddenly he lay dying in the local Catholic hospital of acute hepatitis. After daily updates, the local paper reported his death on July 30, with the headline "A Brave and Noble Virginian Gone." His funeral was filled with all the pomp, circumstance, and procession marchers any hero could have wanted.[91]

After post-war tempers cooled, generations of Washingtonians renewed the affection for George Pickett, based on his life in the Northwest. There aren't many monuments to the Confederate hero of Gettysburg in the East or South, but his name lives on in Washington State: a national park plaque, Mount Pickett on Orcas Island, and in Bellingham, a building and the bridge that became controversial in 2017. The home on the hillside overlooking the bay that he and Mrs. Pickett shared is Washington's oldest building on its original foundation and by extension, Bellingham's oldest structure.[92]

James Tilton never wavered in his godfather commitment, even though he no longer lived in the Northwest. Three months after Pickett's death, he reminisced in a letter to his teenaged godson. He told Jimmie how much his father had loved him and that they had talked a long time about him during their last visit. Pickett had told Tilton of his hope that he could someday bring his first son east for school if he could accumulate enough money. It is pure speculation whether or not the sentimental man George Pickett, with a new family, ever truly wanted the boy to live with them. Or was realistic about what Jimmie's life would be in Virginia. He and Tilton both knew that the biracial boy would find no place in Virginia society, or even in a home with Sallie and her children. Truth or not, the words comforted the boy. Jimmie and Sallie Ann began a correspondence after Tilton told him to write to his stepmother about himself.[93]

Catherine and Aaron Collins

When George Pickett chose Catherine Collins to mother his little boy, a woman came into Jimmie's life who became his most significant influence until his death. She and Aaron have usually been labeled only "*a* Mr. and Mrs. Collins," but their individual characters and histories, combined with the genes of his parents, molded the growing boy.

As colonial elite as Pickett's family was in Virginia, so was Catherine Millard's colonial Quaker family of Pennsylvania. When "The Fighting Picketts of Fauquier County" went to war, it was the Millard men who made their guns at the Hopewell Furnace foundry.[94]

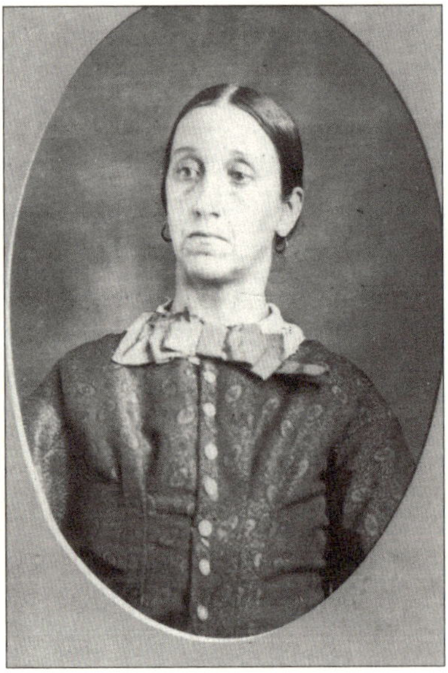

Catherine Millard Collins Walter. *Courtesy of the Pickett House Museum, Bellingham, WA.*

Three years younger than George Pickett, Catherine was never pretty, having a prominent port wine birthmark under her protruding brown eyes, but her neck was long and her hair dark and glossy. Her best features were a generous heart and Quaker simplicity in her personal tastes. She was a trained midwife and nurse, a profession she practiced until her death.[95]

Aaron (sometimes erroneously called Isaac) Collins' parents were civic-minded Baptist abolitionists who fled Kentucky's slavery with ten children for a new Quaker town in Indiana. The men were shortly elected to office and Aaron's sister turned her home into a stop on the Underground Railroad. Though his grandfather had died in an Indian attack, Aaron's values apparently overcame animosity toward indigenous people.[96]

Catherine, age twenty, met and married Aaron, thirty-eight, after she migrated to Indiana with an older sibling who needed help with child care. She kept house for his three adult brothers, and began to care for children in need. No record exists of she and Aaron ever having children or perhaps any who lived.[97]

Ads touting Washington Territory opened new opportunities for a second son who inherited nothing when his father died, and the couple arrived on July 1, 1853. Catherine's valuable midwifery and nursing skills would provide cash until their land claim on Big Skookum Bay produced income. They joined a vanguard group composed of Territorial Indian Agent Michael Simmons's family, David Shelton's logging operation, and William Walter, a bachelor orchardist. All of them were on *Sa'he'wamish* land not yet released by treaty, the same white settlement pattern seen before.[98]

The couple quickly established themselves as pivotal settlers on the south Sound inlets. When the Treaty War started two years after they arrived, Aaron enlisted in the militia, acted as interpreter, and carried mail to isolated cabins. His unit built Fort Skookum on Collins Point where families slept in two log cabins for months, though the conflict never reached them. This may have been the time they first met James Tilton who served as Governor Stevens' adjutant.[99]

Jimmie's future home was a place of unsurpassed beauty. Big Skookum Bay was a nine-mile long, quarter mile-wide "fish hook," rich with steelhead and salmon that fed on annual smelt runs. Oysters and clams revealed their presence on the ebb tide, and deer, cougars, bears, and bobcats roamed the moss-laden woods. The Collins family horizon featured Mount Rainier's white immensity to the east and the Olympic Mountains to the west.[100]

When Catherine and Aaron moved to the inlet, he drolly observed that the scattered settlers were "the worst fool set of people." By the time Jimmie arrived six years later, a community had formed within the Sa'he'wamish territory, knit together by their cedar canoes. Charles Graham's sawmill sat across the inlet's mouth from Collins Point at

"Arcadia." William Walter taught the children, Aaron Collins handled the mail, and generous "Big Mike" Simmons' gristmill up the inlet was the news center and community hall. His brother and several others married native women, and built a mixed community similar to Bellingham Bay. When George Pickett chose the Collins home for his son, he already knew that Jimmie would not be an isolated biracial child, though later writers portrayed him that way.[101]

Jimmie

Jimmie thrived with Catherine, who observers said could not have loved her boy more if he had been her own. By the time he was eleven, he had a younger biracial foster sister, Emmaline Smith, who lived with the family for at least two years and possibly much longer. Catherine took into her family a number of children over the years.[102]

The gifted Jimmie learned Catherine's lessons quickly and built his vocabulary by asking about words in the newspapers that covered walls. Tilton's used atlas opened his world. Most startling was his early artistic talent that set him apart from other children, the gift of his Haida mother. To make up for a spotty supply of pencils and paper, the child used charcoal to draw birds and other pictures on the side of the barn and other farm buildings. People stopped by just to see his art.[103]

In early December 1869, Aaron's leg turned gangrenous from an unrecorded cause. Former Sehome Mine manager (and Territorial Justice) E. C. Fitzhugh's mixed-blood daughter Julianne lived on the next inlet with the John Campbells and arrived to provide constant care. The only father Jimmie Pickett knew died in mid-January. The sensitive twelve-year-old witnessed the formalities of Aaron's two-day "laying out" and burial on Collins Point.[104]

When a family farmer like Aaron died, it put a heavy burden on the survivors if they were to keep their land, but Catherine and the children were not alone for long. The Campbells sent help until Aaron's brother William arrived from Indiana. Their neighbor William Walter, one land claim up the inlet, started to court Catherine. Loneliness and friendship turned to a proposal, and the couple married August 8 the same year. Catherine and the children moved to Walter's home, where Jimmie Pickett came under the influence of a third father figure as he entered adolescence. Catherine's love remained his constant.[105]

William Walter

Pennsylvanian orchardist William Walter served in the militia with Aaron Collins and helped guard the families sheltering on the Collins claim. He taught the inlet's few children in an unused cabin at the Simmons mill and settlers elected him the county's first school superintendent, not a surprise since his was the only school. He became regionally well-known for his lengthy letters to the Olympia paper about agricultural and scientific matters. By 1859 he was a staunch Republican while nearly every other man in Washington was still a Democrat, and when he ran for county assessor, he won only his own vote.[106]

When the Civil War began, men did not rush to join Washington's volunteer infantry regiment. They were trying to make their fortunes, and were emotionally distant from the conflict except as it affected their own families. Not so William Walter at age thirty-seven. His former militia captain, A. W. Swindal, told a territorial politico that he had heard "one abolitionist say that he would volunteer his services for Uncle Abe. His name is Sir William Walter. The governor had better send him a commission as there is no mode prescribed by law for forming a company of one." The Washington regiment never left home, so ignoring the jibes, Walter made his way to Indiana and became the only Mason County man to fight in the Civil War. When he returned with his teenaged nephew Calvin Saeger to the more Republican-friendly atmosphere, voters elected him county commissioner. William Walter became Jimmie's major male influence for the rest of his life.[107]

Jim Pickett

By age twelve, Jimmie was "a boy of more than ordinary attainments generally, with a strong predilection for painting and drawing," according to a friend who knew him then. William wanted him to learn more practical skills and help with the chores, but visions of pictures Jimmie wanted to paint always distracted him. Catherine unwaveringly supported his talent, and Walter was proud of the boy he treated as his son, despite the disdain he still felt for George Pickett.[108]

The young artist drew on smooth split-cedar boards with charcoal, and continued to draw on buildings. He started to simmer and soak berry juices and leaves to make usable inks for his bird paintings. He built a crude desk so he could paint in his room, but never invited the curious little son of Calvin Saeger to visit his retreat, so Allie watched silently whenever Jimmie painted outside. Whole families visited the Walter home to marvel at the untrained artist's natural skill. They probably didn't know about his mother's artistic culture or the artistic bent of his military father. Jimmie grew tall and fair-skinned with dark brown eyes and with his "good and kind disposition," was idolized by local children.[109]

When Jimmie was sixteen, settlers built Kamilche School at Mary and John Campbell's farm an inlet away. The Walters visited but did not send Jimmie to the school, perhaps because William was teaching the boy. The next year the teacher, O. F. Williams, rented the old Collins house. Jimmie still didn't attend the school, but became good friends with the teacher's son Dea. When Williams agreed to stay on for an extra term that winter, Jimmie attended, boarding with the Campbells. He doesn't appear to have been required to do many chores, as the Fitzhugh children did when they lived there. Perhaps the family also supported Jimmie's desire to paint and draw in his spare hours. The Walters may have paid a sufficient boarding fee that he could avoid most chores.[110]

George Pickett died the next summer, but no one recorded how that and Tilton's sympathy letter affected the son who dreamed of a reunion with his illustrious father. However, it was clear to everyone that the intellectual teenager was in need of more and better education. Catherine and William considered how they could help their boy make the best of his talents.

Olympia's newly-opened Union Academy promised to provide regional students "the best possible advantages for education in all branches preparatory to a university course." Possibly with a little cash from Tilton or a tuition break from the trustees, Catherine and William found a way to send Jim there for its first three years. He joined about thirty students, some from Olympia's finest families, plus others like Quimuth's grandsons, the children of Lt. August Kautz, and the murdered Nisqually leader's daughter Kitty.[111]

Catherine and William placed Jim with Calvin and Pamela Hale. The couple possessed an unusual set of experiences that made them ideal people to guide him into his future. Calvin Hale served on the Territorial University's first Board of Regents, had been a legislator and held other civic offices.[112]

Pamela Hale's influence on Jim over three years was perhaps the major source of his growing confidence and belief in his artistic talent. Pamela was the principal of Olympia's public school, a suffragette, and a Unitarian minister. One teacher said of her: "what she did for young people struggling to get an education is beyond my power to tell."[113]

Jim was nineteen when Union Academy opened in 1876 and included him. Either the school had no age limits because of the spotty access to rural education or they saw him as a special case. He took full advantage of the classes while using his off-school hours for chores, art, and hijinks with the two girls also living with the Hales. His diary reflected his zeal: "Sat up till past midnight preparing for tomorrow. I am determined to keep my standing high and as near perfect as possible." He scolded himself when his grades fell short and congratulated himself when they went well. By the second year, his grades were nearly perfect with a focus so tight that when he went home for Christmas, he soon confided to his diary how tired he was of vacation.[114]

Jim's penmanship books illustrate his drive for artistic perfection with rows and rows of elegant letters, numbers, and signature flourishes. Two practice sentences clearly defined his goals: "To excel in art we should excel in patience," and "It is not how much we do, but how well." By year three, he taught art to the primary classes after school. Even when she was elderly, Flora Parsons still fondly remembered her teacher and the butterfly she drew in his class.[115]

Jim spent considerable time walking around the territorial capital sketching. His concentration could blind him. Sitting on a rock and focused on Tumwater Falls one day, he failed to notice the rising tide and had to wade to shore. The incident was so typical that his friends used it to describe his personality.[116]

During that time he used charcoal for portraits based on photographs of Catherine and William, as well as his father in his Civil War general's uniform. It is the only portrait of his father Jim is known to have done.[117]

Jim's reputation spread beyond his school to the Olympia community. He visited A. L. Callow's home several times, and the family thought "it was quite an honor to entertain him."[118]

The adult son of the general and his indigenous wife yearned for real art training. He had corresponded regularly with Pickett's widow who saw herself as his appropriate life guide. He sent Sallie (now calling herself "LaSalle") some sketches with a feeler for art school funds. She vaguely offered to help him get some art lessons, but he should be satisfied with a local teacher, implying he shouldn't get above his station. LaSalle/Sallie wrote that she had shown the pictures to twelve-year-old George Jr. and told him "someone who was very dear to me had drawn them and whom he must love very much and that when he was older I would tell him all about the young artist whom I loved and whom he was to." She closed with an admonition that Jim must "write freely and fully on every subject to your devoted mother, Mrs. Pickett." Clearly, she had yet to inform teenaged George Jr. that he had a half-brother. The closing betrayed her conflicted feelings about just how far into her family she wanted her stepson to come.[119]

When Jim sent his New Year's Day 1878 letter, LaSalle's reply was typical of her manipulative mixture of criticism and support. She scolded him for not writing to thank her for photos she had sent of herself and her son. She added that she was proud of his penmanship award and would be sending him ten dollars for his Christmas gift. It was a substantial sum for the struggling widow and it may only have been a paper promise, something she made often.[120]

It is difficult to say how the image-conscious stepmother truly felt about Jimmie. Her letters to everyone reflect an overwhelming desire to be seen as a hero's gracious widow. The physical distance between the two made it easy for her to say anything without her sincerity being questioned. Catherine Collins Walter chose to believe that LaSalle was fond of her distant stepson.[121]

James Tilton Pickett, Artist

After Jim finished school, the farm boy followed his dream despite LaSalle/Sallie's lack of support, and William's wish that he work in the orchard. He started an oil painting of Captain J. G. Parker's *Messenger* from sketches made of the passing vessel. When he finished, he noted in his diary that he had worked a long time on his first major oil and his feelings about it were different from the anxiety he had felt about school work. "Am elated by my success with my painting of the Messenger. All colors work so much better than I supposed." He knew who he was in this world.[122]

Jim received his first media notice in April 1879, when the Olympia post office put the *Messenger* on display where every resident would see it. People marveled at the amazing work done by a "local" boy, beginning the regional ownership of the artist. The newspaper said: "It is, for an amateur who has never received any instruction in the art, a very creditable production, the sky and water—the most difficult objects in nature to faithfully portray on canvas—being especially well represented."[123]

After Jim raffled off the painting (his first professional art income), it made its way to San Francisco for exhibition at the Merchant's Exchange Building in early July. The *Alta* noted that it was "executed by a half-breed named Jimmy Pickett, aged 18 years, who never received a lesson in drawing or painting, and to do this work he made his own brushes out of hair that he plucked from a cougar's skin. It is a neat little picture, and our artists are invited to pass upon it." Jim was actually twenty-one, and he may or may not have ever made brushes from cougar hair. Seattle's paper reprinted the review under the title "A Local Artist." Now the entire Puget Sound region had taken ownership of Big Skookum Bay's prodigy.[124]

When the painting moved to San Francisco's annual Mechanics Institute Fair, Jim's work received a cash prize, a medal, and more glowing reviews. The fair drew huge crowds to its pavilions where they could experience fine art. The city's art lovers launched Jim's career in a few short weeks.[125]

The Seattle paper revisited the story a year later, after the *Messenger* went on permanent display at the Merchant's Exchange. This time the editor sent a reporter to visit Jim and see what all the fuss was about. The article referred to him as a school boy with "the making of a famous marine painter" and the "*unacknowledged* half-Indian son of the rebel General Pickett" (author's italics). The editor wrote that the "genuine enthusiasm" in San Francisco intensified when the history of "the neglected, uneducated boy painter was made known." Obviously, he never spoke to Catherine Walter, or he twisted facts to be more sensational, thus beginning the erroneous myths about Jim Pickett and his parents.[126]

When William and Catherine took a winter trip back to Pennsylvania, Jim stayed at the house with eight-year-old foster sister Alice Jones and the Wivells, new settlers living there temporarily. Eva Wivell later remembered Jim as "tall, quiet, very good-looking, and kind to shy little girls." With uninterrupted rainy hours to paint, Jim experimented in other mediums and worked on an oil portrait of the

Messenger's sister ship, the *North Pacific.* He portrayed it laboring to cross the Straits of Juan de Fuca in rough seas, and he grew in technique and emotional content.[127]

The Walters arrived home in the spring and were probably surprised to see Jim's expertise demonstrated in the nearly-completed large painting. Captain Parker immediately bought and hung the finished painting on board the *Messenger* (that ship's portrait would never return home from San Francisco). A Seattle newspaperman who saw it effused that the *North Pacific* was superior to the first and "would do credit to any collection or any artist on the coast." He suggested that some wealthy man might do a "noble deed" by loaning Pickett the helping hand his own father refused to extend to develop his genius into a world-wide name. Since George Pickett had been dead for three years, the article again suffered from the lack of consultation with Catherine.[128]

After a summer with friends in a logging camp, Jim moved to the Olympia home of the territory's first dentist and owner of a new photography studio. A. E. Woodard hoped that Jim would become his resident photographer, but the media's lack of color frustrated the artist's creativity and he was never really interested. He lived with the Woodards for two years, taking portraits and developing prints, and seems to have continued to teach art at Union Academy. He used the rest of his time to improve his skills, producing drawings, watercolors, and charcoal works. His small oil landscapes of Mount Olympus and Lake Cushman, and a first sketch of Mount Rainier probably date from those years. Stationery and art supply store owner T. C. Van Epps purchased (or was given) the Mount Rainier sketch, and later bought one of Jim's prize-winning paintings which became one of the family's "treasured possessions."[129]

It was time to strike out into a larger world, perhaps with Pamela Hale's urging. In Jim's case that was Portland, Oregon, the Northwest's largest city with 18,000 residents, a metropolis compared with Olympia's 1,300. He might have felt apprehensive about leaving those who had loved, supported, and mentored him, but his artistic confidence and vision of what could be drew him forward.[130]

Harvey Scott, longtime editor and part-owner of *The Oregonian*, lived as a boy near the Simmons mill on Big Skookum Bay where his family were residents of the colony. He also served in the militia with Aaron Collins and William Walter. He had probably known of Jim's talent for many years. Jim went to work for Scott who was modernizing the paper in 1882 and increasing its content beyond business and politics. He had started a content-heavy Sunday edition for three states, and it constantly demanded advertising and article illustrations, something with which Jim could help.[131]

Jim Pickett may not have known about Oregon's race laws that had produced a discriminatory port city culture. Fewer than six Native Americans lived in Portland. Artist James Tilton Pickett stood out. His roommate William Walker worked at a firm owned by the sons of Joseph Lane, Oregon's first territorial governor and former Copperhead vice-presidential candidate. Walker thought former Confederate Colonel John Lane would be pleased to meet General Pickett's son. "I presented James Pickett to him, but the Colonel was not enthusiastic, hardly looked up. Jim understood." Walker saw Jim as a man "without a blot on his character and much to industry, honesty, and genius." He resented the ill treatment Jim received from Lane and others in the city. Jim didn't mention it when he wrote to Catherine.[132]

The money won in San Francisco encouraged Jim's ambitions, though Walker didn't think his friend truly understood how important the prize was to his career. Jim started going out to the hills where he drew and painted the Cascade volcanoes, and his interest in landscapes bloomed. He again won prizes at the San Francisco Mechanics Fair where a new, block-long building and students' work from the new California School of Design (CSD) brought out larger crowds than ever. Jim sold enough work to open his own Portland studio while continuing his commercial work.[133]

The newspaper job enabled Jim to take professional art lessons, a major reason for his move to Portland. Two artists resided there who became the major names in Northwest landscape painting. James Everett Stuart attended the CSD in its first years, then moved to Portland because he was fascinated by the silvery light on Cascade peaks and misty environment. He became Jim's mentor and friend.[134]

Cleveland Rockwell's work shows the most affinity with Jim's developing style. A U.S. Coastal Survey cartographer and landscapist, he had exhibited his work in San Francisco alongside Jim's. He painted the Northwest's mountain peaks, understood varying sea conditions, and how light changed during the day. The precision Pickett was soon to be called upon to use probably came from Rockwell's influence.[135]

After two successful years at the *Oregonian*, A.G. Walling offered Jim a better-paying job sketching industries, farms, homes, and city buildings for a subscription history of southern Oregon. Walling first sent him to do a "birds-eye" view of Roseburg. He had never attempted the artistic technique by which he would precisely draw the town from an imaginary, overhead perspective, but Walling gave him all the time and support he needed to master the art form.[136]

Jim's engravings for the book showcased his expertise. The backgrounds were as precise and detailed as the structures he drew, and included individualized animals and people for scale. As his confidence grew, he realized that Walling took advantage of him. Paid $45 a month, he told his mother that no one else would have done the assignments for less than $75. He was indignant that the team had to buy new suits "to give the people the impression that we amount to a great deal, whether we do or not." He resented how the office bookkeeper shorted his expenses. Despite this, he contracted to do a bird's-eye view of Cheney, Washington, in the winter, in the snow. When he returned to Portland, he found that his reputation for both fine and commercial art had grown in his absence and he began to take on students as well as commissioned portraits.[137]

Jim finally went home for a summer visit. He took art work to show everyone, but also sketched some landscapes for Walling, and may have done some work for the Seattle newspaper. When he went to Mount Rainier to paint and sketch, Allie Saeger, still his young admirer, wanted to go along but artists are solitary beings and the boy was not invited. He "grieved for days."[138]

Back in Portland, Jim moved in with "just the pleasantest people," Margaret Jones and her family whom he had met in Roseburg. Her boarding house enabled him to work and not worry about his meals, laundry, or belongings. When he had time to paint, Jones assisted him, and her daughter gave him free music lessons. In return, Jim gave the kind and supportive woman art lessons. He made his home with the Jones family whenever he was in Portland until his death.[139]

Catherine Walter may have been dismayed when she read about her son's only irritant. A much older married female student fancied herself his patron, demanded his attention, and offered him loans and buggy rides. She invited him to her Eastern Oregon home where she would give him a horse, "and etc." Escaping his "nuisance" admirer, he and the book crew went back to southern Oregon for the winter. He joined a Roseburg lodge where men competed in dramatics and other entertainments. He wrote Catherine that his health was good, but his memory poor when it came to keeping track of his belongings which were "scattered all over the country."[140]

Portland went into a slump in the fall of 1884 and Jim had no portrait commissions or lithography work. He worried that Mrs. Jones, who had little money herself, would have to loan him enough to get through the winter. To make things worse, he had no savings because when work had been steady, he had spent any extra money on art lessons.[141]

It was a turning point.

Like many young people before and after him, Jim wrote to "Mamma" about his situation. His "awfully good" (but equally short of money) friends were urging him to find the funds to attend art school rather than hang around Portland unemployed. He quoted his mentor James Stuart: "A course at the Art School is something you must have before you are really an artist—and the sooner you take it the better." When Stuart said "Art School" for Jim, he meant the professional one in San Francisco. Jim added "Now that's just what I have been thinking myself."[142]

He made his case to his parents for a loan of all or part of the $300 it would take to study at the School of Design, a large sum for Jim or his family. He pledged to pay interest "when good times come again," which the art school would make possible. He offered the same interest rate the Walters' savings were earning and added that "it would be doing me lots of good…I am to be trusted am I not." He apologized for being unable to earn his own way and didn't want to sit idle when he might be learning. Lastly, he argued that there wasn't much more in Portland for him to learn.

William and Catherine sent their trustworthy son as much as they could of the money they had carefully saved. Jim promised to make the very best use of it and took a steamer for California on New Year's Day. Seasick all the way, he arrived in San Francisco on January 5, 1885, after a storm-tossed voyage. He moved in with a young book agent before classes started and promptly wrote Catherine that he had arrived "at last." Improbably, the farm boy from Mason County, son of an indigenous woman from an artistic culture and a famous general, now lived in a genuine metropolis where he could marvel at the electric lights, cable cars, and Domingo Ghirardelli's chocolate treats.[143]

Jim Pickett was almost certainly the first Washingtonian to attend a professional art school. At last, he would be surrounded by other artists as consumed by their talent as he.

The California School of Design opened in 1874 to train fine art painters, art teachers, and commercial artists held to professional standards. The rigorous curriculum was patterned after the best art schools in Europe and New York, and graduates came to be called "The California School" of painting.[144]

When Jim arrived, the CSD curriculum included elements not usually part of a young art school: art history, materials, rules of proportion, and technique, all required before a student moved to his/her own artistic vision. Founding director and instructor Virgil Williams, who had studied in Italy after teaching art at Harvard, was free with both criticism and praise for his forty students, mostly daughters of wealthy school supporters.[145]

With instructors Thomas Hill and Frederick Schaefer, both building national reputations, the school was adding classes in "life drawing" when Jim arrived, and Mrs. Williams would teach watercolor. It was the first school in either the United States or Europe to take students outside for *plein air* landscape classes. The school also owned 115 plaster casts of classical sculptures donated and purchased from France that made it unique in resources for study.[146]

And so, on January 7, 1885, James Tilton Pickett found himself in suit and tie climbing the stairs to his school above the city's public market. It was the fulfillment of all his dreams.

Mrs. Pickett's half-indigenous son from Big Skookum Bay entered a breathtaking environment. The stairs opened into a long, wide room. Beneath a huge skylight the walls were lined with dark wood cabinets from whose tops small busts looked down. Full-size reproductions of Venus de Milo, Apollo, and the Discus Thrower on their pedestals towered over students seated at easels.[147]

Jim was put to work drawing a foot.

He wrote to "Mamma" the next day, already frustrated. Williams would allow him to bypass engravings since he had experience, but he was told to spend an entire year drawing with black and white crayon (pastels) before studying painting. His course of study was to progress from feet through the body parts until he got to copy a whole body from the plaster statues. Only then would he draw live models, and finally, nature. That didn't fit with Jim's plan and he told Catherine he thought he could learn everything the instructors had to offer in half the time with hard work, "crowding and skipping." He had planned to get a night job but found nothing, so studied calligraphy at a free night school. He also realized that lithography was still the best way to support his fine art career. He wanted to be a "good workman" producing first class work, though he thought most people had no idea how much work and study it took to reach that standard.[148]

Less than five months after he enrolled, Jim quit art school and returned to Portland. Only after he was back in town did he tell his parents. A. G. Walling had again asked him to work for several months at a time when Jim had been unable to find summer work in San Francisco. His money depleted, though Catherine had sent more funds, Jim claimed that he was happy to go back to work and start repaying his parents.[149]

James Tilton Pickett did not tell his parents about the ill-fated meeting with his half-brother George Pickett Jr. The awkward and dispiriting introduction to his one remaining blood relative may have played a larger part in Jim's decision to abandon his art school dreams than his already advanced skills and need to make money did.[150]

Jim found three men waiting for him to join them in founding the Portland Art Club. At weekly meetings, they would support art in Oregon and each other. One was his mentor and friend, the landscapist and portraitist James Everett Stuart (grandson of famed George Washington portrait painter Gilbert Stuart). Edward Espey was younger than Jim and also a former School of Design student who was a landscapist and still life painter. The third new colleague was Grafton Tyler Brown, California's first African American professional artist who was, like Jim, an experienced lithographer and oil painter.

Jim went to work for Walling, and began preparations to exhibit his fine art works at the upcoming new Portland Mechanics Fair in October. His acclaimed portrait of the local steam launch *Mikado* signaled his return to marine art that built a wider Oregon audience. Jim now had an artist community who supported and understood him.[151]

Financial problems continued. Six months after completing months of work on the *History of Benton County*, the printer hadn't paid him. Others were slow to pay for commissioned works, including one man he called a "bilk who refused to pay for half the work." The problems forced him back into a photography studio, this time making enlargements for Frank Abell, Portland's top photographer. Under his tutelage, Jim saw photography's growing opportunities to support his fine art.[152]

When Jim wrote to Catherine in early 1886, Margaret Jones had been nursing him through a bad cold. His unhappiness at not going home for the holidays and his financial woes developed into a lengthy depression. Despite his "blues," he continued to work and turned to perfecting his use of pastels.[153]

The two maladies may have heralded the onset of tuberculosis, which Edward Espey was also fighting. Sunk in depression, Jim didn't write to his parents for months and rarely wanted to see his friends. He tried using an agent to find commissions because there was plenty of work to be had, but the competition among artists had grown stiff. Agents he hired were unreliable or incompetent and the portrait commissions he obtained were at rates too low to pay for his time.[154]

Jim's gloom lifted when T. E. Kane published his detailed portrait of Portland, viewed from across the river, in his new *Kane's Illustrated West*. He was so pleased with the public response that he gave Jim another assignment. In late fall, E. C. Smalley of *The Northwest Illustrated Monthly* sent Jim to sketch the "liveliest little town" of Spokane Falls, Washington, and the rowdy mines above Coeur d'Alene, Idaho. When freezing weather stalled his transportation, Jim walked forty-eight miles in two days to catch the railroad home. Smalley hired him again for some Puget Sound illustrations. Jim's finances recovered, even before Harvey Scott asked him to do illustrations of Portland for a January special feature in *The Oregonian*.[155]

With his new profits, Jim started to astutely buy and sell real estate. He converted his first purchase and the profits from a large painting of Spokane Falls into twelve promising lots near Green Lake in Seattle.[156]

He also pursued another piece of land, the Whatcom lot his father never sold and may have intended for his son all along. He began to correspond with Sallie Ann/LaSalle Pickett about the property. She was slow to respond to his letters and took no action about the land. Despite any Virginia law that forbade non-white offspring from inheriting, Jim knew that he was a legitimate heir in Washington Territory. While it may have been illegal for his father to "officially" marry his mother in 1857, Territorial Chief Justice Roger Greene's 1879 intersession opinion on the nature of the marriage contract legitimized tribal custom marriages and made the offspring of intermarriages lawful heirs.[157] (See Appendix B)

Jim went to Bellingham to take legal possession of his father's lot in the summer of 1888 and probably stayed with Elizabeth and Henry Roeder as usual. In Virginia, LaSalle and George Jr. signed over Lot 1, Block 16 to Jim on July 23. By then, Lot 1 faced the main road north to Ferndale, substantially increasing its value. The local version of the events says that LaSalle only agreed to relinquish it after Jim threatened to sue. There is no documentation or eyewitness statement for that, but Jim gave a valuable painting of Mount Rainier to lawyer Charles Roth (the Roeder son-in-law), who helped him through the legal process for free.[158]

Seven months later, Jim and T. E. Kane arrived back in town to do a birds-eye view of Whatcom that would be far more detailed and skilled than one sold the previous summer. Jim stayed with the Roeders again and enjoyed a lengthy visit with old friends. The *Reveille* expected that when the view was published with Jim's name on it in April 1889, it would trigger big newsstand sales and it did. Jim did additional sketches for Kane's monthly, including one of the remains of his father's fort.[159]

What is most remarkable about Jim's return to his birthplace was not the artwork he completed. It was a singular affidavit among Whatcom County records that he filed at that time with the earlier deed. He swore that his father "left surviving him as his sole heirs at law his wife Sallie C. Pickett *and his two sons*, George E. Pickett *and this affiant* and no other children or other heirs" (author's italics). With those words put into the record, Jim established that his parents were a legally married couple. He might not legally exist in Virginia, but he did in Washington. Jim sold his lot to fellow pioneer son Hugh Eldridge the same

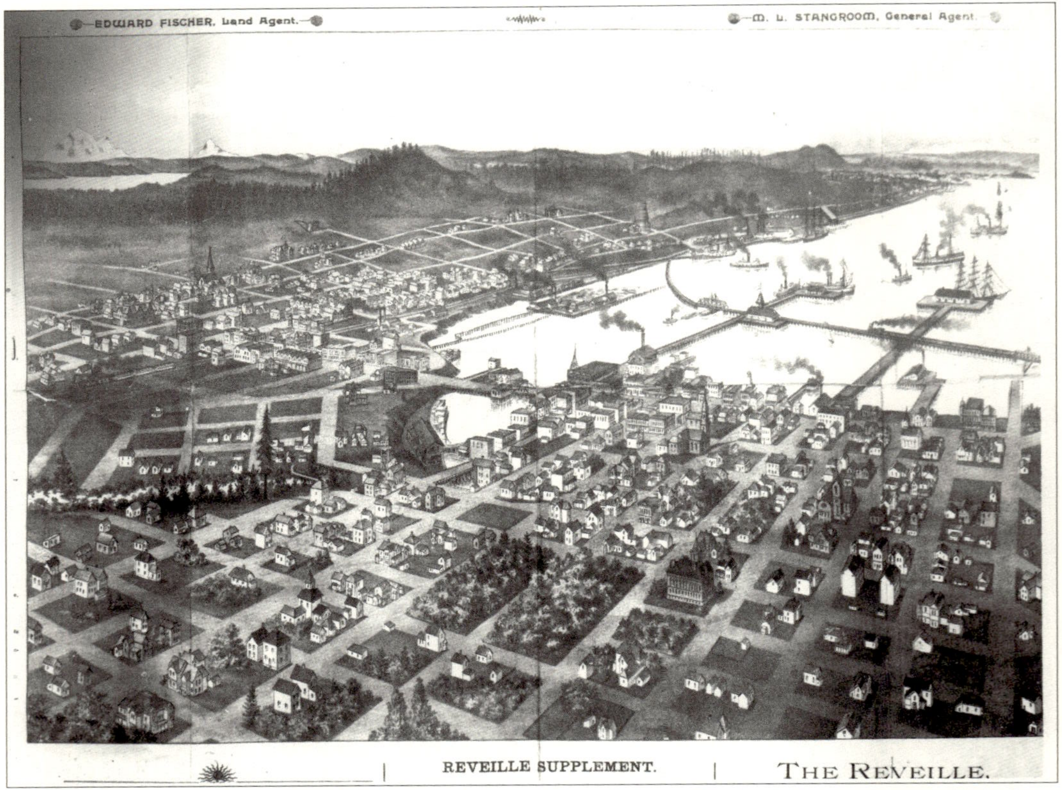

1889 Bird's-eye view of Bellingham, Washington, by James Tilton Pickett of Portland, Oregon. It was published in a supplement to *The Reveille* (Bellingham) to increase sales. The work demonstrated Pickett's precision in lithography and mastery of the bird's-eye view technique at a time when no actual overhead viewpoint was possible. Mt. Baker's position was moved in order to include it. *Galen Biery Collection, Center for Pacific Northwest Studies. Western Washington University, Bellingham, WA.*

day, then bought another in Spokane. A few months later, he bought four lots and a cabin on virtually uninhabited Mercer Island in Seattle's Lake Washington.[160]

The same month (May 1889) Jim bought the new lots, the steamer *Alaskan* sank in stormy seas three days out of Portland with the loss of thirty lives. He had already begun sketches for a painting of the vessel, and had completed drawings of the captain and some officers. He convinced surviving seamen to sit with him and describe the wreck as each experienced it. They frequently broke down and the artist wept with them while he added details. Depression took hold again while Jim scarcely ate or slept until he finished. Every sailor who saw the painting, and many others who viewed it, left Jim's studio in tears. It quickly became his most talked-about work.[161]

Dr. A. C. Panton, one of Portland's top physicians, visited Jim on July 14. It seems likely that Panton had already told him that his tuberculosis was serious and he hadn't much time, given the urgency with which Jim had been working on *The Alaskan*. He immediately signed over his Spokane lot to Margaret Jones for the $600 he said he owed her plus another $100. He must have rarely paid her for the room and board since moving in, and borrowed substantial amounts because the debt was very large for a young artist to ever repay. Though the debt was large, she never asked him to leave, a measure of their friendship and her belief in his talent. The day after he turned over the Spokane lot, the "Great Spokane Fire" obliterated the city's downtown. Jim began work on a painting of the fire from his previous sketches.[162]

Typhoid shortly complicated Jim's tuberculosis. The combination of diseases was enough to quickly be lethal, but his housemate from back home, E. C. McGreavy, always believed that Jim's death was hastened by the stress of working with the shipwreck survivors. Typhoid cases in the burgeoning city occurred so frequently that it was part of the city's accepted environment. There was no modern water or sewer system and the river was severely polluted.[163]

Dr. Panton visited again on August 13 and prescribed "Southern Liver Regulator" for typical early stage symptoms. When he returned a week later, Jim's continuing high fever and extreme abdominal symptoms, on top of tuberculosis, determined the terminal prognosis. The doctor advised Jim to get his affairs in order. The artist made out his will the same day.[164]

Rather than send an urgent telegram, someone wrote a letter to Catherine and William that their boy was very sick. Catherine left for Portland as soon as the letter arrived, but transportation still involved three different voyages. It all took time.[165]

Dr. Panton visited Jim every day for the next nine days, the period when most victims died. His housemates took turns sitting up with him through the long nights when delirium set in and he entered "the typhoid state," lying motionless and exhausted. According to McGreavy, shortly before Jim's death, he asked his friend to read the letters from his father and some from Sallie Ann, including the one describing the general's death and her promise to send Jim the Gettysburg sword.[166]

James Tilton Pickett died at 9:00 p.m. on Friday, August 30, 1889, surrounded by his Portland family. He was not yet thirty-two. Catherine Walter, the only mother he ever knew, did not arrive in time.[167]

After a prominently placed newspaper announcement, his many friends and probably most of Portland's professional artists and photographers attended the afternoon funeral September 1 at the Jones home. His Portland family buried him in a plot Margaret Jones bought at Riverview Cemetery, a short walk from a spot where he often went to sketch and paint the mountain peaks and sunset above the converging rivers.[168]

Both McGreavy and William Walter said that after the burial, some paintings, Jim's letters, and the "Gettysburg sword" were missing. It is impossible to determine if the paintings, never named, were actually stolen or later surfaced. Many of his letters reside in museums and archives, but none from Jim's stepmother regarding the sword, nor any from George Pickett. It is unlikely that Sallie/LaSalle Corbell Pickett, the keeper of her own son's future and the Pickett legend, would have willingly sent Jimmie Pickett the general's dress or battle sword from Gettysburg. However, her husband probably owned Mexican War presentation weapons that she might have substituted and it is always possible that George had asked her to send Jim his shorter everyday sword before his death. McGreavy was in a position to have seen it and read the letters to his dying friend.[169]

The Oregonian death notice called Jim a highly esteemed artist of "considerable genius." The *Mason County Journal* reminded locals of "the first rate artist's" relationship with William Walter (though not of Catherine) and who his father was. The Olympia paper paid a lengthy tribute that said he had "attained a name all over the coast for his talent and skill." The truth of the accolades has been borne out by the prices his works bring on the market and the search by museums for his paintings.[170]

The funeral eulogy appeared in *The Oregonian* a week after the funeral and revealed James Tilton Pickett's less widely known talents. He had been writing prose and poetry which he filed away in scrapbooks, many of which were of a "melancholy and mournful" nature. He once penned a snippet of one of Edgar Allen Poe's popular poems on the back of a canvas and may have been inspired for his own writing.[171]

No publication listed LaSalle and George Pickett Jr. as survivors.

James Tilton Pickett's will revealed his love for the three most important women in his life. He left fourteen Seattle and Mercer Island lots to his "mamma," but no artworks, probably because she already had some. He affirmed his three hundred dollar debt to Catherine, but she denied its existence and refused repayment. He left his father's widow the other two lots on Mercer Island, though nothing to George Jr. Finally, he left Margaret Jones real estate that in his illness he forgot he had sold. More important, he left her all his personal property: cash, books, and art. Some later accused Jones or her son of the theft during the funeral, but she was Jim's executrix and the personal possessions had been willed to her. When the probate grew complicated, she resigned and Jim's realtor, John Cress, took over. He raffled the *Alaskan* painting to pay the bills. It raised $600, six times its appraised value.[172]

In 1901 Catherine and William Walter moved into Shelton at the head of the inlet. The widely respected woman whose mother love sustained Jim Pickett for decades died early the next year of heart disease and without her, William took little interest in life. Two years later, William sat for an interview with Lelah Jackson, a young teacher interested in the Pickett story, and it became the most accurate source of Jim's life story. When he died four years later, the newspaper noted that since the "kindly, honest" pioneer's "adopted son" had died, there were no direct survivors.[173]

George Pickett Jr. married a Gettysburg veteran's daughter—a Union colonel's daughter. He didn't invite his mother to the wedding. When George Pickett III visited the Pickett house in Bellingham in 1938, he said the two grandfathers' history had never been discussed at home. He had never heard of the second Mrs. Pickett, but the family then added her and Jim to the family history and genealogy. Some "Lost Cause" diehards continue to have trouble incorporating the cross-cultural marriage into their hero's legend. In 1998, when a *Washington (DC) Times* feature writer profiled the second Mrs. Pickett and her son, the Daughters of the Confederacy organization rejected the article written by their own regional director.[174]

Mrs. Pickett's red trunk and its contents are now at the Washington State Historical Society. The official army papers disappeared after Lelah Edson saw them in 1904, but the Pickett Bible is still there. Many objects lack original explanation which made them fodder for imaginative writers. For instance, the faded red and white calico dress with shoulder ties is obviously a little girl's, unsuited for December weather, but writers assumed that Jimmie wore it when he was taken to Collins Point. Without evidence, two mismatched white gloves were romanticized as part of the Pickett wedding ceremony. Glove exchange has never been part of army or West Point custom and speculation on their purpose or ownership is fruitless. It seems likely that Catherine used the trunk for some of her own mementoes.[175]

James Tilton Pickett's talent and contributions have frequently been recognized by the fine art world. The man who called himself "a living reminder" of his parents' marriage was one of three hundred artists chosen for a biographical dictionary of important Western artists, as well as a book profiling prominent Oregon artists. His Portland friend Edward Espey died of tuberculosis a few months before he did, but James E. Stuart and Grafton Tyler Brown went on to national careers. It is interesting to note that of the four major figures in Portland's early artist community, Pickett and Brown were classified as non-whites in a state with racial exclusion laws.[176]

Jim gave the only portrait of his father he did to Fort Bellingham's former post sutler Ed Warbass on San Juan Island. After hanging over "Kwan Lama's" fireplace through at least two owners, it passed to the University of Washington Library where it hung in a main hallway for many years. Finally, it was given to the Washington State Historical Society. After a brief appearance at the Whatcom Museum in the 1960s, contradictory records leave its present location unknown.[177]

The Portland Art Museum owns no paintings by James Tilton Pickett or any of his three colleagues. His paintings almost never surface for sale.

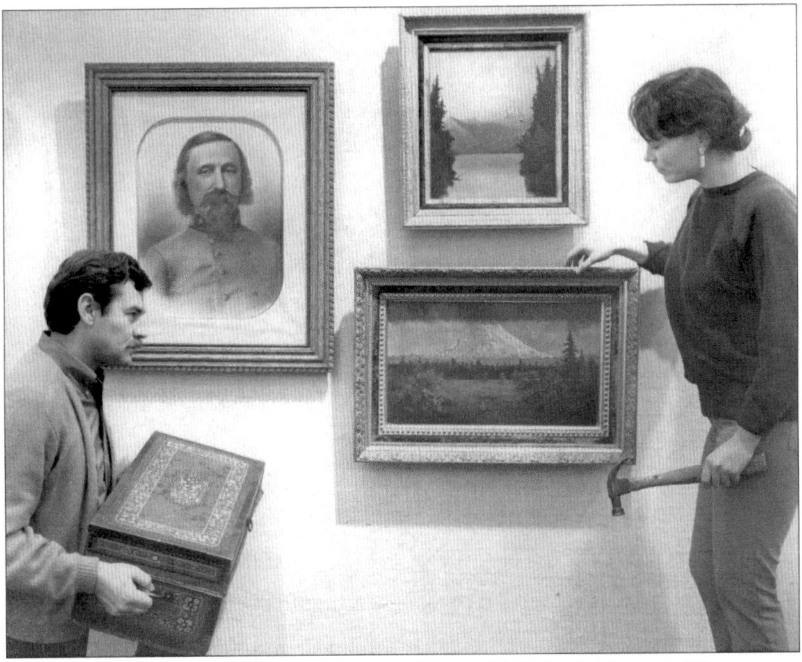

January 1969 Whatcom Museum exhibition of George E. Pickett's history in Whatcom County. The display includes paintings "Mt. Rainier" and top right "Lake Cushman" by his son James Tilton Pickett. The drawing of George Pickett from a photograph is the only known portrait James Tilton Pickett created. At the left, a museum worker holds the red leather Chinese tea trunk owned by Mrs. Pickett, the only remaining memento of her life. "Lake Cushman" and the trunk were on loan from the Washington State Historical Society in Tacoma. *Jack Carver, photographer. #1995.1.954. Whatcom Museum, Bellingham, WA.*

Conclusion

An examination of the four biographies of *Interwoven Lives,* in addition to the four in *Peace Weavers*, shows the breadth of experience of young indigenous women who by their own volition, or at the bidding of their families, married across the cultural line. Married life for some involved unhappiness, endurance, or death. Others had marriages that resulted in decades of lasting partnership and happy family life. Their unpredictability mirrors the fate of marriages in the twenty-first century.

What is also apparent is the simplistic, even blind, view historians have put forth of the life of "community mothers" in new towns that actually began with intermarried couples, not just "the first white woman in town." Women who found themselves straddling the line between their birth families and cultures, and the new society being born in the frontier West, had their own roles to play in birthing communities. Especially when their husbands were county officials or military officers, they were not women ignored on the fringe of town with a ne'er-do-well husband, as history and fiction has presented them. Perhaps they were ignored in later years when the residential population became overwhelmingly white, but they were embedded in the birth of their new communities and made significant contributions, sometimes their own and sometimes in the children they raised to enrich their own hometowns.

Jenny Wynn contributed a strong voice for justice for her Lummi people. She and her husband sent generations of teachers forth to enrich the region's future.

Elizabeth Patterson's death started the sequence of events that would result in the founding of the town of Lynden, and her daughters were the sources of significant literary and business contributions in their own communities.

Mary Allen was a resilient and strong woman whose long-time marriage resulted in the birth of the village of Marietta. The sons who bore the same traits played their own important parts in the early history of Southeast Alaska.

Mrs. George Pickett left no personal name to history after her early death, but she gifted the West with one of its most important early artists. His works enriched published county histories, newspaper illustrations, and included fine art that continues to be treasured by museums and private owners today.

A critical gap in Western history has resulted from the initial tellings of local and regional histories where cross-cultural marriages took place. The possibility that armed conflict was lessened or prevented in some communities by the presence and mediation of indigenous wives has not been fully addressed. Peace reigned in Whatcom County where nearly everyone was an in-law in the two post-treaty years (1855–56) of conflict in Washington Territory. The same lack of armed conflict may be true in some other communities across the Northwest and other frontier states.

These community mothers rightly deserve to have their stories told and contributions recognized. While *Peace Weavers* and *Interwoven Lives* have addressed this gap only in the far northwest corner of the American far northwest corner, there are probably hundreds of like biographies across the western states waiting to be told and integrated into the social history of the frontier. The question follows: what was left out of community histories on the eastern side of the Mississippi River?

Appendix A

Mary Devoes v. Samuel Strange. 3rd District Territorial Court, Jefferson County. Series 2, #173 (1878)

Outgoing Justice Joseph R. Lewis' decision triggered indictments of "Old Settlers" with long tribal custom marriages to native women. Neither Devoes nor Strange was a Native American.

Mary Devoes, an Irish immigrant, sued Samuel Strange for back wages for housekeeping and farm labor after their six-year relationship ended. Strange responded that he didn't owe wages for a common law marriage. She countered that they never were married and his defense would be an illegal contract. Justice Lewis ruled they only had a contract for "open and notorious fornication…in open violation of the law." He dismissed the case.

The law cited (Leg 5 Acts 1866, p. 82) declared that "marriages may be solemnized by any regular ordained minister and priest, Justice of the Peace, District or Probate Judge…a license shall be procured… there can be no legal marriage save only in accordance with the provisions of the statute."

Lewis added: "The rule is based on reason and morality. The plaintiff…asks this court to compensate her by compelling the defendant to pay her the wages of her sin and immorality. She and the defendant are equally guilty and the court…will leave these parties…to wallow in the filth it has found them in."

Appendix B

Territory of Washington, 3rd Judicial District. In the District Court of Whatcom County of the June Term, 1879. *Territory v. Beale:* Indictment for living in open and notorious fornication. Judicial Review by Chief Justice Roger S. Greene. (*Bellingham Bay Mail* 6/14/1879)

After the Lewis decision, and subsequent criminal indictments of long-married tribal custom husbands for "open and notorious fornication," Chief Justice Greene issued a review of the series of contradictory and confusing territorial marriage laws and amendments. Greene's opinion on the nature of the marriage contract ended the criminal proceedings.

Excerpts follow:

"The marriage contract stands, among all contracts, chief. It exists not by the law of a particular nation, but by the law of all nations. It is before all nations, and it is the legitimate source of them all…"

"…where the relationship of parties apparently living together as husband and wife, is in question, the presumptions of the law are always that they are married."

"The great weight of legislative, judicial and speculative authority is that marriage among English-speaking peoples, and particularly throughout the United States, is a civil contract, and needs for its validity nothing more than the mutual assent of two persons legally capable of making and fulfilling such a contract. Such is our English common law. And a statute, therefore, providing for a license, publication, witnesses, an officiating civil or religious officer, or ceremonies of any kind, is not held to make these formalities necessary to constitute a marriage…for it is not the act of the State, but the act of the couple, that makes the wedding."

Notes

Abbreviations in endnotes and bibliography:

CPNWS = Center for Pacific Northwest Studies, Western Washington University, Bellingham, Washington

EMP = Edmond C. Meany Papers. Special Collections, University of Washington Libraries, Seattle, Washington

GLO = General Land Office

HBP = Howard Buswell Papers, CPNWS

HBC = Hudson's Bay Company

JCA = John C. Allen Collection. Clausen Museum, Petersburg, Alaska

JTP = James Tilton Pickett Collection. Washington State Historical Society, Tacoma, Washington

NARA = National Archives and Records Administration

NARA, NW = NARA, Pacific Northwest Region, Seattle

NARA, Seattle = Seattle Federal Records Center

NWEC = Northwest Ethnohistory Collection, CPNWS

OHS = Oregon Historical Society, Portland, Oregon

PNQ = Pacific Northwest Quarterly

PRJ = Percival R. Jeffcott Collection, CPNWS

PSH = Puget Sound Herald

UBC = University of British Columbia, Vancouver, British Columbia

UW = University of Washington, Seattle, Washington

WHQ = Washington Historical Quarterly

WSA, NW = Washington State Archives, Northwest Region. Bellingham, Washington

WSHS = Washington State Historical Society (Research Center). Tacoma, Washington

WSU = Washington State University, Pullman, Washington

WSU MASC = Washington State University Libraries, Manuscripts, Archives, and Special Collections

Introduction

1. Lelah Jackson Edson, *The Fourth Corner* (Bellingham, WA: Whatcom Museum, 1968), 115.

2. *Bellingham Herald*, 8/22/2017, 8/27/2017, 9/3/2017, 9/7/2017, 9/12/2017, 9/13/2017.

3. Robert Poole, "What Became of the Taino?" *Smithsonian* (October 2011), 60; Roberta Brown, remarks, PNW History Conference, 4/4/2014.

4. Devin A. Mihesuah, *American Indians: Stereotypes and Realities* (Atlanta: Clarity Press, 1996), 104; Conrad Richter, *The Light in the Forest* (New York: Alfred A. Knopf, 1953).

5. Robert Morgan, *Lions of the West: Heroes and Villains of the Westward Expansion* (Chapel Hill: Algonquin Books, 2012), 48–50; Mihesuah, *American Indians*, 99.

6. Brown remarks, 4/4/2014; John P. Bowes, *Land Too Good for Indians: Northern Indian Removal* (Norman: Univ. of Oklahoma, 2016), 12.

7. Nancy Isenberg, *White Trash: The 400 Year Untold History of Class in America* (New York: Penguin Books, 2016), 18–19; *Blaine Journal*, 8/9/1888.

8. Coll Thrush, *Native Seattle: Histories from the Crossing-Over Place* (Seattle: Univ. of Washington Press, 2007), 57.

9. Ben Olney to Lucullus McWhorter, undated interview, McWhorter Papers, WSU MASC; "Mrs. Elizabeth Collins' Story," *Polk County (OR) Observer*, 1/1/1927, copy in McWhorter Papers.

10. Lottie Roeder Roth, *History of Whatcom County* (Seattle: Pioneer Historical Publishing Company, 1926), 2:430; Percival Jeffcott, *Nooksack Tales and Trails* (Sedro-Woolley *Courier Times*, 1949), 418.

Chapter 1: Jenny, Defender of the People

1. Harry P. Wynn, interview, *Ferndale Record-Journal*, 1936, copy in Frank Teck Papers, CPNWS; H. B. Williams, *American Reveille*, 6/14/1908; John Tennant, Farm Journal, 9/20–27/1868. William James Collection, Lummi Nation Archives, courtesy of Chief Tsi'lixw (William) James.

2. Al Charles to Howard Buswell, 2/5/1952, and others, HBP, CPNWS.

3. For more information on the Tsi'lixw family, see Wellman, *Peace Weavers* ch. 4. Sea'nult and Tsi'lixw were also brothers-in-law. Wayne Suttles, "Post-Contact Culture Change Among the Coast Salish Indians," *British Columbia Historical Quarterly* 18:1 & 2 (January/April 1954), 32, 59; August Martin to Suttles, 1947–48, Wayne Suttles research papers, courtesy of Dr. Suttles; Julius Charles to Buswell, 4/18/1943, HBP; Wayne Suttles, ed., *Handbook of North American Indians Vol. 7* (Washington, DC: Smithsonian Institution, 1990), 457.

4. Martin to Suttles, Suttles research files; Howard Buswell genealogies, compiled, HBP; Noel Wynne, "Family History of Jennie (Jane) Wynn" (unpub. ms.,

1970), courtesy of Echo Dorr; Aurelia Balch Celestine, Lummi genealogies, NWEC; Julia Wynn Smith to Buswell, several, HBP; Jenny Wynn, Lummi Individual History Card #1056, courtesy of Wynn family; www.royalbcmuseum.bc.ca; Grant Keddie, *Songhees Pictorial* (Victoria: Royal BC Museum, 2003), 14–15.

5. Grant Keddie, Supplement to *Songhees Pictorial*, www.royalbcmuseum.bc.ca, n.p.

6. Family members contributed Jenny's personal name to Howard Buswell; Noel Wynne genealogy chart courtesy of Echo Dorr; compiled genealogies, HBP, CPNWS; Celestine, Lummi genealogies; Archdiocese of Seattle, *Sacramental Register*, vol. 1, Archdiocesan Archives, Seattle; Jenny Wynn, Lummi Individual History Card #1056, courtesy of Wynn family.

7. Jenny Wynn Individual History Card #1056; Martin, 1947 to Suttles; Celestine genealogies; Noel Wynne, 1970, and others; Lizzie Malmberg to Buswell, 7/4/1952; Florence Boone to Buswell, 12/30/1947; Angeline Alexander to Buswell, 1/26/1967; Hallie Lysle Campbell to Buswell, undated notation about remarks, probably 7/1945 interview. All in HBP, CPNWS.

More than one witness named Jenny's sister Harriet as the spurned wife of Henry Roeder. Roeder was interested in the wild hay that grew at the eastern edge of Lummi land, to which Sea'nult's family had claim. Harriet had no surviving children, as did Roeder's wife.

8. Julia Wynn Smith to Buswell, 11/4/1950, 6/24/1951, 3/31/1955; B. F. Shaw to M. T. Simmons, Indian Agent, 10/15/1860. "Correspondence and Accounting Records of the Puget Sound District Agency, 1854–1861 and the Tulalip Agency 1861–1886," RG75 microfilm. NARA, NW; Lummi elder to Tim Wahl, 3/2003.

9. Julia Wynn Smith to Buswell, 8/24/1946, 11/4/1950. Buswell summary of JWS remarks, 6/24/1951. All in HBP.

10. Julia Wynn Smith to Buswell, 11/4/1950, 3/13/1952. Buswell, 6/24/1951; Leland Donald, *Aboriginal Slavery on the Northwest Coast of North America* (Berkeley: Univ. of California Press, 1997), 95.

11. Catherine Clinton, *The Plantation Mistress: Woman's World in the Old South* (New York: Pantheon, 1982), 96; Lummi children's DAR contest essays, 1948, HBP, CPNWS; Wilson Duff, *The Upper Stalo Indians of the Fraser Valley, B.C.* (Victoria: BC Provincial Museum, 1952. Reprint by Indian Education Resources Centre, UBC 1972), 80.

12. A female Lummi elder to author, n.d.; Paula Gunn Allen, *The Sacred Hoop: Recovering the Feminine in American Indian Traditions* (Boston: Beacon Press, 1986), 254.

13. Rina Swentzell in *Western Women: Their Land, Their Lives*, ed. Lillian Schlissel, Vicki L. Ruiz, and Janice Monk (Albuquerque: Univ. of New Mexico Press, 1988), 108; Crisca Bierwort, *Brushed by Cedar, Living by the River: Coast Salish Figures of Power* (Tucson: Univ. of Arizona Press, 1999), 32.

14. Becky Wynn-Thill family history research sources, courtesy of Becky Wynn-Thill.

15. Wynn-Thill family history research; Lynn Larsen and Becky Thill, *Dr. Thomas Wynne's Legacy* (New York: TFG Press, 2002), 29.

16. Charles Woodman, *Quakers Find a Way: Their Discoveries in Practical Living* (Indianapolis: Bobbs-Merrill, 1950), 26; Larsen and Thill, *Dr. Thomas Wynne's Legacy*, 38; Wynn-Thill family history research.

17. Russell F. Weigley, ed., *Philadelphia: A 300-Year History* (New York: W. W. Norton, 1982), 5–6.

18. Liberty Lands Patent Records Book D, v. 80, Wynn-Thill research.

19. Noel Wynne, genealogy chart; Wynn-Thill family history research.

20. Larsen and Thill, *Dr. Thomas Wynne's Legacy*, 130; George DeWan, "The Wretched Prison Ships," Newsday.com, 2/17/2009.

21. Larsen and Thill, *Dr. Thomas Wynne's Legacy*, 130.

22. Letter from Gen. James Potter, 12/15/1777, in Dora H. Develin, *Historic Lower Merion and Blockley* (Philadelphia: George Buchanan Co., 1922), 34; Mary Wood email to Becky Wynn-Thill, 1/4/2002.

23. Geraldine Shastid interview by Wynn-Thill, 7/28/2001; Thomas Wynn (1895) Sons of the American Revolution membership application #6285; Wood to Wynn-Thill, 1/4/2002; Noel Wynne, genealogy chart; Larsen and Thill, *Dr. Thomas Wynne's Legacy*, 130; Wynn-Thill family history research.

24. Joseph Johnson, *Wynnefield, Pennsylvania*, map, 1884, courtesy of Janet Beard.

25. Wynn-Thill emails to author 7/18/2001, 6/21/2001; George Soule, 17th owner, to Geraldine Shastid, related 7/28/2001 to Becky Thill; R. C. Smedley, *History of the Underground Railroad in Chester and the Neighboring Counties of Pennsylvania* (Mechanicsburg, PA: Stackpole Books, 2005).

26. Conflicting birthdates exist, but best evidence indicates that his sister recorded the date incorrectly. Thomas and Hannah Wynne Bible, Genealogical Society of Pennsylvania; Whatcom County (WA) censuses; Thomas Wynn obituary, *The Blade*, 11/12/1896.

27. David H. Fischer, *Albion's Seed: Four British Folkways in America* (NYC: Oxford Univ. Press, 1989), 509–11, 556, 582, 603.

28. S. M. Rea and J. Miller, *Map of Blockley Township, Philadelphia County, PA, 1851.*

29. Wynn-Thill email, 11/28/2001; Rea and Miller, Map of Blockley Township; 1840 U.S. Census, Philadelphia County, PA; Janet Beard email, 6/7/2006; photos/descriptions of Wynnestay, courtesy of Becky Wynn-Thill.

30. Fischer, *Albion's Seed*, 485; Janet Beard research; Wynn-Thill family history research. Elizabeth Harrison, ed., *Philadelphia Merchant: The Diary of Thomas P. Cope 1800–1851* (South Bend, IN: Gateway Editions, 1978), 562.

31. Harrison, *Philadelphia Merchant*, 570; Donald D. Jackson, *Gold Dust* (New York: Alfred A. Knopf, 1980), 70.

32. James Delgado, *To California by Sea: A Maritime History of the California Gold Rush* (Columbia: Univ. of South Carolina Press, 1990), 19–20.

33. Julia Wynn Smith to Buswell, many dates, HBP, CPNWS.

34. Delgado, *To California by Sea*, 42–43.

35. Robert Phelps, "All Hands Have Gone Downtown: Urban Places in Gold Rush California," in Kevin Starr and Richard J. Orsi, eds., *Rooted in Barbarous Soil: People, Culture, and Community in Gold Rush California* (Berkeley: Univ. of California Press, 2000), 127.

36. Julia Smith to Buswell, 11/4/1950, 6/24/1951, 9/12/1956; Henry Roeder letters in W. W. Miller Papers, Yale University.

37. Thomas Wynn photo in 1850, courtesy of Janet Beard; Henry Roeder photo, Whatcom Museum; references to the "Quaker blacksmith" include repeated mentions by Lottie Roth, Howard Buswell, other historians, and newspapers.

38. Teresa Eldridge, "Fifty-five Years on Bellingham Bay," *American Reveille*, 6/14/1908; *Puget Sound Mail*, 10/8/1881.

39. Thomas B. Wynn to Howard Buswell, n.d., HBP.

40. Whatcom County Commissioners Proceedings v. 1, 9/18/1854; 3rd District Territorial Court Journal, 4/17/1855, both at WSA, NW.

41. Treaty of Point Elliott, January 22, 1855. The treaty text can be found online and in many other sources.

42. For more information on E. C. Fitzhugh, see *Peace Weavers* ch. 3; Julia Wynn Smith to Buswell, 8/28/1946, 2/23/1964, HBP.

43. Noel Wynne, genealogy chart and "Family History," and others; Fischer, *Albion's Seed*, 485–98.

44. Janet Beard (descendant of Ruth Wynne Compton) to author, 6/7/2006.

45. Nicholas V. Sheffer, "A Story of Pioneering, 1825–1910," *Lynden Tribune*, 8/1909; Edward Eldridge, "Sketch of Washington Territory, 1880," unpub. ms, Bancroft Library, University of California, Berkeley.

46. Teresa Eldridge, "Fifty-five Years," 6/14/1908.

47. Michael Vouri, *Raiders from the North*, extended manuscript copy, 1995, courtesy of Michael Vouri; H. R. Crosbie, "The San Juan Difficulty," *The Overland Monthly 2, #3* (3/1869), 201–15.

48. Whatcom County Commissioners Proceedings, v. 1; Charles Miles, *Michael T. Simmons* ([Olympia?]: Vivian E. Bower, 1980), 140–41; Mary Lysle, "Christmas, 1854," *Bellingham Herald*, 1905, HBP; *Washington Territory v. Daniel Harris*, #64 (1856), 3rd District Territorial Court.

49. Noel Wynne, genealogy chart.

50. Edward Eldridge, "History of Whatcom County," *Bellingham Bay Reveille*, 10/4/1889; Lysle, "Christmas 1854"; Eldridge, "Sketch of Washington Territory"; Sheffer, *Lynden Tribune*, 8/1909.

51. E. C. Fitzhugh to I. I. Stevens, 4/5/1857, in *WHQ* 1 (1/1907): 56; *Olympia Pioneer-Democrat*, 5/1/1857, in Vouri, "Raiders From the North" ms.; Indian Agent M. T. Simmons, Report, 5/1/1857, NWEC, CPNWS; Elizabeth Roeder obituary, *Reveille*, 2/13/1897; Mary Tawes obituary, *BH*, 1/11/1921.

52. J. Ross Browne, Report, reprinted in *Pioneer-Democrat*, 11/6/1857; Henry Roeder, Diary 1850–1878, Henry Roeder Papers, UW, Special Collections.

53. *Pioneer-Democrat*, 11/6/1857; *Alta California*, 10/7/1857.

54. Sea'nult tombstone, Lummi Cemetery; Fitzhugh to M. T. Simmons, 1/5/1858.

55. Edward Eldridge, "Western Washington Territory," *Whatcom Reveille*, 6/15/1883; Sheffer, *Lynden Tribune* 8/1909.

56. Sam Crockett report in *Pioneer-Democrat*, 5/2/1858; *Northern Light* #4: 2; Fred Beckey, *Range of Glaciers: The Exploration and Survey of the Northern Cascade Range* (Portland: OHS Press, 2003), 11; *Pioneer-Democrat*, 10/2/1858, 10/8/1858; Microsoft Encarta Encyclopedia, "Donati's Comet."

57. *Pioneer-Democrat*, 4/9/1858; Whatcom County Commissioners Proceedings, v. 1, 59, 69.

58. Indian agent M. T. Simmons in *Northern Light* #4, 7/24/1858; M. T. Simmons, *Annual Report, 1859*, NWEC; E. C. Fitzhugh to Fayette McMullen, 6/14/1858.

59. Whatcom County Deeds, "D," 32 and "C," 59.

60. Simmons to Edward Geary, *Annual Report, 1859*; Sheffer, *Lynden Tribune*, 8/1909; *Autobiography of James S. Lawson*, reprinted on www.history.noaa.gov.

61. Inflation calculations are from westegg.com/inflation; Julia Wynn Smith to Howard Buswell, several mentions; Urban Hicks in *Small World of Our Own* by Robert A. Bennett (Walla Walla: Pioneer Press, 1985), 290; Simmons, *Annual Report, 1859*.

62. Simmons, *Annual Report, 1859;* "A Talk With the Indians," *Northern Light #4*, 7/24/1858.

63. Noel Wynne, genealogy chart, and other sources make July 22, 1859, the most likely birthdate; 1860 U.S. Census, Whatcom County; *Pioneer-Democrat* (Olympia), 7/22/1859, 5/25/1860.

64. Whatcom County Commissioners. Proceedings, v. 1, 1/17/1860, 5/10/1860, 7/20/1860, 9/8/1860.

65. *Territory v. Oscar Olney* #245, 246, 247 (1860), 3rd Territorial District Court. WSA, NW; Whatcom County Comm. Proceedings, v. 1, 9/8/1860.

66. *Territory v. Oscar Olney* cases; Whatcom County Comm. Proceedings, v. 1, 9/8/1860, 12/26/1860.

67. Julia Wynn Smith to Buswell, 8/28/1946; Richard White, *Land Use, Environment, and Social Change: The Shaping of Island County, Washington* (Seattle: Univ. of Washington Press, 1980), 81.

68. Dennis Conroy, "Pioneers of Utsalady," *Columbia* 14 (Spring 2000): 7–12.

69. Noel Wynne Genealogy and other records of Thomas B. Wynn. No official baptismal records exist for the children.

70. Washington Superintendent of Indian Affairs, David Crockett Chief's Certificate. Tulalip Papers, WSU MASC. Cage 256, Folder 19.

71. *The Blade*, 12/14/1897; John Tennant, *Farm Journal*, v. 1, Lummi Nation Archives; Thomas Wynn, Patent Application #4529, General Land Office; Peter James to Howard Buswell, 9/9/1946, HBP; Whatcom County Comm. Proceedings, v. 1; Percival Jeffcott to Howard Buswell re: Thomas B. Wynn belief about his parents' marriage and land, HBP.

72. Allan Richardson and Brent Galloway, *Nooksack Place Names: Geography, Culture, and Language* (Vancouver: Univ. of British Columbia Press, 2011), 51–52; Nancy J. Turner, *Food Plants of Coastal First Peoples* (Vancouver: Univ. of British Columbia Press, 1995), 42–43, 56–57.

73. Thomas Wynn GLO file #4529, 1/25/1873; Tennant, Journal, 6/7/1863; Homestead Act of 1862, text on www.nps.gov.

74. *PSH*, 1/3/1861, 3/12/1864; Sample period patent issued in Olympia to Benjamin Ure in 1872.

75. Maxine Stremler (T'ing descendant) to author, 1/21/2009; 1880 U.S. Census, Whatcom County; Julia Wynn Smith to Buswell, 8/28/1946, HBP; Noel Wynne, "Family History."

76. Smith to Buswell, 8/28/1946, 11/4/1950; *Ferndale Record-Journal*, 7/25/1946; *Bellingham Herald*, 8/1946; Tennant Journal, 11/6/1864, 11/13/1864.

77. Thomas Wynn GLO file #4529; Maria Wynn Oxford, *Ferndale Record-Journal*, 7/30/1936, 7/25/1946.

78. 1870 Washington Territorial Census, Products of Agriculture, Whatcom County; Tennant Journal, 1865–1870; *PSH*, 4/30/1863.

79. Noel Wynne, "Family History"; U.S. Census 1870, 1880.

80. 1870 Products of Agriculture; Bernard McDonough Account Books, HBP.

81. Julia Wynn Smith, 6/24/1951, Johanna Tealish Brown, 3/12/1954, John Allen, 3/4/1953, all written to Howard Buswell, HBP; Jay Miller, "Dr. Simon, A Snohomish Slave at Ft. Nisqually and Puyallup," *Journal of NW Anthropology* 36, #2: 145–54; Diamond Jenness, "The Saanich Indians of Vancouver Island," unpub. ms., 1938, 63–64, copy in NWEC, CPNWS; Julius Charles to Wayne Suttles, 4/11/1949, Suttles Research files, courtesy of Dr. Suttles.

82. Julia Wynn Smith to Buswell, 8/28/1946, HBP; Noel Wynne, "Family History"; Tennant, Journal.

83. Johanna Tealish Brown to Buswell, 5/19/1949, 3/12/1954, HBP; Maxine Stremler to author, 1/21/2009; Noel Wynne "Family History"; Patrick George, 1940s, cited in Wayne Suttles, *Coast Salish Essays* (Seattle: Univ. of Washington Press, 1987), 83; 1880 U.S. Census, Whatcom County.

84. Johanna Tealish Brown to Buswell, 5/19/1949, 3/12/1954, HBP; Maxine Stremler to author, 1/21/2009; Noel Wynne "Family History"; Patrick George, 1940s, cited in Suttles, *Coast Salish Essays*, 83; 1880 U.S. Census, Whatcom County.

85. 1870 Products of Agriculture; Tennant Journal, 4/14/1867, and other entries; Maria Wynn Oxford, *Ferndale Record-Journal*, 7/30/1936; Jacqueline B. Williams, *The Way We Ate* (Pullman: Washington State Univ. Press, 1996), 137.

86. For more about James Carr, see *Peace Weavers* ch. 5; Tennant, Journal.

87. *PSH*, 8/26/1859, 4/10/1886; S. D. Howe to C. H. Hale, 9/30/1864, copy in NWEC.

88. See *Peace Weavers* ch. 4 for more explanation.

89. Peter James to Howard Buswell, 3/19/1943, HBP; Old Polan's memory of the 1856 boundary lines, described by Peter James, 9/9/1945, to Buswell; Anonymous Lummi elder to author, n.d.; 1859 Smith and Hurd Survey of Township 38N, R2E, CPNWS; 1860 *Annual Report*, M. T. Simmons to Edward Geary, copy in Tulalip Papers, WSU.

90. Al Charles to Jeff Wilner, 4/26/1973. Oral histories, CPNWS; *PSH* 11/6/1857; James Nesmith, *Annual Report*, 8/1868, copy in NWEC; G. D. Hill, Agent, to E. S. Parker, 9/11/1869. NWEC.

91. Thomas B. Wynn to Percival Jeffcott, recounted to Howard Buswell and in a letter from HB to PRJ, n.d. in Buswell Papers; Tim Wahl to author, 12/2/1999; Whatcom County Deeds M, 595–96.

92. James Nesmith, *Annual Report*, 8/18/1868; G. D. Hill, 9/11/1869; *Annual Report*, Washington Superintendency, 10/1/1871; M. T. Simmons, *Annual Report* 1860, Tulalip Papers, WSU.

93. E. C. Chirouse to R. H. Milroy, 7/1/1873, Tulalip Papers, WSU.

94. Whatcom County Marriage Records, Book B, License 5/23/1873, and Marriage 6/1/1873, pg. 22; Thomas Wynn GLO file #4529.

95. Other mixed couples marrying that season included the John Plasters, the Solomon Allens, the Reuben Bizers, and the C. C. Finkbonners.

96. *Bellingham Bay Mail*, 9/27/1873; Harrison, *Philadelphia Merchant*, 451.

97. Tim Wahl to author, 2/23/1999; Bruce Miller, "Women and Politics: Comparative Evidence from the Northwest Coast" in *Ethnology*, n.d, 370; George Gibbs, "Tribes of Western Washington and Northwest Oregon," in *Contributions to North American Ethnology* (U.S. Department of the Interior, 1877), 1:185; C. C. Finkbonner to S. D. Howe, 8/16/1863, NWEC.

98. Archdiocese of Seattle, Sacramental Register.

99. Noel Wynne, "Family History," 1970.

100. Seattle Archdiocese, Sacramental Register, v. 3, 100.

101. E. C. Chirouse to E. P. Smith, 9/23/1874 in *Report to the Commissioner of Indian Affairs*, copy in NW Ethnohistory Collection.

102. Jeffcott, *Nooksack Tails and Trails* (Ferndale: *Sedro-Woolley Courier Times*, 1949) 154, 163; Neill Mullen, "Chronological History of Whatcom County to 1900" (unpub. ms.), n.p., copy at WSA, NW; McDonough Account Book AA, 90, HBP.

103. Gertrude Matz Alvord interview, undated, unnamed newspaper, Frank Teck Papers, Michael Sullivan Collection, CPNWS.

104. Thomas B. Allen, ed. *We Americans* (Washington, DC: National Geographic Society, 1975), 223–30; James Conaway, *The Smithsonian: 150 Years of Adventure, Discover and Wonder* (Washington, DC: Smithsonian Institution, 1995); www.150.si.edu.

105. James Conaway, *The Smithsonian*, n.p.; National Museum of the American Indian, *Listening to Our Ancestors: The Art of Native Life Along the North Pacific Coast* (Washington, DC: Smithsonian Institution with the National Geographic Society, 2005), 181; Shari Huhndorf, *Going Native: Indians in the American Cultural Imagination* (Ithaca: Cornell Univ. Press, 2001), 27–31.

106. Julia Wynn Smith to Buswell, 3/13/1952, 3/31/1955, 9/12/1956, HBP; Philadelphia County Deed Book LW, #52, 321, 3/20/1876; *Territory v. Daniel Harris* #540 (1876), 3rd Territorial District Court; Jeffcott, *Nooksack Tales and Trails*, 212.

107. "Women Had to Take Care of Cattle When Men Were Away," Annie Klocke newspaper interview, n.d., copy in Frank Teck Papers, Michael Sullivan Collection, CPNWS; Julia Wynn Smith to Buswell, 3/31/1955.

108. *Bellingham Bay Mail*, 4/14/1877; Henry Roeder Diary, 1860; *Weekly Messenger*, 4/25/1871.

109. Whatcom County Deeds M, 597–98 and Deeds 3, 58–59.

110. Harry Wynn in *Ferndale Record-Journal*, 1936, copy in Frank Teck Papers, Michael Sullivan Collection.

111. *Bellingham Bay Mail*, 3/22/1879; Thomas Wynn GLO patent entry #5970; Whatcom County Deeds 3, 59–60.

112. Jeffcott, *Nooksack Tales*, 165; Sophie Walsh, "Alden Academy Fulfilled One Man's Dream of Service," *Anacortes American*, 12/15/1927; Whatcom County Deeds 3, 124; McDonough Acct. Book E., HBP.

113. Julia Wynn Smith, 8/28/1946; Peter James to Howard Buswell, 9/9/1946, HBP; Suttles, "Post-Contact Culture Change," 68; 1884 Surveyor General's Office map of Lummi allotments, Lummi Reservation Library; U.S. and Lummi Reservation censuses 1885–1912.

114. Julia Wynn Smith to Buswell, 8/10/1949; "The Ferndale Tragedy," *Daily British Colonist*, 9/27/1885; *Daily Reveille*, 8/19/1892; *Ferndale Record*, 9/25/1885; *Whatcom Reveille*, 9/25/1885.

115. The still-beautiful historic home was torn down in the name of progress about 70 years later, when a freeway exit for the town of Ferndale was built; Michael Sullivan, slide, and Thomas Wynn House Survey-Inventory Form for community cultural resource survey, undated. Michael Sullivan Collection.

116. Whatcom County Power of Attorney 3, 9–10; Deeds 20, 59–60; *The Fairhaven & Southern Railroad Company v. Julia Wynn and Sallie Wynn* #298 (1890), Whatcom County Superior Court; Sally Wynn, Guardianship, Probate case #272 (1890), Whatcom County; Whatcom County Deeds 28, 410.

117. Maria Wynn Oxford interview in "Present Line Laid Over Old Canfield County Survey," *Ferndale Record-Journal*, 9/30/1936; *Bellingham Bay Express*, 8/23/1890, 10/11/1890, 10/23/1890; *Fairhaven Weekly World*, 10/11/1890; Lelah Jackson Edson, *The Fourth Corner* (Whatcom Museum edition, 1978), 257–59.

118. Maria Wynn Oxford, *Ferndale Record-Journal*, 7/30/1936.

119. Julia Wynn Smith to Buswell, 6/24/1951; Archdiocese of Seattle, Sacramental Records, 4:241, 271.

120. Thomas and Hannah Wynne, Family Bible; *Blaine Journal*, 6/10/1892.

121. Rev. John Wesley Moles to Selina May Hindle, 11/27/1889, courtesy of the Moles family.

122. Philadelphia County Deeds LW, 352, p. 321; Estate information in a deed from Sarah Wynn to Theodore Kraan, #156579, 4/8/1913. Philadelphia Office of Deeds; Julia Wynn Smith to Howard Buswell, 3/13/1952.

123. Whatcom County Death Return #215, Thomas Wynn; *The Blade*, 11/17/1896.

124. *The Blade*, 11/12/1896; *Bellingham Bay Reveille*, 11/13/1896.

125. Whatcom County Marriage Records 2, 182. Sallie Wynn and Frank Vandermark.

126. *In the Matter of the Estate of Thomas Wynn, Deceased* #636 (1897), Whatcom County Probate Court; Deeds 47, 175–76.

127. *M. L. Stangroom, as Administrator of the Estate of Thomas Wynn, Deceased v. Thomas B. Wynn, Harry P. Wynn, Jane Wynn, Julia Wynn and Sallie Vandemark*, #5116 (1897), Whatcom County Superior Court.

128. Depositions of Hannah W. Compton and Sarah S. Wynne, 5/7/1897, Thomas Wynn Probate Case #636.

129. Whatcom County Superior Court Journal, v. "T", 258; Deeds v. 47, 431–33.

130. *Daily Reveille*, 5/22/1897.

131. Henry A. Post Death Return, 12/13/1897; *The Blade*, 12/14/1897.

132. Post also left $1.00 to a brother in New Jersey; *The Blade*, 12/14/1897; Thomas Wynn Probate Case #686; Henry A. Post will, Whatcom County Probate Court Record of Wills, v. 1; Henry A. Post Death Return.

133. Thomas Wynn, Probate Case #686.

134. For more about Caroline Kavanaugh, see *Peace Weavers* ch. 2; Jeffcott, *Nooksack Trails*, 427; Noel Wynne family history, 10/22/1970.

135. Julia Wynn Smith to Buswell, 11/4/1950; Will of Mary Wea'cheloot, 6/11/1898, Record of Wills, v. 1, 127–28; Whatcom Probate Case #723.

136. Lummi Personal History cards #1055 and #1056, Mary Wea'cheloot and Jenny Wynn.

137. The allotment abutted that of her cousin George Swiloos/Placid, the near-lynching victim a few years before. See ch. 3; 1900 and 1910 U.S. Census, Lummi Reservation.

138. Julia Wynn Smith to Buswell, unpub. mss. drafts 1/19/1952, 5/14/1958, HBP; Thomas B. Wynn affidavit 6/12/1918 in Charles Roblin, "Schedule of Unenrolled Indians," U.S. Dept. of Interior, Office of Indian Affairs (1919), Microfilm Roll 3, M1343, NARA, Seattle.

139. Julia Wynn Smith to Buswell, 8/28/1946.

140. Julia Wynn Smith to Buswell, 6/24/1946; Howard Buswell unpub. draft 5/14/1958; Noel Wynne undated letter to unknown recipient in Vandemark family, courtesy of Lisa Mowat.

141. Jenny Wynn Individual History Card; "Jane" Wynn Death Certificate. Whatcom County; Woodlawn Cemetery stone inscription.

142. *In the Matter of the Estate of Wynifred Oxford Grimson*, U.S. Dept. of the Interior, 6/24/1966, courtesy of Echo Oxford Dorr.

143. Alice Biggs, "An Indian Legend from Nooksack," *Bellingham Herald*, 4/15/1905.

144. Lottie Roeder Roth, ed., *History of Whatcom County* (Seattle: Pioneer Historical Pub., 1926) 2:434.

145. Noel Wynne to Jesse Vandemark, n.d.; Roth, *History of Whatcom*, 2:430–37; Lisa Mowat, Interview, 7/12/2008; Echo Oxford Dorr, Interview, 1/4/2000; Marjorie Vandemark to Lisa Mowat quoted in email to author, 7/3/2008.

146. Anna Maria born 7/22/1859 at Sehome. Noel Wynne genealogy; C. F. Hauke memo to Charles Roblin 11/27/1916 re: Wynn children living white. Indian Claims Commissioners Files RG75, Box 259, File 1. NARA, Seattle.

147. Thomas was born at Utsalady 11/16/1862. Noel Wynne, genealogy chart; Roth, *History of Whatcom*, 2: 434–35; Angie Burt Bowden, *Early Schools of Washington Territory* (Seattle: Lowman and Hanford, 1935), 296; Whatcom County Marriage Certificate, 3/25/1896, Bk. 2, 139; *In the Matter of the Guardianship of Mabel Robinson* #684 (1896), Whatcom County Superior Court; *Bellingham Herald*, 7/24/1935, 7/27/1935; Whatcom County Birth Certificates for Baby

Girl Wynn 1906 and others; Noel Wynne to Percival Jeffcott, 4/9/1964; *Bellingham Herald* 7/24/1935 and other issues.

148. Harry Post Wynn born at Sehome 10/8/1866; Roth, *History of Whatcom*, 2:435 and photo; Noel Wynne to Percival Jeffcott, 4/9/1964; Whatcom County Marriage Certificate 6/30/1900, Bk. 3, 167, Return #919; Whatcom County Register of Teachers 1891–1900, Book 1.

149. "Information Regarding Claims Brought by Puget Sound Tribes in 1925," Minutes of Council Meeting 3/24/1925 at Lummi Reservation. Exhibit C, RG 75, Box 259, NARA, Seattle; Noel Wynne, genealogy chart.

150. Julia was born 7/22/1869 on the homestead. Julia Wynn Smith to Howard Buswell, numerous interviews 1946–1956, and notes in his unpub. draft, 5/14/1958.

151. Julia Wynn Smith interviews with Buswell, 1946–1956; Charlie Kahana to Howard Buswell, 4/11/1956.

152. Sallie was born on the farm 9/26/1873. Lisa Mowat emails and 7/2/2008 conversation; Diocese of Seattle Sacramental Register, v. 3, 100; Whatcom County Marriage Record Bk. 2, p. 182, 12/1/1896; Vandemark baby birth certificates, WSA, NW; Christie Hilton obituary, *Bellingham Herald*, 5/10/2015.

153. Sarah S. Wynn Will, 10/9/1919, courtesy of Janet Beard; Janet Beard email to author, 7/5/2006.

154. Rachel Myers, Whatcom Community Foundation, to author, 3/28/2018.

Chapter 2: Elizabeth, Daughter of the Moon

1. Peggy McDonald to author, 12/10/2010, re: the sisters' regular reading of local papers.

2. *Bellingham Reveille*, 4/16/1925; *Bellingham Herald*, 4/28/1925, 4/29/1925.

3. *Bellingham Herald*, 5/8/1925.

4. Phoebe Judson, *A Pioneer's Search for an Ideal Home* (Lincoln: Univ. of Nebraska Press, 1984), 210; Roth, *History of Whatcom County* 1:170; Charles Cline, "Lynden: the Gem City of Years Ago." *Pacific Pilot*, 8/25/1904; Percival Jeffcott, "The First County Dairy Was Scene of Romance and Despair," *Bellingham Herald*, 6/1/1966.

5. Irene Hewitt, "Patkanim Family Tree," copy at Lynden Public Library. Some additional information from Carol Rasmussen; Jack Kidder et al., "The Family Tree of Chief Patkanim," unpub. ms.

6. Hewitt, "Patkanim Family Tree"; Kidder, "The Family Tree of Chief Patkanim"; Bill Kanim deposition, 1923, and Skookum George testimony, *Duwamish, et al. v. U.S.* (1927), U.S. Court of Claims. RG 75, NARA, NW; Relationships also drawn from Cecelia Svinth Carpenter, *Ft. Nisqually, a Documented History* (Tacoma: Tahoma Research, 1986); T. G. Boyden, *Warrior of the Mist* (Spokane:

T. G. Boyden, 1996) and many other sources on family relationships; Fred Beckey, *Range of Glaciers*, 64; Kenneth Tollefson, "In Defense of a Snoqualmie Political Chiefdom Model," *Ethnohistory* 43, #1. Winter 1996, 155.

7. Kenneth Tollefson, "The Snoqualmie, a Puget Sound Chiefdom." *Ethnology* 26 (April 1987): 124–28; Brad Asher, "A Shaman-killing Case on Puget Sound," *PNQ* 86 (Winter 1994–95): 17–24; "American Law and Salish Culture," *PNQ* 86 (Winter 1994–95): 23; Tollefson, "Cultural Survival of the Snoqualmie Tribe," *American Indian Culture and Research Journal* 16, no. 4 (1992): 32–33; Jay Miller, "Back to Basics: Chiefdoms in Puget Sound," *Ethnohistory* 44 (Spring 1997): 383; Phil Wahl and Earngy Sandstrom, interview by author, 6/16/2003; Susie Kanim, 2/25/1927. *Duwamish v. U.S.*, copy in NWEC, CPNWS.

8. Hewitt, "Patkanim Family Tree"; Kidder, "The Family Tree of Chief Patkanim"; Susie Kanim, 2/25/1927; Archdiocese of Seattle, Sacramental Records, 2:3/20/1864; Edmond S. Meany, "Chief Patkanim," *WHQ* 15 (July 1924): 187–99; Tollefson, "In Defense of," 159.

9. Arthur Ballard, with additional material by Kenneth G. Watson, *Mythology of Southern Puget Sound: Legends Shared by Tribal Elders* (North Bend, WA: Snoqualmie Valley Historical Museum, 1999, reprint of 1929 edition), 78.

10. Hewitt, "Patkanim Family Tree"; Kidder, "The Family Tree of Chief Patkanim"; Carpenter, *Fort Nisqually*, 143, 149; Cecelia Carpenter, *The Nisqually, My People* (Tacoma: Tahoma Research Service, 2002), 143.

11. Carpenter, *Ft. Nisqually*, 3, 101, 124; Natalie Roberts, "A History of the Swinomish Community" (unpub. dissertation, UW, 1975), 162; George A. Kellogg, *A History of Whidbey's Island* (Coupeville, WA: Island County Historical Society, 1934, 2001), 15–16; Douglas Deur, *Ebey's Landing National Historical Reserve: An Ethnohistory of Traditionally Associated Contemporary Populations* (Seattle: National Park Service and UW Press, 2009), 28, 30, 49.

12. Julia and Thomas Glasgow's daughters married into the pioneering Gildow and Hastie families on Whidbey Island; A. B. Rabbeson account in H. H. Bancroft, *History of Washington, Idaho, and Montana, 1845–1889* (San Francisco: History Company, 1890), 10–11; Deur, *Ebey's Landing*, 50; Kellogg, *History of Whidbey's Island*, 15; Roberts, "History of the Swinomish," 177; Arthur Denny, *Pioneer Days on Puget Sound* (Seattle: A. Harriman 1908, Shorey Books 1975), 24.

13. William Fraser Tolmie, "History of Puget Sound and the Northwest Coast," (unpub. ms., 1878. Bancroft Library); Carpenter, *Ft. Nisqually*, 146–47.

14. Sandstrom and Wahl, 6/16/2003; Kidder, Patkanim genealogies; U.S. Census, Thurston County 1860, 1870; Kellogg, *History of Whidbey's Island*, 17–18.

15. Carpenter, *The Nisqually*, 107; Carpenter, *Fort Nisqually*, 143–44, 147, 149.

16. Meany, "Chief Patkanim," 192; "Death of a Noted Snoqualmie Indian," *Marysville Globe*, 6/15/1917; Jay Miller, "Back to Basics," 376; James G. Swan, *The Northwest Coast or Three Years Residence in Washington Territory* (New York: Harper, 1857), 395.

17. Roger Newman, "John McPhail, 1809–1876," *The Sequalitchew*, 5/20/2007.

18. David L. Nicandri, *Olympia's Forgotten Pioneers: The Oblates of Mary Immaculate* (Olympia: State Capitol Historical Assoc., 1976) 27; David Wilma, "Dr. Wesley F. Cherry dies following arrest of murder suspect Tom Taylor on March 6, 1854," www.historylink.org.

19. Denny, *Pioneer Days*, 58.

20. George Gibbs, "Proceedings of the Western Washington Treaty (1/10/1855)," in Barbara Lane, *Background of Treaty Making in Western Washington*, copy in NWEC, CPNWS.

21. Susie Kanim testimony, 2/15/1927, *Duwamish v. U.S.*; Bill Kanim deposition, 1923, copy in NWEC, CPNWS.

22. Gibbs, 1/22/1855, in Lane, *Background of Treaty Making;* Susie Kanim and Bill Kanim depositions.

23. Susie Dorsey (1927) in David Cameron, Charles LeWarne, M. Allen May, Jack C. O'Donnell, and Lawrence E. O'Donnell, *Snohomish County: An Illustrated History* (Index, WA: Kelcema Books, 2005), 37.

24. Denny, *Pioneer Days*, 58.

25. Denny, *Pioneer Days*, 65–67; Robert Ruby and John A. Brown, *Indians of the Pacific Northwest: A History* (Norman: Univ. of Oklahoma Press, 1981), 152; Thrush, *Native Seattle*, 45.

26. Denny, *Pioneer Days*, 68.

27. Washington National Guard, Office of the Adjutant General, *Washington Territorial Militia in the Indian Wars of 1855–1856*. "Minutes of Company I, Northern Rangers 11/27/1855," 149.

28. Denny, *Pioneer Days*, 67; Margaret McKibben Corliss, *Fall City in the Valley of the Moon* (Fall City, WA, 1972), 22.

29. Washington National Guard, *Washington Territorial Militia*, "Minutes," 11/29/1855, 150.

30. Nicandri, *Olympia's Forgotten Pioneers*, 35; J. A. Eckrom, *Remembered Drums: A History of the Puget Sound Indian War* (Walla Walla: Pioneer Press, 1989), 116; *Olympia Pioneer-Democrat*, 12/11/1855.

31. Washington National Guard, *Washington Territorial Militia*, "Minutes," 12/12/1855.

32. Sandstrom and Wahl, 6/16/2003.

33. *Pioneer-Democrat*, 1/15/1856, 2/22/1856, 2/29/1856.

34. Alexander Vincent in Bennett, *A Small World*, 208–10; J.J.H. VanBokkelin to Adjutant General James Tilton, 3/10/1856. Washington National Guard, *Washington Territorial Militia*, 69.

35. Carolyn Ruggrath, "The Patterson Family History" (unpub. ms.) and personal Patterson family research.

36. Ruggrath research, James Patterson (Sr.) will, courtesy of Carolyn Ruggrath; Goodspeed Publ. Co., *History of Tennessee* (Chicago, 1887), 883, 886; Goodspeed, *History of Greene County, Tennessee* (Chicago, 1887).

37. Judson, *A Pioneer's Search*, 195; William Speer, *Sketches of Prominent Tennesseans* (Nashville: Albert B. Tavel, 1888), 531.

38. Ruggrath, "Patterson Family History" and research; 1830, 1840 U.S. Census, Greeneville County, SC, and Greene County, TN.

39. Ruggrath, personal research.

40. Anne F. Hyde, *Empires, Nations, and Families: A New History of the North American West, 1800–1860* (Lincoln: Univ. of Nebraska Press, 2011) 270, 388.

41. David Dary, *The Santa Fe Trail: Its History, Legends and Lore* (NY: Penguin Putnam, 2000), xiii; Walker Wyman, "Freighting: A Big Business on the Santa Fe Trail," *Kansas Historical Quarterly* 1 (Nov. 1931): 17–27.

42. Elliott and Moore, *History of Alameda County, California* (San Francisco: 1883), 958; Dary, *Santa Fe Trail*, 173; A. J. Patterson obituary, Ruggrath research.

43. It has been reported that Nathaniel was a rescuer, but his name appears on no list; David Campbell, "Pioneer of 1846: A Sketch of the Hardships Endured by Those Who Crossed the Great Plains in 1846," *Weekly Review* (Porterville, CA), 7/1899. www.philnorf.tripod.com; Elliott and Moore, *History of Alameda County*, 958; Kristin Johnson to author, 8/29/2010.

44. Elliott and Moore, *History of Alameda*, 958; "Captain John C. Fremont," www.militarymuseum.org; Kristin Johnson to author, 8/29/2010.

45. Ruggrath research; Perry McCandless, *History of Missouri* (Columbia: Univ. of Missouri Press), 2:130.

46. Kristin Johnson to author, 8/29/2010; Ruggrath research; Janice Marschner, *California 1850: A Snapshot in Time* (Sacramento: Coleman Ranch Press, 2000), 154, 246–47; Elliott and Moore, *History of Alameda*, 113, 462.

47. Marschner incorrectly identified James Patterson as "Jacob." Ruggrath research; Elliott and Moore, *History of Alameda County*, 958; Newton G. Finley, "Memoirs of Travel," 1922, MF #1206424, item 17, Family History Library, Salt Lake City; Marschner, *California 1850*, 154.

48. Elliott and Moore, *History of Alameda*, 463; Ruggrath research; Paolo Sioli, *History of El Dorado County* excerpts on www.westernlivingcenter.com; Marschner, *California 1850*, 248; George Tinkham, *History of Stanislaus County* (Los Angeles: Historic Record Co., 1921), 50, 189.

49. Andrew Johnson to Franklin Pierce, 3/4/1853, courtesy of Carolyn Ruggrath.

50. Sandstrom and Wahl to author, 6/16/2003; Patkanim family genealogies.

51. Susie Kanim, 2/25/1927; *Duwamish v. U.S.*

52. Washington State did not apologize for the unjust execution until 2004; M. T. Simmons to James Nesmith re: Puget Sound Agency, 6/30/1858. Boxberger Papers, NWEC, CPNWS.

53. Simmons to Nesmith re: Puget Sound Agency, 6/30/1858; *PSH*, 7/20/1858.

54. Long years later, elderly nonnative friends and historians helped the Snoqualmie buy a large stone for the remarkable man's grave. *Pioneer-Democrat*, 11/26/1858; Susie Kanim, 2/25/1927, *Duwamish v. U.S.*; Sandstrom and Wahl to author, 6/16/2003.

55. Whites changed *Tohlt'w* to Tolt, and later "Carnation." Ruth Shelton to Colin Twedell, 9/2/1952. Colin Twedell Papers, NWEC, CPNWS; Tollefson, "The Snoqualmie," 133.

56. Tyler Heiskell diary, 2/13/1856. Tyler Heiskell file, Madera (CA) Public Library.

57. Samuel Colville, *Colville's San Francisco Directory*, 1856/1857 (San Francisco: Monson, Valentine & Co., 1857), 17; Edwin C. Bearss, *Redwood National Park History Basic Data* (National Park Service, 1969), www.cr.nps.gov.

58. U.S. Military Academy, "Index to Cadet Application Papers, 1805–1866," Records of the Adjutant General's Office, RG94 (MF 688) NARA, NW.

59. *PSH*, 8/20/1858; J. Orin Oliphant, "The Cattle Trade on Puget Sound, 1858–1890," *Agricultural History* 7 (1933): 132.

60. Bancroft, *History of Washington*, 359; Kenneth Tollefson, "Political Organization of the Duwamish," *Ethnology* 28 (April 1989), 144; *Ellensburg Record*, 2/6/1957; Corliss, *Fall City*, 27; Percival Jeffcott, "Col. James A. Patterson and Reuben Bizer were Partners at Squahalish Before There was a Lynden," draft ms. and notes, PRJ, CPNWS. The small fort was called Fort Patterson, but seems named for another man.

61. Borst was part of the pioneering Duwamish Valley Collins-Borst family; Corliss, *Fall City*, 31–32; Kate Kanim Borst in Clarence Bagley, *History of King County, Washington* (Seattle: S. J. Clarke, 1929) 1:783; Jeremiah Borst obituary, www.historylink.org; Thrush, *Native Seattle*, 45.

62. Snoqualmie Museum files; Bancroft, *History of Washington*, 368–69.

63. Oliphant, "The Cattle Trade," 132–33.

64. *Pioneer-Democrat*, summer 1860 issues; James Patterson to M. T. Simmons, 6/18/1860; S. S. Bulkley to M. T. Simmons, 6/18/1860, Correspondence and Accounting Records of the Puget Sound District Agency, 1854–1861, NARA, NW.

65. Allan Richardson and Brent Galloway, *Nooksack Place Names* (UBC Press, 2011 edition), 72–73.

66. Agnes James, 8/13/1952, quoting Jack Jimmy in Paul Fetzer field notes, author copy courtesy of Wayne Suttles.

67. Patterson to Simmons, 6/18/1860. Accounting Records of the Puget Sound Agency; Simmons to Geary, *Annual Report*, 7/1860, Tulalip Papers, WSU MASC.

68. Agnes James, 12/12/1950, Fetzer field notes, 1950–1954; E. C. Fitzhugh to Gov. Stevens 1/18/1857 in *Annual Report of the Commissioner of Indian Affairs*, copy in Boxberger Papers, NWEC, CPNWS.

69. See a more complete account of the conflict in *Peace Weavers* ch. 4.

70. George Swanaset Sr. in Fetzer field notes, 7/14/1950; Emily Bizer Cotter, 2/12/1917 affidavit, "Roblin Report of Unenrolled Indians," NARA, NW; Lottie Tom to Fetzer, 11/8/1950; Fetzer notes on language; George Adams to author, 4/29/2010.

71. Suttles, "Post-Contact Culture Change," 41; Swanaset, 9/7/1951, Fetzer field notes; George Adams to author, 3/20/2004.

72. Richardson and Galloway, *Nooksack Place Names*, 64, 73.

73. Patterson to Frank (Benjamin) Shaw, 7/26/1861. Accounting Records of the Puget Sound District Agency, NARA, NW.

74. Roeder diary, 11/28/1861 to 12/1/1861, Henry Roeder Papers, UW Library Special Collections.

75. Patterson genealogies; *PSH*, 6/27/1861, 1/16/1862; Thomas Lately, *The First President Johnson: The Three Lives of the 17th President of the United States of America* (NY: William Morrow, 1968), 101.

76. Patterson and Patkanim genealogies; 1860 U.S. Census, Whatcom County.

77. Judson, *Pioneer's Search*, 211; Judson in C. E. Cline, "Lynden: The 'Gem City' of 20 Years Ago," *Pacific Pilot*, 8/25/1904.

78. Bierwert, *Brushed by Cedar*, 201.

79. John Tennant, farm journal, 6/12/1862, Lummi Nation Archives.

80. Judson, *Pioneer's Search*, 209.

81. Howard Buswell interview notes indicate the Bizer-Descanum relationship. Mrs. Albert Descanum (Sarah) was Clara Tennant's sister; *PSH*, 2/13/1862.

82. Bill Quackenbush (Barkerville Archives) to author, 5/24/2012; Mark Forsythe and Greg Dickson, *The Trail of 1858: B.C.'s Gold Rush Past* (Madeira Park, BC: Harbour Publishing, 2007), 119–20.

83. Oliver Wells, *The Chilliwacks and Their Neighbors*, Ralph Maud, Brent Galloway, and Marie Weeden, eds. (Vancouver: Talonbooks, 1987), 152.

84. *Kwelshan* was the name for the slopes of the volcano; Judson, *Pioneer's Search*, 208–9; Agnes James to Wayne Suttles, 8/13/1952, Suttles research files; Harry M. Majors, ed., *Mount Baker: A Chronicle of its Historic Eruptions and First Ascent* (Seattle: Northwest Press, 1978), 37, quoting the *Pioneer-Democrat*, 12/28/1860; Robert Hawley, *Skqee Mus* (Bellingham: Miller and Sutherlien, 1945), 35, 50.

85. The cabin's exact location is unknown, but one eyewitness located it at about 6th and Front Streets in present-day Lynden. Many photos of the Patterson-Judson cabin exist in books and archives, including Whatcom Museum, CPNWS, Lynden Pioneer Museum.

86. Amelia Dan interview, 1953, NWEC, CPNWS.

87. George Adams to author, 3/20/2004, 4/29/2010; 2003 Nooksack Days flyer; George Swanaset, 9/7/1951, in Fetzer field notes.

88. Louis (Antone) Saquilty, quoted in "Indian Probate Case Revives Ancient History," *Bellingham Herald*, 11/28/1918.

89. Jeffcott, "Col. James Alexander Patterson and Reuben Bizer"; Williams, *The Way We Ate*, 127–28.

90. Williams, *The Way We Ate*, 125–26.

91. Williams, *The Way We Ate*, 128–31.

92. Judson, *Pioneer's Search*, 210–11.

93. Tennant, journal, multiple 1862–1870 entries re: visits to the Patterson home.

94. *PSH*, 3/5/1863.

95. Patterson family genealogy; F. W. Lindsay, *The Cariboo Story* (Kelowna: Regatta City Press, 1958), 13; *Charles Richards v. James A. Patterson and Daniel McClanahan* #377, Series 1 (1863). 3rd District Territorial Court; Henry Roeder Account Book and diary, 1863; Roeder to Elizabeth Roeder, 7/10/1863, both in Roeder Papers.

96. Elizabeth was listed as "Elizabeth Srhaneswoe" on the baptismal record on 9/24/1863, which may have been a mangling of her personal name. Archdiocese of Seattle, Sacramental Records, 2:99.

97. Roeder Account Book, 1863; Bill Quackenbush, Barkerville archivist to author, 5/24/2012.

98. Henry Roeder to Elizabeth Roeder, 7/10/1864, 1/29/1865, Roeder Papers; James Taylor in *American Reveille*, 6/14/1908; Isabel Bescoby, "Society in Cariboo During the Gold Rush," *WHQ* 3 (July 1933): 202.

99. Gordon P. Elliott, *Barkerville, Quesnel and the Cariboo Gold Rush* (Vancouver, BC: Douglas & McIntyre, 1958), 51; John S. Lutz, "Interlude or Industry: Ranching in B.C., 1859–1885," *B.C. Historical News* 13 (Summer 1980): 3–9; Oliphant, "The Cattle Trade," 144; Dolly Patterson Rittenberg interview and Nellie Patterson McDonald in "Sisters Who Will Receive Cup at Pioneers' Picnic Born at Lynden," *Bellingham Herald*, 7/29/1938; Tennant journal, 7/10/1868.

100. Speer, *Sketches of Prominent Tennesseans*, 531–33.

101. Patterson family genealogies; *Bellingham Herald*, 7/29/1938.

102. Tennant journal, 1/1867, 7/14/1867, 1/1869; *Bellingham Herald*, 7/29/1938.

103. For a longer account of the climbs, see *Peace Weavers* ch. 4; Tennant journal, 8/9/1866, 8/23/1866, 8/8/1868, 8/21/1868, 12/24–30/1868.

104. Judson, *Pioneer's Search*, 209–11.

105. Susan Butruille, *Women's Voices from the Frontier* (Boise: Tamarack, 1995), 254ff.

106. George Swanaset, 9/25/1951, Lottie Tom, 11/10/1951, and Agnes James, 9/7/1951, all to Paul Fetzer; Daphne Sleigh, ed., *One Foot on the Border: A History of Sumas Prairie and Area* (Deroche, BC: Sumas Prairie and Area Historical Society, 1999), 99–100; Bob Joe in Wells, *The Chilliwacks*, 53; George Adams to author, 3/20/2004.

107. Judson, *Pioneer's Search*, 211.

108. Tennant journal, 7/14/1867, 7/15/1867.

109. Agnes James to Fetzer, 1950; Drew Crooks, *Past Reflections: Essays on the Hudson's Bay Company in the Southern Puget Sound Region* (Tacoma: Ft. Nisqually Foundation, 2001), 34–43.

110. Sandstrom and Wahl, 6/16/2003.

111. Hawley, *Skqee Mus*, 176–77; Judson, *Pioneer's Search;* Boyd Pratt personal research re: Emmerling, 4/6/2016.

112. Volney Steele, *Bleed, Blister, and Purge: A History of Medicine on the American Frontier* (Missoula MT: Mountain Press, 2005), 277–78; www.raw-milk-facts.com.

113. Dr. Jack Miller, descendant of Johnny Richards, to author; Paul Fetzer Nooksack genealogy chart, CPNWS.

114. Mary Michaelson, *Memory Book: Friends of Aunt Phoebe Reunion* (Lynden WA: Lynden Pioneer Museum, 2006 edition), 98–99; Judson, *Pioneer's Search*, 114–15.

115. Corliss, *Fall City*, 114; *Bellingham Bay Coal Company v. James Patterson*, #625 (1869) and #625 (1870), 3rd District Territorial Court.

116. Whatcom County Auditor, "Record of Marks and Brands, v. 1."

117. Whatcom County Auditor, Conditional Deed Between James Patterson and Phoebe Judson, 3/3/1870, "Deeds G," 208–11.

118. Agreement, James A. Patterson to Holden A. Judson, 3/4/1870, Whatcom County "Deeds F," 133 and "Deeds K," 351–52. The first was filed the day the girls and Phoebe arrived and the second not until 1873 when the survey was done and Judson wanted to file on the land.

119. Judson, *A Pioneer's Search*, 133; Judson, "My Aboriginal Neighbors," *Lynden Tribune*, 1912, printing of paper read to Old Neighbors Club, 1904, Phoebe Judson scrapbook. Lynden Pioneer Museum.

120. Tennant journal, 3/31/1870, 4/7/1870; H. A. Judson, Receipt from the General Land Office, 12/10/1875 in Whatcom County "Deeds M," 514.

121. Whatcom County Power of Attorney, v. 1, 174; 1870 U.S. census, Whatcom County Agricultural Supplement.

122. Whatcom County "Deeds F," 142, 107–8; *Andrew Chambers v. James A. Patterson* judgment, 9/7/1870, District Court Execution Docket Book 1, 222; Mary Michaelson to author, 12/7/2010.

123. Whatcom County "Probate Journal D," 34; "Deeds F," 129, 142–43; *Bellingham Bay Mail*, 10/21/1876.

124. Judson, both *Pioneer's Search* and "My Aboriginal Neighbors."

125. Judson, *Pioneer's Search*, 213; Michaelson, *Memory Book*, 161.

126. Judson, *Pioneer's Search*, 211–12.

127. Judson, *Pioneer's Search*, 213; Peg McDonald to author.

128. Mary Michaelson research; Dan McClanahan will, 1/24/1873, Whatcom County Auditor "Day Book C," 36–37; Lynden Cemetery records; Whatcom "Probate Journal D," 84–85; Probate Journal "Day Book C," 59–61; Judson, *Pioneer's Search*, 231–32.

129. 1880 U.S. Census, Whatcom County; Mary Michaelson research.

130. *Bellingham Bay Mail*, 10/21/1876, 12/9/1876.

131. Whatcom County Auditor, "Mortgages vol. 1," 133–35; Roscoe Sheller, *Ben Snipes: The Northwest Cattle King* (Portland: Binford & Mort, 1957, 1966), 160.

132. 1880 U.S. Census, Washington County, Oregon; Joan Fitch personal research on Ben Catching family; Mary Michaelson research; www.forestgrove-or.gov.

133. James Patterson death notice, *The Daily Mountaineer* (The Dalles, OR), 5/1886.

134. Hawley, *Skqee Mus*, dedication and many additional references.

135. "Petition to the Magistrate of Indian Affairs from the People of Whatcom County, W.T.," 3/25/1874, copy courtesy of Tim Wahl.

136. Phoebe Judson letter, 1/1872, property of Karen Parsons and summarized content courtesy of Mary Michaelson.

137. Judson letter, 1/1872.

138. Whatcom County Auditor, "Marriage Book C," 4; Marriage certificates, 21.

139. Judson, *Pioneer's Search*, 272–73.

140. "Mrs. Dolly Rittenberg, Resident of County 80 Years, is Summoned," *Bellingham Herald*, 4/1943.

141. Whatcom County Auditor, "Deeds 14," 49–51.

142. Mary Michaelson research; *Lynden Pioneer Press*, 12/25/1888, 1/15/1891; Nellie's class photo in Michaelson, *Memory Book*, 142.

143. *Pioneer Press*, several issues; Peggy McDonald to author, 12/10/2010.

144. McDonald family genealogy, courtesy of Peggy McDonald; Clipper Mill letterhead courtesy of Margaret Hellyer; Whatcom County Marriage Book, 2, 225.

145. John McDonald obituary, *Bellingham Herald*, 3/14/1963; Photo of James McDonald courtesy of Peggy McDonald; 1900 U.S. Census, Whatcom County. Peggy McDonald to author, 1/25/2010, 12/10/2010.

146. Whatcom County directories, 1902, etc., WSA, NW region; McDonald research and photo collection; Lynden Museum collections; Mary Michaelson research, 2006.

147. McDonald research.

148. McDonald research; Judson, "My Aboriginal Neighbors."

149. 7/7/1910 postcard re: fire from Phoebe Judson, Edmond Meany Collection, UW; Whatcom County Auditor, "Deeds v. 160," 253.

150. *Bellingham Herald*, 7/24/1938, 7/29/1938.

151. Bayview Cemetery Records, WSA, NW; *Bellingham Reveille*, 12/27/1922; *Deming Prospector*, 12/29/1922; clipping re: Nellie's death, probably from *Bellingham Herald*, undated.

152. Agnes James, 9/7/1951, Lottie Tom, 11/10/1951, George Swanaset, many entries in Fetzer field notes; Sleigh, *One Foot*, 99–100.

Chapter 3: Mary, From the Rapids

1. *Fairhaven Herald*, 3/6/1892.

2. Pronunciation from Mandie Jimmie, Lytton B.C.; Whatcom County marriages Bk. B, 28; Book of Liens "H," 88; Mary Allen, Military Widow Pension Application, 1896, copy in HBP, CPNWS. James Allen Death Certificate, Territory of Alaska #625.

3. Irene Bjerky, "First Peoples of Yale and Spuzzum," unpub. ms. Historic Yale Museum. n.d.

4. Andrea LaForet and Annie York, *Spuzzum: Fraser Canyon Histories, 1808–1939* (Vancouver: UBC Press, 1998), 48; Rich Blacklaws, "Fraser River War: Conflict, Compromise and Consequences," 9/23/2007 Fraser River War Symposium presentation, Lytton, B.C.

5. Annie York, Richard Daly, and Chris Arnett, *They Write Their Dreams on the Rock Forever: Rock Writings in the Stein River Valley of British Columbia* (Vancouver: Talonbooks, 1993), 3.

6. The oldest cemetery in British Columbia was discovered at *Spuzzum*, 15 feet under the surface; Cole Harris, "Fraser Canyon Encountered," *BC Studies* 94 (Summer 1992): 6; Heritage House, *Fraser & Thompson River Canyons* (Surrey, BC: Heritage House, 1986), 58.

7. Bjerky, "First Peoples"; Heritage House, *Fraser and Thompson*, 63.

8. Bjerky, "First Peoples"; Beckey, *Range of Glaciers*, 118.

9. Annie York in Laforet and York, *Spuzzum*, 58; Bjerky, "First Peoples"; 1881 census in Laforet, 179; Mary Charles, 1967 interview, Oliver Wells Collection.

10. Lucy Celestine to Howard Buswell, 5/9/1949, HBP, CPNWS; Robert Boyd, *The Coming of the Spirit of Pestilence* (Seattle: UW Press, 1999), 158.

11. Howard Buswell note 6/6/1942, from conversation with Allen friend who had been told about the gun.

12. Archdiocese of Seattle, Sacramental Records, 4:93.

13. Leslie H. Tepper, *Earth Line and Morning Star: Nlaka'pamux Clothing Traditions* (Hull, Quebec: Canadian Museum of Civilization, 1994), 1.

14. York, Daly, and Arnett, *They Write Their Dreams*, viii, xiv.

15. Jim and Linda Allen personal family research; James E. Davis, *Frontier Illinois* (Bloomington: Indiana Univ. Press, 1998), 180.

16. "Southern Illinois ca. 1812," *Saga of Southern Illinois* 92 (Summer 1982): 20.

17. Theodore Pease, *The Frontier State, 1818–1848* (Urbana: Univ. of Illinois Press, 1987), 160.

18. Solomon Allen claimed the hamlet named for Lafayette as his birthplace, but it didn't become a townsite until after he had left Illinois.

19. 1807 Indiana Territory census; William and Tabitha Allen marriage record, 6/28/1815. Randolph County (IL) Marriage Records v. 1, p. 3, Southern Illinois Archives.

20. J. L. McDonough & Co. *Combined History of Randolph, Monroe, and Perry Counties, Illinois* (Philadelphia, 1883), 106; U.S. Census, Randolph County, 1825, 1850; Archdiocese of Seattle, Sacramental Record, 4:93; C. William Horrell, Henry D. Piper, and John W. Voigt, *Land Between the Rivers: The Southern Illinois Country* (Carbondale: Southern Illinois Univ. Press, 2017), 22.

21. Solomon Allen, Pension File, MexSC # 11651, Veterans Administration, Records of the Mexican War, NARA, copy in HBP, CPNWS.

22. Descendants of Mexican War Veterans, www.dmwv.org; James McCaffrey, *Army of Manifest Destiny: The American Soldier in the Mexican War, 1846–1848* (New York: New York Univ. Press, 1992), 52–53.

23. Solomon Allen Pension file.

24. 1860, 1870 U.S. Census, Randolph County; William Allen, Will 4/5/1864, Randolph County (IL) Probate Records, 1864.

25. John C. Allen to Howard Buswell, 4/14/1948, HBP; Fred Allen affidavit, 5/25/1917. Charles E. Roblin, "Schedule of Unenrolled Indians," U.S. Dept. of the Interior, Office of Indian Affairs, 1919, NARA, NW.

26. John C. Allen to Buswell, 4/14/1958.

27. John C. Allen to Buswell, 4/14/1948.

28. Timetables given by family and second-generation witnesses differ as to when Solomon staked an Oregon claim or whether it was a different Solomon Allen. This version seems to fit the stories and documents best.

29. George F. G. Stanley, *Mapping the Frontier: Charles Wilson's Diary of the Survey of the 49th Parallel, 1858–1862, while Secretary of the British Boundary Commission* (Seattle: UW Press, 1970), 24.

30. Marc Stangroom to "Charly," 6/17/1858. Marc Stangroom Papers, CPNWS.

31. Laforet and York, *Spuzzum*, 75.

32. Laforet and York, *Spuzzum*, 177.

33. Donald Hauka Jr., *McGowan's War* (Vancouver: New Star Books, 2003), 34–35.

34. James Douglas to Lord Stanley, 6/15/1858. In Hauka, *McGowan's War*, 37.

35. *PSH*, 5/14/1858; Frank Allen, interview by author, 8/3/2000; Fred Allen affidavit in Roblin, "Schedule of Unenrolled Indians, 1917"; Rosamond VanMiert, *Settlers, Structures and Ships on Bellingham Bay, 1852–1889* (Bellingham: Rosamond VanMiert, 2004), 90.

36. Agnes Laut, *The Cariboo Trail* (Toronto: Glasgow, Brook and Co., 1921), 11.

37. John C. Allen to Buswell, 4/14/1958.

38. Linguistic usages equate some relationships within the same term.

39. Urban Hicks (1893 essay) in Bennett, *Small World of Our Own*, 292.

40. Jean Barman, "Taming Aboriginal Sexuality: Gender, Power and Race in British Columbia, 1850–1890." *BC Studies* 115/16 (Autumn/Winter 1997–98): 246–47.

41. John C. Allen to Buswell, 4/14/1958; Edith Graham to Buswell, 1/6/1958; Howard Buswell note, 6/6/1942. All in HBP, CPNWS; Laforet and York, *Spuzzum*, 15.

42. Adele Perry, *On the Edge of Empire: Gender, Race and the Making of British Columbia, 1849–1871* (Toronto: Univ. of Toronto Press, 2001), 172; Adele Perry, "Oh I'm Just Sick of the Faces of Men," *BC Studies* 105/6. (Spring/Summer 1995): 39–40.

43. A. W. Arnold in Bennett, *Small World of Our Own*, 286.

44. *Spuzzum*-raised Lena Hope to Oliver Wells, 9/28/1967, Oliver Wells Collection; Perry, *On the Edge*, 61.

45. The Warner land in Skagit County, WA, is now called "Warner's Prairie." Laforet and York, *Spuzzum*, 14.

46. Jenny Wynn's half-sister married a son of Allard (see ch. 1); Hauka, *McGowan's War*, 96–97.

47. For additional information on Thomas York's life in B.C., see Sleigh, *One Foot on the Border*, 102–3. His son Fraser York was later involved in the infamous lynching of Nooksack Indian Louie Sam by Whatcom County men who crossed the border to kill the young man. See Keith Thor Carlson, "The Lynching of Louie Sam," *BC Studies* (Spring 1996): 63–79.

48. Spintlum's daughter married Thomas Hicks, brother of a Washington Territory Indian fighter and newspaperman who had exploited a young woman and left. They established a family. John Hauka to author, 5/7/2009.

49. Laforet and York, *Spuzzum*, 56, 117.

50. Kate Vail to Howard Buswell, 4/27/1948; Buswell notes, 6/6/1942; Chris Siegel to Buswell, 10/29/1956. All in HBP; Williams, *The Way We Ate*, 46.

51. Vail to Buswell, 4/27/1948.

52. Roeder Account Book, 8/15/1861; John Tennant, Farm Journal, 3/13/1862, Lummi Nation Archives, courtesy of Chief Tsi'lixw (William) James; Buswell notes on Mahoney, 1956; San Francisco Committee of Vigilance, 1851 Log Book, copy at San Francisco Public Library; Whatcom County Public Works, Survey Field Notes 1, 7/1859, 25–41.

53. *Territory v. Abner Dunn* #361 (1862), 3rd District Territorial Court.

54. The McLean and Allen homesteads are not exactly the same shape. Henry Roeder Account Books; *PSH*, 2/6/1864, 3/12/1864; John C. Allen, Ledger, Allen Collection, Clausen Memorial Museum (Petersburg, AK), 155; Whatcom County Deeds "N," 147–49; Tennant journal, 2/25/1864.

55. Julius Charles interview, 4/13/1943, HBP, CPNWS.

56. Tennant journal, 7/23/1864, 11/6/1864, 1/23/1866; John C. Allen Ledger, 155.

57. County Commissioners Proceedings 1, 159; Edith Graham 1/6/1958 and 1/9/1958 to Howard Buswell, HBP, CPNWS; John C. Allen to Buswell, 4/13/1948; Fischer, *Albion's Seed*, 771; Melody Graulich, "Violence Against Women: Power Dynamics in Literature of the Western Family" in Susan Armitage and Elizabeth Jameson, *The Women's West* (Norman: Univ. of Oklahoma Press, 1987), 113–14.

58. Edith Graham to Buswell, 1/6/1958, HBP, CPNWS; John Tennant journal, summer 1868; H. B. Williams in *American Reveille*, 6/14/1908; James Kavanaugh, diary, 9/23/1868, copy courtesy of Kavanaugh family.

59. See *Peace Weavers* ch. 2 for Caroline's deer story; Edith Graham to Buswell, 1/6/1958.

60. John C. Allen Ledger, 155.

61. Howard Buswell noted in his research that "someone" told him the story, 1/1958, HBP, CPNWS.

62. 1870 U.S. Census, Whatcom County Agricultural Supplement; Solomon Allen, Homestead Application #432 and Application for Title (1869). General Land

Office records, Olympia WA, courtesy of Tim Wahl; Homestead Certificate #157, Whatcom County Deeds "N," 147–49.

63. Allen Homestead Application; 1870 Washington Territorial Census, Products of Agriculture Schedule; Henry Roeder diaries, 187, Roeder Papers; Tennant journal 1867+.

64. Whatcom County Deeds "N," 148–49.

65. 1880 Washington Territorial Census, Products of Agriculture; *Puget Sound Mail*, 3/27/1880; Whatcom Deeds 1, 136–37; *Whatcom Reveille*, 7/2/1883, 9/7/1883, 7/9/1881; Bernard McDonough Account Books; Howard Buswell research files. Both in HBP.

66. See *Peace Weavers* ch. 5 for Nellie Lane's biography; Constance Lane, delayed birth certificate, 3/7/1880. Whatcom County Clerk, WSA, NW.

67. Chris Siegel to Buswell, 11/7/1956, HBP; Steele, *Bleed, Blister and Purge*, 191; James Teit, *Thompson Indians of B.C.*, Franz Boas, ed. (Merrit, BC: Nicola Valley Museum Archives Assn. reprint, n.d.), 304–5.

68. Edith Graham to Buswell, 1/6/1958; Chris Siegel to Buswell, 11/7/1956, 10/29/1956. HBP.

69. Tennant journals; Siegel to Buswell, 10/29/1956; Frank Wifler to Buswell, 11/27/1950. HBP.

70. Archdiocese of Seattle, Sacramental Records, 3:36.

71. Whatcom County Auditor Book of Liens "H," 88; Whatcom County Marriage Book B, 28, 50, 40; John C. Allen Ledger.

72. Archdiocese of Seattle, Sacramental Records, 3:107, and 4:93, 277.

73. John C. Allen to Buswell, 4/19/1948, HBP.

74. McDonough Account Books, HBP.

75. Sam and John Allen to Buswell, 2/24/1954. Dessie May Dunagan, *History of Ferndale Consolidated School District #502* (Ferndale WA: Ferndale Consolidated School District, 1968), 42–45.

76. John Allen to Buswell, 4/13/1948; Florence Boone to Buswell, 12/30/1947. HBP.

77. John C. Allen, 4/13/1948; Solomon Allen Military Pension Application, 6/13/1887, copy in Buswell Papers; Mary Allen, Widow's Claim for Service Pension, 9/11/1896, copy in Buswell Papers. Both from Military Pension file #11651. All in HBP.

78. McDonough Account Books, HBP.

79. *Puget Sound Mail*, 11/19/1881; copy of Marietta plat 7/4/1883, Buswell Map Collection, CPNWS; *Whatcom Reveille*, 6/23/1883.

80. Marietta plat map 7/4/1883; *Whatcom Reveille*, 9/7/1883; John C. Allen to Buswell, 4/19/1948 and other eyewitness reports re: the naming of the town.

Later secondhand guesses that "Marietta" had something to do with Tennant's own history were erroneous.

81. Mary Jane died 2/6/1887, John C. Allen Ledger, 156; Edith Graham to Buswell, 1/6/1958, HBP.

82. Howard Buswell research notes; Chris Siegel to Buswell, 10/29/1956. HBP.

83. *Whatcom Reveille*, 9/21/1883; Solomon Allen Pension file affidavit, 1/30/1894. HBP.

84. James LeMaster, "Baer Tales," (unpub. ms., 1996), 16–18, courtesy of the author.

85. *Daily Reveille*, 1/1/1892, 1/22/1892.

86. Preferred spelling of "Swe'lus" taken from later name holder's obituary, *Bellingham Herald*, 4/25/2010; *Daily Reveille*, 1/24/1892; *State of Washington v. George Swiloos*, Whatcom County #1347 (1892), WSA, NW.

87. George Swanaset to Paul Fetzer, 9/26/1951. Fetzer field notes, CPNWS.

88. *Fairhaven Herald*, 3/6/1892; *Daily Reveille*, 3/23/1892.

89. *Fairhaven Herald*, 3/13/1892, 3/15/1892; Chris Siegel to Buswell, 10/29/1956.

90. George Swe'lus eventually returned to the Lummi Reservation where he had been a successful farmer. He spent the rest of his life there with his family; *Daily Reveille*, 3/23/1892, 3/31/1892.

91. Solomon Allen to Mary Allen, Whatcom County Deeds 34, 436, 1/21/1895; Solomon Allen death return, WSA,NW.

92. *Bellingham Bay Reveille*, 2/1/1895; Bayview Cemetery Records, WSA, NW.

93. Laforet and York, *Spuzzum*, 185.

94. "Claim of Widow for Service Pension," Solomon Allen Pension File, copy in Buswell Papers; Frank Allen to author, 8/3/2000.

95. *American Reveille*, 1/6/1913; Buswell research notes, HBP; Bayview Cemetery records.

96. Mary Allen to Buswell, undated and quoted to Percival Jeffcott, 4/27/1945, Jeffcott Collection, WSA, NW; Edith Graham to Buswell, 1/6/1958, HBP; Sylvia Van Kirk, "Tracing the Fortunes of Five Founding Families of Victoria," *BC Studies* 115/16 (Autumn/Winter 1997–98): 177.

97. Fred Allen affidavit, 5/5/1917; Roblin, "Schedule of Unenrolled Indians"; Snohomish County (WA) Marriage Certificates Book 1B, 26; Frank Allen to author, 8/3/2000; Robert H. Ruby and John A. Brown, *Esther Ross, Stillaguamish Champion* (Norman: Univ. of Oklahoma Press, 2001).

98. Jim and Linda Allen correspondence; Buswell notes, 6/6/1942, HBP; Whatcom County Birth Returns #1323 and #1322; Brown's Business College files, Centralia (IL) Area Historical Museum; Hyde, *Empire, Nations and Families*, 49, 326–27.

99. Virginia Roberts to author, 2/8/2003; Whatcom County Marriage Returns, Box 1; 1910 U.S. Census, Whatcom County; Mary Allen to John C. Allen, Quit Claim Deed, 12/8/1902, copy in HBP.

100. *The Petersburg Progressive*, 1/3/1914.

101. *Petersburg Progressive*, 6/27/1914, 7/4/1914; Pioneers of Alaska, *Pioneer Profiles: A History of Petersburg Settlers, 1898–1959* (Port Townsend: Sand Dollar Press, 2004), 11; www.petersburg.org.

102. *Petersburg Weekly Report*, 1/8/1916, etc.; State of Alaska Death Certificate, Herbert Allen, #0024; Kathy Pool research and correspondence with author, 2003; Letter to Mary C. Allen, 9/4/1916, John C. Allen Papers, Clausen Memorial Museum; Mary C. Allen obituary, *Alaska Weekly*, 8/31/1945.

103. John C. Allen Ledger, 156, 158; Whatcom County Birth Return 5/28/1894; Buswell research notes; U.S. Census, St. Louis 1900, 1910, 1920: Maggie Kirwam research, C. E. Brehm Library (Mt. Vernon, IL).

104. Snohomish County Marriage Certificate #344, Book B, 108; Whatcom County directories 1901–1904, WSA, NW; Sam Allen, letter to John C. Allen, 12/20/1916, John Allen Papers; Edith Allen obituary, *Alaska Weekly*, 7/20/1945.

105. Corinne Allen school photo, Buswell Papers; Lytton Museum and Archives Newsletter, 11/2001; Jean Barman to author, 2/12/2015.

106. *Ketchikan Times* editorial 7/25/1919; *Petersburg Weekly Report* 7/4/1919, 7/11/1919, 8/22/1919, 9/19/1919.

107. *Alaska Weekly*, 4/26/1946, obituary of James Allen.

108. Pioneers of Alaska, *Pioneer Profiles*, 260; U.S. Commissioner, records of Marriages Certificate Book A, 175; *Petersburg Progressive*, 2/15/1913, 3/8/1913; Patricia Roppel research notes; Kathy Pool research notes; "The Arctic Brotherhood," unpub. ms. courtesy of Valdez Museum Historical Archives.

109. *Alaska Weekly* 4/26/1946. Alaska Death Certificates, Petersburg Book 5: 104.

Chapter 4: Mrs. Pickett, The Commander's Wife

1. Doris McIlroy, "George E. Pickett III Tells of Grandfather's Post-War Romance," *Bellingham Herald* and *Seattle Post-Intelligencer*, 10/21/1938.

2. There was no such defeat, and no "chief" at the time; LaSalle Corbell Pickett, "My Soldier," *McClure's Magazine* 30 (March 1908, #5), 563–64.

3. Hallie Lysle Campbell, 7/1945, to Howard Buswell, HBP.

4. Edward G. Longacre, *Pickett: Leader of the Charge* (Sheppenburg, PA: White Mane Publishing, 1998), 40–41; Lesley J. Gordon, *General George E. Pickett in Life and Legend* (Chapel Hill: Univ. of North Carolina, 1998), 49–53; also many others; Scott C. Sagan & Samuel K. Sagan, "Pickett's Other Charge," *Wall Street Journal*, 6/21/2013.

5. The most reliable accounts are in Edson, *Fourth Corner*, and research by Mary Knight and Jessie Knight Grisdale, J. T. Pickett Collection, WSHS. All of those parties knew and interviewed Jimmy Pickett's foster father, William Walter. Examples of the stereotyped writings are Dolly Connolly's "Jimmie Pickett—the forgotten child," *Tacoma News Tribune & Sunday Ledger*, 12/4/1977, and Alice Watts, "The Life & Hard Times of Jimmie Pickett," *Sunday Olympian*, 9/10/1967.

6. Archie Binns, *The Laurels Are Cut Down* (New York: Literary Guild of America, 1937), 1–10; Edson, *Fourth Corner*, 115.

7. William Walter interview, 1904, in Edson, *The Fourth Corner*, 110, 115.

8. Karen Jones-Lamb, *Native-American Wives of San Juan Settlers* (Decatur Island: Bryn Tirion Publishing, 1994); Sylvia Van Kirk, "Tracing the Fortunes of Five Founding Families of Victoria," (*BC Studies*, Autumn/Winter 1997–8), 149–179; Charles Griffin, *BelleVue Farm Post Journals 1854–1855*, HBC MF 1M16, transcription by Wayne Suttles, courtesy of Mike Vouri; R. V. Peabody to Gov. Isaac Stevens, 1/23/1856 re: Northern wives and M. T. Simmons report, 138–9, both in NWEC, CPNWS; Mary Frances Lysle, "Christmas, 1854," speech copy in HBP, CPNWS; Mike Vouri, "Raiders from the North" (ms. copy, 1995), courtesy of author; Bill Mason and Babe Jewett 9/25/2001 to Jacilee Wray & Mike Vouri; Lucy Beigin obituary 4/14/1898, *Washington Genealogy Society Bulletin* 15 (1984), 10; Michael and Julia Vouri, *Images of America: San Juan Island* (Charleston: Arcadia Publishing, 2011), 91; Bill Rossler to Wayne Suttles, 1946–47. Suttles personal research files courtesy of Dr. Suttles; Lucile McDonald, *Making History: The People Who Shaped the San Juan Islands* (Friday Harbor: Harbor Press, 1990), 73; Wayne Suttles, "The Coast Salish in the Journals," *BC Historical News* (Fall 1999): 10–13; Grant Keddie, *Songhees Pictorial: A History of the Songhees People as Seen by Outsiders, 1790–1912* (Victoria: Royal BC Museum, 2003), 7; E. C. Fitzhugh to W. W. Miller, 8/21/1856, re: payment to Northern men in the militia, W. W. Miller Papers, Beineke Library, Yale University.

9. W. H. Pierce, *13 Years of Travel and Exploration in Alaska*, R. N. DeArmond, ed. (Anchorage: All Alaska Publishing, 1977), 15; Jeanette Taylor, *The Quadra Story* (Madeira Park, BC: Harbour Pub., 2009), 27–36; Mike Vouri email 6/19/2018.

10. Charles Fleurieu (1801) in Erna Gunther, *Indian Life on the Northwest Coast* (Chicago: Univ. of Chicago Press, 1972), 281.

11. Pierce, *13 Years*, 15.

12. Christiancy Pickett Jr., genealogy research, 1998, courtesy of Christiancy Pickett and Martha Boltz; Fischer, *Albion's Seed*, 216; Madeline Devereaux Eckert, comp., "Pickett-Heth-Copland Genealogy" (unpub. ms., 2001), courtesy of George and Ridgeley Copland.

13. The colonel's son, Charles C. Pickett, established a family line whose members have used the name "George" and often confuse their genealogy with that of George E. Pickett; Christiancy Pickett Jr. genealogy chart; R. E. Stivers,

"Turkey Island Plantation," *Virginia Cavalcade* 14 (Autumn 1964): 41–47; Gordon, *General George E. Pickett*, 185; James A. Johnston, *Virginia Magazine of History & Biography*, 60, #3 (7/1952), 242, 251–52; Edwin M. Betts, *Thomas Jefferson's Farm Book* (Thomas Jefferson Memorial Foundation, 1999), 293–94; author visit to Turkey Island, 9/11/2003; W. Asbury Christian, *Richmond, Her Past and Present* (Richmond: L. H. Jenkins, 1912), 46, 57.

14. Dr. James B. McCaw, "McClurg Descent," *William & Mary College Quarterly Historical Papers*, 1 (January 1893), 164–65; Christiancy Pickett Jr. genealogy; Shockoe Cemetery (Richmond) records and biographies, online; online McCaw, McClurg, Johnston, and Pickett researchers' results consistent with each other and other sources.

15. Virginia Dabney, *Richmond: The Story of a City* (Garden City: Doubleday, 1976), 90–91; J. F. Watson, *Calamity at Richmond* (Philadelphia: John W. Watson, 1812), 19; Christian, *Richmond, Her Past*, 81.

16. The Pickett-Johnston wedding was 6/19/1823; Johnston family genealogies, Pickett Society research files, courtesy of Patricia Wood; Louise Pecquet DuBellet, *Some Prominent Virginia Families, vol. 1* (Lynchburg: J. P. Bell Co., 1907), n.p.; www.findagrave.com, Shockoe Cemetery records.

17. www.pickettsociety.com; G. E. Pickett obituary, *Norfolk Virginian*, 7/31/1875; Christiancy Pickett Jr. genealogy; Shockoe Cemetery records.

18. Stivers, "Turkey Island," 41–47; Longacre, *Pickett: Leader of the Charge*, 3–4; Gordon, *General George E. Pickett*, 7; Bertram Wyatt-Brown, *Southern Honor: Ethics and Behavior in the Old South* (New York: Oxford Univ. Press, 1982), 167; Gregg Kimball, "We Are Virginians," CSPAN2, 2/18/2001; Christian, *Richmond, Her Past*, 115.

19. Gordon, *General George E. Pickett*, 7.

20. www.pickettsociety.com; Kimball, "We Are Virginians," CSPAN2, 2/18/2001; Richard F. Selcer, *Faithfully and Forever Your Soldier: General George E. Pickett, CSA* (Gettysburg: Farnsworth House Military Impression, 1995), 7; Harry M. Ward, *Richmond: An Illustrated History* (Northridge CA: Windson Publishing, 1985), n.p.; Christian, *Richmond, Her Past*, 148.

21. Alfred J. Morrison, *The Beginning of Public School in Virginia, 1776–1860*, v. 187 (Virginia State Board of Education, 1917); Christian, *Richmond, Her Past*, 46.

22. Gordon, *General George E. Pickett*, 7; Christian, *Richmond, Her Past*, 124.

23. Andrew Johnson's law partner Archibald Williams introduced him to Lincoln. City of Quincy Abraham Lincoln bicentennial website, "Building on Lincoln's Legacy," 2009.

24. Gordon, *General George E. Pickett*, 9–10.

25. Wyatt-Brown, *Southern Honor*, 190–91; Gordon, *General George E. Pickett*, 10–14; James L. Morrison Jr., *The Best School in the World: West Point 1833–1866* (Kent, OH: Kent State Univ. Press, 1986).

26. Selcer, *Faithfully and Forever*, 11–12; Longacre, *Pickett: Leader of the Charge*, 27; Gordon, *General George E. Pickett*, 27.

27. Longacre, *Pickett: Leader of the Charge*, 28; Selcer, *Faithfully and Forever*, 12.

28. John & Sarah Harrison Minge Bible, usgenweb.com; "Minge Family Register." Family Bible copied by Minge Wilkins, owner. *William & Mary Quarterly*, Series 1, 21 (July 1912): 31–32; George & Ridgely Copland, North Bend plantation, interviews by author, 9/11–12/2003; John W. Minge, "Compiled History of Minge Family and Map of Weyanoke," (unpub. ms.), courtesy of George and Ridgely Copland; Elizabeth Fox-Genovese, *Within the Plantation Household: Black and White Women of the Old South* (Chapel Hill: Univ. of North Carolina Press, 1988) 207.

29. Longacre, *Pickett: Leader of the Charge*, 30; Gordon, *General George E. Pickett*, 34, 194; "Minge Family Register" and other cited Minge genealogical sources; Selcer, *Faithfully and Forever*, n.p.; Shockoe Cemetery biographies.

30. Gordon, *General George E. Pickett*, 37; Shockoe Cemetery records & biographies; *Daily Picayune* (New Orleans), 1/13/1852.

31. Gordon, *General George E. Pickett*, 39–41; Howard Buswell research notes, HBP; Michael Vouri, *The Pig War* (Friday Harbor: Griffin Bay Bookstore, 1999), 198.

32. John Hemphill, *West Pointers in Early Washington* (Seattle: West Point Society of Puget Sound, 1992); *Pioneer-Democrat* (Olympia), 3/21/1856.

33. Fred R. Brown, *History of the 9th U.S. Infantry 1799–1909* (Chicago: R.R. Donnelley and Sons, 1909); Letter to the editor from E. C. Fitzhugh, *Pioneer-Democrat*, 9/28/1855.

34. Edson, *Fourth Corner*, 34–35; Capt. G. E. Pickett to Major William Mackall, Adjutant General, Dept. of the Pacific, 8/1/1857, copy at Oregon Historical Society.

35. *Pioneer-Democrat*, 11/6/1857; Roth, *History of Whatcom County*, v. 1, 73.

36. *Washington Territory v. Thomas Harkey and Richard McCann #65* (1857), 3rd Territorial District Court; Lt. James W. Forsyth to James H. Forsyth, late fall 1856, courtesy of family member Dr. Elizabeth Upton, now at William Clements Library, Univ. of Michigan; Pickett to Mackall, 8/1/1857; James W. Forsyth to his sister Ada Forsyth 4/30/1859, courtesy of Dr. Elizabeth Upton; Roth, *History of Whatcom v. 1*, 73. For more on Robert Davis, see *Peace Weavers*, ch. 2.

37. Jack Brown, *The Semiahmoo People*, unpub. thesis, www.members.shaw.ca; Suttles, "Post-Contact Culture," 29–102; Kent D. Richards, *Isaac I. Stevens: Young Man in a Hurry* (Pullman: Washington State Univ. Press, 1993), 268; E. C. Fitzhugh to W. W. Miller, 8/21/1856, re: Northern mercenaries, copy in HBP.

38. Charles Wilson, 3/3/1859, in Stanley, *Mapping the Frontier*, 46.

39. Ben Olney to Lucullus McWhorter, McWhorter Collection, WSU MASC; Blanche Eskin, "Mrs. Elizabeth Collins' Story," *The Polk County Observer*,

1/1/1927; Carpenter, *The Nisqually, My People*; Van Kirk, "Tracing the Fortunes," 149–79; John Adams, *Old Square Toes and His Lady* (Victoria: Horsdal and Shubart, 2001), 87.

40. Howard Buswell noted in a letter to Edson 6/27/1955, that "you have authority for your stand," HBP; Clinton, *The Plantation Mistress*, 103; Edson, *Fourth Corner*, 116; William Walker to George H. Himes, 8/1930, James Tilton Pickett file, OHS.

41. See also *Peace Weavers* ch. 2 for the story of Lt. Davis and wife Caroline; N. V. Sheffer, *Port Townsend Leader*, 12/17/1905; George Kinley (Kennerly) to Lelah Edson, *Fourth Corner*, 115; Anne P. Streeter to author, 3/9/2012; author's personal research on Cecelia and Caleb Kennerly.

42. "City of Whatcom, Bellingham Bay," illustration by S. F. Baker in *California Magazine*, v. 3 (8/5/1858), California State Library.

43. Jessie Grisdale to Bernice Sapp, 7/15/1943, Pickett Collection, WSHS; Thomas Vaughn & Bill Holm, *Soft Gold: The Fur Trade & Cultural Exchange on the Northwest Coast of America* (Portland: OHS, 1982), 20; Robin Fisher, *Contact and Conflict: Indian-European Relations in B.C., 1774–1890* (Vancouver: UBC Press, 1992), 5–7.

44. Clinton, *Plantation Mistress*, 177.

45. E. C. Fitzhugh to Gov. Isaac Stevens, 4/5/1857, in *WHQ* 1 (January 1907): 56; Alexandra Harmon, *Indians in the Making: Ethnic Relations and Indian Identities around Puget Sound* (Berkeley: Univ. of California, 1998), 95.

46. Tom Edwards, "The Civil War and Benjamin Stark," PNW Historians Guild Conference speech, 3/1/2008.

47. John Nevin King to mother, 12/25/1857, King Family Papers, Illinois State Historical Society; C.B.R. Kennerly to S. F. Baird, 1/7/1858, Spencer F. Baird Papers, Smithsonian Institution Archives; Anne P. Streeter, *Joseph S. Harris and the U.S. Northwest Boundary Survey, 1857–1861* (Bloomington, IN: Trafford Publishing, 2013), 101.

48. *Washington Territory v. Edward French* #86 (1857) 3rd District Territorial Court. WSA, NW.

49. C.B.R. Kennerly to S. F. Baird, 12/31/1857, Baird Papers, Smithsonian Institution Archives.

50. Lorraine McConaghy and Judy Bentley, *Free Boy: A True Story of Slave and Master* (Seattle: UW Press, 2013).

51. E. C. Fitzhugh to M. T. Simmons, 1/5/1858, Tulalip Papers re: winter, WSU MASC; Simmons to Commissioner of Indian Affairs, 12/31/1857, re: Fitzhugh's reports, copy in NWEC.

52. John N. King to Sarah King, 10/12/1857, King Family Papers; J. Ross Browne, *Indian Affairs in the Territories of Oregon and Washington* (Fairfield WA: Ye Galleon Press, 1977, reprint of special report), 14 (original, H.R. Exec. Doc.

#39. 35 Cong I Session [1858], 10); Fitzhugh to Simmons, 1/5/1858, Simmons to Commissioner of Indian Affairs, 12/31/1857; Fred Beckey, *Range of Glaciers*, 299–300.

53. Robert C. Fay, 6/30/1858, Annual Report, Commissioner of Indian Affairs, 240, copy in NWEC; Boyd, *The Coming of the Spirit of Pestilence*, 20.

54. Edson, *Fourth Corner*, 110; Fitzhugh to Simmons, 3/1858.

55. A small "lower class" native in-ground cemetery was below the Pickett house, but it was an unlikely choice because she was an elite woman whose people used tree burials. When Bayview Cemetery was founded in the 1880s and a railroad came through Dead Man's Point, remains were disinterred and gathered into a single box or bag and re-buried in an unknown plot there; *Northern Light* #11 (9/11/1858), 4.

56. Edson was told that Mrs. Pickett had a married sister on San Juan Island, but efforts to find a "Dan and Maggie Ross" there have been fruitless.

57. Special Order #68, *Fort Bellingham Post Returns*, 5/1858. Microfilm, WSA, NW; Letter 7/29/1858, William Henry Royle Papers, WSHS.

58. The lot at the corner of F Street and Dupont is the site of the later "Pickett Building"; Edward M. Coffman, *The Old Army: A Portrait of the American Army in Peacetime, 1784–1898* (New York: Oxford Univ. Press, 1986), 84–86; Whatcom County Deeds B, 94, 96–7, Deeds E, 24, 77.

59. *Fort Bellingham Post Returns*, 6/1858; *Alta California*, 6/9/1858.

60. Gordon, *General George E. Pickett*, 53; Dr. Blair Burwell to Virginia Pickett, 7/21/1858; Virginia Pickett to Burwell, 7/21/1858, both in Virginia Pickett Burwell Papers, Swem Library, College of William & Mary.

61. Burwell to Virginia Pickett, 8/4/1858.

62. J. W. Forsyth to Ada Forsyth, 4/30/1859, courtesy of Dr. Elizabeth Upton.

63. The summary narrative of Pig War events is taken from several of historian Michael Vouri's definitive books on the dispute, most notably *The Pig War*, but also including his personal research and several other works. The dispute's British perspective is presented in Vouri's *Outpost of Empire: The Royal Marines and the Joint Occupation of San Juan Island* (Seattle: UW Press, 2004); *PSH*, 8/5/1859.

64. *PSH*, 8/12/1859; Pickett to AAG Alfred Pleasanton, rec'd 7/27/1859, NARA RG567, MF Reel #609; Court martial of Lt. John C. Howard, Records of the Judge Advocate General, RG 153, Court Martial Card Files 1809–1894, NARA; Camp Pickett Post Returns, 6/1861, Records of the War Dept., Office of the Adjutant General, NARA.

65. John Nevin King letter, 12/11/1859, King Family Papers.

66. Butruille, *Women's Voices*, 108.

67. Edson, *Fourth Corner*, 119; Accounts, James Tilton Pickett Collection, WSHS.

68. B. F. Shaw to 'Armstrong,' 8/6/1860, re: Pickett's pleasure in hearing about his boy. W. W. Miller Papers.

69. *PSH*, 5/25/1860; Shockoe Cemetery records; Pickett genealogies.

70. Vouri, *Outpost of Empire*, 52.

71. G. E. Pickett to Maj. Benjamin Alvord, 2/13/1861, OHS; Christopher Rossler to Eldridge Morse, 1881 interview, Bancroft Mss P-B 30–54, #44, Bancroft Library, University of California Berkeley; Gregg Kimball, *American City, Southern Place* (Athens: Univ. of Georgia Press, 2000), 228–29; Camp Pickett Post Returns, 5/1861, NARA Microfilm, WSA, NW.

72. Gordon, *George E. Pickett*, 65.

73. *Pioneer-Democrat*, 5/17/1861, 5/21/1861, 5/24/1861, 5/30/1861.

74. Special Order #9, General Order #13, in Camp Pickett Post Returns, 6/1861; Mike Vouri, "Pig War to Civil War: George Pickett and James Alden, Jr.," endnote 16, 17, ms. copy 2008, courtesy of author; Roxanne Dunbar-Ortiz, *An Indigenous People's History of the U.S.* (Boston: Beacon Press, 2014), 133.

75. Hugh Goldsborough arrived in 1850 on the *Massachusetts*, commanded by his brother and future Admiral, Louis Goldsborough; acceptance of the resignation (6/25/1861) published in General Order #64, series 1861, House of Representatives, 39th Congress, 6/1/1866; Pickett to Goldsborough, 7/2/1861, copy in Edson, *Fourth Corner*, 117; Harry Deegan, *History of Mason County* (H. W. Deegan, 1960), 5; R. V. Peabody to W. W. Miller, 7/16/1861, re: payment for children's foster care; W.W. Miller Papers.

76. Vouri, *The Pig War*, 205; *The Northwest*, 7/18/1861; Brown, *History of the Ninth Infantry*; Vouri, *Outpost of Empire*, 52; Edson, *Fourth Corner*, 111–12; James Tilton to Catherine Collins, 8/8/1861, copy in Thomas Bibb manuscript, Pickett collection at WSHS, as well as in Edson, 117; the location of the original is unknown to author.

77. Tilton to Collins, 8/8/1861; James Tilton Pickett Collection, WSHS.

78. Tilton to Collins, 8/8/1861.

79. Years before, Eldridge (born Alexander Braid Munro) took the name of a no-show ship crewman in order to get to the United States from Scotland; *PSH*, 2/13/1862; Vouri, *The Pig War*, 247; Pickett, "My Soldier," 563–64; Mike Vouri email, 6/19/2018, re: Sam Barron.

80. James Tilton to Catherine Collins, 8/8/1861, Edmund Meany Collection, UW, copy in Edson, *Fourth Corner*, 117.

81. Tilton to Collins, 8/8/1861; photo at WSHS and Whatcom Museum.

82. Tilton to Collins, 9/23/1861, copy in Edson, *Fourth Corner*, 118; George Pickett letter in Arthur Crew Inman, ed., *Soldier of the South: General Pickett's war letters to his wife* (NY: Houghton Mifflin Co., 1928), quoted in Howard Buswell notes, HBP, CPNWS; McIlroy, "George E. Pickett III Tells of Grandfather's Post-War Romance," *Bellingham Herald*, 10/21/1938.

83. Frank S. and Anne Page Johns, "Chimborazo Hospital and J. B. McCaw, Surgeon-in-chief," *Virginia Magazine of History and Biography* 62 (April 1954); Chimborazo Hospital Employee List, copy at Richmond Battlefield Park.

84. Longacre, *Pickett, Leader of the Charge*, 122–27, 133; Selcer, *Faithfully and Forever*, 32.

85. Marriage, 9/15/1863, in LaSalle Pickett obituary, *Washington Post*, 3/23/1931; also *PSH*, 5/23/1864.

86. Longacre, *Pickett, Leader of the Charge*, 164, 170; Gordon, *George E. Pickett*, 154.

87. R. A. Brock, *The Appomattox Register* (New York: Antiquarian Press, 1962, reprint of 1887 edition), 70–71; James L. Morrison Jr., ed. *Memoirs of Henry Heth* (Westport, CT: Greenwood Press, 1974), 65.

88. James Tilton to Aaron Collins, 9/26/1865, though he used the erroneous name "John," EMP; James Tilton to Catherine Collins, 6/4/1864, reprinted in Edson, *Fourth Corner*, 118.

89. Portland friends saw letters from George to his son, but they have disappeared; Tilton to A. Collins, 9/26/1865; Accounts, Pickett Collection, WSHS.

90. Born healthy, David Corbell Pickett lived only until 1873 when he died from an injury. Pickett to Ben Stark, 3/16/1866. Benjamin Stark Papers, OHS; Advertisement, www.pickettsociety.com; condolence letters to the Picketts, courtesy of Patricia Wood, 4/17/2012.

91. *Norfolk Virginian*, 7/30/1875, 7/31/1875, 8/2/1875; St. Vincent's Hospital death record, 7/30/1875, courtesy of Patricia Wood, 4/17/2012; *Bellingham Bay Mail*, 8/28/1875.

92. Washington Territory House of Representatives, 1/9/1860, copy in EMP, UW.

93. Tilton had an impeccable patriot lineage. His great-uncle was the nation's first Surgeon General and he owned a lock of George Washington's hair, which he presented to the Olympia Masonic Lodge. He gained unwanted notoriety in 1860 when his young slave stowed away on a ship to join Victoria's black community. *GLO Surveyor Personal Notes*, www.olsonengr.com; James Tilton to James Tilton Pickett, 11/10/1875, EMP; McConaghy and Bentley, *Free Boy*, ch. 5.

94. In a strange historic twist, Catherine's great-grandfather's brother married Abraham Lincoln's great-grandfather's sister, although she may have never known the odd connection. "The Millard Family of Berks County, Pennsylvania." www.ancestry.com/genMillard.

95. Catherine Millard, born 6/9/1828, Benjamin & Elizabeth Millard family Bible, James T. Pickett collection, WSHS; Obituary 1/17/1902, *Shelton Journal*.

96. Aaron Martin Collins, born 11/29/1809, John and Jane Collins family Bible, courtesy of JoEllen McConnell; Weston A. Goodspeed & Charles Blanchard, *History of Whitley & Noble Counties, Indiana* (Chicago: F. A. Battey and Co., 1882), 122, 243; S. P. Kaler and R. H. Maring, *History of Whitley County,*

Indiana (B. F. Bowen and Company, 1907), 321; Lewis Pub. Co., *Memorial Record of Northeastern Indiana* (Chicago: Lewis Publishing, 1896), 180; James D. Adams, "Tomahawks, Indians and the Stake," *The Bulletin*, Whitley County Historical Society, 4/1966; Jo Ellen McConnell research; G. M. Fleck, *The Cuppy House* (no pub., 1954), 3–8; John Campbell diary, 10/3/1870, John Campbell Papers, UW Library Special Collections.

97. Notes from Collins family courtesy of Llyn De Danaan, 11/15/2010; Marriage record 9/21/1848, Indiana State Library database "Indiana Marriages through 1850," 1850 U.S. Census, Whitley County, IN.

98. John Collins will, 1849, *Whitley County, Indiana Will Record*, v. 1, 25–27; Aaron Collins to James Collins, 12/8/1853, GLO Records, land claim T20N Sec16 & 21, R2W. Both in Gene MacKenzie Collection, courtesy of Tim Wahl.

99. Mason County Museum Indian War file, Muster Roll; Washington National Guard, Office of the Adjutant General, *History of the Washington National Guard, v. 2. "Washington Territorial Militia in the Indian Wars of 1855–56"* and Index to Military Records, Letters 669, 670; Longacre, *Pickett, Leader of the Charge*, 140–41, 855–56; Aaron Collins to James Collins, 6/6/1856, 8/1856, Gene MacKenzie Collection; Charlotte Simmons Koontz interview, 3/23/1920, in Edmund S. Meany, *Living Pioneers of Washington* (Seattle Genealogical Society, 1995).

100. www.historylink.org; *PSH*, 12/19/1861; Frank Mossman in F. H. and J. R. Loutzenhizer, eds., *Told by the Pioneers, vol. 2* (WPA Project 5841, Secretary of State, 1938), 217–18.

101. By 1879 there were 38 biracial children living on the inlet; Aaron Collins to James Collins, 12/8/1853, Gene MacKenzie Collection; Mason County Historical Society timeline; Bowden, *Early Schools of Washington Territory*, 331–32; Miles, *Michael T. Simmons*, 111–14, 191; Sheffer, "A Story of Pioneering"; *Pioneer-Democrat*, 1/7/1859; 1879 Mason County Territorial Census.

102. 1870 U.S. Census, Mason County; 1871 Territorial Census; Dr. Thomas Bibb research, 1930s–40s, James Pickett Collection, WSHS; William Walter in Edson, *Fourth Corner*, 120.

103. Edson, *Fourth Corner*, 119; Bibb research, Pickett Collection, WSHS.

104. Aaron Collins died on 1/15/1870, John Campbell diary, 12/1869–1/17/1870, Campbell Papers.

105. The digital Mason County marriage record says August 11, 1878, but is a misreading of the shape of the zero. Catherine's obituary (*Shelton Journal*, 1/17/1902) agrees with other evidence for 1870; 1870 U.S. Census, Mason County; Campbell diary, 4/4/1870, 1/1871.

106. "Pioneer William Walter Dies," *Shelton Journal*, 12/25/1908; compiled biography and land records, Mason County Museum; Michael Fredson, *Oakland to Shelton: The Sawdust Trail* (Belfair, WA: Mason County Historical Society, 1976), 11; *Pioneer-Democrat*, ?/22/1859, 3/1/1859, 9/16/1859, 9/9/1859; Edson, *Fourth Corner*, 119.

107. Wm. Walter served in the 150th Indiana Infantry; A. W. Swindal to W. W. Miller, 5/27/1862, Miller Papers; "The Strange Life of Artist Jimmie Pickett," *Shelton-Mason County Journal*, 10/28/1976; Deegan, *History of Mason County*, n.p.; William Walter obituary, *Shelton Journal*, 12/25/1908; Catherine Walter obituary, *Shelton Journal*, 1/17/1902; Sharon Saeger Matthews, "New York-to-Shelton: The Hard Way," *The Sunday Olympian*, 6/22/1975, p. 3; Henry G. Langley, *1867 Pacific Coast Directory* (San Francisco: Langley Publishing, 1867).

108. Eva Wivell, "Journey to Homestead in Agate," *Shelton Journal*, 1951; George Blankenship, *Lights and Shades of Pioneer Life on Puget Sound By a Native Son* (self-published, 1923), 16–17; "Pioneer William Walter Dies," *Shelton Journal*, 12/25/1908.

109. Edson, *Fourth Corner*, 119; Alvin Saeger to Jessie Knight Grisdale, in a letter to Thomas Bibb, 4/12/1933, Bibb papers in Pickett Collection, WSHS; W. D. Campbell to Jessie Knight, 4/18/1933, Pickett Collection, WSHS; Grisdale to Bernice Sapp, 7/15/1943, Pickett Collection, WSHS.

110. John Campbell Diary, 10/13/1873–4/7/1875; Edson, *Fourth Corner*, 120.

111. Bowden, *Early Schools of Washington*, 152; Gordon Newell, *Rogues, Buffoons and Statesmen* (Seattle: Hangman Press, 1975), 100; James T. Pickett diaries, Pickett Collection, WSHS; historicfortsteilacoom.org.

112. *Whatcom Reveille*, 6/15/1883; T. O. Abbott, *Real Property Statutes of Washington Territory from 1843 to 1889* (Olympia: State Printing and Publishing Co., 1892), 438; *Pioneer-Democrat*, 3/29/1862; *PSH*, 5/30/1864; J. G. Parker in Bennett, *A Small World of Our Own*, 78.

113. *Whatcom Reveille*, 11/19/1881; Bowden, *Early Schools of Washington*, 151–52.

114. James T. Pickett Diary; Thomas Bibb research notes. Both in Pickett Collection, WSHS; Bowden, *Early Schools*, 151–52.

115. J. T. Pickett penmanship books; Thomas Bibb research notes. Both in Pickett Collection, WSHS; Bowden, *Early Schools*, 152.

116. Edson, *Fourth Corner*, 121.

117. William and Catherine Walter portraits, Mason County Museum.

118. A. L. Callow to Jessie Knight Grisdale, 4/11/1933. Pickett Collection, WSHS.

119. Howard Buswell notes, 1/22/1947, re: letter from George Pickett in the WSHS Collection, since lost; LaSalle Pickett to James T. Pickett, 5/2/1876, and others, EMP.

120. Sallie Ann (LaSalle) Pickett to James Tilton Pickett, 2/9/1878. EMP.

121. W. D. Campbell to Jessie Knight Grisdale, 4/8/1933, Pickett Collection, WSHS.

122. James T. Pickett diary and Thomas Bibb research, WSHS; E. W. Wright, ed., *Lewis & Dryden's Marine History of the Northwest* (Portland: Lewis & Dryden, 1895), 243.

123. *Washington Standard*, 4/18/1879.

124. *The San Francisco Alta*, 7/7/1879; *Daily Intelligencer*, 7/24/1879.

125. *Washington Standard*, 8/1/1879; *Mechanics Institute San Francisco*, pamphlet, San Francisco Public Library.

126. *Daily Intelligencer*, 5/19/1880.

127. Walter journal, 10/22/1879–1882, Pickett Collection, WSHS; *Daily Intelligencer*, 5/19/1880; Eva Wivell, "Journey to Homestead in Agate," *Shelton Journal*, 1951 excerpt from 1948 unpub. ms.

128. William and Catherine Walter Journal 1879–1882, Pickett collection, WSHS; *Daily Intelligencer*, 5/19/1880.

129. 1880 U.S. Census, Mason County; Thomas Bibb research, Jessie Knight Grisdale undated note regarding information from Eva Wivell's mother; A. E. Woodard to Grisdale, 4/25/1933. Arley Van Epps to "Anne" at WSHS, quoted in letter to Grisdale, all in Pickett Collection, WSHS; copy of magazine portrait of Maude Branscombe, *Mt. Olympus, Lake Cushman*, Pickett Collection, WSHS.

130. Walter journal, 7/14/1881, list of letters sent, Pickett Collection, WSHS.

131. Harvey Scott's sister was Northwest suffragette and author Abigail Scott Duniway; Miles, "Michael T. Simmons," 112; Llyn De Danaan to author, 11/11/2010; Pioneer Historical Publ. Co., *History of Oregon* (1922), 2:5–7; Harry Stein, "The Oregonian," *Oregon Encyclopedia*, Portland State Univ., www.oregonencyclopedia.org.

132. 1880 U.S. Census, Multnomah County, OR; www.portlandonline.com; William Walker to George H. Himes, 8/1930, Pickett File, OHS.

133. Walker to Himes, 8/1930. OHS, "Register of Artists"; "The San Francisco Art Boom: 1860s–1880s," www.siskiyous.edu; Thomas Bibb research, Pickett Collection, WSHS.

134. Thomas Bibb research, Pickett Collection, WSHS; OHS, "Register of Artists"; JTP to Catherine Walter, 11/4/1884, Mason County Museum.

135. Franz Stenzel, *Cleveland Rockwell, Scientist and Artist, 1837–1907* (Portland: OHS, 1972), chapter 6; www.branrudfineart.com.

136. A. G. Walling, comp., *History of Southern Oregon* (Portland: A. G. Walling, 1884); JTP to Catherine Walter, 11/24/1883, typescript in EMP, UW; Carolyn Marr, "Birdseye Views," *MOHAI Old News* (Autumn 2001): 11.

137. JTP to Catherine Walter, 11/24/1883, 9/29/1884, EMP; 2/26/1884, Mason County Museum.

138. *Tacoma Daily Ledger*, 6/12/1884; Allie Saeger to Jessie Knight Grisdale, in letter to Thomas Bibb, 4/12/1933. Pickett Collection, WSHS.

139. JTP to Catherine Walter, 2/26/1884, Mason County Museum.

140. JTP to Walter, 2/26/1884; JTP to Catherine Walter, 4/6/1884, Daughters of the Pioneers Collection, Bellingham.

141. JTP to Catherine Walter, 11/4/1884, Mason County Museum.

142. Stuart became a highly successful artist whose work was popular with European collectors and American industrialists. JTP to Catherine Walter, 11/4/1884.

143. Edson, *Fourth Corner*, 119; JTP to Catherine Walter, 11/28/1884, 1/8/1885, EMP.

144. Today the San Francisco Institute of Art; Raymond L. Wilson, "The First Art School in the West: The San Francisco Art Association's California School of Design." *The American Art Journal* 14 (Winter 1982): 42–54; www.siskiyous.edu, "The San Francisco Art Boom: 1860s–1880s."

145. Edward Bosqui, *Memoirs* (Oakland: Holmes Book Co., 1952); "The School of Design," *Alta California*, 12/28/1880; wwwgracehudsonmuseum.org.

146. San Francisco Art Association/San Francisco Art Institute records, San Francisco Public Library; Wilson, "The First Art School," 49.

147. Wilson, "The First Art School," 48 and photo.

148. JTP to Catherine Walter, 1/8/1885.

149. JTP to Catherine Walter, 5/14/1885, EMP.

150. Hallie Lysle Campbell to Howard Buswell, 7/1945, HBP.

151. Ginny Allen and Jody Klevit, *Oregon Painters: The First Hundred Years (1859–1959)* (Portland: OHS Press, 1999) 124, 152–53, 294; *Oregon Register of Artists*, OHS; "Portland Mechanics Fair," *Pacific Rural Press*, 11/3/1888; Wright, *Lewis & Dryden's Marine History*, 335.

152. David D. Fagan, *History of Benton County, Oregon* (Portland: David D. Fagan, 1885); JTP to Catherine Walter, 1/12/1886, Mason County Museum; "Frank G. Abell," www.oldoregonphotos.com.

153. JTP to Catherine Walter, 1/12/1886, Mason County Museum.

154. JTP to Catherine Walter, 5/7/1886, Mason County Museum; E. C. McGreavy to Jessie Knight Grisdale, 8/9/1933, Pickett Collection, WSHS.

155. *Kane's Illustrated West*, 1886, 1887; JTP to Catherine Walter, 12/4/1886, Pickett Collection, WSHS; *The Northwest Illustrated Monthly*, 6/1887.

156. Series of 1890 letters between John Cress, Catherine Walter, and Margaret Jones; John and Catherine Cress to JTP, 3/21/1889, both in Pickett Collection, WSHS; email to CW from Spokane County Auditor re: Lot 4, Blk 6, Mt. View Addition; King County Recorder, *Deeds* 55, 168.

157. JTP to Catherine Walter, 12/14/1887, Pickett Collection, WSHS; Thomas Ritchie, *Revised Code of the Laws of Virginia*, vol. 1, 1819.

158. Whatcom County *Deeds* 9, 325–26; Edson, *Fourth Corner*, 124; Charles and Lottie Roeder Roth's family later donated the painting of Mt. Rainier to the Whatcom Museum. It remains the only Pickett painting in Whatcom County.

159. Edson, *Fourth Corner*, 124; *Bellingham Bay Reveille*, 3/1/1889, 3/8/1889, 4/19/1889.

160. Whatcom County *Deeds* 9, 325–26, Affidavit #3289 and *Deeds* 8, 219; Spokane County *Deeds*, 3/23/1889; King County *Deeds* 73, p. 468; 1889 King County Assessment Roll.

161. E. C. McGreavy to Jessie Knight Grisdale, 8/9/1933, Pickett Collection, WSHS; William Walter to Edson, *Fourth Corner*, 120.

162. James Tilton Pickett probate file, Multnomah County, Oregon, copy courtesy of Martha Boltz; Spokane County Deeds, JTP to Margaret Jones, 8/3/1889.

163. McGreavy to Grisdale, 8/9/1933, Pickett Collection, WSHS; City of Portland Bureau of Planning & Sustainability, *City of Portland Civic Planning, Development & Public Works 1851–1965: A Historic Context*; www.historicalthreads.blogspot.com, "Swimming in the Willamette River in and near Portland."

164. Ad in *The Louisiana Democrat*, 8/31/1881; www.mayoclinic.com, "Typhoid Fever"; JTP Probate File; JTP Will 8/21/1889, Multnomah County, OR, copy courtesy of Martha Boltz.

165. Edson, *Fourth Corner*, 119–20.

166. McGreavy to Grisdale, 8/9/1933.

167. Death notice, *The Oregonian*, 8/31/1889; Rev. David Wetzel, "In Memoriam," *The Oregonian*, 9/8/1889.

168. Death notice, *Oregonian*, 8/31/1889; Riverview Cemetery records, OHS; application for burial permit, JTP probate file; McGreavy to Grisdale, 8/9/1933.

169. All letters except the two are at Mason County Museum, WSHS, the EMP at UW, and the Daughters of the Pioneers, Bellingham; William Walter in Edson, *Fourth Corner*, 120; McGreavy to Grisdale, 8/9/1933.

170. *Mason County Journal*, 9/6/1889; *Washington Standard*, 9/6/1889.

171. The stanza from Poe's 1844 poem "Dreamland" is on the back of Pickett's painting at WSHS, *Shipwreck on the Northwest Coast*; Wetzel, "In Memoriam"; Gwen Perkins, "Dreamland: The Lost Worlds of James Tilton Pickett," *Columbia* (Summer 2012): 21.

172. J. T. Pickett Will; McGreavy to Grisdale, 8/9/1933.

173. Catherine Walter obituary, *Shelton Journal*, 1/17/1902; "Pioneer William Walter Dies," *Shelton Journal*, 12/25/1908; Edson in *The Bellingham Herald*, 4/25/1911, and *The Fourth Corner*.

174. Research materials re: the Pickett-Christiancy marriage, collection of Suzann Pickett Zbar, courtesy of The Pickett Society; McIlroy, "George E. Pickett III Tells…"; Christiancy Pickett Jr. genealogy charts, 1998; Christiancy Pickett Jr., interview by Martha Boltz, 9/9/1999; Martha Boltz, "LaSalle Pickett's Battle to Buff Husband's Image," *Washington Times*, 3/14/1998.

175. Edson, *Fourth Corner*, 120; Jessie Knight Grisdale to Bernice Sapp, 7/15/1943, Pickett Collection, WSHS; author correspondence with West Point Archives re: glove traditions.

176. Doris Ostrander Dawdy, *Artists of the American West: A Biographical Dictionary* (Chicago: Swallow Press, 1974), 1:182; Allen and Klevit, *Oregon Painters*, 255–56; William Walker to George H. Himes, 8/1930. OHS.

177. Minnie Little to Jessie Knight Grisdale, 7/11/1933, Pickett Collection, WSHS; UW Library and WSHS provenance records re: portrait of George E. Pickett; Whatcom Museum photo #9144.

Bibliography

Sources cited only once, or in passing, in the notes are usually not included in this bibliography unless an important general source.

Abbott, T. O. *Real Property Statutes of Washington Territory from 1843 to 1889*. Olympia, WA: State Printing and Publishing, 1892.

Adams, George. Conversations with author re: Nooksack history, language, culture.

Adams, John. *Old Square-Toes and His Lady: The Life of James and Amelia Douglas*. Victoria, BC: Horsdal and Schubart, 2001.

Alaska, Territory of. Bureau of Vital Statistics. Marriage and Death Certificates.

Allen, Frank. Papers and interview by author 8/3/2000 re: Mary and Solomon Allen. Courtesy of Frank Allen.

Allen, Ginny, and Jody Kleirt. *Oregon Painters, the First Hundred Years (1859–1959)*. Portland: Oregon Historical Society Press, 1999.

Allen, James (Jim) and Linda. Personal research re: Allen family genealogy and history. Courtesy of Jim and Linda Allen.

Allen, John C. Collection. Clausen Museum, Petersburg, AK.

Allen, Solomon. Military Pension File, MexSC#11651. Veterans Administration Records of the Mexican War, NARA. Copy in HBP.

Archdiocese of Seattle. Sacramental Records, vols. 1–4. Archdiocesan Archives, Seattle, WA.

Armitage, Susan, and Elizabeth Jameson. *The Women's West*. Norman: University of Oklahoma Press, 1987.

Asher, Brad. *Beyond the Reservation: Indians, Settlers, and the Law in Washington Territory, 1853–1889*. Norman: University of Oklahoma Press, 1999.

Bagley, Clarence B. *History of King County, Washington*. Seattle: S. J. Clarke, 1929.

Baird, Spencer F. Papers. Smithsonian Institution Archives. Washington, DC.

Bancroft, H. H. *History of Washington, Idaho and Montana, 1845–1889*. San Francisco: The History Company, 1890.

Barman, Jean. *French Canadians, Furs, and Indigenous Women in the Making of the Pacific Northwest*. Vancouver: University of British Columbia Press, 2015.

Bayview Cemetery Records. City of Bellingham. WSA, NW.

Beard, Janet. Personal research re: Wynne family. Courtesy of Janet Beard.

Beckey, Fred. *Range of Glaciers: The Exploration and Survey of the Northern Cascade Range*. Portland: Oregon Historical Society, 2003.

Bennett, Robert A. *A Small World of Our Own*. Walla Walla: Pioneer Press, 1985.

Bibb, Thomas. Research papers. JTP.

Bierwert, Crisca. *Brushed by Cedar, Living by the River: Coast Salish Figures of Power*. Tucson: University of Arizona Press, 1999.

Bjerky, Irene. "First Peoples of Yale and Spuzzum." Unpublished manuscript. Historic Yale Museum. Yale, BC.

Boltz, Martha. Personal research and correspondence re: George E. Pickett. Courtesy of Martha Boltz.

Bowden, Angie Burt. *Early Schools of Washington Territory*. Seattle: Lowman and Hanford, 1935.

Boxberger, Bruce. Papers. NWEC.

Boyd, Robert. *The Coming of the Spirit of Pestilence: Introduced Infectious Diseases and Population Decline Among Northwest Coast Indians, 1774–1874*. Seattle: University of Washington Press, 1999.

Brown, (Captain) Fred R. *History of the Ninth U.S. Infantry, 1799–1909*. Chicago: R. R. Donnelley and Sons, 1909.

Brown, Roberta. "One Tribe Among Many: Concepts of American Citizenship Among Washington Territory's French Canadian Pioneers and Founders." Pacific Northwest History Conference, 4/4/2014.

Brown's Business College. Files. Centralia Area Historical Museum, Centralia, IL.

Browne, J. Ross. *Indian Affairs in the Territories of Oregon and Washington*. Fairfield, WA: Ye Galleon Press, 1977. Reprint of 1858 report.

Burwell, Virginia Pickett. Papers. Swem Library Special Collections, College of William and Mary.

Buswell, Howard. Papers. CPNWS.

Butruille, Susan G. *Women's Voices from the Western Frontier*. Boise, ID: Tamarack Books, 1995.

Calloway, Brenda C. *America's First Western Frontier: East Tennessee*. Johnson City, TN: Overmountain Press, 1989.

Camp Pickett (San Juan Island) Post Returns. Records of the War Dept., Office of the Adjutant General 1859–1861. NARA. Microfilm copy at WSA, NW.

Campbell, John. Papers. University of Washington Libraries, Special Collections.

Carhart, Edith. *A History of Bellingham*. Bellingham: Argonaut Press, 1926.

Carlson, Keith Thor, ed. *A Sto:lo Coast Salish Historical Atlas*. Seattle: University of Washington Press; Vancouver: Sto:lo Heritage Trust; Chilliwack BC: Sto:lo Nation, 2001

Carpenter, Cecelia Svinth. *Fort Nisqually: A Documented History of Indian and British Interaction*. Tacoma, WA: Tahoma Research Service, 1986.

———. *The Nisqually, My People*. Tacoma, WA: Tahoma Research Service, 2002.

Celestine, Aurelia Balch. "Genealogy of the Sea'nult Family, 1917." Box 6, NWEC.

Christian, W. Asbury. *Richmond: Her Past and Present*. Richmond, VA: L. H. Jenkins, 1912.

Clinton, Catherine. *The Plantation Mistress: Woman's World in the Old South*. New York: Pantheon, 1982.

Coffman, Edward M. *The Old Army: A Portrait of the American Army in Peacetime, 1784–1898*. New York: Oxford University Press, 1986.

Conaway, James. *The Smithsonian: 150 Years of Adventure, Discovery and Wonder*. Washington DC: Smithsonian Institution, 1995.

Coontz, Stephanie. *Marriage, A History: From Obedience to Intimacy or How Love Conquered Marriage*. New York: Viking, 2005.

Copland, George and Ridgeley. Collection and interview by author, 9/2003 re: Minge and Pickett family history. North Bend Plantation, VA. Courtesy of George and Ridgeley Copland.

Corliss, Margaret McKibben. *Fall City in the Valley of the Moon*. Fall City, WA: Margaret McKibben Corliss, 1972.

Dary, David. *The Santa Fe Trail: Its History, Legends and Lore*. New York: Penguin Putnam, 2000.

Daughters of the Pioneers. Collection. Pickett House Museum, Bellingham, WA.

Dawdy, Doris Ostrander. *Artists of the American West: A Biographical Dictionary*, vol. 1. Chicago: Swallow Press, 1974.

Deegan, Dr. Harry W. *History of Mason County*. Shelton, WA: Dr. Harry W. Deegan, 1960.

Delgado, James P. *To California by Sea: A Maritime History of the California Gold Rush*. Columbia: University of South Carolina Press, 1990.

Denny, Arthur. *Pioneer Days on Puget Sound*. Seattle: Shorey Books, 1975. First published 1888.

Deur, Douglas. *Ebey's Landing National Historical Reserve: An Ethnohistory of Traditionally Associated Contemporary Populations*. Seattle: National Park Service and University of Washington Press, 2009.

Donald, Leland. *Aboriginal Slavery on the Northwest Coast of North America*. Berkeley: University of California Press, 1997.

Dorr, Echo Oxford. Personal records and interview by author, 1/4/2000, re: Wynn family. Courtesy of Echo Dorr.

Dunagan, Dessie May. *History of Ferndale Consolidated School District #502*. Ferndale, WA: FCSD #502, 1968.

Dunbar-Ortiz, Roxanne. *An Indigenous Peoples' History of the United States*. Boston: Beacon Press, 2014.

Duwamish, et al. v. U.S. (1927) F-275. Washington DC: U.S. Court of Claims. Copy in NWEC.

Edson, Lelah Jackson. *The Fourth Corner.* Seattle: Craftsman Press. Whatcom Museum edition, 1978. First published 1951 by Cox Brothers.

Eldridge, Edward. "Sketch of Washington Territory." Unpublished manuscript. Bancroft Library, University of California, Berkeley.

Eldridge, Teresa. "Fifty-five Years on Bellingham Bay." *American Reveille*, 6/14/1908. Reprinted in Carhart, *History of Bellingham.*

Elliott and Moore. *History of Alameda County, California.* San Francisco: Elliott and Moore, 1883.

Elliott, Gordon R. *Barkerville, Quesnel and the Cariboo Gold Rush.* Vancouver: Douglas and McIntyre, 1958.

Eskin, Blanche. "Mrs. Elizabeth Collins' Story." *Polk County (OR) Observer*, 1/1/1927. Copy in Lucullus McWhorter Papers, Washington State University Libraries, MASC.

Fetzer, Paul. Field notes. Author's copy courtesy of Dr. Wayne Suttles (originals now at University of Washington Libraries, Special Collections).

Fischer, David Hackett. *Albion's Seed: Four British Folkways in America.* New York: Oxford University Press, 1989.

Fisher, Robin. *Contact and Conflict: Indian-European Relations in British Columbia, 1774–1890.* Vancouver: University of British Columbia Press, 1992.

Fitch, Joan. Personal research re: Ben Catching. Courtesy of Joan Fitch.

Forsyth, James W. Letters. Author's copies courtesy of descendant Dr. Elizabeth Upton (now in University of Washington Libraries, Special Collections).

Forsythe, Mark, and Greg Dickson. *The Trail of 1858: British Columbia's Gold Rush Past.* Madeira Park, BC: Harbour Publishing, 2007.

Fort Bellingham Post Returns. Records of the War Dept., Office of the Adjutant General 1859–1861. NARA. Microfilm copy at WSA, NW.

Fox-Genovese, Elizabeth. *Within the Plantation Household: Black and White Women of the Old South.* Chapel Hill: University of North Carolina Press, 1988.

Fredson, Michael. *Oakland to Shelton, the Sawdust Trail.* Belfair and Shelton WA: Mason County Historical Society, 1976.

Gibbs, George. "Proceedings of the Western Washington Treaty." In Lane, Barbara. "Background of Treaty-Making in Western Washington." Copy in NWEC.

Goodspeed Publishing. *History of Greene County, Tennessee.* Chicago: Goodspeed, 1887.

———. *History of Tennessee.* Chicago: Goodspeed, 1887.

Gordon, Lesley J. *General George E. Pickett in Life and Legend.* Chapel Hill: University of North Carolina Press, 1998.

Graybill, Andrew R. *The Red and the White: A Family Saga of the American West.* New York: Liveright (W.W. Norton), 2013.

Harmon, Alexandra. *Indians in the Making: Ethnic Relations and Indian Identities around Puget Sound.* Berkeley: University of California Press, 1998.

Harrison, Eliza Cope, ed. *Philadelphia Merchants: The Diary of Thomas P. Cope, 1800–1851.* South Bend (IN): Gateway Editions, 1978.

Hauka, Donald Jr. *McGowan's War.* Vancouver: New Star Books, 2003.

Hawley, Robert E. *Skqee Mus or Pioneer Days on the Nooksack.* Edited by P. R. Jeffcott. Bellingham: Whatcom Museum (Craftsman Press), revised edition, 1971. First published 1945 by Miller and Sutherlen.

Heitman, Francis. *Historical Register and Dictionary of the U.S. Army from its Organization, 9/29/1789–3/2/1903.* 2 vols. Washington DC: Government Printing Office, 1903.

Heritage House. *Fraser and Thompson River Canyons.* Surrey BC: Heritage House, 1986.

Hewitt, Irene. "Patkanim Family Tree," (2003). Copy at Lynden Pioneer Museum.

Hyde, Anne F. *Empires, Nations and Families: A New History of the North American West, 1800–1860.* Lincoln: University of Nebraska Press, 2011.

Ingersoll, Thomas N. *To Intermix with Our White Brothers: Indian Mixed Bloods from the Earliest Times to the Indian Removals.* Albuquerque: University of New Mexico Press, 2005.

Jackson, Donald Dale. *Gold Dust.* New York: Alfred A. Knopf, 1980.

Jagodinsky, Katrina. *Legal Codes and Talking Trees: Indigenous Women's Sovereignty in the Sonoran and Puget Sound Borderlands, 1854–1946.* New Haven: Yale University Press, 2016.

James, Chief Tsi'lixw (William) (Lummi). Interviews and conversations with author re: Lummi history, culture, and language.

James, Frances Lane. Interviews and conversations re: Lane family history and Lummi culture.

Jeffcott, Percival R. "Colonel James A. Patterson and Reuben Bizer were Partners at Squahalish before there was a Lynden." Unpublished manuscript draft and notes. Box 8, PRJ, CPNWS.

———. *Nooksack Tales and Trails.* Ferndale: Sedro-Woolley Courier Times, 1949. Reprint, Sincyrly Ours Publishing: 1995.

Jeffrey, Julie Roy. *Frontier Women: "Civilizing" the West? 1840–1880.* New York: Hill and Wang, 1979. Revised edition, 1998.

Jenness, Diamond. "The Saanich Indians of Vancouver Island." Unpublished manuscript. Ethnology Archives, Canadian Museum of Civilization, ca. 1938. Copy in Box 37, NWEC.

Jetté, Melinda Marie. *At the Hearth of the Crossed Races: A French-Indian Community in 19th Century Oregon, 1812–1859*. Corvallis: Oregon State University Press, 2015.

Johnson, Kristin. Correspondence re: Patterson family history.

Jones-Lamb, Karen. *Native American Wives of San Juan Settlers*. [Decatur Island, WA]: Bryn Tirion Publishing, 1994.

Judson, Phoebe Goodell. "My Aboriginal Neighbors." *Lynden Tribune* reprint c. 1912 of paper read to Old Neighbors Club, 1904. Phoebe Judson scrapbook. Lynden Pioneer Museum.

———. Letter 1/1872 to unknown person. Courtesy of Karen Parsons.

———. *A Pioneer's Search for an Ideal Home*. Lincoln: University of Nebraska Press, 1984. Originally published 1925.

Kane's Illustrated West. 1886, 1887 issues re: Pickett lithographs. Portland, OR.

Kavanaugh, James. Diary, 1863–1885. Transcribed by Miriam Tschida. Edited by Mary Ellen Mulcahy. Original at Samish Nation Archives, Anacortes, WA. Note: Excerpted transcription previously published in the *Anacortes American*, 1913. Paraphrased excerpted version by Soroptomists (1930s) at Skagit County Museum.

Keddie, Grant. *Songhees Pictorial: A History of the Songhees People as Seen by Outsiders, 1790–1912*. Victoria: Royal British Columbia Museum, 2003.

———. *Supplement to the Songhees Pictorial*. www.royalbcmuseum.bc.ca.

Kellogg, George A. *A History of Whidbey's Island*. Coupeville, WA: Island County Historical Society, 2001 reprint. First published 1934 by George A. Kellogg.

Kidder, Jack, et al. "The Family Tree of Chief Patkanim." Unpublished manuscript. Courtesy of Earngy Sandstrom.

Kimball, Gregg D. *American City, Southern Place: A Cultural History of Antebellum Richmond*. Athens: University of Georgia Press, 2000.

King County Recorder. Records. Seattle, WA.

King, John Nevin. Letters, 1857–1873. King Family Papers. Illinois State Historical Library, Springfield, IL.

Laforet, Andrea, and Annie York. *Spuzzum: Fraser Canyon Histories, 1808–1939*. Vancouver: University of British Columbia Press, 1998.

Lane, Barbara. *Background of Treaty Making in Western Washington*. Washington DC: Institute for the Development of Indian Law, 1977. Copy in Box 34, NWEC.

Lanham, Dr. Howard. Correspondence re: pre-Civil War army bladed weaponry.

Larsen, Lynn, and Becky Wynn-Thill. *Dr. Thomas Wynne's Legacy*. New York: TFG Press, 2002.

Laut, Agnes C. *The Cariboo Trail*. Toronto: Glasgow, Brook, 1921.

LeMaster, James. "Baer Tales." Unpublished manuscript, 1996. Courtesy of James LeMaster.

Limerick, Patricia Nelson. *The Legacy of Conquest: The Unbroken Past of the American West*. New York: W.W. Norton, 1987.

———. *Something in the Soil: Legacies and Reckonings in the New West*. New York: W.W. Norton, 2000.

Lindsay, F.W. *The Cariboo Story*. Kelowna, BC: Regatta City Press, 1958.

Longacre, Edward G. *Pickett: Leader of the Charge*. Shippensburg, PA: White Mane, 1998.

Lummi Tribe (Nation). *Nooh-whlummi: A Brief History of the Lummi*. Lummi Tribe, undated.

Lutz, John S. "Interlude or Industry: Ranching in British Columbia, 1859–1885." *BC Historical News* 13, no. 4 (Summer 1980): 2–11.

Lynden Pioneer Museum. Collections. Lynden, WA.

Lysle, Mary Frances. "Christmas, 1854." Speech given at P.L.F. Club, 1905. Copy in Box 4, HBP.

MacKenzie, Gene Geske. Collins family letters. Transcription by Candace Wellman. Courtesy of Gene MacKenzie and Tim Wahl.

Majors, Harry M., ed. *Mount Baker: A Chronicle of its Historic Eruptions and First Ascent*. Seattle: Northwest Press, 1978.

Mansfield, Joseph. "Report of the Inspector of Fort Bellingham, 12/28/1858." NARA, Seattle.

Marschner, Janice. *California 1850: A Snapshot in Time*. Sacramento: Coleman Ranch Press, 2000.

Mason County Museum. Collections. Shelton, Washington.

McCaffrey, James. *Army of Manifest Destiny, the American Soldier in the Mexican War 1846–1848*. New York: New York University Press, 1992.

McConaghy, Lorraine and Judy Bentley. *Free Boy: A True Story of Slave and Master*. Seattle: University of Washington Press, 2013.

McConnell, Jo Ellen. Personal research re: Aaron Collins. Courtesy of Jo Ellen McConnell.

McDonald Family genealogy research. Courtesy of James and Peggy McDonald.

McDonald, Nellie Patterson. Family history collection. Courtesy of James and Peggy McDonald.

McDonough, Bernard. Account Books. HBP.

McIlroy, Doris. "George E. Pickett III Tells of Grandfather's Post-War Romance." *Bellingham Herald*, 10/21/1938.

McWhorter, Lucullus. Papers. Washington State University Libraries, MASC.

Meany, Edmond S. "Chief Patkanim." *Washington Historical Quarterly* 15, no. 2 (July 1924): 187–99.

———. Collections. University of Washington Libraries, Special Collections, Seattle.

———. *Living Pioneers of Washington*. Seattle: Seattle Genealogical Society, 1995.

Michaelson, Mary Margaret, ed. *Memory Book: Friends of Aunt Phoebe Reunion, May 29, 2006*. Lynden WA: Lynden Pioneer Museum, 2006 edition.

———. Personal research re: Judson and Patterson families. Courtesy of Mary Michaelson.

Mihesuah, Devon A. *American Indians: Stereotypes and Realities*. Atlanta: Clarity Press, 1996.

Miles, Charles. *Michael T. Simmons*. [Olympia, WA?]: Vivian E. Bower, 1980.

Miles, John C. *Koma Kulshan: The Story of Mt. Baker*. Bellingham, Chuckanut Editions, 2010, revised edition. First published by Mountaineers Press, 1984.

Miller, Dr. Jack. Interviews with author, 2002, re: Johnny Richards at Sqweha:lich.

Miller, Jay. "Back to Basics: Chiefdoms in Puget Sound." *Ethnohistory* 44, no. 2 (Spring 1997): 375-87.

Miller, William Winlock. Papers. Beineke Library, Yale University. New Haven, CT.

"Minge Family Register." *William and Mary Quarterly*, Series 1, vol. 21 (July 1912): 31-33.

Morgan, Robert. *Lions of the West: Heroes and Villains of the Westward Expansion*. Chapel Hill, NC: Algonquin Books of Chapel Hill, 2012.

Mowat, Lisa. Personal research and interview by author 7/12/2008 re: Wynn family. Courtesy of Lisa Mowat.

Mullen, Neil. "Chronological History of Whatcom County to 1900." Unpublished manuscript, 2002. Courtesy of Neil Mullen.

Newman, Roger. Personal research re: Washington Territory marriage laws. Courtesy of Roger Newman.

Nicandri, David. *Olympia's Forgotten Pioneers: The Oblates of Mary Immaculate*. Olympia: State Capital Historical Association, 1976.

Northwest Ethnohistory Collection (NWEC), CPNWS.

Northwest Federation of Indians (NFAI). Records. RG75. NARA, Seattle.

Northwest Oral History Collection, CPNWS.

Oliphant, J. Orin. "The Cattle Trade on Puget Sound, 1858-1890." *Agricultural History* 7 (1933): 129-49.

Oregon Historical Society. "Register of Artists." OHS.

Pascoe, Peggy. *What Comes Naturally: Miscegenation Law and the Making of Race in America.* New York: Oxford University Press, 2009.

Perry, Adele. *On the Edge of Empire: Gender, Race, and the Making of British Columbia, 1849–1871.* Toronto: University of Toronto Press, 2001.

Pickett, Christiancy Jr. Correspondence and conversation with Martha Boltz re: the second Mrs. Pickett's name. Courtesy of Martha Boltz.

———. Pickett family genealogy charts, 1998. Courtesy of Christiancy Pickett and Martha Boltz.

Pickett, James Tilton. Collection. WSHS Research Center.

———. Probate file, 1889. Multnomah County, OR. Copy courtesy of Martha Boltz.

———. Vertical file folder. OHS.

Pickett, LaSalle Corbell. "My Soldier." *McClure's Magazine* 30, no. 5 (March 1908): 563, 564.

Pierce, W.H. *13 Years of Travel and Exploration in Alaska.* Anchorage: All Alaska Publishing, 1977.

Pioneers of Alaska Igloo #26 and Auxiliary #10. *Pioneer Profiles: A History of Petersburg Settlers, 1898–1959.* Port Townsend, WA: Sand Dollar Press, 2004.

Pool, Kathy. Personal research, interviews, correspondence re: Allen family. Courtesy of Kathy Pool.

Pratt, Boyd. Personal research re: Emmerling family. Courtesy of Boyd Pratt.

Puget Sound District Agency. "Correspondence and Accounting Records of the Puget Sound District Agency, 1854-1861 and the Tulalip Agency 1861-1886." RG75 Microfilm. NARA, Seattle.

Quackenbush, Bill (Barkerville Archives). Correspondence re: Henry Roeder, 5/24/2012.

Raibmon, Paige. *Authentic Indians: Episodes of Encounter from the Late 19th Century Northwest Coast.* Durham, NC: Duke University Press, 2005.

Rasmussen, Carol. Personal research re: Patkanim genealogy. Courtesy of Carol Rasmussen.

Rea, S. M. and J. Miller. Map of Blockley Township, Philadelphia County, PA, 1851.

Richardson, Allan. "Nooksack Indian Homesteading: A Study of Settlement Ethnohistory." Bellingham: CPNWS, revised edition 1978.

Richardson, Allan and Brent Galloway. *Nooksack Place Names: Geography, Culture, and Language.* Vancouver: University of British Columbia Press, 2011.

Riley, Glenda. *Building and Breaking Families in the American West.* Albuquerque: University of New Mexico Press, 1996.

———. *Women and Indians on the Frontier 1825–1915*. Albuquerque: University of New Mexico, 1984.

Roberts, Natalie. "A History of the Swinomish Tribal Community." Unpublished dissertation, University of Washington, 1975. University of Washington Libraries, Seattle.

Roblin, Charles E. "Schedule of Unenrolled Indians." U.S. Dept. of the Interior, Office of Indian Affairs, 1919. MR3, M1343. NARA, Seattle.

Roeder, Henry. Papers. University of Washington Libraries, Special Collections. Seattle.

Roppel, Patricia. Personal research re: Allen family. Courtesy of Patricia Roppel.

Roth, Lottie Roeder. *History of Whatcom County*. 2 vols. Seattle: Pioneer Historical Publishing, 1926.

Ruggrath, Carolyn. "The Patterson Family History." Unpublished manuscript and personal research. Courtesy of Carolyn Ruggrath.

Sandstrom, Chief Earngy (Snoqualmoo). Interview by author 6/16/2003, re: Patkanim family history, Treaty War.

San Francisco Art Institute. SFAI and San Francisco Art Association records. MF1888. San Francisco (CA) Public Library.

San Francisco Committee of Vigilance, 1851. Log Book. Box 1. Bancroft Library, University of California, Berkeley.

Schlissel, Lillian, Vickie Ruiz, and Janice Monk, eds. *Western Women: Their Land, Their Lives*. Albuquerque: University of New Mexico Press, 1988.

Selcer, Richard F. *Faithfully and Forever Your Soldier: General George E. Pickett, CSA*. Gettysburg PA: Farnsworth House Military Impressions, 1995.

Sheffer, Nicholas V. "A Story of Pioneering 1825–1910." *Lynden Tribune*, 8/1909.

Shockoe Cemetery (Richmond, VA). Records and Biographies. www.findagrave.com.

Shoemaker, Nancy, ed. *Negotiators of Change: Historical Perspectives on Native-American Women*. New York: Routledge, 1995.

Simmons, Michael T. Annual Reports to Commissioner of Indian Affairs 1857, 1858, 1859, 1860. Copies in NWEC.

Sleigh, Daphne, ed. *One Foot on the Border: A History of Sumas Prairie and Area*. Deroche, BC: Sumas Prairie and Area Historical Society, 1999.

Smedley, R.C. *History of the Underground Railroad in Chester and the Neighboring Counties of Pennsylvania*. Mechanicsburg, PA: Stackpole Books, 2005. First published 1883.

Smith, Sherry L. *The View from Officer's Row: Army Perceptions of Western Indians*. Tucson: University of Arizona Press, 1990.

Snohomish County (WA) Auditor. Records. WSA, NW.

Snoqualmie Valley Historical Museum. Files re: Patterson. North Bend, WA.

Southern Illinois Archives. Randolph County records, U.S. Census records. Southern Illinois University, Carbondale, IL.

Speer, William S. *Sketches of Prominent Tennesseans*. Nashville: Albert B. Tavel, 1888.

Spokane County (WA) Assessor. Records and correspondence. Spokane, WA.

Stangroom, M. L., administrator of the estate of Thomas Wynn, deceased v. Thomas B. Wynn, Harry P. Wynn, Jane Wynn, Julia Wynn, and Sallie Vandemark. #5116 (1897). Whatcom County Superior Court, Bellingham, WA.

Stanley, George F. G., ed. *Mapping the Frontier: Charles Wilson's Diary of the Survey of the 49th Parallel 1858–1862, while Secretary of the British Boundary Commission*. Seattle: University of Washington Press, 1970.

Starr, Kevin, and Richard J. Orsi, eds. *Rooted in Barbarous Soil: People, Culture, and Community in Gold Rush California*. Berkeley: University of California Press, 2000.

State of Washington v. George Swiloos (George Placid) #1347 (1892). Whatcom County Superior Court. WSA, NW.

Steele, Volney. *Bleed, Blister and Purge: A History of Medicine on the American Frontier*. Missoula, MT: Mountain Press, 2005.

Sterne, Netta. *Fraser Gold 1858! The Founding of British Columbia*. Pullman: Washington State University Press, 1998.

Stivers, R.F. "Turkey Island Plantation." *Virginia Cavalcade* 14, no. 2 (Autumn 1964): 41–47.

Stremler, Maxine. Interview by author 1/21/2006 re: Thomas T'ing family history.

Sullivan, Michael. Collection. CPNWS.

Suttles, Wayne. *Coast Salish Essays*. Seattle: University of Washington Press, 1987.

———, ed. *Handbook of the North American Indian: Volume 7, Northwest Coast*. Washington, DC: Smithsonian Institution, 1990.

———. "Post-Contact Culture Change Among the Lummi Indians." *BC Historical Quarterly* 18, no. 1 and 2 (Jan–April 1954): 29–102.

———. Personal research files, interviews, correspondence, and conversations with author. Courtesy of Dr. Suttles.

Swindle, Lewis J. *The Fraser River Gold Rush of 1858 as Reported by the California Newspapers of 1858*. Victoria: Trafford Publishing, 2001.

Taylor, Jeanette. *The Quadra Story: A History of Quadra Island*. Madeira Park, BC: Harbour Publishing, 2009.

Teck, Frank. Papers. In Michael Sullivan Collection, CPNWS.

Teit, James Alexander. Edited by Franz Boaz. *The Thompson Indians of British Columbia*. Merrit, BC: Nicola Valley Museum Archives Association reprint. No first date listed.

Tennant, John. Farm journals 1862–1872. William James Collection, Lummi Nation Archives. Lummi Reservation, WA. Used with permission of Chief Tsi'lxw (William) James.

Tepper, Leslie H. *Earth Line and Morning Star: Nlaka'pamux Clothing Traditions.* Hull, Quebec: Canadian Museum of Civilization, 1994.

Thrush, Coll. *Native Seattle: Histories from the Crossing-over Place.* Seattle: University of Washington Press, 2007.

Tollefson, Kenneth. "In Defense of a Snoqualmie Political Chiefdom Model." *Ethnohistory* 43, no. 1 (Winter 1996): 145–71.

———. "The Snoqualmie: A Puget Sound Chiefdom." *Ethnology* 26, no. 2 (4/1987): 121–36.

Tremaine, David. *Indian and Pioneer Settlement of the Nooksack Lowland, Washington to 1890.* Bellingham, WA: CPNWS, 1975.

Tulalip Papers. Washington State University Library Special Collections. Pullman, WA.

Turner, Nancy J. *Food Plants of Coastal First Peoples.* Vancouver: University of British Columbia Press, 1995.

———. *Food Plants of Interior First Peoples.* Vancouver: University of British Columbia Press, 1997.

———. *Plant Technology of First Peoples of British Columbia.* Vancouver: University of British Columbia Press, 1998.

Turner, Nancy J., Lawrence C. Thompson, M. Terry Thompson, Annie Z. York. *Thompson Ethnobotany: Knowledge and Usage of Plants by the Thompson Indians of British Columbia.* Victoria: Royal British Columbia Museum, 1990.

U.S. Census 1830–1930: Alaska Territory; Greene County, TN; Marion County, IL; Multnomah County, OR; Philadelphia County, PA; Randolph County, IL; St. Louis, MO; Whitley County, IN; Washington State and Territory: Lummi Reservation, Mason, Thurston, Whatcom counties.

U.S. General Land Office Records (Olympia, WA). Copies courtesy of Tim Wahl.

U.S. Military Academy. "Index to Cadet Applicaton Papers 1805–1866." Records of the Adjutant General's Office. RG 94. NARA.

U.S. Surveyor General. Lummi Reservation Allotment Map, 1884. Copy at Northwest Indian College Library, Lummi Reservation, WA.

Unruh, John Jr. *The Plains Across: The Overland Emigrants and the Trans-Mississippi West, 1840–1860.* Urbana: University of Illinois, 1979.

Valencius, Conevery Bolton. *The Health of the Country: How American Settlers Understood Themselves and Their Land.* New York: Basic Books, 2002.

Van Kirk, Sylvia. *Many Tender Ties: Women in the Fur Trade Society, 1670–1870.* Norman: University of Oklahoma Press, 1980.

———. "Tracing the Fortunes of Five Founding Families of Victoria." *BC Studies* 115/116 (Autumn/Winter 1997/98): 149–79.

Van Miert, E. Rosamond Ellis. *Settlers, Structures and Ships on Bellingham Bay, 1852–1889*. Bellingham: Rosamond Van Miert, 2004.

Virginia Historical Society. Collections. Richmond, VA.

Virginia State Library. Collections. Richmond, VA.

Vouri, Michael. *Outpost of Empire: The Royal Marines and the Joint Occupation of San Juan Island*. Seattle: Northwest Interpretive Association, 2004.

———. *The Pig War: Standoff at Griffin Bay*. Friday Harbor, WA: Griffin Bay Bookstore, 1999 edition.

———. "To Resign or Not: Southern Officers in Washington Territory on the Eve of the Civil War." Manuscript copy courtesy of Michael Vouri. HistoryLink.org essay 20570. www.historylink.org/File/20570.

Wahl, Phillip. Interview by author 6/16/2003 re: Patkanim family, Treaty War.

Wahl, Tim. "Historic Land Areas of the Lummi Reservation." Unpublished manuscript, 2013. Courtesy of Tim Wahl.

———. Personal research re: Whatcom County and Lummi Reservation geography. Courtesy of Tim Wahl.

Walling, A.G., compiler. *History of Southern Oregon comprising Jackson, Josephine, Douglas, Curry and Coos Counties*. Portland: A.G. Walling, 1884.

Ward, Harry M. *Richmond: An Illustrated History*. Northridge, CA: Windsor Publications, 1985.

Washington National Guard. Office of the Adjutant General. "Washington Territorial Militia in the Indian Wars of 1855–1856." Minutes of Company I, Northern Rangers.

Washington Territorial Census: 1860, 1870, 1871, 1879, 1880, 1887.

———. Products of Agriculture, Whatcom County: 1870, 1880.

Washington Territorial Court, 3rd District. Records. Jefferson County Superior Court Clerk. WSA, NW.

Washington Territory Superintendent of Indian Affairs. Records. NARA, NW. Copies in CPNWS.

Washington Territory v. Daniel Harris #64 (1856). 3rd District Territorial Court.

Washington Territory v. Oscar Olney #245, 246, 247 (1860). 3rd District Territorial Court.

Wellman, Candace. *Peace Weavers: Uniting the Salish Coast through Cross-cultural Marriages*. Pullman: Washington State University Press, 2017.

Wells, Oliver. Collection. Chilliwack City Archives. Chilliwack, BC.

Wells, Oliver. *The Chilliwacks and Their Neighbors*. Edited by Ralph Maud, Brent Galloway, and Marie Weeden. Vancouver: Talonbooks, 1987.

Whatcom County (WA). Records: Auditor, County Clerk, County Commission, Probate Court, Superintendent of Schools, Superior Court Clerk. WSA, NW and microfilm at courthouse.

Whatcom County (WA) Public Works. "Survey Field Notes vol. 1, July 1859."

Williams, Jacqueline. *The Way We Ate: Pacific Northwest Cooking 1843–1900*. Pullman: Washington State University Press, 1996.

Wilson, Raymond L. "The First Art School in the West: the San Francisco Art Association's California School of Design." *The American Art Journal* 14, no. 1 (Winter 1982): 42–55.

Wood, Mary. Correspondence re: Merion Meeting House, Philadelphia, 2002.

Wood, Patricia. Collection and personal research re: Pickett family. Courtesy of Patricia Wood.

Wright, E.W., ed. *Lewis and Dryden's Marine History of the Pacific Northwest*. Portland: Lewis and Dryden, 1895.

Wyatt-Brown, Bertram. *Southern Honor: Ethics and Behavior in the Old South*. New York: Oxford University Press, 1982.

Wynn, Jenny ("Jennie Winn"). Individual History Card #1056, Census #L-452. Bureau of Indian Affairs. Copy courtesy of a Wynn family member.

Wynn, Thomas. Probate Case File #636 (1897). Whatcom County Clerk microfilm. Bellingham, WA.

Wynn(e), Thomas and Hannah Sharp. Family Bible. Genealogy Society of Pennsylvania.

Wynne, Noel. "Family History of Jennie (Jane) Wynn." Unpublished manuscript, 1970. Courtesy of Wynn family.

———. Genealogy chart, 1970. Courtesy of Echo Oxford Dorr.

Wynn-Thill, Becky. Personal research files re: Thomas Wynn family history. Courtesy of Becky Wynn-Thill.

York, Annie, Richard Daly, and Chris Arnett. *They Write Their Dreams on the Rock Forever: Rock Writings in the Stein River Valley of British Columbia*. Vancouver: Talonbooks, 1993.

Zbar, Suzanne Pickett. Pickett family papers. Via emails with Patricia Wood re: LaSalle Pickett.

Index

About the Author

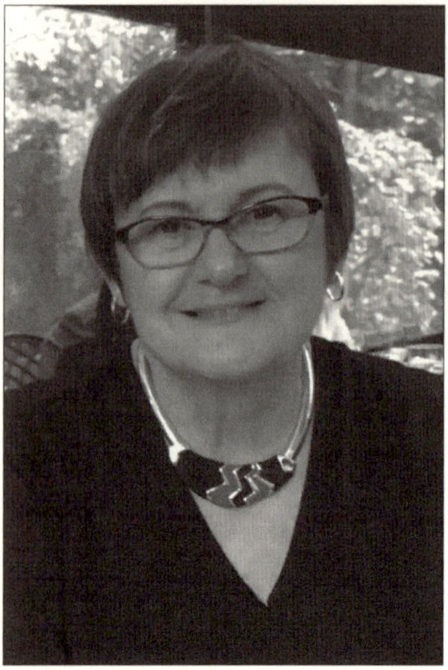

While working with researchers at the Washington State Archives, Candace Wellman discovered that about 80–90 percent of all marriages in Whatcom County's early decades were cross-cultural. The husbands included nearly every community founder and official, yet history writers mentioned only white women as founding mothers. She became determined to illuminate the hidden history surrounding these relationships.

Over twenty years and working with nearly two hundred collaborators, Wellman, an expert in research methods, sociology, history, and genealogy, scrutinized old sources and searched for new ones, particularly legal cases. Focusing on cross-cultural couples, she found evidence that, except in rare cases, local and regional historians stereotyped and ignored the Frontier West's intermarried women.

Interwoven Lives is Wellman's second book. Her first, *Peace Weavers: Uniting the Salish Coast Through Cross-Cultural Marriages* (WSU Press, 2017), was awarded the 2018 WILLA Literary Award for Scholarly Non-Fiction by the organization Women Writing the West.

Wellman holds bachelor's degrees in sociology from Washington State University and history/secondary education from Western Washington University, and pursued graduate work in sociology. Born and raised in Washington, the Bellingham resident is a local history consultant and speaks regularly about women's history and regional settlement.